FUNDAMENTALS OF INSURANCE

Dr. P.K. Gupta

M.Com., Ph.D. (Finance), FICWA, FCS, CFA, FIII
Associate Professor (Finance & Risk Management),
Center for Management Studies,
Jamia Millia Islamia, New Delhi.

Himalaya Publishing House
ISO 9001 : 2015 CERTIFIED

First Edition : 2004
Reprint : 2006
Reprint : 2008
Second Revised Edition : 2011
Reprint : 2013
Reprint : 2015
Reprint : 2017
Reprint : 2023
Reprint : 2025
Reprint : 2027

Published by : Mrs. Meena Pandey
for **HIMALAYA PUBLISHING HOUSE PVT. LTD.,**
Vishal Industrial Estate, 1st Floor, Office No. 63/64,
Bhandup Village Road, Subhash Nagar (Opp. CEAT Tyres),
Nahur (W), Mumbai - 400 078. **Phone:** 022-35131464/65/66/67
E-mail: himpub@bharatmail.co.in; **Website:** www.himpub.com

Branch Offices :

New Delhi : "Pooja Apartments", 4-B, Murari Lal Street, Ansari Road, Darya Ganj, New Delhi - 110 002. Phone: 011-23270392, 23278631; Fax: 011-23256286

Nagpur : Kundanlal Chandak Industrial Estate, Ghat Road, Nagpur - 440 018. Mobile: 09325409992, 09325908881

Bengaluru : Plot No. 91-33, 2nd Main Road, Seshadripuram, Behind Nataraja Theatre, Bengaluru - 560 020. Phone: 080-41138821; Mobile: 09379847017, 09379847005

Hyderabad : No. 3-4-184, Lingampally, Besides Raghavendra Swamy Matham, Kachiguda, Hyderabad - 500 027. Phone: 040-27560041, 27550139

Chennai : No. 34/44, Motilal Street, T. Nagar, Chennai - 600 017. Mobile: 09380460419

Pune : "Laksha" Apartment, First Floor, No. 527, Mehunpura, Shaniwarpeth (Near Prabhat Theatre), Pune - 411 030. Phone: 020-24496323, 24496333; Mobile: 09370579333

Cuttack : Plot No 5F-755/4, Sector-9, CDA Market Nagar, Cuttack - 753 014, Odisha. Mobile: 09338746007

Kolkata : 3, S.M. Bose Road, Near Gate No. 5, Agarpara Railway Station, North 24 Parganas, West Bengal - 700 109. Mobile: 09674536325

DTP by : Avinash

Printed at : Geetanjali Press Pvt. Ltd., Nagpur. On behalf of HPH (P).

Dedicated to the

Sacred memory of my father

Insurance is now fast growing area of academic study or profession. The recent financial crisis has witnessed the indispensable need of professionals in the area of risk management. Due to the complexity of the dynamic environment, new insurance products are evolving as well as the existing business models of insurance companies are undergoing significant change. After liberalisation of the economy, large number of alternative products and financial services have evolved that paved the way for the potential and unconventional entrants to penetrate the financial market through innovative higher product profile and portfolios, resulting into a sudden spurt in the demand of insurance professionals. The study of insurance as an academic discipline in new form is an obvious outcome. More and more academic institutions all over the countries are offering highly specialised insurance programmes to cater to this demand.

Since my first edition in 2004, many universities and institutions in India and abroad have introduced insurance as a specialised formal area of study both at graduate and postgraduate level. The edition of 2004, reprinted 2006 have been quite successful on the basis of feedback from the readers and the mentors.

Changes from the first Edition

The edition of 2011 in new form is an attempt to a give a more in-depth view of the insurance business and risk concepts. The chapter of risk has been split into more elaborate two chapters. Chapter 5 relating to mathematics of insurance has been introduced. The chapter on life are three covering various aspects of life insurance business. The earlier chapter 16 on insurance business nationalisation has been removed and merged with insurance business economic environment. All the tables, graphs have been amended with new statistics available till 2009. The non-life unit has been systematically arranged with comprehensive information.

I hope that the new edition of the book shall be useful to the students and as well as the trainers. I expect and would be highly obliged, if I receive comments and criticism from the readers. This would further help me in improving the book.

Organisation of the Book

The book is organised into 4 units.

Unit I introduces the concept of risk management to the readers. It conceptualises the risk definitions, classes of risk and the methods of handling risk and attempts to provide an overall view of the risk management and control systems.

Unit II deals with various aspects of insurance management. Chapter 3 and 4 give a framework of insurance basics and underlying principles respectively.

Chapter 5 has been deliberately introduced to give an idea of insurance mathematics. Chapter 6 and 7 deal with the insurance legal framework. Chapter 9 and 10 deal with underwriting and rating of insurance products.

Unit III deal with the life insurance business covering the life insurance players and products, claim settlement and procedural aspects, group insurance and life assurance management.

Unit IV focuses on non-life category. It covers the history of general insurance, the players and their performance, product wise the various non-life insurance categories. Attempt has been made to provide the statistics to the maximum possible extent.

Acknowledgements

I am inspired by my mother and my wife Rachna Gupta who strongly suggested me write a book on the subject from a pure student's perspective. I am indebted to my brother who has provided valuable suggestions to the organisation of text and its contents. I am indebted to my mother, sisters and family members especially my beloved Tinku, Chinki, Pintoo and Minkoo who have made sacrifices at all levels in various forms and contexts for timely completions of this book.

I also thank my Ph.D. supervisor, Dr. B.L. Surolia, who has provided me presentation skills, which, I feel is the most important tool in any literary work.

I am thankful to Prof. D.K. Agarwal, Dean (Academics), IIM Shillong for building motivation to update and revise the text of the book.

I thank from my heart Mr. Vijay Rawat at Delhi office who provided me immense support and motivation for timely completion of this edition.

I am thankful to my colleagues and staff members at Centre for Management Studies, JMI. I would be failing in my duty if do not thank my colleagues and staff of various libraries who have helped at various stages in provision of statistics and other information required for the book.

The last but not the least, my thanks are due to the academicians at various institutions and insurance companies who provided me an idea as to contents and other valuable suggestions.

New Delhi

June 2011 **P. K. Gupta**

CONTENTS

UNIT I RISK BASICS

UNIT II INSURANCE MANAGEMENT

UNIT III LIFE INSURANCE

UNIT IV NON-LIFE INSURANCE

BRIEF CONTENTS

UNIT I
RISK BASICS

CONCEPT OF RISK

Chapter Objectives

- The Concept of Risk
- Risk vs. Uncertainty
- Types of Risk
- Pure Risk and its Management
- Financial Risk and its Management

Introduction

Human beings are considered the most intelligent creatures on this earth. The thinking power available to human beings is enormous and this has led human beings to define their style of living and distinguish between good and bad situations. The criteria for deciding whether the situation is good or bad depend upon *individual's perception*. However, one thing is sure — *that human beings always prefer and strive for happy situations and wants to avoid the adverse ones.* Actually, the zeal to be happy always has given birth to the jargon **risk!**

1.1 The Concept of Risk

People express risk in different ways. To some, it is the chance or possibility of loss, to others, its may be uncertain situations or deviations or what statisticians call dispersions from the expectations. Different authors on the subject have defined risk differently. However, in most of the terminology the term risk includes exposure to adverse situations. The indeterminateness of outcome is one of the basic criteria to define a risk situation. Also, when the outcome is indeterminate, there is a possibility that some of them may be adverse and therefore need special emphasis. Let us have a look at the popular definitions of risk.

According to the Dictionary, risk refers to the possibility that something unpleasant or dangerous might happen.[1]

"Risk is a condition in which there is a possibility of an adverse deviation from a desired outcome that is expected or hoped for."[2]

"At its most general level, risk is used to describe any situation where there is uncertainty about what outcome will occur. Life is obviously risky."[3]

Risk may be objective or subjective. *Objective Risk* is defined as the relative variation of actual loss from expected loss. For example, assume that a property insure has 10,000 houses insured over a long period and, on average 1% or 100 houses, burn each year. However, it would be rare for exactly 100 houses to burn. In some years, 90 houses may burn, in other years 110 houses may burn. Thus, there is a variation of 10 houses or 10%, from the expected number of 100. This relative variation of actual loss from expected loss is known as objective risk.

Subjective Risk is defined as uncertainty based on a person's mental condition or state of mind. For example, a customer who was drinking heavily in a bar may foolishly attempt to drive home. The driver may be uncertain whether he will arrive home safely without being arrested by the police for drunk driving. This mental uncertainty is called subjective risk.

There is no single definition of risk. Economists, risk theorists, statisticians and actuaries each have there own concept of risk.

"At its most general level, risk is used to describe any situation where there is uncertainty about what outcome will occur. Life is obviously risky."

- S.E Harrington

"Risk is a measurable uncertainty."

- Frank Knight

"Risk is an objectified uncertainty regarding the occurrence of an undesirable event."

- A.M. Willet

"Risk may be defined as combination of hazards measured by probability". *- Lrving Fisher*

According to Federation of Insurance Institute, "Risk can be thought of as the degree of variation in the possible outcome from an uncertain event or as the variable in the possible outcomes."

According Life Insurance Corporation (LIC) of India, risk may be defined as "a condition where there is a possibility of an adverse deviation from a desired outcome that is expected or hoped for, there is no requirement that the possibility be unmeasurable, only that it must exist."

In business, risks include changing demand, price falls, change in desire and taste of consumers, change in market conditions, high competitions, new inventions, and heir development, fire, flood, accident and etc.

---

1. *Macmillan English Dictionary,* Macmillan Publishers Ltd. 2002, p. 1227.
2. Emmett J. Vaughan, *Risk Management*, John Wiley & Sons Inc., 1997, p. 8.
3. S.E. Harrington and G.R. Michaus, *Risk Management and Insurance,* McGraw-Hill, 1999, p. 3.

In insurance practice, risk is used for perils or loss producing events. Any risk bearing object needs to be insured so as to cover its unexpected losses caused by uncertain events.

The degree of risk refers to the likelihood of occurrence of an event. It is a measure of accuracy with which the outcome of a chance event can be predicted.

In most of the risky situations, two elements are commonly found:

1. The outcome is uncertain, i.e., there is a possibility that one or other(s) may occur. Therefore, logically, there are at least two possible outcomes for a given situation.
2. Out of the possible outcomes, one is unfavorable or not liked by the individual or the analyst.

1.2 Risk vs. Uncertainty

Uncertainty is often confused with the risk. Uncertainty refers to a situation where the outcome is not certain or unknown. Uncertainty refers to a state of mind characterised by doubt, based on the lack of knowledge about what will or what will not happen in the future.[4]

Uncertainty can be perceived as opposite of certainty where you are assure of outcome or what will happen. Accordingly, some weights or probabilities can be assigned into risky situations but uncertainty; the psychological reaction to the absence of knowledge lacks this privilege.

Decision under uncertain situations is very difficult for the decision-maker. It all depends upon the skill, the judgement and of course luck.

Uncertainty being a perceptual phenomenon implies different degrees to different person. Assume a situation where an individual has to appear for the first in the newly introduced insurance examination.

(A) an individual student undergone a training in insurance.

(B) an individual with training or experience in insurance.

A's perception towards uncertainty (of performance in examination) is different from that of B. Nonetheless, in both situations, the outcome that is the questions which will be asked in the examination are different.

1.2.1 Loss and Chance of Loss

A risk refers to a situation where there is the possibility of a loss. What is a loss?

Loss has been defined in many ways. *Loss in accounting sense means that portion of the expired cost for which no compensating value has been received.*[5]

Loss refers to the Act or instance of losing the detriment or a disadvantage resulting from losing.[6]

4. Vaughan, *op. cit.*, p. 7.
5. M.N. Arora, *Cost Accounting,* Vikas Publishing House, 2000, p. 122.
6. *Oxford Advance Learner's Dictionary,* Oxford University Press, 1984, p. 504.

Loss means being without something previously possessed.[7]

The chance of loss refers to a fraction or the relative frequency of loss. The chance of loss in insurance sense is the probability of loss. For example, assume there are 10,000 factories in the insurance pool which may be affected due to earthquake and on the basis of past experience, 5 have been affected, then the probability of loss is 0.0005. The whole game of insurance business is based on the probability of loss. If the insurer estimates correctly, he wins else loses or is forced to close the business.

From the insurer's perspective, it is the probability of loss that essentiates the need for insurances. The probabilities of losses may be *ex-post* or *ex-ante*. In practice, the *ex-ante* probabilities are widely used for undertaking risk in insurance business. The chance or probabilities of loss estimation requires accounting for causes of losses popularly characterised as *perils* and *hazards*.[8]

1.2.2 Perils

A peril refers to the cause of loss or the contingency that may cause a loss. In literary sense, it means the serious and immediate danger.[9] Perils refer to the immediate causes of loss. Perils may be general or specific, e.g., fire may affect assets like building, automobile, machinery, equipment and also, humans. Collusion may cause damage to the automobile resulting in a financial loss.

1.2.3 Hazards

Hazards are the conditions that increase the severity of loss or the conditions affecting perils. These are the conditions that create or increase the severity of losses. Economic slowdown is a peril that may cause a loss to the business, but it is also a hazard that may cause a heart attack or mental shock to the proprietor of the business. Hazards can be classified as follows:

1. **Physical Hazards:** Property Conditions — consists of those physical properties that increase the chance of loss from the various perils. E.g., stocking crackers in a packed commercial complex increases the peril of fire.
2. **Intangible Hazards:** Attitudes and Culture — Intangible hazards are more or less psychological in nature. These can be further classified as follows:
   (*a*) *Moral Hazard*: Fraud — These refer to the increase in the possibility or severity of loss emanating from the intention to deceive or cheat. For example — putting fire to a factory running in losses. With an intention to make benefit out of exaggerated claims, deliberately indulging into automobile collusion or damaging it or tendency on part of the doctor to go for unnecessary checks when they are not required, since the loss will be reimbursed by the insurance company.

---

7. M.S. Dorfman, *Introduction to Risk Management and Insurance,* Prentice-Hall, 2002, pp. 4-5.
8. Dorfman, *op. cit,* p., 5.
9. *Oxford Advance Learner's Dictionary, op.cit.* p. 622.

(*b*) *Morale Hazard*: Indifference — It is the attitude of indifference to take care of the property on the premise that the loss will be indemnified by the insurance company. So, it is the carelessness or indifference to a loss because of the existence of insurance contract. For example — smoking in an oil refinery, careless driving etc.

(*c*) *Societal Hazards*: Legal and Cultural — These refer to the increase in the frequency and severity of loss arising from legal doctrines or societal customs and structure. For example, the construction or the possibility of demolition of buildings in unauthorised colonies.

1.3 Types of Risks

Risk can be classified into several distinct categories. The following are the major categories:

1. Financial and non-financial risk
2. Static and dynamic risk
3. Fundamental and particular risk (or) group and individual risk
4. Pure and speculative risk.
5. Quantifiable and non-quantifiable risks

Financial and Non-financial Risks

If any risk is concerned with financial loss, it is termed as financial risk. Financial risk involves the simultaneous existence of three important elements of a risky situation.

1. Some one is adversely affected by the happening of an event.
2. The assets or income is likely to be exposed to a financial loss from the occurrence of the event.
3. Peril can cause the loss. For example, loss accrued in case of damage of property, theft of property, loss of business any financial losses. This is financial risk, output can be measured in monetary terms.

When the possibility of a financial loss does not exist, the situation can be referred to as non-financial in nature. For example, risk in the selection of career, risk in the choice of course of study etc. they may or may not have any financial implications. These types of risk are difficult to measure.

As per the insurance is concerned, risk is involved with financial loss.

Individual and Group Risks

A risk is said to be a *group* risk or *fundamental* risk if it affects the economy or its participants on a macro basis. These are impersonal in origin and consequence. They affect most of the social segments or the entire population. These risk factors may be socio-economic or political or natural calamities, e.g., earthquakes, floods, wars, unemployment or situations like 11th September attack on US etc.

Individual/particular risks are confined to individual identities or small groups. Thefts, robbery, fire etc. are risks that are particular in nature. Some of these are insurable. The methods of handling fundamental and particular risks differ by their very nature, e.g., social insurance programmes may be undertaken by the government to handle fundamental risks. Similarly, fire insurance policy may be bought by an individual to prevent against the adverse consequences of fire.

Pure and Speculative Risks

Pure risk situations are those where there is a possibility of loss or no loss. There is no gain to the individual or the organisation. For example, a car can meet with an accident or it may not meet with an accident. If an insurance policy is bought for the purpose, then if accident does not occur, there is no gain to the insured. Contrarily, if the accident occurs, the insurance company will indemnify the loss.

Speculative risk is defined as a situation in which either a profit or loss is possible. For example, investing in share market as I situation of speculation risk. If the prices of the shares increase, the person who bought the shares will gain. If the prices decreases, he will definitely loose. Horse racing, investing money in others are some examples of speculative risk.

The distinguishing characteristics of the pure and speculative risks are:

1. The pure risks are generally insurable while speculative ones are not.
2. The law of large number can be applied more easily to pure risk than to speculative risk. It is more difficult to apply the law of large number to speculative risk to predict the future loss.
3. The society may benefit from a speculative risk, even though a loss occurs but it is harmful if a pure risk is present and a loss occurs. For example, a firm may develop a new technology for producing inexpensive computers. As a result, the competitors may be forced to produce computers at a lower price. Consequently, the society benefits. However, society normally does not benefit when a loss from a pure risk occurs, such as a flood, or earthquake that devastates an area.

Static and Dynamic Risks

Dynamic risks are those resulting from the changes in the economy or the environment. Economic variables like inflation, income level, price level, technology changes and etc. since the dynamic risk emanates from the economic environment, these are very difficult to anticipate and quantify. Dynamic risk involves losses mainly concerned with financial losses. These risks affect the public and society. These risks are the best indicators of progress of society, because they are the results of adjustment or misallocation of resources.

On the other hand, static risks are more or less predictable and are not affected by the economic conditions. Static risk involves losses resulting from the destruction of an asset or changes in its possession as a result of dishonesty or human failure. Such financial losses arise, even if there are no changes in the economic environment. These losses are not useful for the society. These arise with a degree of regularity over time and as a result, are generally predictable. Example for static risk includes possibility of loss in a business, unemployment after undergoing a professional qualification, loss due to act of others ect.

Dynamic Risk	Static Risk
1. Losses are not easily predictable.	1. Losses can be predicted.
2. These results from the changes in economic environment.	2. These occur even if there is no change in economic environment.
3. These are not caused by insurance	3. These can be covered by insurance.
4. These risks benefit the society.	4. These risks don't benefit the society.

Quantifiable and Non-quantifiable Risks

The risk which can be measured using numerical scales are known to be quantifiable while the situations which may result in repercussions like tension or loss of peace are called as non-quantifiable.

The newer classification of risk adopted by financial institutions and also insurance companies is: (*a*) credit, (*b*) market, (*c*) operational and (*d*) other. These are discussed in detail in next section.

1.4 Pure Risks and Its Management

Since pure risks are generally *insurable*, the discussion on risk in various chapters of this book is skewed towards pure risks only.

1.4.1 Classification of Pure Risk

On the presumption that insurable pure risks being *static* can be classified as follows:

Exhibit 1-1

Personal Risks

Personal risks are risks that directly affect an individual. They involve the possibility of the complete loss or reduction of earned income. There are four major personal risks.

Risk of Premature Death: Premature death is defined as the death of the household head with unfulfilled financial obligations. If the surviving family members receive an insufficient amount of replacement income from other sources or have insufficient financial assets to replace the lost income, they may be financial insecure. Premature death can cause financial problems only if the deceased has dependents to support or does with unsatisfied financial obligations. Thus, the death of a child aged 5 is not premature in the economic sense.

Risk of Insufficient Income During Retirement: It refers to the risk of not having sufficient income at the age of retirement or the age becoming so that there is a possibility that individual may not be able to earn the livelihood. When one retires, he looses his earned income. Unless he has sufficient financial assets from which to draw or has access to other sources of retirement income such as social security or a private pension, he will be exposed to financial insecurity during retirement.

Risk of Poor Health: It refers to the risk of poor health or disability of a person to earn the means of survival, For example, losing the legs due to accident, heart surgery, which will cost lakhs, etc. Unless the person has adequate health insurance, private savings or other sources of income to meet these loss, he will be financially insecure. The loss of insecurity, if the disability is severe. In case of long-term disability, things will become worst and some one must take care of the disabled person. The loss of earned income can be financially vary painful.

Risk of Unemployment: The risk of unemployment is another major threat to financial security. Unemployment can result from business cycle downswings, technological and structural changes in the economy, seasonal factors and etc. Employers are increasingly hiring temporary or part-time workers to reduce labor costs. Being temporary employees, workers lose their employee benefits. Unless there is adequate replacement income or past savings on which to draw, the workers (unemployed, part-time, temporary) will be financially insecure. In the period, past savings and unemployment benefits may be exhausted.

Property Risks

It refers to the risk of having property damaged or lost because of fire, windstorm, earthquake and numerous other causes. There are two major types of loss associated with the destruction or theft of property.

Direct Loss: A direct loss is defined as a financial loss that results from the physical damage destruction, or theft of the property. For example, physical damage to a factory due to fire is known as direct loss.

Indirect or Consequential Loss: An indirect loss is a financial loss that results indirectly from the occurrence of a direct physical damage or theft loss. For example, apart from the financial loss resulted from the profit for several months while the factory as rebuilt. Extra expenses are also indirect loss to operate regardless of cost. Otherwise they will lose their customers. Therefore it is necessary to set up a temporary operation at some alternative location and extra expenses would occur. There are the indirect expenses resulted from the damage of the factory.

Liability Risks

These are the risks arising out of the intentional or unintentional injury to the persons or damages to their properties through negligence or carelessness. Liability risks generally arise from the law. For example, liability of the employer under the workmen's compensation law or other labour laws in India.

In addition to the above categories, risks may also arise *due to the failure of others.* For example, the financial loss arising from the non-performance or standard performance in a contract — in engineering/construction contracts.

1.4.2 Methods of Handling Pure Risk

Risk is burden not only to the individuals but to society as well. Thus, it is important to examine some techniques for meeting the problem of risk. There are five major methods of handling risk.

1. Avoidance of risk.
2. Loss control.
   (a) Loss prevention.
   (b) Loss reduction.
3. Risk Retention.
4. Non-insurance Transfers
   (a) Transfer of risk by contracts.
   (b) Hedging price risks
   (c) Incorporation of a business firm.
5. Insurance

1. Avoidance of Risk

Avoiding the risk or the circumstances which may lead to losses is one method of handling risk. For example, one can avoid the risk of death or disability in a plane crash by refusing to fly. It is not possible to find a formula to avoid risk completely, but to a great extent the risk can be reduced. For example, if you avoid plane, you have to drive yourself or take train/bus which are also not appealing. Losses from fire can be completely avoided by constructing a fireproof building for stocking products. Avoiding the visit to the border area at the time of war tensions is another example.

2. Loss Control

It is another important method of handling risk. Loss control consists of certain activities that reduce the frequencies and severely of losses. Thus, loss control has two major objectives: loss prevention and loss reduction.

(a) Loss Prevention: Loss prevention aims at reducing the probability of loss so that the frequency minimised/prevented by using safely lockers, number of heart attacks can be reduced, if individuals reduce their weight, diet, etc., accidents can be reduced is also important for business firms. Machine breakdown can be reduced by periodic inspections by engineers. Strict security measures in airports can reduce hijacking of aircrafts by terrorists.

(b) Loss Reduction: Even though strict loss prevention can reduce the frequency of losses, some losses will inevitably occur. Thus, the second objective of loss control is to reduce the severity or a loss after it occurred. For example, keeping firefighting equipments will reduce the severity of loss from fire. Keeping first-aid box will reduce the severity of injury.

3. Risk Retention

An individual or a business firm retains all or part of a given risk, i.e., retains the obligations to pay for part or all of the losses. For example, a transport company may decide to retain the risk that cash flows will drop due to increases in the price of oil. Retention is done with a formal plan to fund losses can be paid by the firm. It is the easiest and cheapest way of dealing with relatively small losses by paying out of one's own resources whenever they occur or by creating some fund to meet such losses if their magnitude is somewhat large.

In general, Risk retention is appropriate for low severity risks where potential losses are relatively small. For example, A House owner may retain the small part of the risk of damage to the house (small repairs). The motorist may wish to retain the risk of low severely accidents. Even if a person has purchased a mediclaim policy, he can pay for small medical expenses and he does not need to claim from the insurance company.

4. Non-insurance Transfers

Some type of risks involving loss can be shifted or transferred to other's shoulders. Risk is transferred to a party other than a insured company. A risk can be transferred by several methods. Following are some major methods of risk transfer.

(a) Transfer of Risk by Contract: Unwanted risk can be transferred by contracts. For example, the risk of defective computers can be transferred to a service provider through annual maintenance contract. The contractor is responsible for all repairs and maintenance. The risk of price increase in the construction material can be transferred to the builder by having a fixed price in the contract.

(b) Hedging Price Risk: This is a technique for transferring the risk of unfavorable price fluctuations to a speculator by purchasing and selling forward contracts on an organized exchange. These contracts can be used to hedge risk, i.e., they may be used to offset losses that can occur from changes in interest rates, commodity prices, foreign exchange rates, etc. Firms that use oil in the production process are subject to losses from unexpected increase in oil prices. Similarly, oil producers are subject to loss from unexpected decrease in oil prices. Both firms can hedge their risk by entering into a forward contract that requires the oil producer to provide the oil user with a specified future delivery date at a predetermined price (known as forward price), regardless of the market price of oil. Oil price may be increasing or decreasing, but the supplier sells the oil at the agreed price.

(c) Incorporation of Business Firm: If a firm is a sole proprietorship, owner,s personal assets can be attached by creditors for satisfaction of debts. If a firm incorporates, personal assets cannot be attached by creditors for payment of the firm's debts. In essence, by incorporation, the liability of the stockholders is limited, and the risk of the firm having insufficient assets to pay business debts is shifted to the creditors.

5. Insurance

Even if we try to avoid, control and prevent, still the risk will exist. Therefore, insurance is the most practical method for handling a major risk. The risk is transferred to the insurer. The basic objective of insurance is to transfer the risk of a person to the insurance company which has easily similar risks. As such for handling risks which involve large financial losses or which are dangerous and uncontrollable by any single person, insurance is a mean of shifting such risks to insure in consideration of a nominal cost called premium. In fact, among the various methods of handling risks, insurance is the only widely used method.

1.5 Financial Risk and Its Management

Financial Risk is the risk arising from the changes in the values of measurable financial variables. For example, Financial risk is that a company will not have adequate cash flow to meet financial obligations. In a corporate financing context, financial risk is the additional risk a shareholder bears when a company uses debt in addition to equity financing. Companies that issue more debt instruments would have higher financial risk than companies financed mostly or entirely by equity. Finance theory prescribes that a firm undertakes activities that maximize shareholder value. A firm cannot create value for shareholders by taking on project that shareholders could do for themselves at the same return. This implies that firm managers should not hedge risks that investors can hedge for themselves. Since financial markets are not perfect, firm managers likely have many opportunities to create value for shareholders using financial risk management.

Sources of Financial Risk

An organization may be faced with the following financial risks:

1. Risk arising from organization's exposure to changes in market prices, viz., interest rates, exchange rates, commodity prices.
2. Risk arising from actions of, and transactions with, other organizations such as vendors, customers, and counterparties in derivative transactions.
3. Risk arising from the internal actions or failures of the organization, particularly people, processes and systems.

Financial risk in business organizations arises from transactions of financial nature including sales purchases, investments and loans and various other business activities. It can arise as a result of legal transactions, new projects, mergers and acquisitions, debt financing, the energy component of cists, or through the activities of management and other stakeholders. Fluctuations in the value of financial variable comprised in these activities reduces value giving risk to financial risk.

Classification of Financial Risk

On the basis of above, James Lam (2001) has suggested the following classification of risk:

(a) Credit: Credit risk is the risk that a customer, counterparty, or supplier will fail to meet its obligations. It includes every thing from a borrower default to supplier's missing deadlines because of credit problems. Credit Risk is the change in value of a debt due to changes in the perceived ability of counterparties to meet their contractual obligations (or credit rating). Also known as default risk or counterparty risk, credit risk is faced by lending institutions like banks, investors in debt instruments of corporate houses, and by parties involved in contractual agreements like forward contracts. There are independent agencies that assess the credit risk in form of credit ratings.

Credit rating is an opinion (of the credit rating agency) on the ability of the organization to perform its contractual obligations (pay the principle and/or interest of the loan) on a timely basis. Each level of rating indicates a probability of default. International credit rating agencies (like Moody's, Fitch, and S&P) use quantitative models along with their experience to predict the credit ratings. Credit scoring models of banks and lending institutions use stock prices (if available), financial performance and sector-specific data, and macroeconomic forecasts to predict the credit rating.

Credit risk can be transferred using credit derivatives, and also by securitization. For business organizations, swaps and structured notes are useful financial products to hedge.

(*b*) *Market*: Market risk is the risk that process will move in a way that has negative consequences for a company. Market Risk is the change in value of assets due to changes in the underlying economic factors such as interest rates, foreign exchange rates, macroeconomic variables, stock prices, and commodity prices. All economic entities that own assets face market risk. For example, bills receivable of software exporters that are denominated in foreign currencies are exposed to exchange rate fluctuations; while value of bonds/government securities owned by investors depend on prevailing interest rates. Organizations with huge exposures, either have a dedicated treasury department, or outsource market risk management to banks.

Modeling market risk requires forecasting the changes in the economic factors, and assess their impact on the asset value. Amost popular measure for expressing market risk is Value-at-Risk, which is 'the maximum loss' from an unfavorable event, within a given level of confidence, for a given holding period. Various financial instruments like options, futures, forwards, swaps etc. can be used effectively to hedge the market risk. Availability of huge data on various markets has facilitated the development of many sophisticated models.

(*c*) *Operational:* Operational risk is the risk that people, processes, or systems will fail or that an external event will negatively affect the company. Practically speaking, all organizations face operational risk. For a financial institution/bank, operational risk can be defined as the possibility of loss due to mistakes made in carrying out transactions such as settlement failures, failures to meet regulatory requirements, and untimely collections. No concrete model of managing credit risk is available till today. Still lot of research is being done in this direction.

(*d*) *Other*: Other risks are extensions of the above-mentioned categories, viz., business risk is the risk that future operating results may not meet expectations and also, organizational risk is the risk that arises from a badly designed organizational structure or lack of sufficient human resources.

Financial Risk Management Process

The financial risk management process in every organization involves the following logical steps (Gupta, June 2004):

- *Defining Objectives/Establishing Context*: Drawing a structure of the operating environment, both external and internal, overview of the organization mission, objectives, stakeholders' interests and the developing the risk management context activities and their relationships across business segments.
- *Identifying the Risk Exposures*: Documenting the conditions and events that represent material threats to the organization's achievement of its objectives or represent areas to exploit for competitive advantage.
- *Evaluating the Risk Exposures*: Analyzing/Quantifying Risks the risk-probability distributions, computing Value-at-Risk (VaR)[10] etc. (Linda, 2004).

10. VaR is the maximum possible loss that can occur in a situation at a given confidence level.

- *Analysing Solutions:* Aggregating all risk distributions, reflecting correlation and portfolio effects, and expressing results in terms of impact on the organization's key performance indicators, prioritizing risks and determining the feasibility of various risk management alternatives. It includes feasibility analysis of the various alternatives and developing strategies for controlling or exploiting the various risks.
- *Implementation and Review:* Implementing the solutions and continuous appraisal of the performance of the risk management strategies.

The assessment of financial risk hinges around the probability of adverse events. There are events that have a low probability of occurring but result in a high loss. Risk is not always possible to eliminate, it is better to hedge to transfer to reduce its severity.

Financial Risk Modeling

Financial risk modeling is the practice of measuring risks in various domains of finance, viz., financial markets, banking, insurance etc. It is the most important part of pricing financial instruments and also helps in regulation of financial activities like investment banking, and lending. The following matrix gives an illustration of the various risk measurement models (detailed description is out of the preview of this book).

Risk Type	Measurement Models	Manage/Hedge/Transfer
Market Risk	Nelson-Seigel Svennson Model, Cubic B-Spline, Cox, Ingersoll & Ross Model, Vasicek Model, Black Kara, Risk metrics	Derivatives (Options, Futures, Swaps etc.)
Credit Risk	*Structural Models* - Black & Scholes, Merton Model,Black & Cox, Geske, Delianedis & Geske*Reduced form Models* - Litterman & I ben, Jarrow & Turnbull, Duffie& Singleton *Products* - KMV, Creditmetrics, Credit Portfolio View, Credit Risk+, Loan Analysis System etc.	Credit Derivatives, Securitization
Operational Risk	Scorecard, Simulation, Causal Modeling etc.	Insurance

Source: www.decisioncraft.com/dmdirect/financial.htm

The risk management strategies highlighted above keeps on changing in view of the market conditions, business environment changes or changes in the political conditions.

1.6 Rationale for Risk Management

The rationale for risk aversion can usefully be segmented into four categories:

(a) Managerial Self-interest

(b) The Non-linearity of Taxes

(c) The Cost of Financial Distress

(d) The Existence of Capital Market Imperfections

(a) Managerial Self-interest

Managers have limited ability to diversify their own personal wealth position, associated with stock holdings and the capitalization of their career earnings associated with their own employment position. Therefore, they prefer stability to volatility because, other things equal, such stability improves their own utility, at little or no expense to other stakeholders.

(b) The Non-linearity of Taxes

Beyond managerial motives, firm level performance and market value may be directly associated with volatility for a number of other reasons. The first is the nature of the tax code, which both historically and internationally is highly non-linear. By reducing the effective long-term average tax rate, activities which reduce the volatility in reported earnings will enhance shareholder's value.

(c) The Cost of Financial Distress

Firms may also be concerned about volatility of earnings because of the consequences of severely negative deviations from expected value and their implications for corporate viability.

(d) Capital Market Imperfections

Conventionally, external financing is more costly than internally generated funds due to many number of capital market imperfections. These may include discrete transaction costs to obtain external financing, imperfect information as to the riskiness of the investment opportunities present in the firm, or the high cost of the potential future bankruptcy state. In the case of mutual insurers, who have little access to the capital market, this line of argument is particularly compelling. At the same time, the firm has an investment opportunity set which can be ordered in terms of net present value.

The volatility of profitability causes the firm to seek external finance to exploit investment opportunities when profits are low. The cost of such external finance is higher than the internal funds due to the market's higher cost structure.

Key Terms

- Financial Risk
- Market Risk
- Risk Modeling
- Value Maximization
- Static Risk
- Speculative Risk
- Peril
- Credit Risk
- Operational Risk
- Value at Risk
- Risk
- Dynamic Risk
- Event
- Hazard

Questions for Review

1. Discuss the various types of financial risk and how they can be managed.
2. Explain the logical steps in financial risk management.
3. Define risk. List some ways in which risk creates an economic burden for society.
4. Differentiate between the following type of risk:
   (a) Pure versus speculative
   (b) Static versus dynamic
   (c) Subjective versus objective.
5. Give an example of a risk that is both pure and static.
6. An insurable loss is:
   (a) An event that has not been predicted.
   (b) An exposure that cannot be easily measured before the event has occurred.
   (c) An unexpected reduction of economic value.
   (d) Being without something one has previously possessed.
7. Differentiate between a peril and a hazard and give an example of each.
8. For each of the following hazards, state the peril to which the hazard relates.
   (a) A drunken driver of a truck
   (b) A person with damaged kidneys
   (c) A house with poor quality of electricity cable fittings.
   (d) An unlocked car in no-parking area.
9. "Pure Risks are always insurable." Comment.

Suggested Readings

1. Dun and Bradstreet, Financial Risk Management, 2007, Tata McGraw-Hill, Delhi.
2. Gupta, P.K., Insurance & Risk Management, 2004, Himalaya Publishing House, Mumbai.
3. Emmett Vaughan and Therese Vaughan, *Essentials of Risk Management and Insurance,* John Wiley and Sons Inc., 2002.
4. M.W. Jones-Lee, *The Economics of Safety and Physical Risk,* Basic Blackwell Ltd., 1989.
5. M.W. Jones-Lee, *The Value of Life,* The University of Chicago University Press, Chicago, 1976
6. Margot Naylor, *The Truth about Life,* George Allen and Unwin Ltd., London, 1971.
7. Mark S. Dorfman, *Fundamentals of Insurance*, Prentice-Hall, 2002.
8. Scott E. Harrington and Gregory R. Niehaus, *Insurance and Risk Management*, Irwin/McGraw-Hill, 1999.

❑❑❑

RISK MANAGEMENT AND CONTROL

CHAPTER

Chapter Objectives

- Risk Management
- Risk Control
- Risk Financing
- Risk Management Objectives
- Risk Management Process
- Risk Management : Guidelines and Responsibilities
- Levels of Risk Management
- Risk Management Information Systems (RMIS)
- Risk Management by Individuals
- Process of Risk Management by Individuals
- Personal Risk Management Strategies
- Factors Affecting Individual's Demand for Insurance
- Corporate Risk Management
- Risk Management and Derivatives

Introduction

The future is largely unknown. Most business decision-making takes place on the basis of expectations about the future. Making a decision on the basis of assumptions, expectations, estimates and forecasts of future events involves taking risks. Risk has been described as the *"sugar and salt of life"*. This implies that risk can have an upside as well downside. People take risk in order to achieve some goal they would otherwise not have reached without taking that risk. On the other hand, risk can mean that some danger or loss may be involved in carrying out an activity and therefore, care has to be taken to avoid that loss. This is where Risk Management is important, in that it can be used to protect against loss or danger arising from a risky activity.

2.1 Risk Management

Risk management is an integrated process of delineating specific areas or risk, developing a comprehensive plan, integrating the plan, and conducting ongoing evaluation.

Risk management is the identification, assessment, and prioritization of risks followed by coordinated and economical application of resources to minimize, monitor, and control the probability and/or impact of unfortunate events. The International Organization for Standardization (ISO) has identifieed the following principles of risk management. Risk management should:

a. create value

b. be an integral part of organizational processes

c. be part of decision making

d. explicitly address uncertainty

e. be systematic and structured

f. be based on the best available information

g. be tailored

h. take into account human factors

i. be transparent and inclusive

j. be dynamic, iterative and responsive to change

k. be capable of continual improvement and enhancement

The risk management process involves the following logical steps:

1. Defining the objectives of the risk management exercise
2. Identifying the risk exposures
3. Evaluating the exposures
4. Critical analysis of risk management alternatives and selecting one of them
5. Implementation and review.

The job of risk management can, therefore, be broken down into three elements, which follow each other in a logical sequence:

- Risk analysis
- Risk control
- Risk financing

Because the conditions under which firms operate change, the risk management process has a necessity to be dynamic. All three elements of the process have therefore to be continuing reassessment and monitoring of the results.

Exhibit 2.1

Risk Managment Process

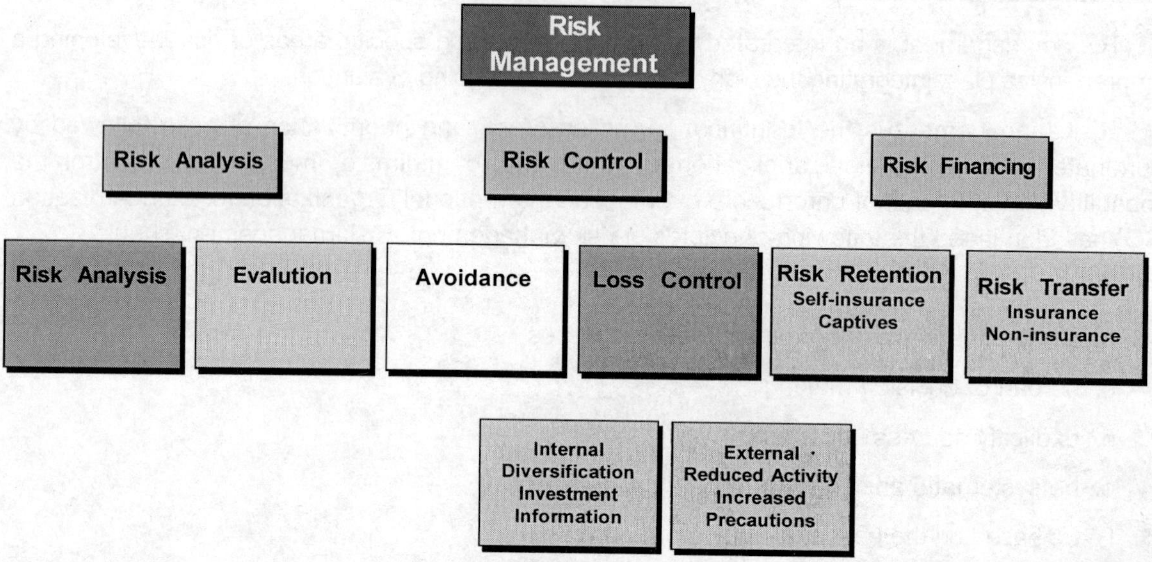

Risk Management

Risk Analysis | Risk Control | Risk Financing

Risk Analysis | Evalution | Avoidance | Loss Control | Risk Retention Self-insurance Captives | Risk Transfer Insurance Non-insurance

Internal Diversification Investment Information | External · Reduced Activity Increased Precautions

All Risk Manager's believe that *"prevention is better than cure"*. It is better not to have suffered a loss than to suffer and collect under an insurance policy. Insurance will not compensate for all losses; for example, time spent dealing with the claim loss of client base and reputation. There is also a growing body of evidence to suggest that a significant proportion of firms never fully recover from the effects of a major loss and have to be wound-up within a short time even if fully insured.

Risk Identification

The first step in the process is to anlalyse the risk to which an organisation may be exposed. Risk analysis has to prime elements — the identification of risk and its evaluation.

Risk Identification requires knowledge of the organization, the market in which it operates, the legal, social, economic, political, and climatic environment in which it does its business, its financial strengths and weakneses, its vulnerability to unplanned losses, the manufacturing processes, and the management systems and business mechanism by which it operates. Any failure at this stage to identify risk may cause a major loss for the organisation. Risk identification provides the foundation for risk management. The various methods of risk identification are:

- Checklist Method
- Financial Statement Method
- Flow Chart Method
- On-site Inspections

- Interactions with Others
- Contract Analysis
- Statistical Records of Losses

Risk Evaluation

Risk Evaluation breaks down into two parts, the assessment of:

- The probability of loss occurring, and
- Its severity

The underlying logic of risk management is that "Risk Reduces Value". Therefore, in order to quantify risk, value-at-risk is the most popular measure.

Value-at-Risk

Value is measurable variable that depicts one's desire or state of affairs in a given set of circumstances. Since circumstances never remain same for any identity, whatever value is perceived or created is always at risk (Value-at-risk).

VaR measures the worst expected loss over a given horizon under the normal market conditions at a given confidence level.

In its most general form, the Value-at-Risk measures the potential loss in value of a risky asset or portfolio over a defined period for a given confidence interval. Thus, if the VaR on an asset is $ 100 million at a one-week, 95% confidence level, there is a only a 5% chance that the value of the asset will drop more than $100 million over any given week. In its adapted form, the measure is sometimes defined more narrowly as the possible loss in value from "normal market risk" as opposed to all risk, requiring that we draw distinctions between normal and abnormal risk as well as between market and non-market risk.

While Value-at-Risk can be used by any entity to measure its risk exposure, it is used most often by commercial and investment banks to capture the potential loss in value of their traded portfolios from adverse market movements over a specified period; this can then be compared to their available capital and cash reserves to ensure that the losses can be covered without putting the firms at risk.

To estimate the probability of the loss, with a confidence interval, we need to define the probability distributions of individual risks, the correlation across these risks and the effect of such risks on value. Simulations are widely used to measure the VaR for asset portfolio.

There are three key elements of VaR – a specified level of loss in value, a fixed time period over which risk is assessed and a confidence interval. The VaR can be specified for an individual asset, a portfolio of assets or for an entire firm.

A one-day VAR of $10mm using a probability of 5% means that there is a 5% chance that the portfolio could lose more than $10mm in the next trading day.

Exhibit 2.2

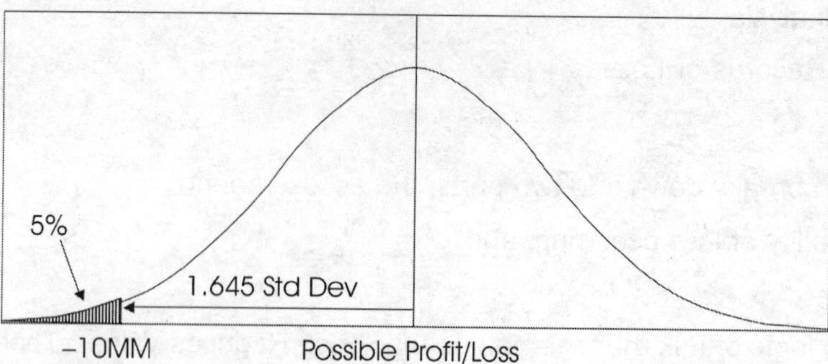

VaR Methodologies

- Historical Simulations Approach
- Variance-Covariance Approach
- Monte-Carlo Simulation

Supplementing VaR

VaR estimation can be made more robust by the techniques like: (a) *Stress Testing:* Hypothetical estimation of various market scenarios, valuation of the impact, development of contingency plans, or (b) *Sensitivity Analysis:* Hypothetical changes in the value of the individual market factor, use of pricing models to compute the overall value, formulating strategies for the combined impact.

2.2 Risk Control

Risk control covers all those measures aimed at avoiding, eliminating or reducing the chances of loss-producing events occurring, or limiting the severity of the losses that do happen. Here, one is seeking to change the conditions that bring about loss-producing events or increase their severity. Though some measures call for little more than common sense, often-considerable technical knowledge is required, for which the risk manager will need to turn to experts in the particular field.

Risk can be controlled either by avoidance or by controlling losses. Avoidance implies that either a certain loss exposure is not acquired or an existing one is abandoned.

Loss control can be exercised in two ways:

(*a*) One way is to enhance and monitor the level of precautions taken to minimise the losses due to exposures.

(*b*) Another is to control and minimise the risk operations, internal risk control techniques include diversification and/or investments in getting information of loss exposures so as to control them.

Risk management objectives differs from individual to individual and organisation to organisation. However, as a concept these can be segregated into two:

(*a*) Before occurrence of losses — these can be of following types:

(*i*) Reduction in worry and fear

(ii) Economical ways of handing risk

(iii) Overcome legal obligations

(b) After occurrence of losses:

(i) Survival

(ii) Congruence with mission and objectives

(iii) Optimising social effects

2.3 Risk Financing

When the risk exposure for an organisation exceeds the maximum limit that the organization can bear, it becomes necessary to either transfer or reduce risk. However, there is cost involved in both of these exercises. If the method adopted is insurance, the consequential impact on taxes and profits also becomes important. Risk Financing, therefore, refers *to the manner in which the risk control measures that have been implemented shall be financed.*

It has to be recognized that in the long run, an organization will have to pay for its own losses. The primary objective of risk financing is *to spread more evenly over time cost of risk in order to reduce the financial strain* and possible insolvency which random concurrency of large losses may cause. The secondary objective is *to minimise risk costs.*

Essentially, an organization can finance its risk cost in three ways:

- Losses may be charged as they occur to current operating costs; or
- *Ex-ante* provision may be made for losses, either through the purchase of insurance or by building up a contingency found to which losses can be charged; or
- When losses occur they may be financed with loans, which are repaid over the next few months or years.

Risk financing includes the following alternatives:

Risk Retention

Risk retention implies that the losses arising due to a risk exposure shall be *retained* or *assumed* by the party or the organization. Risk retention is generally a deliberate decision for business organizations inherited with the following characteristics:

(a) The consequential losses are small;

(b) Losses are shown as operating expenses or can be funded with retained profits.

Self-insurance

Self-insurance is one of the forms of planned retention by which the part or full of the exposure arising due to a risk factor is retained by the firm. Self-insurance programmes differ from the other programmes in the sense of the formal arrangements made. It acts as an alternative to buying insurance in the market or when a part of the claim is not insured in the commercial market. It may be done by keeping aside funds to meet insurable losses. The main reason for self-insurance is that the organization believes it has large funds to finance losses and the opportunity cost of transfer is less than the cost of insurance.

Benefits of Self-insurance

(*a*) *Saves transaction costs* — It helps to save cost in the form of amount payable to insurer for overheads and profits, commissions and taxes and the social loading (arising from the statutory requirements) inherent in the premium.

(*b*) *Accuracy of predictions* — The risk managers in the organization think that they are better judges of the adverse exposures and can estimate better than the insurers.

(*c*) *Investment of funds* — Since insurance companies invest large chunk of funds in various securities and the returns arising therefrom is not reflected in the rates charged by the insurers, the cost reduction becomes obvious for the insured.

(*d*) *Minimisation of disputes* — Self-managed funds enhances satisfaction to the insured and reduces the conflicts in claims settlement. Also, there is a direct incentive to reduce and control the risk of loss.

Captive Insurance

Captive insurance companies represent a special case of risk retention. *A captive insurance company* is an entity created and controlled by a parent, whose main purpose is to provide insurance to its corporate owner. The ideology behind this method is that the parent company may save in terms of overhead costs and profits which would otherwise be charged by the insurance company. Also, the insured companies claim premiums as expenses, which may lead to advantages in terms of differential cash flows. These captives may either be *pure captives or group captives.*

A pure captive is an insurance company established by the parent (generally into non-insurance business) organization to provide insurance cover to itself or its subsidiary or affiliated organizations.

Group captives are those formed by a group of companies for providing insurance cover to control their respective and collective risks. In US terminology, these are also known as "trade association insurance companies."

Motives Behind Captives

(*a*) *Optimized loss prevention benefits:* The benefits enduring from loss prevention are available directly to the insured.

(*b*) *Economies of scale:* Groups with several subsidiaries can enjoy the benefit of perfectly tailored insurance products made available to cover risks.

(*c*) *Non-availability of insurance:* Captives provide to cover risk exposures for which covers are otherwise not available in the market.

(*d*) *Stability of earnings:* The captives reduce the chances of adverse impact of sudden fluctuations in profits on the firm.

(*e*) *Cost and tax advantages:* Obviously, as said earlier, captives reduce cost of risk financing and provide gains in the regime of differential taxes.

Risk Transfer

Risk transfer implies that the exposed party transfers whole or part of the losses consequential to risk exposure to another party for a cost. The insurance contracts fundamentally involve risk transfers. Apart from the insurance device, there are certain other techniques by which the risk may be transferred. Some of the these have been discussed in detail in Chapter 7.

(*a*) *Insurance:* Insurance is a contractual transfer of risk. The insurance company agrees to indemnify the losses arising out an occurrence predetermined and charges some cost for this act, called as premium. The insurance method of risk transfer is most appropriate when the severity of losses is very high.[1] Since the important constraint, i.e., the cost of transfer prevails, the suitability of this method depends upon the *size* of the organization and *affordability.*

(*b*) *Non-insurance transfers:* Out of the various methods of non-insurance risk transfers, the most common are:

(*i*) Hold harmless agreements or indemnity agreements are the contractual relationships specifying that all losses shall be borne by the designated party, e.g., a landlord contracting that all losses shall be borne by the tenant. These agreements by themselves do not reduce original risk.[2] The form and jurisdiction of hold harmless agreements varies from contract to contract.

(*ii*) Incorporation is another method by which, for example, the sole proprietorship firm or partnership firm can convert themselves into companies and reduce the liability on them. To quote, the liability of a proprietorship firm is unlimited compared to that of a company limited by shares — the liability of the members is limited to the extent of capital contributed by them.

(*iii*) Hedging can be used to transfer speculative risk. The popular of the instruments used in hedging are derivative contracts.

(*iv*) Diversification across business or geographic locations justified or coupled with synergies or economies of scale can also significantly reduce risk in aggregate.

2.4 Risk Management Objectives

As discussed earlier, risk management is an integrated process of describing specific areas of risk, developing a comprehensive plan, integrating the plan and conducting ongoing evaluation. It is a process that identifies loss exposures faced by an organization and selects the most appropriate techniques including insurance for treating such exposures.

Risk management should not be confused with insurance management. Risk management is broader concept and includes all techniques for treating loss exposures, in addition to insurance. Risk management has important objectives. These objectives can be classifieds follows:

(*a*) Preloss Objective: Following are the objectives before the loss.

(*i*) *Reduction in worry and fear:* The risk management should be able to reduce anxiety and fear in the mind of the likely exposed unit and should be able to enhance value without constraints on operating activities.

1. Dorfman M.S., *Introduction to Risk Management and Insurance,* Prentice-Hall 2002, pp. 58.
2. J.S. Trieshman *et. al., Risk Management and Insurance,* South-Western College Publishing, 2001, pp. 84-85.

(*ii*) *Economy:* This means that the firm should prepare for potential losses in the most economical way. This preparation involves an analysis of the cost safety programmes, insurance premium paid and the costs associated with the different techniques for handling losses.

(*iii*) *Meeting legal obligations:* The next objective is to meet any legal obligations. Risk managers must see that all these obligations are met or not. For example, government regulation may require a firm to install safety devices to protect workers from harm, to dispose hazardous waste materials, property etc.

(*b*) Post Loss Objective: Following are the objective of risk management after a loss occurs.

(*i*) *Survival:* The most important post loss objectives is survival of the firm. If a loss occurs, the firm cannot be totally shut down. The firm should be able to resume the operations or at least partial operations within some reasonable time period so that the firm will survive in the market.

(*ii*) *Continued operation:* Even if a loss occurs, the firms mainly service provider should be able to continue their operations,. For example, public utility firms such as airlines, banks, bakeries and dories must continue to operate even after a loss. Otherwise business will be lost to competitors.

(*iii*) *Stability of earning:* The next post loss objective is stability in earning. If the firm continues to operate, then there will be a stability in the earning of the firm. The firm will have to face substantial additional expenses to achieve this goal. The firm can shift their operations to another location.

(*iv*) *Continued Growth:* After the stability is earning. The company can show a continuous growth. It can develop new products and enter into new markets. They can acquire or merge with another company. The risk manager must consider the effect that a loss will have on the firm's ability to grow.

(*v*) *Optimizing Social Effects:* The objective of social responsibility of risk management is to minimize the effects that a loss will have on other person and on socially. A severe loss can adversely affect employees, suppliers, creditors and the community in general. For example, a severe loss that shut down a plant in a small town for an extended period can cause considerable economic distress in the town.

2.5 Risk Management Process

Risk management is the process of identification, analysis and control of those risks. Risk management involves the following steps.

1. Defining the Objective of Risk Management: The first step in the risk management is to define the objective. Risk management is widely used by corporations, small employers, farmers, government bodies and even by individuals. Different risky situations result in different kind of losses. Loss from accident is significantly differ from loss from firm when risk managers deal with these risks, they must have certain objectives, produce and post loss.

2. Identifying Potential Losses: The next step is to identify the potential loss exposures. Risk managers must have the knowledge about the firm, the market in which it operates, the legal, social, economical and political environment in which it operates the firm's financial background and also the business mechanism. Then the risk may cause a major loss for the organization. Property loss, liability loss, business income lose, death or disability, retirement or unemployment, robbery and etc are some of the major loss exposures using some sources of flow charts, financial statements, on-site physical inspection and interaction with exports.

3. Evaluating the Potential Losses: Next step as to evaluate and measure the impact of the losses. This step involves an estimation of the potential frequency and security of losses. Loss frequency refers to the probable number of losses that may occur during some given time period. Loss servile refers to the probable size of the losses.

Once the frequency and security of each type of loss exposures are estimated, various loss exposures can be ranked according to their relative importance. Because a loss exposure with high potential is much more Important than an exposure with small loss potential. Also the estimation of frequency and security of loss will help the risk manager to select most appropriate each exposure. For example, if certain losses occur regularly and are fairly predictable, they can be budgeted out of the firm's income and treated as normal operating expenses.

So, the loss severity is more important than the loss frequency. Because a single catastrophic loss will wipe out the entire firm. Therefore, it is important to consider the maximum possible loss that can result from a single event. For example, if a plant is totally destroyed in a earthquake, the total loss may be 20 lakhs. But occur more than in 50 years. So, the risk manager ignores the event which occurs so infrequently. Thus, the potential losses should be evaluated, even if they occur frequently or infrequently.

4. Selecting Appropriate Techniques for Losses: The next step in the risk management process is to select the most appropriate technique for treating loss exposures. These techniques can be broadly classified as risk control and risk financing.

(*a*) *Risk Control:* Risk control is a technique in which no monetary compensation is involved. Loss controls are those actions which reduce the expected cost of losses by reducing the frequency and severity of losses major risk control techniques involve the following:

(i) Avoidance

(ii) Loss prevention

(iii) Loss reduction

(*b*) Risk Financing: Risk financing refers to the manner in which the risk control measures that have been implemented shall be financed. It refers to techniques that provide for the funding of losses after they occur. Major risk financing techniques include the following:

(i) Risk retention

(ii) Non-insurance transfers

(iii) Commercial insurance

5. Implementing and Reviewing the Programme: To have an effective risk management programme, a risk management policy statement is necessary. This statement outlines the risk management objectives of the firm as well as the company policy with respect to the treatment of loss exposures. In addition to this, a risk treatment manual can be developed. This manual describes the details of the programme. It is a very useful tool for training new employees of the firm. This manual also includes important information's such as procedures to follow in an emergency. The risk manager should have cooperation with other financial departments like marketing, production, finance, HR, ect.

Finally, the risk management programme must be periodically reviewed and evaluated to determine whether the objectives are being attained. Risk management costs, safety programmes must be carefully monitored. Loss records must be periodically examined to detect any changes in frequency and severity.

2.6 Risk Management: Guidelines and Responsibilities

General Risk Management Guidelines

- All human activity involving technical devices or complex processes entails some element of risk.
- Hazards can be controlled; they are not a cause for panic.
- Problems should be kept in perspective.
- Judgments should be based upon knowledge, experience and mission requirements.
- Encouraging all participants in an operation to adopt risk management principles both reduces risk and makes the task of reducing it easier.
- Good analysis tilts the odds in favor of safe and successful operation.
- Hazard analysis and risk assessment do not replace good judgment: they improve it.
- Establishing clear objectives and parameters in risk management works better than using a cookbook approach.
- No one best solution may exist. Normally, there are a variety of alternatives, each of which may produce a different degree of risk reduction.
- Tact is essential. It is more productive to show a mission planner how he can better manage risk than to condemn his approach as unworkable, risky, unsafe or unsound.
- Seldom can complete safety be achieved.
- There are no "safety problems" in planning or design, only management problems that may cause accidents, if left unresolved.

Risk Management Responsibilities

Managers

- Are responsible for effective management of risk.
- Select from risk reduction options recommended by staff.

- ❑ Accept or reject risk based upon the benefit to be derived.
- ❑ Train and motivate personnel to use risk management techniques.
- ❑ Elevate decisions to a higher level when it is appropriate.

Staff

- ❑ Assess risks and develop risk reduction alternatives.
- ❑ Integrate risk controls into plans and orders.
- ❑ Identify unnecessary risk controls.

Supervisors

- ❑ Apply the risk management process.
- ❑ Consistently apply effective risk management concepts and methods to operations and tasks.
- ❑ Elevate risk issues beyond their control or authority to superiors for resolution.

Individuals

- ❑ Understand, accept and implement risk management processes.
- ❑ Maintain a constant awareness of the changing risks associated with the operation or task.
- ❑ Make supervisors immediately aware of any unrealistic risk reduction measures or high-risk procedures.

2.7 Levels of Risk Management

The risk management process operates on three levels. Although it would be preferable to perform an in-depth application of risk management for every operation or task, the time and resources may not always be available. The three levels are as follows:

Time-critical

Time-critical risk management is an "on the run" mental or verbal review of the situation using the basic risk management process without necessarily recording the information. This time-critical process of risk management is employed by personnel to consider risk while making decisions in a time-compressed situation. This level of risk management is used during the execution phase of training or operations as well as in planning and execution during crisis responses. It is also the most easily applied level of risk management in off-duty situations. It is particularly helpful for choosing the appropriate course of action when an unplanned event occurs during execution of a planned operation or daily routine.

Deliberate

Deliberate Risk Management is the application of the complete process. It primarily uses experience and brainstorming to identify risks, hazards and develops controls and is therefore most effective when done in a group. Examples of deliberate applications include the planning of upcoming operations, review of standard operating, maintenance, or training procedures, and damage control or disaster response planning.

Strategic

This is the deliberate process with more thorough hazard identification and risk assessment involving research of available data, use of diagram and analysis tools, formal testing, or long-term tracking of the risks associated with the system or operation (normally with assistance from technical experts). It is used to study the hazards and their associated risks in a complex operation or system, or one in which the hazards are not well understood. Examples of strategic applications include the long-term planning of complex operations, introduction of new equipment, materials and operational, development of tactics and training curricula, high risk facility construction, and major system overhaul or repair. Strategic risk management should be used on high priority or high visibility risks.

2.7.1 Areas of Personal Risk Management

In our personal lives, we will face risk in:

- investments we make
- the impact of death or disability on our lives and those of our immediate family
- health risks and the costs associated with health care
- the business environment (more so for some of us than others).

2.8 Risk Management Information Systems (RMIS)

In view of the growing competition in the insurance sector, risk managers are now feeling a dire need of computer information systems that will help them hold down their costs.

"They also (Risk Managers) want computer applications that are customized to meet their unique needs, and they are seeking true Web-based systems that facilitate the sharing of loss information and reports with managers in remote locations. In the current market, risk managers are demanding the ability to pluck credible data from their information systems."

"Risk management information systems are software tools designed to assist risk managers in their functions. Traditional RMIS software emphasizes claim management, safety monitoring, and financing losses. Other tools available in a RMIS are management of insurance policies, exposure data and insurance certificates.

An enterprisewide RMIS system can help managers with a wide array of functions. At the outset, once connected to an organization's existing information systems, the RMIS gathers information from all these various systems into one database. There, the data can be analyzed from various angles to get different perspectives on the risks the organization faces.

With this rich database and analysis tool, various custom reports can be produced not just for a risk manager, but also for managers throughout the organization, giving them a detailed look at their exposures.

Initially, in the late 1960s and early 1970s, risk management information technology was limited to systems utilizing mainframe computers that allowed insurers to print out summaries of claim losses as a courtesy to their larger policyholders. These primitive loss run were often months behind real time, contained numerous errors, and were difficult to read. Moreover, they contained little useful information, the only exception being the total incurred loss figures for any particular claim.

Nevertheless, these computer print-out loss runs were the precursor of client reports that risk managers, or "insurance managers" as they were called then, were beginning to request with greater frequency. As their superiors demanded more and more financial information about the nature of losses driving their premium costs, obtaining such information was vital."

RMIS can be used for the following:

1. Reporting

Creation of reports that summarize loss payments and estimates of future losses. Accounting and finance departments use these reports in preparing the organization's financial statements.

2. Examination of Causes of Accidents

By identifying the reasons for accidents, risk managers can determine where safety and loss prevention expenditures would be most helpful. A large number of employees or customers slipping and falling in a certain area may warrant a review of clean-up procedures or a study of the costs for installing special carpet.

3. Review of Claims Adjustment Process

Risk managers use RMIS to evaluate the performance of claims adjusters by comparing actual results to standards. Typical evaluation areas are promptness of initial contact, case settlement time, amount paid for type of injury, and accuracy of the adjuster's case value estimate.

The emergence of internet as a critical tool for business communication and services has rapidly impacted RMIS, as many vendors have "Web-enabled" new and existing products to take advantage of the Internet's broad availability and low end-user maintenance costs. The internet has also permitted older legacy systems to remain viable in the marketplace because end-users work with a newer, standard interface even though processing may be occurring on a mainframe or other older computer system.

Software products have also been introduced to serve special application needs, such as catastrophe simulation software to assist in examining the effects of disasters on a group of exposed properties, and hazardous material tracking programmes to record the uses and locations of potentially hazardous items.

2.8.1 Risk Manager Tasks and Responsibilities

Risk manager is a person who performs the risk management function in an organization by whatever name called. He is responsible for overall risk management activities including risk control and financing. They are also sometimes responsible for employee benefit plans. The responsibilities of risk manager vary with the organization size.

In most of the professional organizations, RMIS are computerized, in such cases risk manager has to force relatively new problems.

- data impurity
- lacks of service

- software incompatibility
- mapping errors (when changing vendors)
- poor system documentation
- obsolescence
- bugs
- hardware incompatibility
- system inflexibility
- proprietary problems (only the creator knows how the system is put together)

The possible remedies are:

- solid assessment of needs
- comprehensive and clear specifications
- good contract negotiation
- reference checks, including on-site inspection
- financial check (especially important if relying solely on the vendor for support)
- source code (the actual programming code for the system, especially useful should the vendor go out of business)
- standard software configuration, such as DOS or Windows
- internal access to systems expert
- solid vendor account team

2.8.2 Some RMIS Vendors

Independent, claims administration-oriented RMIS vendors

CARE System Corp.

GenSource Corp. (formerly CIC).

Nichols Engineering (formerly Conway).

These three vendors offer solid property/causality claims administration software for large self-insureds and TPAs on a global basis.

Broker and TPA-based RMIS Vendors

- Crawford RSG.
- Envision/Near North Risk Technologies Inc.
- J&H Marsh & McLennan Inc.'s STARS
- Sedgwick Information Systems

Insurer/TPA-based Vendors

- IG.
- Chubb.

- CIGNA (ESIS Inc.)
- RISKTRAC Inc. (Liberty Mutual Group).

2.8.3 Organization of Risk Management Department

The organizational structure of a large risk management department in a corporate form or organization may be as follows on next page. (Exhibit 2.3)

In small organisations, the risk management job is confined to the president or the owner. In medium type organisations, the risk handling job is entrusted to the chief financial officer or someone at middle level management position.

In large business organization, the risk management department is headed by a top official generally director, who is also a member of the board of directors. He is duly supported by an analyst, generally a professional who is entrusted with all risk research responsibilities. Below the chain are middle level managers designated by the respective risk management methods., viz., prevention and loss control, insurance etc.

Exhibit 2.3

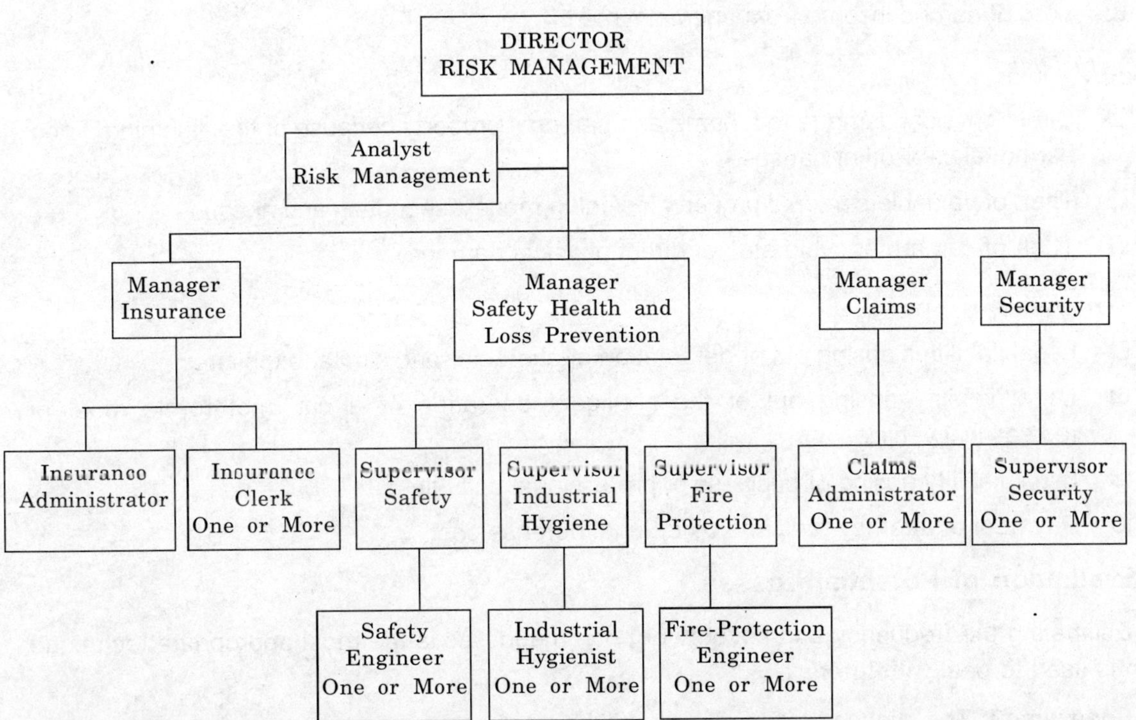

2.9 Risk Management by Individuals

Risk Management is an indispensable tool since it is considered as a complex task that requires a lot of analytical skills. For its effectiveness, risk management programme should be reviewed periodically to analyzes whether the objectives are been attained.

Individual risk management refers to the identification of pure risk faced by an individual or family and to the selection of most appropriate technique for treating such risk. In order to reduce risk element, certain basic steps have been allowed under individual risk management process:

- Potential losses must be identified.
- Potential losses should be evaluated in terms of loss frequency and loss severity.
- Appropriate methods for treating loss exposures must be selected.
- The risk management programme must be implemented and properly administered.

(A) Identification of Potential Losses

The process of risk management for individuals begins with identifying of potential losses which can arise due to the following risks:

Personal Risk

- Risk arising due to loss of earned income to the family because of premature death of family head.
- Insufficient income and financial assets during retirement.
- Loss of earned income from unemployment.

Property Risk

- Direct physical damage to a home and personal property because of fire, lightning, flood, earthquake, or other causes.
- Theft of valuable personal property including money, securities and antiques.
- Theft of car, motor cycle etc., or direct physical damage.

Liability Risk

- Legal liabilities arising out of defamation of character and similar exposures.
- Legal liability arising out of the negligent operation of a car, motorcycle, boat or recreational vehicle.
- Legal liability arising of business or professional activities.
- Payment of attorney fees and other legal defense cost.

(B) Evaluation of Potential Losses

Estimating the frequency and severity of potential losses is the most appropriate technique which is used to deal with the risk.

For example: The chance that your home will be totally destroyed by certain natural clamity – thunder, storm, flood, earthquake etc. is relatively small, but the severity of the loss can be catastrophic. Such losses should be insured because of their catastrophic potentials. Certain techniques such as retention are more appropriate for handling situations where loss frequency is high and loss severity is low, such losses should not be insured.

(C) Selecting the Appropriate Techniques for Handling Losses

Losses are managed by selecting the most appropriate method for handling potential losses. Some of the methods are discussed below:

(1) Loss Control: Is a method by which frequency and security of losses are controlled.

For example: Car theft can be prevented by locking the car, removing the key from the ignition and installing anti-theft device. Wearing a helmet reduces the severity of a head injury in a two-wheeler accidents. Having a fire extinguisher on the premises reduces the severity of a fire.

Thus, occurrence of any loss could be controlled by having loss control devices properly installed.

(2) Avoidance: Apart from controlling losses, the other substitute for preventing losses to occur is a avoidance method for handling potential losses.

Example: You can avoid risk by not travelling on a lonely road in the night and not to drive a vehicle with poor brakes.

(3) Retention: Retention means the amount of loss that you bear it at all some loss occurs. Risk Retention can also be further classified into:

Active Risk Retention: Which is you are aware of the risk and plan to retain part or all of it.

Example: You can retain losses of your car by buying Motor Insurance of your car in case the car meets with an accident or eventually if it gets stolen.

Passive Risk Retention: Risk on the other hand could also be retained passively because of ignorance, indifference, or laziness. This could be dangerous if the retained risk could result in catastrophic loss.

(4) Noninsurance Transfers: Non-insurance transfer is an instrument by which a pure risk is transferred to a party other than an insurer.

For example: Risk associated with a defective music system is transferred to a retailer by purchasing an extended warranty contract that makes the retailer responsible for repairs after warranty expires.

(5) Insurance: It is one of the cheapest mode generally used by individuals for risk management. Individual use life and non-life coverages for personal, property and liability risks.

(D) Review the Programme Periodically

The risk management programme must be reviewed periodically to find out deviations, if these deviations are significant, it requires a modification or complete renewal of the whole model.

2.10 Process of Risk Management by Individuals

Risk Management is an indispensable tool since it is considered as a complex task that requires a lot of analytical skills. For its effectiveness, risk management programme should be reviewed periodically to analyzes whether the objectives are been attained.

The personal risk management process applied to the loss exposures of the individuals and families. They are generally least expected to implement a plan, and expect insurance to take care of all possible exposures.

Individual risk management refers to the identification of pure risk faced by an individual or family and to the selection of most appropriate technique for treating such risk. In order to reduce risk element, certain basic steps have been allowed under individual risk management process:

- Potential losses must be identified.
- Potential losses should be evaluated in terms of loss frequency and loss severity.
- Appropriate methods for treating loss exposures must be selected.
- The risk management programme must be implemented and properly administered.

(i) Identifying Potential Losses: The first step is to identify all potential losses that can cause serious financial problems. Financial losses can result from the following:

- Loss of earned income to the family because of the premature death of the family head.
- Insufficient income and financial assets during retirement.
- Medical bills and the loss of earnings during an extended period of disability.
- Loss of earned income from unemployment.

(ii) Evaluating Potential Losses: The second step is to evaluate the potential losses, i.e., to estimate the frequency and severity of potential losses so that the most appropriate technique can be used to deal with the personal risk. Loss frequency refers to the probable number of losses that may occur during some given time period. Loss severity refers to the probable size of losses that may occur. If these two are not evaluated accurately, then it will be very difficult to adopt the appropriate technique to handle the risk.

(iii) Selecting the Appropriate Technique: The third step is to select the most appropriate technique for handling each potential loss. The major methods for potential losses are:

(a) Avoidance

(b) Risk control

(c) Risk retention

(d) Non-insurance transfers

(e) Insurance

(a) Avoidance: Avoidance is one method for handling a potential loss. It means a certain loss exposure is never acquired or an existing loss exposure is abandoned. For example, one can avoid being mugged in a high crime rate area by staying out of the area. The major advantage of avoidance is that the chance of loss is slightly reduced. However, one cannot be able to avoid all losses. For example, a company may not be able to avoid the premature death of a key executive.

(b) Risk Control: Risk control refers to the activities that reduce both the frequency and severity of losses. For example, one can reduce the risk of an auto accident by driving within the speed limits, taking a safe driving course, and driving defensively. Risk control also aims at reducing the severity of a loss. For example, wearing a helmet reduces the severity of a head injury in a motorcycle accident. Wearing a seal bell reduces the severity of an injury in a car accident.

(c) Retention: Retention means that one retains part or all of a loss if it occurs. For example, one can retain the small expenses; say medical expenses like normal check-ups, blood test etc. He or she can set aside a certain amount from their income to meet these. Retention can be done if the problem is not serious. Retention can be either active or passive. Active risk retention means that one is aware of the loss exposure and plans to retain all or part of it. Passive retention is the failure to identify a loss exposure, failure to act, no forgetting to out. Retention can be effectively used when not other method is available.

(d) Non-insurance Transfers: Non-insurance transfers are methods other than insurance by which a pure risk is transferred to a party other than an insurer. For example, periodic (say, half-yearly) medical check-ups for the workers by the owner of the plant. This can be done through an agreement between the employer and employees. Non-insurance transfers often cost less than insurance. In Non-insurance transfers, the potential loss may be shifted to someone who is a better position to exercise loss control.

(e) Insurance: In a personal risk management programme, people must rely heavily on insurance as the major method for dealing with risk. Insurance is appropriate for loss exposures that have a low probability of loss but for which the severity of loss is high. Insurance policies fulfill the needs of the public.

(iv) Peridic Review: The last step is to implement and review the programme periodically. At least every two or three years, one should determine all major risks are adequately covered. One should also review the programme at major events in his/her life such as divorce, birth of a child, purchase of a house, change of jobs or death of spouse or family member.

2.11 Personal Risk Management Strategies

A personal risk management strategy should ensure that assets are protected and debts are cleared in the event of the unforeseen death, major accident or major illness of a key financial member(s) of a family or partnership. This entails personal protection insurance. In much the same way as one would insure a home or car, one should insure for the protection of income, accumulated wealth and lifestyle.

There are four key forms of personal protection insurances:

Life Term Insurance

Life Term Insurance (often called Term Insurance) pays a lump sum benefit to the policy owner upon the death of the life insured, where this occurs during the term of the insurance cover (this can be up to age 99).

Term insurance is usually taken out in order to repay liabilities, such as mortgage, credit cards, etc., cover funeral costs, pay-off credit cards and, in the event of the death of the main breadwinner, provide a substitute income stream for the spouse so that the current standard of living may be maintained. This is especially important where dependent children are involved.

Total and Permanent Disability (TPD) Insurance

TPD insurance provides a lump sum upon medical confirmation that the insured person is totally and permanently disabled based on the definition provided in the policy document. This type of policy is generally sold as an additional benefit to term life insurance.

It is important to be clear about how the life company defines the total and permanent disability in the context of you being able to continue to work in your current capacity. This definition will assist in the selection of particular products for recommendation. Generally, in order to claim on TPD, you must be off work for at least six months and, in the opinion of the medical practitioners, unlikely to ever work again; or have irrecoverably lost the use of both eyes, legs, arms or one of each.

Trauma (Critical Illness) Insurance

Modern medicine can keep more people alive following major traumas. Trauma insurance pays you a lump sum in the event of a major trauma such as a major heart attack, cancer or stroke. Most life offices also pay the benefit under trauma in the event of death. Statistics show that we will suffer some major illness or trauma during our lifetime and that we are three times more likely to suffer a condition such as heart attack, cancer, stroke or bypass surgery than to die.

Most of us will survive the trauma but many are not able to continue working. In that case their income stream, upon which they rely for their livelihood, ceases.

Trauma insurance is designed to ensure that lifestyle suffers as little as possible by paying at and when the need is highest, therefore aiding recovery.

Income Protection Insurance

Most people state that their greatest physical asset is their home. They see the importance of insuring their home building and contents but most overlook their most valuable asset, their income. Your ability to earn an income between now and retirement determines what you and your family are able to do day to day.

Income Protection cover is designed to provide you with a regular monthly income whilst you cannot work due to sickness or accident. You are able to protect up to 75% of your gross income, inclusive of any packaged benefits such as car and superannuation.

2.12 Factors Affecting Individual's Demand for Insurance

Individuals demand for insurance depends on various factors, sometimes particular to an individual. However, following factors are generally common:

(1) Price for risk transformation — the cost of insurance *vis-a-vis* other products.

(2) Perception towards losses – if the individual feels that insurer's calculation of risk and expected losses is better than his own, he will opt for insurance cover.

(3) Income and wealth states – insurance demand, logically, is positively correlated with the income and wealth of the potential insured.

(4) Social insurance programmes – if as per individual's satisfaction good social programme by government or other public agencies are available, demand for private insurance will be lower.

(5) Nature of losses — insurance covers for non-monetary losses like mental tension and pain, psychological suffering are generally not very common and also legal structure takes care of these partially, e.g., Specific Relief Act.

2.13 Corporate Risk Management

Risk management by business firm differs substantially from risk aversion by individuals. Diversification is one of the strategy pursued by the business firms to tackle risk by spread into number of businesses. Individual shareholders diversify risk by spreading their investments in various stocks. However, for a given firm, the perception is different. What is important is the variability of cash flows for the firm being a separate entity. Though "corporate insurance contracts and shareholder's diversification are alternative mechanisms for diversifying pure risk for shareholders." Yet, "any corporate activities that reduce the variability of corporate cash flows will not necessarily reduce the shareholders' risk, because shareholders already may have diversified away the risk."

"Business insurance purchases can: (1) provide an efficient method of purchasing claims processing and loss control services; (2) reduce the expected cost of financing losses; (3) reduce the likelihood that the firm will have to raise costly external capital for new investment projects and thereby increase the likelihood that it will adopt good investment projects; (4) reduce the likelihood of financial distress and thereby improve the terms at which the firm will be able to contract with other claimants, such as employees suppliers, lenders and customers; and (5) reduce expected tax payments."

Doubts are sometimes raised whether the diversification by shareholders is cheaper or the insurance mechanism. Since the cost of buying a mutual fund is lower than an individual stock, it look a cheaper option compared to insurance where the prices include margin and administrative costs. But, even if the shareholders are diversified, insurance can enhance value by restricting losses.

2.13.1 Corporate Risk Management Models

Corporate Risk Management, in a classical sense, has been viewed in terms of cost management primarily focusing on financial risks. However, in present scenario, the focus has changed to holistic view rather than as a narrow approach. "Risk management can be viewed as a means to improve efficiency of other activities of the firm. Or, a firm may extend its internal risk management process for providing risk management products demanded by its customer."

Corporate Risk Management as a Control Exercise

Risk controlling firms use risk management or internal management and control. In these firms, the focus is on cost/loss aspects, popularly known as negative effects of risk, rather than as a business opportunity. The main areas of concern in these firms are:

(*a*) Maintenance of risk tolerance levels as per expectations of stockholders;

(*b*) Using risk control tools enhances efficiency of their business operations;

(*c*) Maintenance of sound governance process which should provide support required for the design, implementation and evaluation and fine-tuning of the risk management process.

2.13.2 The Process

In case of business organisation, following process of risk management modeling is generally followed:

(1) To analyse the risk profile of the firm and the changes brought by fluctuations in the factors that influence the cash flows relating to assets and liabilities.

(2) To restructure the factors depending on the nature of the risk and organizational strategies to manage them.

(3) To develop a model, dynamic in nature which keeps a continuous watch on actual risk undertaken, relative to that targeted.

(4) Comparison of actuals with targets calls for corrective action and application of suitable risk transformation products.

The process of risk management need to be aimed not only to meet the requirements of internal policies and guidelines but also to improve the efficiency at other activities of the firm.

Thus, the process of 'risk management' is dynamic in nature, however it gives managers an opportunity to realign goals and ensure that the needs of the firm and design of the risk management system fits together.

2.13.3 Types of Risk Managing Firms

Business firms, on the basis of risk perception, can be classified as follows:

(*a*) *Risk controllers* are the firms which use risk management for purely internal control purposes.

(*b*) *"Efficient enhancers* are firms that use their risk control tools to operate their business more efficiently. They focus more on the strategic issues relating to risk management rather than tactical or implementation issues, which are the main issues of concern of the risk controllers."[3] Generally, these firms use customized software solutions.

(*c*) *Risk transformers* are optimistic and view the risk management as a business opportunity and the main focus area is on design of new financial products for risk management.

2.14 Risk Management and Derivatives

The Derivatives are the most modern financial instruments in hedging risk. All over the world, derivatives is the key part of the financial system. The term "Derivative" indicates that it has no independent value, i.e., its value is entirely "derived" from the value of the underlying asset. The underlying asset can be securities, commodities, bullion, currency, livestock or anything else. In other words, Derivative means a forward, future, option or any other hybrid contract of pre-determined fixed duration, linked for the purpose of contract fulfillment to the value of a specified real or financial asset or to an index of securities. With Securities Laws (Second Amendment) Act, 1999, Derivatives has been included in the definition of Securities. The term Derivative has been defined in Securities Contracts (Regulations) Act, as:

A Derivative includes:

- a security derived from a debt instrument, share, loan, whether secured or unsecured, risk instrument or contract for differences or any other form of security;
- a contract which derives its value from the prices, or index of prices, of underlying securities.

Derivative markets can be broadly classified into two types:

- ❑ Commodity derivative markets
- ❑ Financial derivative markets

In commodity derivative markets, the trade contract for the underlying asset is a commodity. It can be agricultural commodity like wheat, soybean, cotton, rapeseed, pepper, chana, mustard seed etc. or precious metals like gold, silver, mega silver etc. Due to the bulky nature of the underlying assets, physical settlement in commodity derivative creates the need for warehousing. In case of commodities, the quality of the underlying asset can vary largely. In financial derivative markets, the trade contracts for the underlying asset is a financial asset. It can be equity, interest rates and exchange rates. Financial derivatives are used to hedge the exposure to market risk.

2.14.1 Types/Classification of Derivatives

Derivatives can be classified into four types:

- Forwards
- Futures
- Options
- Swaps

Forward Contract

In a forward contract, two parties agree to do a trade at some future date, at a price and quantity agreed today. No money changes hands at the time the deal is signed. The agreed upon price is called the forward price. In a forward market the transfer of ownership occurs on the spot, but the delivery of the commodity or instrument does not occur until some future date.

Example: A wheat farmer may wish to contract their harvest at a future date to eliminate the risk of a change in prices by that date.

Features of forward contracts:

- ❑ They are bilateral contracts and hence exposed to counterparty risk.
- ❑ Each contract is custom designed, and hence is unique in terms of contract size, expiration date and the asset type and quality.
- ❑ The contract price is generally not available in public domain.
- ❑ The contract has to be settled by delivery of the asset on expiration date.
- ❑ In case, the party wishes to reverse the contract, it has to compulsorily go to the same counterparty.

Futures Contract

Futures contract means a legally binding agreement to buy or sell the underlying security on a future date. Future contracts are the organized/standardized contracts in terms of quantity, quality (in case of commodities), delivery time and place for settlement on any date in future. The contract expires on a pre-specified date which is called the expiry date of the contract. On expiry, futures can be settled by delivery of the underlying asset or cash. Cash settlement enables the settlement of obligations arising out of the future/option contract in cash. The agreed upon price is called the future price.

Important features of a futures contract:

Originally, future trading was exclusively concentrated in agricultural commodities due to the seasonal nature of its supply. But nowadays, future trading has extended to financial instruments with greater intensity.

- *Use of standard contracts:* The important feature of future contract is the standardization of contract. The standardization of the contract fetches the potential buyers and sellers and increases the marketability and liquidity of the contracts.
- *Clearing House:* An organization called Futures exchange will act as a clearing house. In futures contract, the obligation of the buyer and seller is not to each other but to the clearing house in fulfilling the contract which ensures the elimination of the default risk on any transaction.
- *Margin Requirements:* The clearing house requires the participants to keep margin money, normally ranging between 5% to 10% of the face value of the contract.
- *Time spreads:* There is a relationship between the spot price and future price of the contract. The relationship also exists between prices of future contracts which are on the same commodity or instrument but which have different expiry dates. The difference between the prices of two contracts is known as the time spread.
- *Simple pay-off positions in Futures:* In futures market, the pay-off can be either positive or negative.

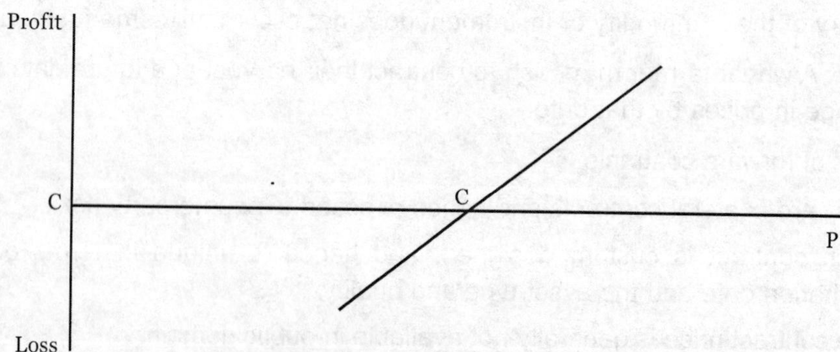

Figure 1: Buyer's Pay-off

where C = contract price and P = price of security

The buyer of the contract has an obligation to purchase the underlying instrument at a price of C. When the spot price is above the contract price, the buyer will buy the instrument for the price C and sell the instrument for higher spot price, thus making a profit. When the spot price is below the contract price, a loss is made by the buyer of the contract.

The seller of the contract makes a profit when the contract price is above the spot price (the seller will purchase the instrument at the spot price and sell at the contract price) and makes a loss when the spot price is above the contract price.

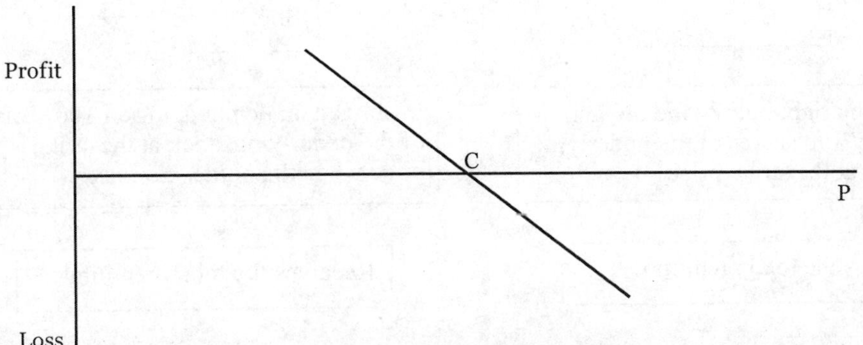

Figure 2: Seller's Pay-off

Options Contract: Option contract is a type of Derivatives Contract which gives the buyer/holder of the contract the right (but not the obligation) to buy/sell the underlying asset at a predetermined price within or at end of a specified period. The buyer/holder of the option purchase the right from the seller/writer for a consideration which is called the premium. The seller/writer of an option is obligated to settle the option as per the terms of the contract when the buyer/holder exercises his right. The underlying asset could include securities, an index of prices of securities etc.

European and American Options

If an option that is exercisable on or before the expiry date, it is called *American option*. The holder can exercise the right anytime between purchase date and expiration date. An option that is exercisable only on expiry date is called *European option*. In this case, the holder of the option can only exercise his right on the expiration date. The price at which the option is to be exercised is called *Strike price or Exercise price*.

Call and Put Options

Call Option: A call option is the right (not the obligation) to buy the commodity or security at a specific price called the exercise price.

Rights and obligations of the holder and writer of a call options is given in the following figure.

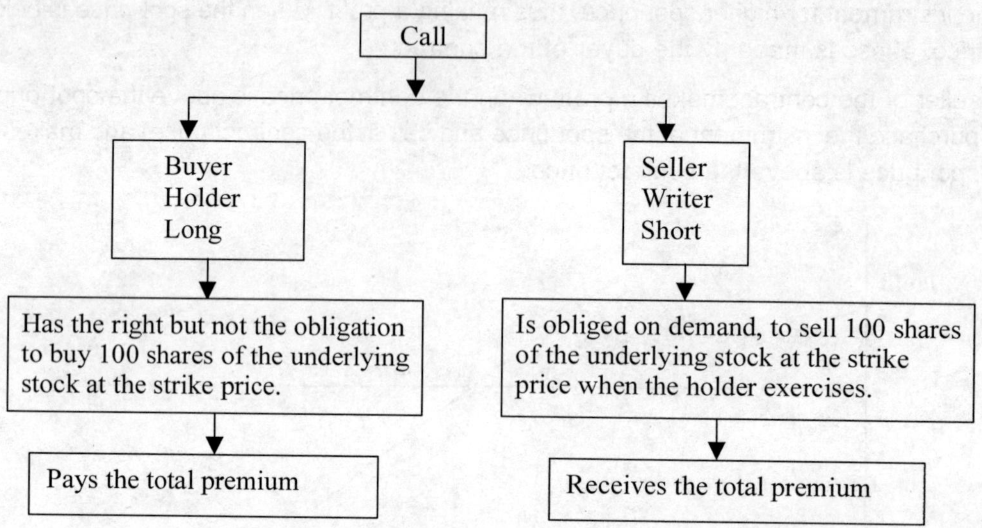

Expectations, rewards and risks of holder and writer of a call option is as follows:

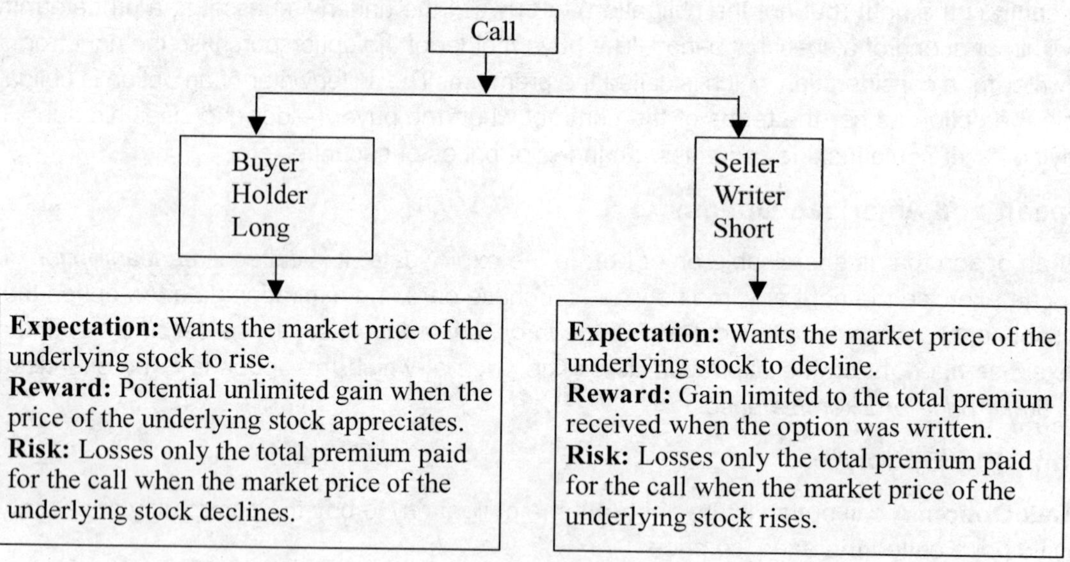

Put Option: option to sell is called *Put option.*

Rights and obligations of the holder and writer of a put options is given in the followibg figure:

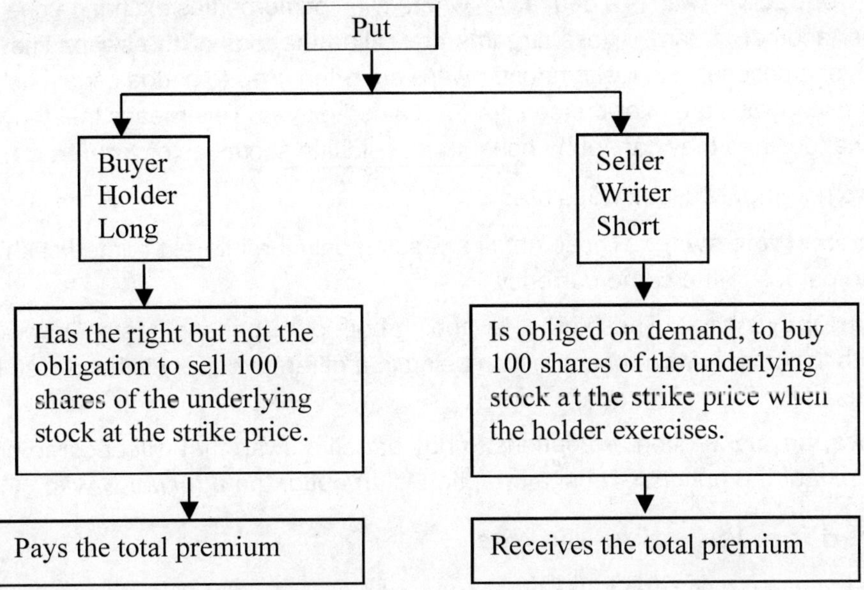

Expectations, rewards and risks of holder and writer of a put option is as follows:

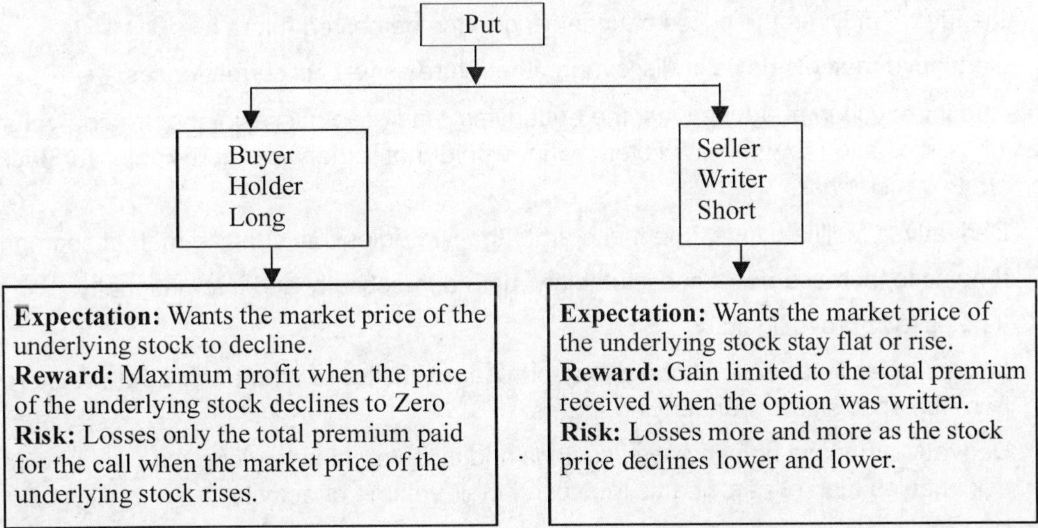

Difference Between Futures and Options

FUTURES	*OPTIONS*
Future contract involve obligations.	Option contracts involve rights.
Future contracts have symmetric risk.	Options have asymmetric risk.

The prices are affected by the prices of the underlying asset. Prices are affected by the prices of the underlying asset, time, interest rate, volatility etc.

Swap Contract: A swap is a derivative, where two counterparties exchange one stream of cash flows against another stream. These streams are called the legs of the swap. The cash flows are calculated over a notional principal amount. Swaps are often used to hedge certain risks, for instance, interest rate risk. Swaps are over-the-counter (OTC) derivatives. This means that they are negotiated outside exchanges and they cannot be bought and sold like securities or **futures contracts.**

The two commonly used swaps are:

- **Interest rate swaps**: These entail swapping only the interest related cash flows between the parties in the same currency.
- **Currency swaps:** These entail swapping both principal and interest between the parties, with the cash flows in one direction being in a different currency than those in the opposite direction.
- **Swaption:** Swaption are options to buy or sell a swap that will become operative at the expiry of the options. Thus, a swaption is an option on a forward swap.

2.14.2 Need for Derivative Markets

- The derivative market helps to transfer risks from those who have them but may not like them to those who have an appetite for them.
- Prices of an organized derivative market reflect the perception of market participants about the future and lead the prices of underlying to the perceived future level.
- Derivative markets helps in discovering the future as well as current prices.

With the introduction of derivatives, the underlying market witnesses higher trading volumes because of participation by more players who would not otherwise participate for lack of arrangement to transfer risk.

- Derivatives facilitate investment and arbitrage strategies that straddle market segments.
- It helps to increase asset substitutability, both domestically and internationally.
- It helps to improve liquidity.
- It helps to facilitate the creation of pay-off characteristics at a lower cost that would result from the acquisition of underlying assets.
- Derivative markets help increase savings and investment in the long run. The transfer of risk enables market participants to expand their volume of activity.
- Derivative trading act as a catalyst for new entrepreneurial activity. Derivatives have a history of attracting many bright, creative and well educated people with an entrepreneurial attitude.

2.14.3 Risks Involved in Derivatives market

There are several risks inherent in financial transactions. Derivatives are used to separate risks from traditional instruments and transfer these risks to parties willing to bear these risks. The fundamental risks involved in derivative business include:

Credit Risk

This is the risk of failure of counterparty to perform its obligation as per the contract. Also known as default or counterparty risk, it differs with different instruments.

Market Risk

Market risk is a risk of financial loss as a result of adverse movements of prices of the underlying asset/instrument.

Liquidity Risk

The inability of a firm to arrange a transaction at prevailing market prices is termed as liquidity risk. A firm faces two types of liquidity risks:

- Related to liquidity of separate products
- Related to the funding of activities of the firm including derivatives.

Legal Risk

Derivatives cut across judicial boundaries, therefore the legal aspects associated with the deal should be looked into carefully.

Operating Risk

It involves errors, omissions, loss of important documents, frauds, forgeries, delays in settlement, loss of dividends and other corporate actions etc.

2.14.4 Participants in the Derivative Markets

- **Hedgers:** Operators, who want to transfer a risk component of their portfolio. Hedgers face risk associated with the price of an asset. They use the futures or options markets to reduce or eliminate this risk. Example: farmers.
- **Speculators:** Operators, who intentionally take the risk from hedgers in pursuit of profit. Speculators are participants who wish to bet on future movements in the price of an asset. Futures and option contracts can give them leverage, by putting in small amounts of money upfront, they can take large positions on the market. As a result of this leveraged speculative position, they increase the potential for large gains as well as losses.
- **Arbitrageurs:** Operators who operate in the different markets simultaneously, in pursuit of profit and eliminate mispricing. If for example, they see the futures price of an asset getting out of line with the cash price, they would take offsetting positions in the two markets to lock in the profit.
- **Day traders:** Day traders are speculators who take positions in futures or options contracts and liquidate them prior to the close of the same trading day.
- **Floor trader:** A floor trader is an exchange member or employee, who executes trade by being personally present in the trading ring or pit and they have no place in electronic trading system.
- **Market maker:** A market maker is a trader, who simultaneously quotes both bid and offer price for a same commodity throughout the trading session.

There are two distinct groups of derivative contracts, which are distinguished by the way they are traded in market:

(i) Over-the-counter (OTC) derivatives are contracts that are traded (and privately negotiated) directly between two parties, without going through an exchange or other intermediary. Products such as swaps, forward rate agreements, and exotic options are almost always traded in OTC from Exchange-traded derivatives are those derivatives products that are traded via specialized derivatives exchanges or other exchanges. A derivatives exchange acts as an intermediary to all related transactions, and takes initial margin from both sides of the trade to act as a guarantee. Products like futures, options etc. are traded on exchanges.

2.14.5 Risk Management via Derivatives

Derivatives can be used to transfer risk by taking the opposite position in the derivative (futures) market against the underlying assets. Derivatives are used both by speculators and hedgers. Speculators may trade with other speculators as well as with hedgers. In most financial derivatives markets, the value of speculative trading is far higher than the value of true hedge trading. As well as outright speculation, derivatives traders may also look for arbitrage opportunities between different derivatives on identical or closely related underlying securities. Other uses of derivatives are to gain an economic exposure to an underlying security in situations where direct ownership of the underlying security is too costly or is prohibited by legal or regulatory restrictions, or to create a synthetic short position. In addition to directional plays (i.e., simply betting on the direction of the underlying security), speculators can use derivatives to place bets on the volatility of the underlying security. This technique is commonly used when speculating with traded options.

Let us look at some examples of risk management using financial derivatives.

Short Hedge Using Options

A short hedge in the options market is referred to as the purchasing of a put option. Entering into (short) hedge in the options market can reduce the price risk associated with selling an output/ asset that will arise in future. For example, a producer knows he will be selling the output three months from now but is afraid of prices. He can enter the options market and partially offset any loss in value (decrease in price) with a gain in option value.

Short Hedge Example with Futures

One can enter the futures market and offset any loss in value (decrease in price) with a gain in the futures market. So, the price can be locked in advance.

Long Hedge Example with Options

A long hedge in the options market is accomplished by purchasing a call option. For example, a manufacturer needs to buy raw material two months from now. It can enter the options market and partially offset any loss in value (increase in price) with a gain in the options value.

Hedging via Options vs. Futures

Options provide market players with a powerful strategy to protect themselves from the potential negative affects of market fluctuations. Despite being expensive or risky, options serve as a cost-effective and economical practice to hedge against market exposures. In contrast, the buying or selling futures or forwards is bit inflexible way of dealing with a dynamic and ever-changing market because they lock the price. Options offer flexibility and can be tailored to provide pay-offs that match end-users' exposures more closely, and also suit their tolerance to risk, mirror corporate policy as well as satisfy their accounting and compliance requirements. Additionally, options can reflect users' general outlook on the market. They can enable users to benefit from a favorable market move while being fully hedged against an undesired market fluctuation. All this can be done cost-effectively and, frequently, at a lower final cost than using forwards.

Managing Interest Rate Risk with Derivatives

An important business risks for corporations is unexpected fluctuation in the cost of funding the company's operations through debt financing — borrowing from bank or corporate bonds. The company may want to benefit falling interest rates and likely to hedge against higher interest rates. This can be done through an interest rate swap whereby the company can swap fixed to floating or floating top fixed rate.

Another popular interest rate derivative used by companies to manage the cost of their debt capital is the interest rate cap option. In buying an interest rate cap, the corporation limits its debt service cost while retaining some of the benefit of potential falling interest rates.

2.14.6 Derivatives as Tools of Risk Management

Relation between the values of derivatives and their underlying assets: When the values of underlying assets change, so do the values of derivatives based on them. For some derivative instruments such as swaps and futures, the relation between the underlying assets and the instrument is straightforward, i.e., if the product price changes the instrument price also changes. In a currency future contract, the price to be paid when the currency delivered will be fixed by the future contract, the value of the currency delivered will fluctuate depending on the movements of the underlying currency. Thus, the value of the future contract depends on the value of the underlying currency. The relation between values of the underlying asset and option are more complicated, but the values of the option and underlying assets are still be related. Due to this unique quality, the derivatives appear similar to real commodities for many traders.

It is easier to take short position in derivatives than in other assets: As all transactions in derivatives take place in future specific dates, it is easy for the investor to sell the underlying assets, i.e., in an asset if he is obligated to deliver the asset in future. The short position means taking stand for selling the underlying asset, with or without possessing the asset he can take view of the market or product which is not possible in any other asset.

Exchange traded derivatives are liquid and have low transaction cost: Exchange traded derivatives are more liquid and have lower transaction costs than other assets. They are more liquid because they have standardized terms and low credit risk. Furthermore, their transaction costs are low due to high volume in trade and due to high competition. In addition, margin requirement in the exchange traded derivatives is relatively low, which reflects that the risk associated with this instrument is low.

It is possible to construct portfolio, which is exactly needed, without having the underlying assets: Derivatives can be constructed or combined to closely match specific portfolio requirement. For example, suppose a firm with a floating rate loan needs to limit its exposure to sharp increases in the interest rate. The firm can purchase a derivative called an interest rate cap. This derivative pays the firm the difference between the floating rate of interest and a predetermined maximum called the cap rate whenever the floating rate exceeds the cap. Similarly, the lender can protect the decrease in the interest rate by buying the floor.

The derivative product seller pays the lender the difference between a predetermined maximum rate called the floor rate whenever the floating rate falls below the floor rate.

Key Terms

- ❒ Risk Analysis
- ❒ Risk Transfer
- ❒ Self-insurance
- ❒ Risk Retention
- ❒ Risk Identification
- ❒ Forwards
- ❒ Swaps
- ❒ Short and Long Positions
- ❒ Hedging
- ❒ Demand-based Pricing
- ❒ Idea Generation
- ❒ Classification of Products
- ❒ Concept Testing
- ❒ Risk Control
- ❒ Pure Risk
- ❒ Risk Financing
- ❒ RMIS
- ❒ Diversification
- ❒ Futures
- ❒ Hedging
- ❒ Speculation
- ❒ Product Design
- ❒ Product Development
- ❒ Market Analysis
- ❒ Intermediaries
- ❒ Competition-based Pricing

Questions for Review

1. A risk manager stated "If a risk is to be properly controlled, it must be perceived, and it must be appreciated in terms of probable frequency and possible severity." The writers went on to give two examples as follows:
   (*a*) A company brings together in two airplane flights nearly all of its dealers and distributors from a certain country.
   (*b*) Another company makes a special contract with the government of a foreign country to set up a factory in that country. Special machinery is to be sent by ship and customs duty is to be waived if the machinery arrives by a certain date.

For each of these situations, indicate the potential loss exposure for the company.

2. What data would be most helpful to include in a risk management information system designed particularly for an automobile manufacturers? How might the RMIS requirement for such a firm differ from those of an amusement theme park? Explain.
3. List and explain three desirable risk management goals likely to be found in risk management and control process.
4. What are the steps in developing a risk management plan? Why is the order of the steps important? Which step is the most difficult to accomplish?
5. Explain how does enterprise risk management process differs from traditional form of risk management.
6. Define a captive insurer and explain why captive insurers are formed.
7. Explain the basic factor that a risk manager must consider if commercial insurance is used in a risk management programme? List and explain the three main category of loss control activities.
8. Distinguish between: (a) forwards and futures and (b) options and futures.
9. Briefly explain the various types of derivatives. How derivatives can be used as effective tools of risk management?
10. Briefly explain the new product development process. Do you think that pricing is an integral part of product development?
11. List the major areas of concern for insurers in India with reference to product development and customization.

Suggested Readings

1. Emmett Vaughan and Therese Vaughan, *Essentials of Risk Management and Insurance,* John Wiley and Sons Inc., 2002.
2. G.E. Rejda, *Principles of Risk Management and Insurance,* Pearson Education Inc., 2002.
3. Kenneth A. Froot, *The Financing of Catastrophic Risk,* The University of Chicago Press, 1999.
4. Robert I. Mehr, *Fundamentals of Insurance*, Irwin, 1986.
5. Scott E. Harrington and Gregory R. Niehaus, *Insurance and Risk Management,* Irwin/ McGraw-Hill, 1999.
6. Kolb Robert W. (2000), *Futures, Options, and Swaps,* Blackwell Publishers.
7. Hull John C. (2003), *Options, Futures, and Other Derivatives*, Pearson Education.
8. D.C. Srivastava, *et al.*, *Indian Insurance Industry — Transition and Prospects,* New Century Publication.

Web Resources

- www.erisks.com
- www.insure-magic.com
- www.sra.org
- www.rmis.org
- www.aria.org

❑❑❑

UNIT II
INSURANCE MANAGEMENT

CHAPTER

INSURANCE BASICS

Chapter Objectives

- Definition of Insurance
- Costs and Benefits of Insurance
- Elements of an Insurable Risk
- Insurance as a Macro-economic Issue
- Kinds of Insurance

Introduction

Insurance is conventionally the most popular method of risk transfer. It is used to hedge against the risk of a contingent, uncertain loss. Insurance transaction involves the insured assuming a guaranteed and known relatively small loss in the form of payment to the insurer in exchange for the insurer's promise to compensate the insured in the case of a financial (personal) loss.

Insurance contracts are of various types covering the risk of life and physical assets. Insurance business is of critical imporance to the economy in the form of savings and investment generation.

3.1 Definition of Insurance

The term "insurance" can be defined in both financial and legal terms. The financial definition focuses on an arrangement that redistributes the cost of unexpected losses. That is, the collection of a small premium payment from all exposed and distributed to those suffering loss. The legal definition focuses on a contractual arrangement whereby one party agrees to compensate another party for losses. The financial definition provides for the funding of the losses whereas the legal definition provides for the legally enforceable contract that spells out the legal rights, duties and obligations of all the parties to the contract. Let us have a look at these definitions.

In Financial Sense

Insurance is a social device in which a group of individuals (insureds) transfer risk to another party (insurer) in order to combine loss experience, which permits statistical prediction of losses and provides for payment of losses from funds contributed (premiums) by all members who transferred risk.

In Legal Sense

A contract of insurance is a contract by which one party in consideration of the price paid to him proportionate to the risk provides security to the other party that he shall not suffer loss, damage or prejudice by the happening of certain specified events. Insurance is meant to protect the insured against uncertain events which may cause disadvantage to him. Life insurance, however, is a distinctive type of insurance where there is certainty of the payment of a specified amount either on the death of the insured or on the maturity of the policy whichever is earlier.[1]

3.2 Costs and Benefits of Insurance

The purpose of insurance mode of risk transfer is to provide economic protection against the losses that may be incurred but to chance events such as — *(a)* death, *(b)* disability, *(c)* economic losses. One party (the insurer) for a set amount of money, (premium) agrees to pay the other party (insured or beneficiary), a sum of money (benefit) upon the occurrence of an event which may or may not occur. Insurance provides economic protection against losses that may be incurred due to chance events that may or may not occur during the effective time of the contract called a policy. The insurance of business organizations is essential in the sense that adverse events, if not guarded, may affect — the business itself, the business owner or owner's personal property and may also threaten the continued operation of the business and threaten the owner's financial well-being.

Insurance Device

The fundamental characteristics of insurance are:

(a) It involves transfer of risk from the individual to the group, and

(b) There is a sharing (pooling) of losses on some equitable basis such that fortuitous losses will be indemnified (paid).

More specifically, the cost and benefits of insurance are:

Benefits

- Reimbursement for losses
- Reduction in tension and fear
- Avenue for investment — life insurance investment officer attractive return.
- Prevention of losses

1. *Insurance Laws and Practice,* Vidhi Publications, 2002, p. 2.1.

- Credit multiplication
- Costs of insurance to society
- Cost of business operations — social wastage of resources
- Fraudulent and exaggerated claims — malacious and undesirable transfer of wealth

3.3 Elements of an Insurable Risk

For pure risk to be insurable, it should possess the following characteristics:

Large Numbers of Exposure Units

The theory of insurance is based on law of large numbers. Therefore the prime necessity for a rise to be insurable is that there must be a sufficiently large number of homogeneous exposure in order that losses are reasonable predictable. Also, the probabilistic estimates used by the insurance company, by logic, assume large number of units in a distribution and insurance products are priced accordingly.

Define and Measurable (Calculable) Loss

The losses are fairly predictable and can be measured in money terms. Loss of peace of mind, tension etc. or loss of life cannot be indemnified.

Determinable Probability Distribution

The probability distribution of the happening of adverse event is determinable. This condition is necessary to establish the free premium according to the theory of equivalence. If there is not determinable distribution, there is no question of issuing a cover by an insurance company.

Random (Fortuitous) Loss

The adverse event may or may not occur in future and once which the insurance company has not control. Naturally, if the event is non-random or the loss has occurred in the past, there is no question of insurance.

Also, it is important to note that randomness is ensured by underwriters who guard against adverse selection — the tendency of the poorer than average insured to seek or continue insurance coverage.

Non-catastrophic Loss

The losses should be non-catastrophic. Not all the units in a homogeneous group will be subject to an adverse event. Recall that if all the units meet losses, the company will be ruined only few out of a large group will be exposed.

Premium should be Economically Feasible

Since, the insurance pool is structured to be sufficiently large, the price charged by the insurer for buying the risk is generally low. It should be sufficient to cause the rich for the insurer as well as viable for the insured.

Insurance versus Gambling

If gambling events were insurable, the gambler would be put in the enviable position of being unable to lose because if it is head, he wins else if fails, he collects the money from insurance company. Since the insurance premium must include the charge for the losses and the expenses of operating the insurance pool, the resulting premium must be more than the mathematically fair value of the potential loss. Moreover, the gambler presumably enjoys the risk of gambling and therefore would be unlikely to pay the premium needed for transferring the risk being enjoyed. Law prohibits the use of insurance for gambling purposes because fraud and murder would increase thus making a social device prohibitively expensive and therefore making the system fail. In summary, the gambling can be distinguished from an insurance contract in the following ways:

(a) Gambling creates risk while insurance transfers an existing risk.

(b) Gambling deals with speculative risk — there might be gains or losses, while insurance deals with pure risk.

3.4 Insurance as a Macroeconomic Issue

Insurers can promote efficiency in the financial system as follows:

(1) Mobilisation of Scattered Resources: The money collected from the scattered and distant policyholders by way of premium is pooled and invested in projects which would otherwise have not been possible. This reduces the transaction cost of financing and eases the pressure on other financial intermediaries.

(2) Creation of Liquidity: Instead of policyholders directly landing their money to entrepreneurs and projects, the money is lent on their behalf by the insurance company. This creates liquidity in the system and in case the adverse event occurs, money is immediately paid to the insured without time-lags.

(3) Economies of Scale: The bulk funds invested in large and infrastructure projects promote economies of scale, promoter economic development and growth and other technological innovation.

Insurance and GDP

The relationship between the insurance density and GDP is direct. Insurance density varies directly with GDP.

Insurance and Income Redistribution

Life insurance essential serves to transfer funds from currently employed persons via premium payments to unemployed persons, and thereby helps alleviate the problem of economic distress. Insurance proceeds on an important element in the economic well-being of dependents. Government-sponsored insurance programmes strive to comprehensively achieve social goals while private programme provide attractive alternative to public welfare system.

Inflation, Business Cycles and Insurance

Inflation and business recessions directly reduces the real purchasing power and network of the people respectively. Insurance can provide a cover to these, yet the negative side is the adverse impact on the financial performance of companies.

Population Changes and Insurance

Population changes materially affects the insurance industry because of the economic consequences of changing rates of birth, death, marriage and family formation. The shifting age distribution affects the kinds and amount of insurance the people will buy.

Fiscal Policy

Fiscal Policy affects in Insurance sector in the following form:

1. Government spending
2. Taxation
3. Direct Controls on the business systems
4. Moral Suasion (assistance).

3.5 Kinds of Insurance

The commonly known insurance covers can be categorized as follows:

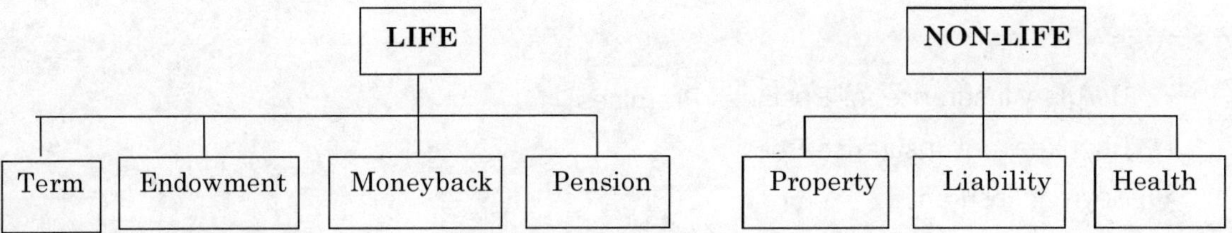

NON-LIFE INSURANCE

Property

Personal and business property insurance covers the risks against fire, marine, theft and burglary. The types of insurance under this category are:

- Home Insurance/Domestic cover
- Business insurance
- Commercial Insurance

Liability

This protects the insured against injury or damage claims made by a third party. The types of insurance under this category are:

- Automobile insurance
- Workers' compensation
- Liability insurance
- Aviation insurance

Health

In case of an illness or injury suffered by the insured or his/her dependents, health insurance covers their medical expenses incurred. The types of insurance under this category are: (a) Hospital Insurance and (b) Medical cover.

Few examples of general (Non-life) insurance policies are:

Health

- Medi-claim Policy
- Personal Accident — Individual
- Personal Accident — Family
- Group Accident Insurance
- Jan Arogya Bima Policy
- Bhavishya Arogya Policy
- Traffic Accident policy

Business

- Burglary insurance for Business Premises
- Shopkeepers' Insurance Policy
- Keyman Insurance
- Partnership Insurance
- Workmen's Compensation Insurance
- Fidelity Guarantee Insurance
- Professional Indemnity Insurance
- Machinery Breakdown Policy
- Boiler Explosion Insurance Policy
- Contractor's Plant and Machinery Insurance Policy
- Contractor's All Risks Policy
- Industrial All Risks Policy
- Air Transit Insurance Policy
- Inland Transit Insurance Policy
- Loss of Stock in Cold Storage Insurance Policy
- Product's Liability Insurance

Fire Insurance

- Fire Insurance policy
- Fire Consequential Loss Policy

Travel

- Overseas Mediclaim Policy
- Videsh Yatra Mitra
- Baggage Insurance Policy
- Executive Travel Insurance
- Suhana Safar

General Insurance

- Money Insurance
- Television Insurance Policy
- Pager Insurance Policy
- Mobile Phone Insurance

LIFE INSURANCE

Life Insurance products can be broadly divided into 9 categories, which include disabled, moneyback, pension women, girl child, couple, endowments, whole life and child insurance.

Moneyback

- Jeevan Sanchay
- Moneyback with Profits Policy
- Jeevan Surabhi

Pension

- New Jeevan Dhara
- Jeevan Suraksha with Life Cover
- Jeevan Suraksha without Life Cover plan
- Jeevan Suraksha Endowment Plan

Women, Girl Child and Couple

- Jeevan Saathi — for married couples
- Jeevan Saritha — for married couples
- Jeevan Sneha — for woman only
- Jeevan Sukanya — for the girl child

Endowment

- Jeevan Shree
- Endowment Policy without Profits
- Endowment Policy with Profits
- Limited Payment Endowments with Profit

- Jeevan Mitra
- Jeevan Mitra — Triple Cover
- Bima Kiran
- Jeevan Ariha

Whole Life

- Whole Life Policy with Profits
- Limited Payment Whole Life
- Convertible Whole Life

Child Insurance Policy

- Jeevan Kishore
- Children's Deferred Assurance Plan
- New Children's Deferred Assurance Plans
- Bal Vidya

Key Terms

- ❒ Contribution
- ❒ Indemnity
- ❒ Catastrophic
- ❒ Gambling
- ❒ Subrogation
- ❒ Fortuitous
- ❒ Insurable Risk
- ❒ Assurance

Questions for Review

1. Define insurance. Briefly explain the costs and benefits of insurance.
2. List the various life and non-life insurance covers available in India.
3. Write short notes on:
   (1) Principle of Subrogation
   (2) Principle of Contribution
4. Distinguish between assurance and insurance in view of principle of indemnity.

Suggested Readings

1. Douglas Caddy, *Legislative Trends in Insurance Regulation,* Texas A&M University Press, 1986.
2. Fredricke G. Crane, *Insurance Principles and Practice,* John Wiley, 1980.
3. H.L. Muller-Lutz, *Basic Principles of Insurance Management,* International Insurance Monitor, N.Y., 1966.

4. H.S. Dennenberg, R.D. Elers, J.J. Melone and R.A. Zetten, *Insurance Concepts — Basic and Legal,* Prentice-Hall, Englewood Cliffs, 1974.
5. Jorg Finsinger and Mark V. Pauly, *The Economics of Insurance Regulation,* Macmillan Press Ltd., 1986.
6. R.A. Blanchard, *Risk and Insurance and Other Papers,* 1965.
7. G.E. Rejda, *Insurance and Risk Management,* Pearson Education, 2002.

Web Resources

- www.insure.com
- www.fool.com
- insurance.yahoo.com
- www.montana.edu
- www.bimaonline.com

❑❑❑

CHAPTER

PRINCIPLES OF INSURANCE

Chapter Objectives

- Principles of Insurance
- Related Concepts

Introduction

Insuarnce contracts operate under a well defined set of principles known as insurance principles. Adherence to these peinciples is essential for validity and performnace opf insurance contract and serves the interest of both the parties.

4.1 Principles of Insurance

Principle of Indemnity

The principle of indemnity implies that *on the happening of an event insured against, the Insured will be placed by the insurer in the same pecuniary (monetary) position that he/she occupied immediately before the event. Indemnity means that the insured person is placed, financially, in the same position, as he was before the loss.*

Indemnity does not imply that the insured will be indemnified to the full falue of his loss, e.g., a person whose factory is destroyed by fire cannot recover for loss of profits or against any liability that may arise from the fire unless he has appropriate policies in place specifically designed to deal with these losses.

Indemnity can be achieved through the following methods:

1. Cash
2. Reinstatement, e.g., where a building is destroyed, insurers may reinstate it.

3. Repair, e.g., where a motor vehicle is partially damaged.
4. Replacement — instead of paying cash a replacement item may be tendered.
5. New for old-used for household contents. This is not a violation of the principle of indemnity as there is no principle of law that requires indemnity to be determined in terms of the market value of the asset.
6. Valued policies-in terms of which the insurer and the insured agree before hand on the value to be paid sentimental rather than a commercial value, e.g., jewellery, works of art etc.

The non-life insurance covers viz. Property and Liability are basically contracts of indemnity. However, the indemnity must not be construed as an instrument to profit. The indemnity goes along with two checks:

(a) to prevent the insured from benefiting under the contract

(b) to reduce the impact of moral hazards

The exceptions to the application of indemnity are found in Personal Accident Policies, Agreed Value policies in Marine Insurance and valuables and reinstatement policies like in Engineering policies. These are also contracts of indemnity but by a special application of the principle, the measure of indemnity is decided at the time of entering into the contract itself in the event of a claim the insured must:

- prove that he/she has sustained a monetary loss
- prove the extent and value of his/her loss
- transfer any rights which he/she may have for recovery from another source to the Insurer, if he/she has been fully indemnified.

Example

In a valued (marine) policy, if there is damage/loss to the cargo, the claim is limited to the value expressed in the policy cover irrespective of the actual value of the cargo lost or damaged. The settlement of the loss will be subject to: (*a*) Sum insured, (*b*) Average and (*c*) Excess/Deductible.

It is important to note that the contract of life insurance is not as such Insurance, but it is in the nature of assurance. This is logical in the sense that life cannot be indemnified, instead if a person dies, then under the contract of life insurance the sum assured will be paid by the insured.

Utmost Good Faith (Ubrrima Fides)

- Insurance contracts are characterized by information asymmetries between the parties. Generally, the insured knows more about the risk to be insured than the insurer. To rectify this imbalance, the law compels disclosure of information between the parties.
- To act in good faith entails that parties must deal openly and honestly with each other without suppressing material facts that may influence the judgment of the other party.

Under the contract of insurance, the insured is duty bound to disclose all material facts relating to the risk to be covered.

Utmost good faith is a positive duty voluntarily to disclose, accurately and fully, all facts material to the risk being proposed, whether requested or not.

The duty to act in good faith applies to all types of insurance contracts. In contracts of sale, the maxim *caveat vendito* applies meaning let the buyer beware. This maxim places an obligation on the buyer to take all reasonable steps to verify that the item he intends to buy meets his expectations. In insurance, this maxim does not apply.

A material fact is a fact, which would influence the mind of a prudent underwriter in deciding whether to accept a risk for insurance and on what terms. Both the parties to a contract are expected to observe good faith. However, the good faith assumes utmost importance when Material Facts are concerned and therefore utmost good faith should be observed on matters relating to material facts. Examples of material facts in various classes of insurance are:

1. *Motor:* Details of any young drivers
2. *Household:* Details of any commercial use of private dwelling house
3. *Commercial:* Previous losses/hazards
4. *Life:* Details of Heart Diseases

Some facts though material need not be disclosed. Thus, the insured has no obligation to disclose the following facts:

1. Any circumstance that diminishes the risk.
2. Any fact known or presumed to be known by the insurer.
3. Facts on which insurers have waived information.

Duty of disclosure applies to both the *Proposer* and the *Insurer*. Duty of disclosure operates at:

- inception — until the date cover is confirmed by the Insurers
- renewal — up to the renewal date mid-term
- alterations — until the Insurers confirm cover in respect of the alterations.

The duty of disclosure lasts for the duration of the negotiations and terminates when the contract is concluded. Material facts that come to light after the contract has been concluded are deemed to be part of the risk that the insurer would have assumed.

To avoid liability on grounds of non-disclosure, the onus is on the insurer to prove that:

1. The undisclosed facts were material.
2. The facts were within the actual or presumed knowledge of the insured.
3. The facts were not communicated to the insurer.

Upon discovering the non-disclosure, the insurer must exercise the right to repudiate the contract within a reasonable time.

Breach of utmost good faith is essentially a violation of "*Consensus ad idem*", a prerequisite for a valid contract. The breach may relate to: (*a*) misrepresentation or (*b*) non-representation.

Intentional misrepresentation may be termed as fraudulent and the intentional non-disclosure may be termed as concealment of facts. When misrepresentation or non-representation is unintentional, it may be termed as breach of general duty. The utmost good faith is vital from an insurer's perspective. It is important for the insurer to decide about:

(*a*) Acceptance or rejection of a proposal

(*b*) Pricing of the insurance cover

(*c*) Contribution to indemnity

(*d*) Powers of subrogation under the contract

(*e*) Imposition of conditions and warranties.

Subrogation

Subrogation in general, means the legal right of one person, having indemnified the other in a contractual obligation to do so, to stand in the place of another and avail of all the rights and remedies of the another, whether enforced or not.

It entitles the Insurer who has granted an indemnity to receive after payment of a loss the advantage of every right of the Insured. Subrogation condition is a corollary to the principle of Indemnity. A loss may occur accidentally or by the action or negligence of third party (not workmen). The property owners have a right to proceed against the offending third party to recover the loss/damage and also under their insurance policy but not under both. If the insured opts to recover the loss under the insurance policy which is faster and does not involve litigation, he will surrender his rights against the third parties in favour of the insurers signing a 'Letter of subrogation' on an appropriate stamp paper.

An exception to this are life insurance policies wherein insured/beneficiaries can claim under an insurance policy and also proceed against the offending third party.

The insurer must exercise the right of recovery in the name of the Insured (prevents the Insured from obtaining more than one indemnity).

Example

The Insurer of an importer of electrical goods receives a claim in respect of a faulty toaster. The Insurer pays the claim but takes over the insured's rights to claim back against the manufacturer. The insurance company can proceed with this claim in the Insured's name.

Subrogation rights only apply where there is a legal liability under the policy, i.e., where policy cover existed and the claims are paid. However, the policy conditions customarily provide for such subrogation rights before the claim payment. However, recovery from third parties can be made only if claim is paid.

Subrogation has a number of sub-principles namely:

- The insurer cannot be subrogated to the insured's right of action until it has paid the insured the made good the loss.
- The insurer can be subrogated only to actions which the insured would have brought himself.

- The insurer must not prejudice the insurer's right of subrogation. Thus, the insured may not compromise or renounce any right of action he has against the third party if by doing so he could diminish his loss.
- Subrogation against the insurer. Just as insured cannot profit from his loss, the insurer may not make a profit from the subrogation rights. The insurer is only entitled to recover the exact amount they paid as indemnity nothing more. If they recover more, the balance should be given to the insured.
- Subrogation gives the insurer the right of salvage.

Insurable Interest

The Insured must have an insurable interest in the subject matter of insurance, i.e., he/she must benefit by its safety or be prejudiced by its loss.

It is the legal right to insure arising out of financial relationship recognised under law, between the insured and the subject matter of insurance.

Insurable interest distinguishes contracts of insurance from gambling in order to define the legitimate area of insurance business.

Insurance interest is required for all types of insurance and its absence renders the contract void and hence unenforceable.

Insurance contracts without insurable interests have no sanction of the law as they amount to speculation The owner of a property has absolute insurance interest. When a person insures a property, what is insured therein, is his interest in that property. By this principle, insurance interest exists to other parties like lessor, lessee, financiers, etc., but their interest is limited to the extent of their financial commitment only. The leading Roman-Dutch law case on insurable interest is *Littlejohn v. Norwich Union Fire Insurance Society 1905 TH 374* where it was held that if the insured can show that he stands to lose something of an appreciable commercial value by the destruction of the thing insured then his interest will be an insurable one. The Court went further to state that as a general rule insurable interest should exist at the time of taking the policy and at the time the loss is incurred.

If a person has insurable interest in an asset at the time of taking the policy but loses the interest thereafter, e.g., if he sells the car, the policy ceases to have any validity. The insurable interest must exist both at the time of the proposal and at the time of claims. However, in the case of marine insurance contracts, which are assignable without the consent of the insurers, insurable interest must exist at the time of loss only (Marine insurance contracts are governed by Marine Insurance Act of 1963). Insurable Interest may be created either by:

Obligation to Insure

(*a*) By Statute

(*b*) By Contract

(*c*) By Custom

Option to Insure

(*a*) Owners

(*b*) Mortgagors

(*c*) Lessors

(*d*) Trustees

(*e*) Tenants

Example

Everybody would have an insurable interest in their own personal possessions, e.g., car, watch. An employee would have no insurable interest in their desk at work but the employer has. A husband has insurable interest in his wife.

Insurable interest can be acquired in various ways notably:

1. Ownership
2. Legal possession
3. Custody of property belonging to others, e.g., bailees.
4. Marriage-spouses have an insurable interest in each other's life.
5. A lien-holder has insurable interest in the property subject to the lien.
6. A debt creates insurable interest between debtor and creditor.
7. An employer has an insurable interest in the life of an employee.

In life insurance, the general rule is that insurable interest need only exist at the time of taking the policy. Thus, if A who is married to B takes a life policy on his life and they later divorce, the policy will pay on B's death even if technically insurable interest no longer exists because the parties divorced.

Proximate Cause

It is defined as the active efficient cause that sets into motion a train of events, which bring about a result, without the intervention of any force started and working actively from a new and independent source. Therefore, there must be an efficient cause, which brings about a loss with no other intervening cause, which breaks the chain of events. A loss could be due to a cause of causes. In the chain reaction, it is the dominant cause, which would be the proximate cause to be considered for the purpose of a claim. It is always the duty of the insured to prove that the loss arose out of the insured peril, which is proximate.

Example

Firemen remove undamaged stock from a burning building to avoid its involvement in the fire. It is stacked in the open yard and subsequently damaged by rain. Was the proximate cause of the damage the fire or the rain? If the rain damage occurred before the Insured had an opportunity to protect it, then the proximate cause of the damage would be the fire. However, if the stock were left unprotected for an unreasonably long period, the rain would be a new and independent cause of damage.

If there are more than one cause operating together and one of the cause is excepted peril, the claim shall not be payable under the policy. However, if the results of the operation of an insured peril can be separated from the excluded peril, the claim shall be payable in respect of insured peril.

Example

During the war period, a bomb was dropped on a factory, which caused fire to the factory. The proximate cause of loss in this case is enemy action and not fire.

In *Etherington v. Lancashire and Yorkshire Accidental Insurance Co. (1909),* a man fell from a horse and sustained injuries that prevented him from moving. As a result, he contracted pneumonia due to lying in the wet and died.

The proximate cause of his death was held to be the fall not pneumonia.

Similarly if furniture is thrown out of a burning house to arrest the spread of the fire and its damaged in the process, the proximate cause of the damage would be the fire.

If the insured makes a *prima facie* case that the loss was proximately caused by an insured peril the insurer is obliged to indemnify unless they can prove that an exception applies.

Contribution

Contribution condition is a corollary to the Principle of indemnity. If an insured obtains more than one policy covering the same risk, he cannot recover the same loss from more than one source so that more than 'Indemnity' does not benefit him. Although the Insured may affect more than one policy to cover the same property or interest, he/she cannot recover in total more than a full indemnity. Contribution condition checks that each policy pays only a rateable portion under each separate policy. Application of contribution principle can arise only when the policies:

- Cover the same peril
- Cover the same subject matter
- Are effected by or on behalf of the same Insured

Example

An insured loses his/her watch on holidays. He/she has holiday insurance and All Risks Cover on his/her household policy. The cost of the claim should be shared under both policies.

Example

If an insured has taken three policies from insurers X, Y and Z for ₹ 5,00,000, ₹ 5,00,000 and ₹ 2,00,000 respectively, an the loss to the property due to the operation of the insured peril is ₹ 1,20,000, then the ratio of contribution will be 5: 5: 2. Hence, the claim payable by X, Y and Z will be ₹ 50,000, ₹ 50,000 and ₹ 20,000 respectively.

In the same example if the value of the property at the time of loss was ₹ 15,00,000 then the indemnity in respect of X, Y and Z shall be reduced proportionately by the factor {Sum Insured/ Actual Value}. Such cases shall be deemed to be cases of under insurance and the under cover shall be construed to *self-insured* by the insured. Hence, the losses shall be borne by the parties X, Y, Z and insured as ₹ 16,667, ₹ 16,667, ₹ 6,667 and ₹ 10,000 respectively.

4.2 Related Concepts

Arbitration

When liability under the policy is admitted but the quantum is disputed, the insured cannot rush to a Court of law without first referring the dispute to Arbitration as per 'Indian Arbitration and Reconciliation Act — 1996'. In keeping with the provisions of the Act, the insured may appoint an arbitrator to be followed by appointment of another arbitrator by the insurers. They can also appoint a single arbitrator, to represent both of them. If the two separate arbitrators cannot reach an agreement, both the arbitrators can appoint a third arbitrator called umpire. The award of the arbitrators is binding on both the parties to the dispute and cannot be challenged unless a point of law is involved. The jurisdiction of Arbitration proceedings is within Indian territory. However, when foreign funding is involved, the financiers who are also joined in the policy as co-insured, may insist upon conducting the Arbitration proceedings in their own country. In such a case, the insurers may agree to modify the arbitration condition suitably.

Average

Average is a concept used by insurers to deal with underinsurance occurs when an item is insured for less than its market value.

In terms of the common law, the general rule is that a person who underinsures his property is entitled to the full amount of his loss whether total or partial subject to the limits of the policy in the absence of any provision in the policy to the contrary, e.g., if a house worth ₹ 50,00,000 is insured for ₹ 3,00,000 and a loss of ₹ 1,00,000 occurs the insured in the absence of an average clause in the policy would be entitled to ₹ 1,00,000. By implication, therefore, average is an alien concept to the common law.

Reduced to its logical conclusion, average entails that if there is underinsurance the insured shall be his own insurer to the extent of the underinsurance. This means the insured will bear part of the loss as a penalty for underinsurance.

Because average is not recognized by the common law, its application in insurance is not automatic. Insurer would have to include the average condition in the policy for average to apply

In marine insurance, the term average has a meaning to that ascribed to it in property. Insurance in marine average may mean one of two things:

1. General average sacrifice
2. General average expenditure.

   * The formula for average is: Sum insured/Market value × Loss sustained.

Average only applies to contracts of indemnity hence since life insurance contracts are not contracts of indemnity all concepts derived from indemnity, like subrogation, contribution and average do not apply to life policies.

The rationale behind average is that the insured should pay a premium that is commensurate with the risk he introduces to the pool to avoid prejudicing other contributors.

Key Terms

- ❒ Contribution
- ❒ Indemnity
- ❒ Catastrophic
- ❒ Gambling
- ❒ Subrogation
- ❒ Fortuitous
- ❒ Insurable Risk
- ❒ Assurance

Questions for Review

1. Define insurance. Briefly explain the costs and benefits of insurance.
2. List the various life and non-life insurance covers available in India.
3. Write short notes on:
   (1) Principle of Subrogation
   (2) Principle of Contribution
4. Distinguish between assurance and insurance in view of principle of indemnity.

Suggested Readings

1. Douglas Caddy, *Legislative Trends in Insurance Regulation,* Texas A&M University Press, 1986.
2. Fredricke G. Crane, *Insurance Principles and Practice,* John Wiley, 1980.
3. H.L. Muller-Lutz, *Basic Principles of Insurance Management,* International Insurance Monitor, N.Y., 1966.
4. H.S. Dennenberg, R.D. Elers, J.J. Melone and R.A. Zetten, *Insurance Concepts — Basic and Legal,* Prentice-Hall, Englewood Cliffs, 1974.
5. Jorg Finsinger and Mark V. Pauly, *The Economics of Insurance Regulation,* Macmillan Press Ltd., 1986.
6. R.A. Blanchard, *Risk and Insurance and Other Papers,* 1965.
7. G.E. Rejda, *Insurance and Risk Management,* Pearson Education, 2002.

Web Resources

- www.insure.com
- www.fool.com
- insurance.yahoo.com
- www.montana.edu
- www.bimaonline.com

❒❒❒

CHAPTER

MATHEMATICAL APPLICATIONS

Chapter Objectives

- Probability and its Use in Insurance
- Dual Application of Law of Large Numbers
- Pooling in Insurance
- Mortality Table
- Calculation of Life Premium

Introduction

The bread and butter of the insurance industry is based on the probability and statistics. Actually speaking, the insurance game is a game of probability. One, who correctly estimates wins, otherwise loses. The Insurance actuaries constantly face a trade off when determining the premium to charge for coverage: the premium must be high enough to cover expected losses and expenses, but low enough to remain competitive with premiums charged by other insurers. Actuaries apply statistical analysis to determine expected loss levels and expected deviations from these loss levels. Through the application of the law of large numbers, insurers reduce their risk of adverse outcomes.

5.1 Probability and Its Use in Insurance

The probability of an event refers to the chances of its occurrence of the total set of possible occurrences. For a given pool of automobile covers sold by an insurance company, it is important to find out for the underwriter, what is the chance of occurrence of an automobile accident? If he correctly estimates the probability, the correct cost of bearing the risk, i.e., the premium will be charged from the clients, otherwise, if adverse happens the claims may *ruin* the company.

Probability is mathematically defined as follows:

"If an event A can happen in '*m*' ways out of '*n*' equally likely mutually exclusive and exhaustive ways, then the probability that the event will happen is $\frac{m}{n}$." That is, probability is the ratio of the number of favourable outcomes to the total number of possible outcomes.

$$P(A) = \frac{\text{Number of outcome favourable to the event A}}{\text{Total number of possible outcomes}}$$

i.e., $$P = \frac{m}{n}$$

The probability of non-occurrence of the event *A* is given by:

$$q = p \text{ (not } A)$$

i.e., $$q = \frac{n - m}{n}$$

i.e., $$q = 1 - \frac{m}{n}$$

i.e., $$q = 1 - p.$$

In practical life the probability lies between the two extremes 0 and 1. When $p = 0$, it denotes impossibility of the event taking place, i.e., the event cannot take place. On the other hand, when $p = 1$, it denotes certainty, i.e., the event is bound to take place. Consider a well-shuffled deck of s_2 cards. When a card is drawn at random, any one can come out. Thus, there are s_2 possible ways. Out of s_2 cards, 13 cards are of diamond suit. Thus, there are 13 ways favourable for getting a diamond card when a card is drawn. The probability that the card drawn is a diamond is $\frac{13}{52}$, i.e., $\frac{1}{4}$. This means that we have a 25% chance of drawing a diamond card.

A *probability distribution* or a *theoretical frequency distribution* is the distribution of all possible outcomes of a random variable (A random variable is a variable whose outcome is uncertain). For example, suppose a coin is tossed, either there can be head or a tail. The coin was tossed 50 times and the following observations *cumulatively* were noted for 10, 20, 30, 40 and 50 experiments:

No. of Experiments	10	20	30	40	50
Heads	4	9	13	18	24
Tails	6	11	17	22	26
Probability of a head	40%	45%	43.33%	45%	48%

We all know that if we increase the number of trials such that it approaches infinity (¥), the probability of getting a head will be 50%. The logical conclusion which flows from this illustration is that by increasing the number of experiments for a given random variable, *the probability of the occurrence for a given outcome can be accurately estimated and used for decision making.* Risk management decisions need to be made prior to knowing what the actual (realized) outcomes of key variables will be. A manager does not know beforehand which outcomes of random variable affecting the firm's profits will occur. Nevertheless, he or she must make decisions. Once the outcomes are observed, it is usually easy to say what would have been the best decision. However, we cannot evaluate decisions from this perspective, which is why probability distribution are so important. Probability distribution tell us all the possible outcomes and the possible outcomes and the probability of those outcomes. Information about probability distribution is needed to make a good risk management decision.

5.1.1 Probability Distributions

Probability distributions can either be discrete or continuous. A discrete distribution can take limited values which can be listed, however a continuous can take any value within a given range. In insurance, we use the three popular variable distributions — the Binomial, the Normal and the Poisson. In each of these distributions, it is assumed that events occur in a random fashion, meaning that the probability that any one event will occur is equal to the probability that any other event will occur. It is also assumed that events are independent of each other, in other words, when one event occurs; the probability that a second event will occur is not changed.

5.1.2 The Binomial Distribution

Assuming the probability of occurrence of an event is *p*. Then the probability *q* that the event will not occur can be stated by the equation $q = 1 - p$. Using the following formula, we can calculate how often an event will happen, i.e. the probability of *r* events in *n* possible times is:

$$\frac{n!}{r!(n-r)!} \times p^r q^{n-r}$$

Note that the expression n! is read "*n* factorial" and refers to a successive multiplication of the numbers *n, n* – 1, *n* – 2 ....1. The means and variance of binomial distribution are *np* and *npq* respectively.

5.1.3 The Normal Distribution

As the number of observations increases, the binomial distribution may be used to approximate what is called the normal distribution, which is a very useful type of mathematical distribution. If shown graphically in figure, it is perfectly bell shaped. If its mean and standard deviation are known, the distribution is said to be completely defined.

It should be noted that the binomial distribution requires variables to be discrete (i.e., there is either a loss or no loss). With the normal distribution the variables may be continuous having a value of any number from O to infinity. As a result normal distribution can be applied in more situations and is more versatile and often more realistic than the binomial distribution.

5.1.4 The Poisson Distribution

The poisson distribution is another theoretical distribution that is useful in risk management applications. For example, auto accident, fires, and other losses tend to occur in a way that can be approximated with the Poisson distribution. The probability of an event under the Poisson distribution can be estimated using the following formula:

Where p = the probability that an event n occurs

r = the number of events for which the probability estimate is needed

m = mean = expected loss frequency

e = a constant, the base of the natural logarithms, equal to 2.71828

The mean '*m*' of a poisson distribution is also its variance. Consequently, its standard deviation *s* is equal to *m*.

Poisson distribution is best to be used when the probability of occurrence of an event is small and the population size is very large. Now let us take an example to illustrate the use of probability. Assume that for a given life insurance group of 5 members, the premium charged is ₹ 3,000 and the coverage (sum assured) is ₹ 90,000. If one of those five persons is likely to die in a given period, we are interested in finding whether there will be profit or loss to the insurance company.

Total Premiums collected = ₹ 3,000 × 5

= ₹ 15,000

Expected value of losses $= \sum_{i=1}^{n} \times ipi$

$= 90{,}000 \times \frac{1}{5}$

= ₹ 18,000

Since expected values of losses > total premiums collected, the pricing was improper.

5.2 Dual Application of Law of Large Numbers

It implies from the above discussion that a large sample will improve our estimates of the underlying probability. Even in the case of priori probabilities where the probability is known, it must be applied to large number of trials if we expect actual results to approximate in true probability. Therefore, in the case of empirical probabilities, the requirements of a large number has dual application:

- To estimate the underlying probability accurately, the insurance company must have a sufficiently large sample, the more accurate will be the estimate of the probability.
- Once the estimate of the probability has been made, it must be applied to a sufficiently large number of exposure units to permit the underlying probability to work itself out.

In this sense, to the insurance company, the law of large numbers means that the larger the number of cases examined in the sampling process, the better the chance of that actual experience will approximate a good estimate of the probability.

In making predictions on the basis of historical data, the insurance company assumes that things will happen in the future as they have happened in the past. But it may not be true. It is likely that the probability involved is constantly changing. Since the insurance company bases its rates on the expectation of future losses, it must be concerned with the extent to which actual experience is likely to deviate from the predicted results. For the insurance, risk is measured by potential deviation of actual from predicted results.

It should be noted that although probability theory plays an important role in the operation of insurance, insurance does not always depend on probabilities and predictions. It is only when insurance is to be operated on an advance premium basis, with the participants paying their share of losses in advance, the probability theory and predictions become important.

Insurance is about spreading the risks. From the perspective of an insurance company, represents the probability of compensation payouts being greater than the premium revenue, resulting in a net loss to the company. In general, the insurers risk is reduced if there are many individuals or business taking up insurance. A large pool of policyholders would reduce the administration cost of processing a policy. A large pool would also reduce average insurance premiums because the revenue required to meet the claims is spread over a large number of policyholders. The general assumption is that claims do not increase proportionately with the number of policyholders.

Therefore it is the probability that must be correctly estimated otherwise, the insurance company may default or go into liquidation.

5.3 Pooling in Insurance

Pooling of risks is the underlying feature of insurance. Insurance companies try to make a group or pool of homogenous exposures with a view to reduce the losses arising from that exposure. It is most advantageous when the losses are uncorrelated. When the group agrees to bear the losses in some proportion, the burden on a given member is reduced. This has the effect of loss distribution for the group flater and flater.

The application of large numbers and pooling suggests that normal curve becomes flater any flater when the members are added to a group – logically, because of reduction in the variance and likely concentration towards mean (μ).

5.3.1 Forms of Pooling

Bulk Buying

One form of pooling is known as "bulk buying" which enables a group of individuals or businesses to collectively purchase insurance. The group collectively obtains the services of an insurance broker to find an appropriate underwriter to provide the insurance cover.

Self-insurance

Another form of pooling is self-insurance. This is where individuals or businesses group together to provide their own insurance through the establishment of mutual funds. Members contribute to the mutual fund, which is used to pay for any compensation payouts.

The funds may also reinsure part of the liability against the probability of big compensation payouts. This form of reinsurance policy is used in high cost and high-risk areas such as aviation and marine insurance.

Mutual funds are often established by an industry body for the benefits of its members. For example, the legal profession and local governments in states of USA have their own mutual funds, which provide insurance cover for their members.

Expertise is required in the establishment of a mutual fund. It is important to consult an expert in this area before deciding if it is appropriate for the business or group. Insurance brokers will be able to provide advice on such matters.

5.3.2 Cost and Benefits of Pooling

Insurance pooling enables small companies or community groups to gain access to insurance, otherwise which is not available to them individually.

Pooling to facilitate bulk buying can increase the ability of individuals and business to negotiate better terms and conditions, including premiums, from the insurer. This is because risk is spread across all policyholders in the pool and loss expectancies are reduced. This could lead to lower premiums or containment of future premium increases. As pool size increases, loss expectancies become more predictable, and insurers would be more comfortable in allowing premiums to stabilize. Pooling can also provide an opportunity to attract insurers back to the market.

Advantages of Pooling

In cases where the community or group gets together and pools their funds, the following advantages are obtained:

- Coverages are specialized for and geared to exposures faced by the individuals pooling in their money for insurance purposes.
- Stability Pooling is not subject to the market whims of the standard insurance market.
- No taxes or fees are required to be paid (in some cases).
- Profits belong to members of the Pool, and they are distributed as per the policy document or consensus as the case may be.
- Members are able to participate in claims handling.
- Flexibility of coverage forms, more customization leads to flexibility.
- Emphasis on Loss Control, including on-site surveys. Safety Committee Set-up.
- Funds are invested in the focused area or location and are less susceptible to market fluctuations.

Besides the above there are other advantages that come by way of pooling:

- Pools offer favourable coverages, terms conditions, and limits tailored to the needs of the public entity participants.
- Pooling spreads the risk of a severe financial loss over a group, rather than being borne by one entity.

- ❑ The combined purchasing power of pool members gives each member group more clout when negotiating terms and conditions for excess insurance.
- ❑ Pool premiums are generally more stable, since the pool is somewhat insulated from the regular fluctuations of the insurance market.
- ❑ Pool participants have ownership in any equity that the pool accumulates.
- ❑ Pool members have a significant voice in how the pool is operated, since the policy-making board is composed of representatives of its members.
- ❑ Data regarding losses are provided to members on a regular basis.
- ❑ Claims handling is dictated by the pool's claim philosophy, and members have a voice in how claims are resolved.
- ❑ Services, especially risk control, are tailored to the needs of its members.

Administrating the Pool

A group representative (industry association, a lobby or a person or organization which is willing and able to represent the group) could perform the role of coordinating the insurance requirements of the pool. An industry association or lobby group would also provide the focal point for attracting members to participate in the pool.

Effective Pool

A pool to facilitate bulk buying has to be sufficiently big to increase the ability to negotiate premiums and to spread the risks. An adequate pool size depends on the type of activities and the levels or risk being insured. In general, high risk and high cost activities would require a bigger pool relative to low risk activities.

A pool cannot cater to a wide range of risks. The spread of risks for the group should ideally be small so that subsidization of the high-risk policyholder by the low risk policyholder is minimized. In addition the insurers should know that they are in for a long haul.

A small "bulk buying" pool has less bargaining power and the ability to negotiate lower premiums. A small group wishing to form a pool insurance purpose may have to consider joining other groups of similar activities and risk levels, to increase the size of the pool. For example, a state industry association may join up with another state or with the national industry association to increase the size of the pool.

Intergovernmental pooling is a risk financing mechanism based on cooperative agreements among public entities to provide for many of their risk financing needs through a jointly owned programme. This programme while very successful abroad (mainly USA and Europe) is yet to catch up stem in India. Pooling involves group self-insurance and/or group insurance purchasing. (Now, public entity pools account for almost 40 per cent of the insurance marketing for the countries specified above).

The financial viability of a private insurance pool depends on the balance between **premium income and losses.** If losses are consistently greater than premium income, a private insurer may default on the contract, leaving the insured worse off than if no insurance had been available.

Financial balance is also important to most government insurance programs, the ones mentioned above and all of the largest ones because they are intended to protect the insured from losses without simply shifting those losses to others.

Multinational Pooling – is another Concept that has been Gaining Importance

Multinational pooling is a technique that allows organizations with multiple operations around the world to consolidate their employee benefit insurance contracts in these countries with a local insurer of an international insurance network. Principal among the merits multinational pooling can offer are:

- Economies of scale and purchasing power
- Global experience rating
- Financial cost savings
- Improved underwriting terms and conditions
- Annual reporting
- A management tool and information base.

But in case of insurance pooling by multinationals of MNC's there are more complexities involved and regular check on management is vital.

Pooling is appropriate in situations when individuals or business are unable to obtain insurance on their own or when insurance is expensive. In the majority of the cases, these would be areas, which the insurance industry at large are not targeting.

5.4 Mortality Table

In life insurance, certain asssumptions have to be made by the insurer about the interest rates, mortality rates and the expenses which will be incurved in the year to come for the purpose of fixing the premium rates or assessing the liabilities under the insurance contracts. It is important to have a correct estimate of these factors as otherwise the results deducted from the assumptions made may not be reasonably close to the actual experience of the insuner. He depends upon the mortality experience of the insuned lives observed inb the recent past as a basis for estimating the probabilities of survival and deaths.

If it is observed that out of 1000 lives all aged 35, 20 die within one year, *i.e.,* before attaining the age 36, the observed mortality rate at age 35 works out to $\frac{20}{10000}=0.002$ and is denoted by q_{35}. The mortality rates at various ages are determined in the same manner.

A mortality table represents a record of mortality observed in the past and is arranged so as to show the probabilities of death and survival at each separate age. A large number of persons are selected at a particular age and number of deaths are observed each and every year. Each year's number of living is the previous year's number of living minus previous year's number of dying. As the persons go on dying year after year the, number of living goes on shrinking. When the last person dies, it is reduced to zero and the mortality table ends there.

The following are the two major mortality tables:

(*a*) LIC (1970-73) Ultimate Table

(*b*) H^m Table (Makehan Graduation)

5.4.1 Construction of Mortality Table

The main objective for having a mortality table for an insurer is to work out the probabilities of deaths and survivors to enable him to make a reasonably accurate estimate of his liabilities under the insurance contracts and also to calculate premium to be charged. The past experience from which the table is constructed will never be exactly reproduced in future. There will be fluctuations in different directions at different ages but on the whole the estimates in respect of mortality rates may be close to the actual experience. So, the mortality table should be constructed to represent the past experience as accurately as possible. The following are the two methods of construction of mortality table.

(i) On Generation Basis: In this method, we select a large number of persons at an attained age. The attained age means the age nearer to the birth date. For example, persons of age 14 years 6 months to 15 years 6 months will be treated as the age of 15 years. The selected persons of this attained age will be observed each and every year and the number of deaths will be recorded during the year. The observation will be continuing till all the persons selected are dead. Preparation of such table is very difficult, because it requires a long period to construct the table and constant watch on the selected persons is practically impossible. A lot of money and manpower will be required to record number of deaths every time. To avoid these difficulties, death rate is calculated on yearly basis.

Mortality Table (on Generation Basis)

Age	*Number of Living*	*Number of Deaths*	*Mortality Rate*	*Survival Rate*
25	987095	1263	0.00128	0.00872
26	985832	1252	0.00127	0.99873
27	984580	1250	0.00127	0.99873
28	983330	1268	0.00129	0.99871
29	982062	1286	0.00131	0.99869

(ii) On Yearly Basis: In this method, the death rate is calculated for every age. Separate sample is taken for each age. The number of death during the age is recorded and the mortality rate is calculated. By this method, we can construct the mortality table within the duration of one year. For example, 5000 persons are taken at age 25, 4000 persons at age 26, 6000 persons at age 27, 10000 persons at age 28 and 3000 persons at age 29. The number of deaths observed at these ages are 10, 16, 18, 60 and 15 respectively. The following table summarizes the mortality rates at the above ages.

Age	*Number of Living*	*Number of Deaths*	*Mortality Rate*	*Survival Rate*
25	5000	10	0.002	0.998
26	4000	16	0.004	0.996
27	6000	18	0.003	0.997
28	10000	60	0.006	0.994
29	3000	15	0.005	0.995

5.4.2 Components of a Complete Mortality Table

Apart from the ordinary mortality table, the insurers use complete mortality table. Generally, the H^m Makeham graduation mortality table is used. All the components of this complete mortality table is discussed below:

***(i)* Column (*x*):** It denotes the age of prospects. The mortality table can start from any age (5, 8, 10 etc.) depending upon the requirement of the insurer and continue to 100-120 years and required by the insurers.

LIC (1970-73) ultimate table starts from the age 15 and ends at the age 103. The H^m table starts from the age 0 and ends at the age 102.

***(ii)* Column (l_x):** It indicates the number of living persons at the beginning of each year (*x*). If the table starts from age 0, then the number in l_x column against this age, say l_0 is any convenient number like 10,00,000 or even an arbitrary number like 2714321 and represents the numbers of persons of age 0., i.e., the number of persons just born having fixed the starting number l_0 any other number l_x in the column appearing against age *x* gives the number of persons living out of the l_0 persons born who reach the age *x*. Thus, l_{30} is the number of persons who reach age 30. In case of LIC (1970-73), ultimate table, l_{30} is 980776.

***(iii)* Column (d_x):** It indicates the number of persons dying between the age *x* and *x* + 1. The number of survivors at the age *x* + 1 is given by $l_{x+1} = l_x - d_x$.

$$\boxed{d_x = l_x - l_{x+1}}$$

For example, the number of deaths at the age of 30 is given by:

$$d_{30} = l_{30} - l_{31}$$

Similarly, we can calculate the number of death between two particular years.

The number of deaths between age 40 and 45 is given by:

$$\sum_{x-40}^{44} dx = d_{40} + d_{41} + d_{42} + d_{43} + d_{44}$$

$$= (l_{40} - l_{41}) + (l_{41} - l_{42}) + (l_{42} - l_{43}) + (l_{43} - l_{44}) + (l_{44} - l_{45})$$

$$= l_{40} - l_{45}$$

$$= 963206 - 946656$$

$$= 16550$$

$$\sum_{x-a}^{b} dx = l_a - l_{b+1}$$

***(iv)* Column (q_x):** It indicates the probability that a person aged *x* dies within 1 year, i.e., before reaching the age *x* + 1.

$$\therefore q_x = \frac{\text{number of deaths between age x and x + 1}}{\text{total number of livings at age x}}$$

i.e., $q_x = \frac{d_x}{l_x}$

i.e., $q_x = \frac{l_x - l_{x+1}}{l_x}$

q_x is called the rate of mortality at age *x*. For e.g., from the LIC (1970-73) table, the rate of mortality at age 30.

i.e., $q_{30} = \frac{d_{30}}{l_{30}}$

$= \frac{1314}{980776}$

= 0.00134.

(v) Column (p_x): It indicates the survival rate. It gives for successive ages the probability that a life survive to age *x* + 1.

$$p_x = \frac{\text{number of survivors to age x + 1}}{\text{total number living at age x}}$$

$$p_x = \frac{l_{x+1}}{l_x}$$

For example, from the H^m table.

$$p_{30} = \frac{l_{31}}{l_{30}}$$

$$= \frac{88994}{89685}$$

= .99229.

Clearly, the probability that a person aged *x* will die within 1 years and the probability that he will survive for 1 year or the complementary probabilities.

i.e., $p_x + q_x = 1$.

We know that, $q_x = \frac{d_x}{l_x}$

$\Rightarrow$ $q_x = \frac{l_x - l_{x+1}}{l_x}$

$\Rightarrow$ $q_x = 1 - \frac{l_{x+1}}{l_x}$

$$\Rightarrow \quad q_x = 1 - p_x$$

$$\Rightarrow \quad p_x + q_x = 1$$

(vi) Column (U_x): It represents the force of mortality at age *x* is defined as the limiting value of the normal yearly rate of mortality at age *x* over a small interval δt. In practice, the smallest interval be considered is 1 day.

$$\delta t = \frac{1}{365} \text{ year}.$$

The deaths between age *x* and $x + \frac{1}{365}$ are $l_x - l_x + \frac{1}{365}$ and the rate of mortality at age *x* per day is $\frac{l_x - l_{x+1/365}}{l_x}$ and the corresponding yearly rate is $365 \times \left(\frac{l_x - l_{x+1/365}}{l_x}\right)$.

(vii) Column (L_x): It represents the number of persons in the population between *x* and *x* + 1, i.e., the number of survivals at the middle of age *x* and *x* + 1. It is also denoted by (l_x + ½).

$$L_x = \frac{1}{2}(l_x + l_{x+1})$$

Now $$l_{x+1} = l_x - d_x$$

$$L_x = \frac{1}{2}(l_x + l_x - d_x)$$

$$= \frac{1}{2}(2l_x - d_x)$$

$$\boxed{L_x = l_x - \frac{1}{2}d_x.}$$

In H^m table, at age x = 50, l_x = 72795, d_x = 1144.

$$L_x = l_x - \frac{1}{2}d_x$$

$$= 72795 - \frac{1}{2} \times 1144$$

$$= 72795 - 572$$

$$= 72223.$$

(viii) Column (T_x): It denotes the total number of persons living at any time who are aged *x* or more. Total number of survivors at any age is equal to the summation of number of persons living between mid of age *x* and at the end of the table i.e.,

T_x = number of persons living between *x* and *x* + 1 + ...

number of persons living between $x + 1$ and $x + 2$ + ...

number of persons living between $x + 2$ and $x + 3$ + ...

i.e., $T_x = L_x + L_{x+1} + L_{x+2} + \ldots\ldots$

$$= \frac{1}{2}(l_x + l_{x+1}) + \frac{1}{2}(l_{x+1} + l_{x+2}) + \frac{1}{2}(l_{x+2} + l_{x+3}) + \ldots\ldots$$

$$= \frac{1}{2}l_x + l_{x+1} + l_{x+2} + l_{x+3} + \ldots\ldots$$

$$\therefore \quad T_x = \frac{1}{2}l_x + N'_{x+1}$$

where, $N'_{x+1} = l_{x+1} + l_{x+2} + l_{x+3} + \ldots.$

For e.g., from thc H^m table, at age 89.

$$N'_{89+1} = l_{89+(90)} + l_{91} + l_{92} \ldots l_{101}$$

= 1273 + 871 + 575 + 366 + 222 + 129 + 71 + 37 + 19 + 9 + 4 + 1.

= 3577

$$T_{89} = \frac{1}{2}l_{89} + N'_{90}$$

$$= \frac{1}{2}1800 + 3577$$

= 900 + 3577

= 4477.

***(ix) Column (lx)*:** This symbol is known as the complete expectation of life. *lx* represents the expectation of life.

The expectation of life at age *x* is the average number of complete years of life lived by each person age *x* after reaching age *x*. Out of l_x lives, l_{x+1} reach age $x + 1$, i.e., each of l_{x+1} lives completes 1 year after age *x*. Similarly, each of l_{x+2} completes 2 years after reaching age *x* and so on.

The total number of completed years lived by l_x persons is given by:

$l_{x+1} + l_{x+2} + l_{x+3} + \ldots$

The average number of complete years that each peron aged *x* will live is given by:

$$l_x = \frac{l_{x+1} + l_{x+2} + l_{x+3}}{l_x}$$

$$l_x = \frac{N'_{x+1}}{l_x}.$$

This expectation of life is called the complete expectation of life as it takes into account only complete years of lives and ignores fraction of the year lived in the year of death.

If the fractions are taken into account, we get the complete expectation of life denoted by l°_{x}.

∴ the additional number of years of life to be included in respect of the fractional years is given by:

$$= \frac{1}{2}d_x + \frac{1}{2}d_{x+1} + \frac{1}{2}d_{x+2} + ...$$

$$= \frac{1}{2}(d_x + d_{x+1} + ...)$$

$$= \frac{1}{2}l_x.$$

$$\therefore \quad l_x = \frac{N_{x+1} + \frac{1}{2}l_x}{l_x}$$

$$\boxed{l_x = \frac{T_x}{l_x}.}$$

$$\Rightarrow \quad e^0_{20} = \frac{N'_{x+1}}{l_x} + \frac{1}{2}\frac{l_x}{l_x}$$

$$\Rightarrow \quad e^0_x = l_x + 1/2.$$

For example in H^m table

$$e^0_{20} = \frac{T_{20}}{l_{20}}$$

$$= \frac{4044238}{96061}$$

= 42.101.

5.4.3 Probabilities of Survival and Death

The mortality table can be used for calculating the various probabilities of survival and death.

(a) np$_x$: It indicates the probability that the person aged *x* survives *n* years. When *n* it *I*, it is denoted by p_x.

$$\therefore \quad np_x = \frac{\text{no. of persons living at age x + n}}{\text{no. of persons living at age x}}.$$

$$\boxed{np_x = \frac{l_{x+n}}{l_x}.}$$

(*b*) mq_x: This symbol denotes the probability that a person aged *x* dies within the next '*m*' years.

$$\therefore \quad mq_x = \frac{\text{total no. of persons dying between age x and x} + \text{m}}{\text{total no. of persons living at age x}}.$$

$$\boxed{mq_x = \frac{l_x - l_{x+m}}{l_x}.}$$

$$mq_x = \frac{l_x}{l_x} - \frac{l_{x+m}}{l_x}.$$

$$\therefore \quad mq_x = 1 - mp_x.$$

(*c*) m/q_x: This symbol denotes the probability that a person aged *x* will die: between the age *x* + *m* and *x* + *m* + 1

$$\therefore \quad m/q_x = \frac{\text{total no. of persons dying between x} + \text{m \& x} + \text{m} + 1}{\text{total no. of living at age x}}.$$

$$\boxed{m/q_x = \frac{l_{x+m} - l_{x+m+1}}{l_x}}$$

$$\Rightarrow \quad m/q_x = \frac{d_{x+m}}{l_x}.$$

(*d*) m/nq_x: This symbol represents the probability that a person aged *x* dies within '*n*' years following '*m*' years from now, i.e., between the years of age *x* + *m* and age *x* + *m* + *n*.

$$\therefore \quad m/nq_x = \frac{\text{total no. of deaths in between age x} + \text{m and x} + \text{m} + \text{n}}{\text{no. of living at age x}}.$$

$$\therefore \quad m/nq_x = \frac{l_{x+m} - l_{x+m+m}}{l_x}.$$

The probability that a person aged *x* will survive between the age *x* + *m* and age *x* + *m* + *n* is given by:

$1 - m/nq_x$

Illustration 1. Find the following probabilities that:

(*a*) a life aged 30 survives 10 years.

(*b*) a life aged 30 dies within next 10 years.

(*c*) a life aged 30 dies after 10 years.

(Use LIC mortality table).

Solution. (*a*) the probability that a life aged 30 survives 10 years, i.e., = $^{10}P_{30}$.

$$= \frac{l_{30+10}}{l_{30}} \qquad \left[\because {}_np_x = \frac{l_{x+n}}{l_x}.\right]$$

$$= \frac{l_{40}}{l_{30}} = \frac{963206}{980776}$$

= 0.9821.

(*b*) the probability that a person aged 30 dies within next 10 years.

i.e., $10q_{30}$

$= 1 - 10p_{30}$

= 1 – 0.9821

= 0.0179

alternatively $\quad 10_{q30} = \dfrac{l_{30} - l_{30+10}}{l_{30}}$

$$= \frac{980776 - 963206}{980776}$$

= 0.0179.

(*c*) the prob. that the person aged 30 dies after 10 years i.e.,

= 1 – the probability that the person died within 10 years.

= 1 – 0.0179

= 0.9821.

Illustration 2. Using the LIC (1970–73) ultimate table, find the following probabilities that —

(*a*) a life aged 35 dies within 12 years.

(*b*) a life aged 40 dies not earlier than 12 years and not later than 15 years.

(*c*) a life aged 52 survives 12 years.

(*d*) a life aged 52 will not dies between 65 and 70.

Solution. (*a*) Probability that a life aged 35 dies within 12 years.

$= 12q_{35}$

$$= \frac{l_{35} - l_{35+12}}{l_{35}} \qquad \left[\because {}_nq_x = \frac{l_x - l_{x+n}}{l_x}\right]$$

$$= \frac{l_{35} - l_{47}}{l_{35}}$$

$$= \frac{983550 - 937401}{973550}$$

= 0.0371.

(*b*) probability that life aged 40 dies not earlier than 12 years and not later than 15 years i.e.,

$$= 12/3q_{40} \qquad \begin{bmatrix} n = 40; \\ m = 12; \\ m + n = 15; \\ n = 3; \end{bmatrix}$$

$$= \frac{l_{40+12} - l_{40+12+3}}{l_{40}} \quad \left[\because m/nq_x = \frac{l_{x+m} - l_{x+m+n}}{l_x}\right]$$

$$= \frac{l_{52} - l_{55}}{l_{40}} = \frac{904837 - 876999}{963206}.$$

= 0.029.

(*c*) The probability that a life aged 52 survives 12 years.

$= 12p_{52}$

$$= \frac{l_{52+12}}{l_{52}} \quad \left[np_x = \frac{l_{x+n}}{l_n}\right]$$

$$= \frac{l_{64}}{l_{52}} = \frac{738825}{904837} = 0.8165.$$

(*d*) The probability that a life aged 52 will not dies between age 65 and 70, i.e.,

= 1 – probability that a life aged 52 will dies between 65 and 70.

$$= 1 - 13/5q_{52} \qquad \begin{bmatrix} x = 52 \\ x + m = 65 \Rightarrow m = 13 \\ x + m + n = 70 \\ \Rightarrow n = 5 \end{bmatrix}$$

$$= 1 - \frac{l_{52+3} - l_{52+13+5}}{l_{52}}$$

$$= 1 - \frac{l_{65} - l_{70}}{l_{52}}$$

$$= 1 - \frac{904837 - 591285}{904837}$$

$$= 1 - \frac{126151}{904837}.$$

= 1 – 0.1394

= 0.08606.

Illustration 3. Fill up the blanks in the following portion of a life table.

x	l_x	d_x	q_x	p_x
10	1000000	...	0.00409	...
11	...	...	0.00370	...
12	...	...	...	0.99653
13	...	...	...	0.99658
14	...	...	0.00342	...

Solution. We know that

$$q_x = \frac{d_x}{l_x} \Rightarrow d_x = q_x \times l_x$$

$$p_x = 1 - d_x$$

$$l_{x+1} = l_x - d_x$$

For age 10:

$$d_{10} = q_{10} \times l_{10} = 0.00409 \times 1000000 = 4090$$

$$P_{10} = 1 - q_{10} = 1 - 0.00409 = 0.99591$$

For age 11:

$$l_{11} = l_{10} - d_{10} = 1000000 - 4090 = 995910$$

$$d_{11} = q_{11} \times l_4 = 0.00370 \times 995910 = 3685$$

$$P_{11} = 1 - q_{11} = 1 - 0.00370 = 0.99630$$

For age 12:

$$l_{12} = l_{11} - d_{11} = 995910 - 3685 = 992225$$

$$q_{12} = 1 - P_{12} = 1 - 0.99653 = 0.00347$$

$$d_{12} = q_{12} \times l_{12} = 0.00347 \times 992225 = 3443$$

Similarly

$$l_{13} = 988782;\quad q_{13} = 0.00342;\quad d_{13} = 3382$$

$$l_{14} = 985400;\quad d_{14} = 3370;\quad P_{14} = 0.99658$$

The complete table is

x	l_x	d_x	q_x	p_x
10	1000000	4090	0.00409	0.99591
11	995910	3685	0.00370	0.99630
12	992225	3443	0.00347	0.99653
13	988782	3382	0.00342	0.99658
14	985400	3370	0.00342	0.99658

Illustration 4. Find the probability that of 2 persons A and B aged 30 and 35 respectively:

(*a*) both died before attaining age 55

(*b*) both die after attaining age 60.

(*c*) A dies before 65 while B dies after 60.

(*d*) atleast one of them survives to age 70.

Solution. (*a*) probability of both A and B dies before attaining age 50 and 55.

$= P\,(A \text{ dies}) \times P(B \text{ dies})$

$= 25q_{30} \times 20q_{35}$

$$= \left(\frac{l_{30} - l_{30+25}}{l_{30}}\right) \times \left(\frac{l_{35} - l_{35+20}}{l_{35}}\right)$$

$$= \left(\frac{l_{30} - l_{55}}{l_{30}}\right) \times \left(\frac{l_{35} - l_{55}}{l_{35}}\right)$$

$$= \left(\frac{980776 - 876889}{980776}\right) \times \left(\frac{973550 - 876889}{973550}\right)$$

$$= \frac{103887}{980776} \times \frac{96661}{973550}$$

$= 0.1059 \times 0.0993$

$= 0.0105$

(*b*) probability that both died after attaining 60 years i.e.,

$= P(A \text{ died after } 60) \times P(B \text{ dies after } 60)$

$= (1 - 30q_{30})\,(1 - 25q_{35})$

$$= \left(1 - \frac{l_{30} - l_{60}}{l_{30}}\right)\left(1 - \frac{l_{35} - l_{60}}{l_{35}}\right)$$

$$= \left(1 - \frac{980776 - 811640}{980776}\right)\left(1 - \frac{973550 - 811640}{973550}\right)$$

= (1 – 0.17245) (1 – 0.16631)

= 0.8276 × 0.8337

= 0.68897

(*c*) *P*(*A* dies after 65 yrs and *B* dies after 60 yrs)

= *P*(*A* dies before 65) X *P*(*B* dies after 60)

= 1 × 2, (*say*)

1. *P* (*A* dies after 65)

$= 35q_{30}$

$$= \frac{l_{30} - l_{30+35}}{l_{30}} = \frac{l_{30} - l_{65}}{l_{30}}$$

$$= \frac{980776 - 717436}{980776}$$

= 0.2685 /–

2. *P*(*B* dies after 60)

= 0.8337 (before (6))

Required prob. = 1 × 2

= 0.2685 × 0.8337

= 0.2238

(*d*) *P* (atleast one of them survive to 70)

= 1 – *P*(Both dies before 70)

= 1 – [*P*(*A* dies before 70) X *P*(*B* dies before 70)]

P(*A* dies before 70) = $40q_{30}$

$$= \frac{l_{30} - l_{70}}{l_{30}}$$

$$= \frac{980776 - 591285}{980776}$$

$$= \frac{389491}{980776} = 0.3971$$

$P(B \text{ dies before } 70) = {}_{35}q_{35}$

$$= \frac{l_{35} - l_{70}}{l_{35}}$$

$$= \frac{973550 - 591285}{973550}$$

$$= \frac{382265}{973550} = 0.3927$$

Required probability $= 1 - (0.3971 \times 0.3927$

$= 1 - 0.1559$

$= 0.8441$

5.5 Calculation of Life Premium

Life assurance is a guarantee or a promise to pay a particular benefit designed by a living person. The insurer who offers assurance and the life assured who seeks protection, are the two parties entering into a contract of life assurance. The insurer experts to review the premiums from the life assured. The life assured, in return, experts the payment of promised benefits. The values of there two expertations at the commencement of the contract should be identical, if no party is to loose in the transaction. Appropriate premium for any particular benefit is arrived at on the basis of the equation of present values of both life insurance benefit and premium payable.

The premium is of two types:

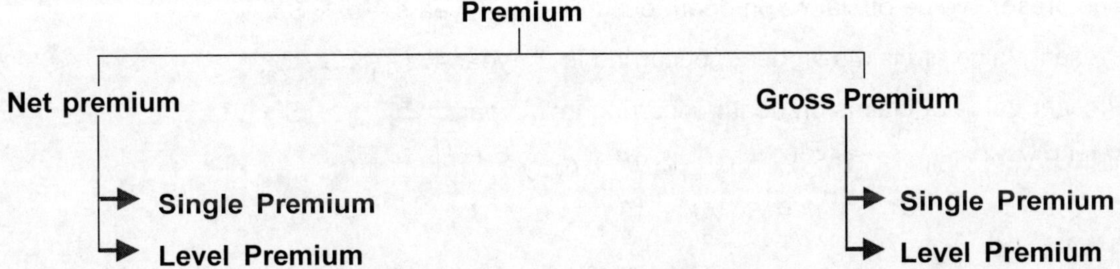

New premium is based in the mortality and interest rates. The gross premium includes the net premium and loading. Loading is the process of adding the expenses to net premium. These expenses include the expenses that vary with the amount of policy such as stamp fee and medical examiner's fee business such as salaries and establishment charges. Single premium is paid in one lump sum while the level premium is paid periodically in instalments, *i.e.*, yearly, half-yearly, quarterly or monthly. Firstly, net single premium (NSP) is calculated and other premium are based on this calculations.

This is the simplest type of contract whereby payment is made only when the life assured dies within the term specified. Nothing will be paid if the death does not occur darring the designated term. This is called term assurance or temporary assurance. The premium is received in advance and will not be returned if the life insured survives. The death claims will be paid at the end of the year in which the death occurs and not at the end of the term.

In case of 1 years, we know $d_x = l_x \times q_x$

Total amount of claim payable = no. of deaths × amount of policy

$$= d_x \,.\, S$$

$$\text{premium} = s\frac{d_x}{l_x}$$

If the insurer earns interest at '*i*' %, then the premium will be the present values of $s.\frac{d_x}{l_x}$.

$$\therefore \text{ Premium} = s\frac{d_x}{l_x}(1+i)^{-1}$$

i.e., $$\text{PNSP} = \text{S.V.}\frac{d_x}{l_x} \quad \text{where} \quad v = (1+i)^{-1}$$

In case the term is more than 1 years, consider a temporary assurance of person aged *x* at entry for the term of '*n*' years.

The present value of claims of death at a particular age = no. of death × amount of claims × present value of Re. 1.

PV of Re. 1 is called discounting factor.

Let *S* be the amount of policy or sum assured and let *i* be the discounting rate.

The present value of claims on death occurring in 1st years = $d_x \times S \times V$

Present value of claims on death occurring in 2nd year = $d_{x+1} \times S \times V^2$

Present value of claims on death occurring in '*n*' years = $d_{x+n-1} \times S \times V^2$

Total P.V. of claim $= d_x\, S\, V + d_{x+1}\, S\, V^2 + d_{x+2}\, S\, V^3 + \ldots + d_{x+n-1}$

$$= S\,[Vd_x + V^2 d_{x+1} + V^3\, d_{x+2} + \ldots V^n \,.\, d_{x+n-1}]$$

$$\text{Premium} = \frac{\text{Total P.V. of claim}}{\text{Total no. of livings at age x}}$$

i.e., $$\text{NSP} = S\left[\frac{Vd_x + V^2 d_{x+1} + V^3 d_{x+2} + \ldots V^2 d_{x+n-1}}{l_x}\right]$$

i.e., $$\boxed{\text{NSP} = S\,A'_{x.\overline{n}|}}$$

If the insurer does not earn interest, then

$$NSP = S\left[\frac{d_x + d_{x+1} + ...d_{x+n-1}}{l_x}\right].$$

Illustration 5. 2000 persons all age 50 years are insured from ₹ 1,00,000 for 1 year If the rate of mortality (q_{50}) is 0.004, calculate the *NSP* of this term assurance:

(*i*) if the insurer earns no interest.

(*ii*) if the insurer earns interest at 6%.

Solution. $l_{50} = 2000$

$$q_{50} = 0.004$$

$$\therefore \quad d_{50} = l_{50} \times q_{50}$$

$$= 2000 \times 0.004$$

$$= 8$$

Total amt. of claim = 8 × 100,000

= 8,00,000

$$\text{Premium} = \frac{8,00,000}{2000} = 400.$$

Present value of total claims = $8 \times 1,00,000 \times (1.06)^{-1}$

$= 8,00,000 \times (1.06)^{-1}$

= 754717.

$$\therefore \quad \text{Premium} = \frac{754717}{2000}$$

= ₹ 377.35

Illustrations 6. Consider a group of 10,000 persons all aged 35 seeking an amount of ₹ 1,00,000 to their families in case of death during the next 10 years.

x	35	36	37	38	39	40	40	42	43	44	45
l_x	10,000	9972	9941	9907	9869	9827	9780	9728	9671	9608	9538
d_x	28	31	34	38	42	47	52	57	63	70	75

Calculate the Net Single premium for their term assurance, if:

(*i*) the insurer earns interest @ 6% p.a.

(*ii*) the insurer earns no interest.

Solution. (*i*) In case of 6% p.a. rate of interest:

no. of livings at age 35, $l_{35} = 10,000$

Policy amount 5 = ₹ 1,00,000

interest rate, i = 6% = 0.06

no. of years, n = 10 years.

Year	*Age x*	l_x	d_x	$V^n = (1.06)^{-n}$ $d_x \times V^n \times S$	*P.V. of Claim*
1	35	10,000	28	0.94340	26,41520
2	36	9972	31	0389000	27,59,000
3	37	9941	34	0.83962	28,54,710
4	38	9907	38	0.79209	30,09940
5	39	9869	42	0.74726	31,38,490
6	40	9827	47	0.70496	33,13,310
7	41	9780	52	0.66506	34,58,310
8	42	9728	57	0.62741	35,76,240
9	43	9671	63	0.59190	37,28,970
10	44	9608	70	0.55839	39,08,730
				Total	**3,23,89,220**

Present value of total claims = 32389220

No. of insured (l_x) = 10,000

$$\therefore \quad \text{NSP} = \frac{32389220}{10,000}$$

= 3238.92

(*ii*) In case of no interest,

$$\text{NSP} = S\left(\frac{d_x + d_{x+1} + \ldots d_{x+n+1}}{l_x}\right)$$

= 1,00, 000 [28 + 31 + 34 + 38 + 42 + 47 + 52 + 57 + 63 + 70]

$$= \frac{1,00,000 \times 462}{10,000}$$

= ₹ 4620.

Key Terms

- ❑ Pool
- ❑ Probability
- ❑ Self-insurance
- ❑ Poisson Distribution
- ❑ Survival rate
- ❑ Construction of Mortality Table
- ❑ Law of Large Numbers
- ❑ Bulk Buyer
- ❑ Binomial Distribution
- ❑ Mortality Rate
- ❑ Mortality Table
- ❑ Components of Mortality Table

- ❑ Expectation of Life
- ❑ Premium
- ❑ Net Premium
- ❑ Loading
- ❑ Gross Premium
- ❑ Term Assurance
- ❑ Whole Life Assurance
- ❑ Pure Endowment Assurance
- ❑ Endowment Assurance
- ❑ Double Endowment Assurance

Questions for Review

1. "Insurance is a dual application of law of large numbers." Discuss.
2. Define Pooling. Briefly explain the advantages of pooling to insurance institutions.
3. Explain how mortality table is constructed.
4. What are the components of a complete mortality table?
5. Derive the relation: $p_x + q_x = 1$.
6. What is net premium? How does it differ from Gross premium?
7. Write a short note on Endowment Assurance.
8. How does term assurance differ from whole life assurance?
9. Find the probability that:
   (*i*) a life aged 35 will die between the age 45 and 50;
   (*ii*) a life aged 35 will not die between 45 and 50;
   (*iii*) a life aged 35 will die in the 10th year from now;
   (*iv*) a life aged 35 will not die in the 10th year from now.

   Ans.: (*i*) 0.0277; (*ii*) 0.9723; (*iii*) 0.0041; (*iv*) 0.9959
10. Given the following rates of mortality, what is the probability that a person aged 65 will die between ages 69 and 70?

Age	*Rate of Mortality*
65	0.035
66	0.040
67	0.045
68	0.050
69	0.055

Ans.: 0.04623

11. Using the LIC (1970-73) ultimate table, compute the following probabilities.
    (*i*) Probability that a life aged 40 survives 10 years;
    (*ii*) Probability that a life aged 40 dies within the next 10 years.
    (*iii*) Probability that a life aged 40 dies after 10 years.

    Ans.: (*i*) 0.9548; (*ii*) 0.0452; (*iii*) 0.9548

12. Of two persons *A* aged 35 and *B* aged 42, find the probability that:
   (*i*) *A* and *B* both survive 10 years
   (*ii*) *A* and *B* both die within 10 years
   (*iii*) One of the two lives survives 10 years while the other dies within that period.
   (*iv*) Atleast one survives 10 years.

Ans.: (*i*) 0.9189; (*ii*) 0.0015; (*iii*) 0.0796; (*iv*) 0.9985

14. Fill up the blanks in the following portion of a life table:

x	l_x	d_x	q_x	P_x
20	1000000	—	0.0050	—
21	—	—	0.0045	—
22	—	—	—	0.9960
23	—	—	—	0.9965
24	—	—	—	0.9970
25	—	—	0.0025	—

Ans.:

$d_{20} = 5000$ $l_{22} = 990522$ $l_{24} = 983107$

$P_{20} = 0.9950$ $d_{22} = 3962$ $d_{24} = 2949$

$P_{21} = 995000$ $q_{22} = 0.0040$ $q_{24} = 0.0030$

$d_{21} = 4478$ $l_{23} = 986560$ $l_{25} = 980158$

$P_{21} = 0.9955$ $d_{23} = 3453$ $d_{25} = 2450$

$q_{23} = 0.0035$ $P_{25} = 0.9975$

15. From the following data, find the number of livings at age 43.

x	l_x	d_x	q_x
40	—	400	0.006
41	—	—	0.007
42	—	—	0.008
43	—	—	—

Ans.: 65277

16. Calculate the value of an assurance of ₹ 1000 for a person aged 25 under which the sum assured is payable in case of death between ages 28 and 30 or on survival to age 30 years from the following data with 6% interest

x:	35	36	37	38	39	40	41	42	43	44	45
l_x:	10000	9972	9941	9907	9869	9827	9780	9728	9671	9608	9538
d_x:	28	31	34	38	42	47	52	57	63	70	75

Ans.: ₹ 740.62

17. Consider the following data:

x:	25	26	27	28	29	30
l_x:	97380	97088	96794	96496	96194	95887
d_x:	292	294	298	302	307	313

(*i*) ignoring interest and expenses

(*ii*) allowing a rate of 6% per annum

(*a*) The value of temporary assurance of ₹ 10,000 for 2 years for a person aged 26.

(*b*) The value of endowment assurance of ₹ 10,000 for 4 years 15to a person aged 26.

(*c*) The value of pure endowment assurance of ₹ 500 for a person aged 28 receivable on attaining age 0.

Ans.: (*i a*) ₹ 60.98; (*i b*) ₹ 10,000; (*i c*) 496.84
(*ii a*) ₹ 55.87; (*ii b*) 7929.04 (*ii c*) 442.19

18. Calculate the net annual level premium for a double endowment assurance of ₹ 100 for a person aged 60 years, the assured benefit being ₹ 100 in the case of his death before attaining age 63 and ₹ 200 if he survives to age 63. Use the following mortality table and 5% rate of interest.

x:	60	61	62	63	64	65
l_x:	1000	980	958	933	900	860
d_x:	20	22	25	33	40	45

Ans.: 59.69

19. The ent premium of an endowment assurance of ₹ 1000 for a person aged 30 for a term of 25 years is ₹ 30.97. Calculate the office premium making the following provisions

(*a*) Initial expenses at ₹ 40 per ₹ 1000 sum assured

(*b*) Renewal expenses at 8% of Office premium

(*c*) Constrant expenses of ₹ 2.50 per ₹ 1000 sum assured

(Given $a_{40:\ 241}$ = 15.64) **Ans.:** ₹ 39.16

Suggested Readings

1. Hanes U. Garber, *Life Insurance Mathematics,* Springer, 1997.
2. *Mathematical Basis of Life Insurance,* IC 61, Insurance Institute of India, Mumbai, 1999.
3. Hillary S. Seal, *Survival Probabilities — The Goal of Risk Theory,* John Wiley and Sons Ltd., 1978.
4. Karl Borch, *Research Papers in Insurance Models,* Lexington Books, 1974.
5. Statistics, IC 62, *Insurance Institute of India*, Mumbai, 1999.
6. G.H. Monney, *The Valuation of Human Life*, The Macmillan Press Ltd., 1977.
7. S.M. Ross, *Stochastic Processes,* Wiley, 1967.
8. Harrington and Niehaus, *Insurance and Risk Management,* McGraw-Hill, 1999.

Web Resources

- www.math.ethz.ch
- www.statsoftinc.com
- www.probability.net
- www.socstats.saton.ac.uk

❑❑❑

CHAPTER

INSURANCE CONTRACTS AND PROVISIONS

Chapter Objectives

- Insurance Contracts
- Indian Contract Act, 1872 Applications
- Insurance Contracts – Important Features
- Elements of Insurance Contract
- Maxims Applicable to Insurance Contracts
- Agency

Introduction

Insurance is made available to the public through the medium of contracts that detail the rights and duties of the parties to the insurance agreement. These contracts may range from implied or oral agreements, as in the binders given by fire and casualty insurance agents, to formal written contracts issued by companies.

Most of the insurance contracts are expressed in writing even when an oral binder initiates the transaction.

Insurance contracts are complicated because of the technical nature of the subject-matter, the statutory requirement that certain language be employed, and the need to avoid terms that may be construed as ambiguous. However, the need for legal clarity may lead to a contract that is beyond the comprehension of the typical insurance consumer. Furthermore, the technical nature of many contracts often distracts from the mutual understanding of its terms by the parties to the contract.

6.1 Insurance Contracts

Insurance contract can broadly be classified into two categories: *(a)* life and *(b)* non-life insurance. The subject-matter of life insurance is life of the assured. In a life policy, the life is covered for a certain amount which is payable on the maturity of the policy or on the death of policyholder whichever is earlier. The amount is payable on death to the nominee/legal heir of the deceased.

Non-life insurance can again be categorised according to the uncertainties and events covered by the respective policies. Some examples of non-life insurance policies are householders' insurance and fire insurance. Personal accident insurance is linked to human life hence would not strictly fall in the category of non-life insurance though the characteristic of uncertainty which attracts to non-life insurance is manifested even in personal accident and medical insurance policies respectively.

The primary law governing contracts of insurance is the Indian Contract Act, 1872. However, there many issues not covered by the said Act. This may relate to torts, consumer rights, transfer of property, agency issues etc. discussed in the following paragraph.

Torts and Crimes

Torts

A tort is a private wrong. It occurs whenever someone acts or fails to act in such a manner that an individual's peace of mind or right are jeopardized. It refers to any individual's action that effectively deprives another of his right to security of person, reputation, or property. Technically, each tort is defined in terms of specific statutory or common law requirements, and these vary substantially in different jurisdictions. Negligence, assault, battery, libel, slander, trespass, fraud, and false imprisonment are examples of torts. Torts differ from crimes in that the latter are public wrongs. A crime is any act that the legislature determines to be punishable by law. The same act may include all of the elements of a particular tort and a particular crime, in which case there exists a public remedy in the form of punishment prescribed by law and a private remedy that is often in the form of monetary damages.

Torts are important in insurance because they are a major source of loss covered by liability insurance. The automobile insurance policy is essential because it provides for payment of judgments awarded by the courts in negligence cases as well as the costs of litigation or claims settlement. The comprehensive personal liability insurance policy covers losses arising from negligent conduct unrelated to the care, custody, or control of the automobile or to business pursuits. The comprehensive general liability insurance policy covers losses occurring as a direct result of negligence in many business situations.

Crimes

Some crimes that are recognized by statute are specific to insurance, while others are relevant to insurance law because they are crimes committed to obtain funds illegally from insurance companies. A few example of crimes are:

(*a*) *Rebating:* passing of commission/incentives by agents to prospective insureds to purchase on insurance policy.

(*b*) *Twisting:* inducing an individual to terminate are life insurance policy in order to buy another to the disadvantage of the insured.

(*c*) *Filing of false claims:* attempt to collect money from an insurance company when there is no loss or the padding or inflation of claims by procuring excessive and fraudulent estimates of damages.

(*d*) *Unlicensed insurance activity*: unlicensed person engaging in any insurance transaction that requires licensing (guilty of a misdemeanor).

(*e*) *Defamation:* publication of material that might tend to lessen public confidence in the institution of insurance.

(*f*) *Asson*: felonious burning of property of another to defraud an insurance company.

(*g*) *Homicide:* when the beneficiary of a life insurance policy swindles the insured for the purpose of obtaining the proceeds of the policy or otherwise.

(*h*) *Breach of trust*: agents using or mingling the client's insurance premiums with their own funds.

(*i*) *Unfair discrimination:* charging of different rates by a single insurance company to similar risk class.

(*j*) *Conspiracy:* dishonest agent conspires with his client to defraud the insurance company by misrepresentation, by filing false claims or falsifying documents.

6.2 Indian Contract Act, 1872 Applications

Insurance contracts are agreements between insurance companies and insured for the purpose of transferring from insured to the insurer a part of the risk of loss arising out of contingent event. Therefore, all the provisions of Indian Contract Act, 1872, in general are applicable to insurance contracts. Under Section 10 of the Indian Contract Act, following conditions are necessary to form a valid contract:

(*a*) Agreement between two parties

(*b*) Lawful object

(*c*) Capacity to contract

(*d*) Consideration

(*e*) Possibility of performance etc.

Offer and Acceptance

The offer for entering into insurance contract generally come from the insured (proposer). The insurance company may also propose to make the contract. In order to constitute a valid acceptance, offer and its acceptance must fulfil the requirements as prescribed by the Indian Contract Act, 1872. Whether the offer is made by the insurer or insured, the moot point is acceptance.

Any act that precedes it is an offer or a counter-offer. All that precede the offer or counter-offer is an invitation to offer. In insurance, the publication of prospectus, the canvassing of the agents are invitations to offer. When the proposer proposes to enter the contract, it is an offer and if there is any alteration in the offer that would be a counter-offer. If this alteration or change (counter-offer) is accepted by the proposer, it would be an acceptance. In absence of counter-offer, the acceptance of offer will be an acceptance by the insurer. At the moment, the notice of acceptance is given to other party, it would be a valid acceptance.

On acceptance of the proposal by the insurer, a valid and binding contract comes into existence. If the insurer indicates a higher premium than the normal as per proposal or conditions of acceptance are different from the standard ones, such indication tantamounts to a counter-offer which the proposer may or may not accept. It is necessary that in order to make a binding contract of insurance, the parties must agree upon every material term affecting the agreement.

In case of Life insurance, a valid and binding contract comes into existence upon payment of first premium. When a proposal form duly filled in by the proposer is accepted by the insurer, the acceptance communicated to the proposer is in reality a counter-offer indicating that the proposal will be accepted on payment of the premium and communication of the assent of the proposer to special terms, if any. Unless the proposer assents to or complies with the terms of insurer, no contract would come into existence.

Every contract of insurance must be in writing and must comply with the provisions of the Indian Stamp Act. An oral or informal contract gives the insured a right to call for a stamped policy, even after the loss insured against has occurred in view of the Indian Stamp Act, 1899.

An issuance of a policy may some time takes after acceptance of risk in view of underwriting and administrative procedures. The issuers may issue a cover note for a stipulated period which is also a valid evidence of contract.

Legal Object

For a valid contract, the object of the agreement should be lawful and must not be prohibited by any law. Any subject-matter of contract that is: (*i*) not forbidden by law, or (*ii*) is not immoral, or (*iii*) opposed to public policy, or (*iv*) which does not defeat the provisions of any law, is lawful. The subject-atter of insurance in the proposal form and also the consideration should be legal. If there is any contract to defraud the insurer rather than based on round principles of indemnity, the contract is void.

Mistake and Misrepresentation

A contract of insurance is a contract *uberrimae fidei*, i.e., is based on the principle of utmost good faith. If utmost good faith is not observed by either party insurer or insured, the contract may be avoided by the other.

Capacity to Contract

The rules laid down under the Indian Contract Act, 1872, defining the contractual capacity of the parties apply generally to insurance contracts in the same manner as they apply to other types of contracts.

Every person is competent to contract: (*a*) who is of the age of majority according to the law, (*b*) who is of sound mind, and (*c*) who is not disqualified from contracting by any law to which he is subject.

The capacity of an insurer to enter into contracts of insurance depends upon its constitution.

A minor is, therefore, incompetent to contract, and a contract with a minor is a nullity; but under certain circumstances, an insurer may issue a policy on the life of a minor. Under the system of deferred assurance policies, the insurance contract is with a parent or legal guardian, who is competent to contract.

Consideration

For insurance contracts, consideration is in the form of premium to be paid by the insured and a promise to pay, compensate or indemnify in accordance with the terms and conditions incorporated in the policy, on the part of the insurer. A premium is the price for the risk undertaken by the insurers. It is the consideration receivable by the insurers from the insured in exchange for their undertaking to pay the sum insured in case the event insured against takes place.

Amount of premium is not the criteria, but a contract without payment of premium is void.

Free Consent

Parties entering into the contract should enter into the contract by their free and genuine consent. The consent shall be free with it is not caused by: (1) coercion, (2) undue influence, (3) fraud, (4) misrepresentation, or (5) mistake. When there is no free consent except fraud, the contract becomes voidable at the option of the party whose consent was so obtained. In case of fraud, the contract would be void. The proposal for free consent, must sign a declaration to this effect, the person explaining the subject-matter of the proposal to the proposer must also accordingly make a written declaration on the proposal.

The proposer must fully disclose all material information and sign a declaration in the proposal. Also, the insurer must fully disclose the product details to the proposer.

Examples of Material Circumstances in Marine Insurance

1. Concealing the nationality of the insured when such nationality is of importance [*Associated Oil Carriers Ltd. v. Union Ins. Society of Canton* (1917) 2 K.B. 184].
2. The fact that the ship had developed a leak before the insurance was effected [*Russel v. Thorton* 1859 20 L.R. Ex. 9].
3. The fact that the goods carried on the ship are grossly overvalued when the ship is insured. [*Ionidies* v. *Pender* (1874) L.R. 7. Q.B. 531].

Discharge of Contract

A contract terminates in the following situations:

1. **Performance:** *When all the terms of the contract* in terms of performance have been carried out. Payment of premium and payment of claim by respective parties.
2. **Release:** *When one party to the contract* agrees to excuse performance by the other party after breach of the contract by the latters. Denial of a claim by insured on account of fraud.
3. **Discharge:** (*a*) ***Discharge by implied consent or impossibility of performance:*** *The law does not compel a man to do the impossible thing. Contract* is discharged when performance becomes impossible:

(*i*) Due to destruction of the subject-matter;

(*ii*) Due to death or incapacity of the promisor in a contract for personal services;

(*iii*) Due to subsequent change of legislation;

(*iv*) Due to non-existence or cessation of a state of affairs, the existence or continuance of which formed the basis of the contract; and

(*v*) Due to such an alternation of circumstances as to bring about complete frustration of the commercial object.

(*b*) ***Discharge by tender:*** *Where on party is ready and willing to perform his promise and has offered to do so at the right time and place, but the other party does not accept performance, the contract* is discharged by tender or 'attempted performance'.

4. **Void Contracts:** *When an agreement is discovered to be void.*
5. **Breach of Contract:** *When a contract has been broken.* Where the insured has committed such a breach the insurer can terminate the contract of insurance.
6. **Novation:** *If the parties to a contract* for it or rescind or later it, the original contract need not be performed.

6.3 Functions of Insurance Contracts

The principle functions of an insurance contract are:

(1) to define the risk that is to be transferred;

(2) to state the conditions under which the contract applies and

(3) to explain the procedure for settling losses.

Nature of Contract

An insurance contract as four attributes:

(*a*) *Entirety:* All the terms and conditions are to be found in the policy document. If the terms and conditions are oral or not stated explicitly, they are difficult for parties to prove.

(*b*) *Personal:* The contact follows the person, the insured, rather than property.

(*c*) *Unilateral*: After the insured pays the premiums, the performance is obligatory on one party, i.e., the insurer.

(*d*) *Aleatory*: Performance is conditioned upon an event that may or may not happen

6.4 Elements of Insurance Contract

The four basic elements to every insurance contract are:

(a) **Application:** An application is required for every contract of insurance. In the application, which is an offer to enter into a contract, the prospective insured sets forth the facts and figures required by the insurance carrier's underwriting department. The application may be brief and oral, or of any length and in written form. In life insurance, the application itself becomes a part of the contract.

(b) Binders: A binder is a memorandum specifying some of the details of the property or liability policy to be issued by the company. It is memorandum of insurance issued pending delivery of the formal policy. The binder may be oral or written and may be given either by an agent or a company. A broker, not being an agent of an insurance company, cannot issue binders. The binder is usually a temporary document and ordinarily would remain in force no more than ten days. For example, in automobile insurance, a car buyer wants immediate coverage. By binding the insurance company to the risk, the agent need not wait for the insurance to become effective.

Binders are not used in life insurance. Given the long-term nature of the contract and the insurer's inability to cancel a life insurance policy, the life insurer requires an opportunity to examine the application (and possible the applicant) before being bound to a lifetime contract. However, in place of binders, the life insurance agent can provide the applicant with a receipt (assuming the first premium installment is paid) that will provide varying insurance benefits depending on the nature of the receipt.

(c) Policy Forms: These are formal written contract of insurance that sets forth all of the terms of the agreement. The policy had four parts:

(i) *Heading:* It is the declaration page and identifies the risk by specifying the name of the issued, the address location of the risk, period covered by the policy, description of the subject being insured, the amount of insurance the amount of the premium, and any warranties of representations made by the insured.

(ii) *Body:* It is the contract itself containing the various clauses pertaining to agreements exclusion and condition.

(iii) *Back:* It specifies the rights of the insured and the duties of the insurer. The condition, and stipulations define the rights and duties of the parties aside from injury agreement.

Standardization of policy forms is an ongoing process, and most insurance contracts have uniform language for the greater part of their terms. Such standardization makes possible economies of operation, statistical uniformity, and better communication between the insured, his agent, and the insurance company. Where language has been standardized, determination of the meaning of the words and phrases by the courts reduces the chance a misunderstanding.

(iv) *Endorsement:* An endorsement is a form that is used to modify the policy contract Endorsements may extend or restrict coverage, permit transfers of interest in property, transfer coverage, transfer coverage from one place to another, increases or decreases limits of coverage, provide for assignment of policies or changes in beneficiary designations, provide for changes in settlement options elected, or in any other legal manner permit amendments to the contract.

Endorsement are usually done by party forms or by embossing through rubber stamps of the desired alteration.

6.5 Maxims Applicable to Insurance Contracts

The following maxims are elemental to insurance contracts and their interpretation:

(*a*) *Uberrimae fidii:* Utmost good faith

(*b*) *Spes successions:* hope of succession — direct and not hope of insurable interest.

(*c*) *Causa proxima:* the proximate and immediate cause of loss is important.

(*d*) *Pari Delicto:* parties to be equally blamed — in case of illegal policies, the premium cannot be recovered/returned.

(*e*) *Salus Populist supermen*: the regard for pubic interest and welfare is the highest in law.

(*f*) *Rao ipsa loquitor:* the thing speaks for itself for example in case of accidents, the circumstances of the case and not more occurrence of the events has to be seen.

6.6 Agency

The law relating to agency is part of the Indian Contract Act. An agent is defined as "a person employed to do any act for another, or to represent in dealings with third persons."

The person for whom such an act is done or who is so represented is called the Principal. Section 226 of the Contract Act states that "Contracts entered into through an agent, an obligation arising from acts done by an agent, may be enforced in the same manner, and will have the same legal consequences as if the contracts has been entered into and the acts done by the principal in person". A contract of agency may be made in writing or verbally. When it is in writing, it is in the form of power of attorney. Following provisions are worthnoting:

- An agent cannot lawfully employ another to perform acts, which he has expressly or implied undertaken to perform personally, unless by ordinary custom of trade or from the nature of the agency, a sub-agent must be employed. This involves the general maxim of law that a delegatee cannot further sub-delegate. A "sub-agent" is a person employed by, and acting under the control of, the original agent in the business of the agency.
- Where a sub-agent is properly appointed, the principal is, represented by the sub-agent and is bound by and responsible for his acts as if he were an agent originally appointed by the principal.
- The agent is responsible to the principal for the acts of the sub-agent.
- The sub-agent is responsible for his acts to the agent, but not to the principal, except in cases of fraud of wilful wrong.
- If an agent does something on behalf of the principal but without his knowledge or authority, the principal may elect to ratify the action or to disown it. A principal ratifying any unauthorized act done on his behalf ratifies the whole of the transaction of which such act formed part.

If an agent deals on his own account in the business of the agency, without first obtaining the consent of his principal and acquainting him with all material circumstances which have come on his own knowledge on the subject, the principal may repudiate the transaction, if the case shows either that any material fact has been dishonestly concealed from him by the agent or that the dealings of the agent have been disadvantageous to him.

If an agent does a criminal act, the principal is not liable to the agent, either upon an express or an implied promise, to indemnify him against the consequence of that act.

Where an agent does more than he is authorized to do, and what he does beyond the scope of his authority cannot be separated from what is within it, the principal is not bound to recognize the transaction.

In the absence of any contract to that effect, an agent cannot personally enforce contracts entered into by him on behalf of his principal nor is he personally bound by them.

Termination of Agency: An agency is terminated by the principal revoking his authority; or by the agent renouncing the business of the agency; or by the business of the agency being completed; or on the death of either the principal or the agent.

Agent's Duty: An agent is bound to conduct the business of his principal according to the directions given by the principal, or in the absence of any such directions, according to the custom which prevails in doing business of the same kind at the place where the agent conducts such business. When the agent acts otherwise and any loss is caused, he must make it good to his principal, and if any profit accrues, he must account for it.

Misrepresentations made or frauds committed by agents acting in the course of their business for their principals have the same effect on agreement made by such agents as if such misrepresentations or frauds has been made or committed by the principals; but misrepresentations made or frauds committed by agents in matters which do not fall within their authority, do not affect their principals.

Key Terms

- ❒ Contract
- ❒ Indemnity
- ❒ Causa Proxima
- ❒ Void Contracts
- ❒ Crime
- ❒ Binders
- ❒ Exempted Insurers

Questions for Review

1. Briefly summarise the various legal provisions applicable to insurance business in India.
2. Write short notes on:
   (a) Licensing of insurance companies
   (b) Elements of insurance contracts
   (c) Maxims applicable to insurance contracts.
3. "Insurance business is partially regulated in India." Do you agree? Give reasons for your answer.

Suggested Readings

1. Anoop K. Kaushal and S.K. Mohanty, *Insurance Law Manual,* Universal Law Publishing Co. Pvt. Ltd., 2002.
2. Kenneth S. Abraham, *Distributing Risk — Insurance, Legal Theory and Public Policy,* Yate University Press, 1986.
3. J.E. Grieder and W.T. Breadles, *Law and the Life Insurance Contract,* Richard D. Irwin, 1968.
4. *Practice of General Insurance,* Insurance Institute of India, Mumbai, 1999.
5. M.N. Srinivasan, *Principles of Insurance* Law, Wadwa & Company, Nagpur, 2006.

Web Resources

- www.irdaindia.org
- www.bimaonline.com
- www.indiacore.com
- www.insuranceinstituteindia.com

❑❑❑

CHAPTER

INSURANCE LAWS

Chapter Objectives

- Insurance Act, 1938
- Life Insurance Corporation Act, 1956
- General Insurance Business (Nationalisation) Act, 1972
- Insurance Regulatory and Development Authority Act, 1999

Introduction

Insurance is a federal subject in India. The insurance business is primarily regulated by two statutes:

(*a*) Insurance Act 1938

(*b*) Insurance and Regulatory Development Authority Act, 1999.

The Insurance business is classified into four classes :

(1) Life Insurance business

(2) Fire Insurance Business

(3) Marine

(4) Miscellaneous insurance

Life Insurers transact life insurance business and the rate is transacted by General Insurers. Apart from this, GIC and its subsidiaries are regulated by General Insurance Business (Nationalization) Act, 1972 and LIC of India being regulated by The Life Insurance Corporation Act, 1956. The text of IRDA Act, 1999, General Insurance Business (Nationalisation) Act, 1972 and Life Insurance Corporation Act, 1956 is given in Annexure 9A, 9B and 9C respectively. Regulation of Insurance business provides the insurance market with direction, management control and correction. Insurance, generally, all over the world is widely regulated. This is because of the following reasons:

(*a*) Widespread severe impact of insurer solvency. Since solvency ensures that insurance transactions are certain ad predictable, promotion and maintenance of insurer solvency are at the heart of all regulatory activity. Insureds are generally incapable of self protection and if the insurance company becomes insolvent, the results may be disastrous. Insurance generally mobilise savings, and therefore they bear a kind of fiduciary relationship as that of a banker and customer, and therefore, it requires public regulation.

(*b*) Unequal knowledge and bargaining power of the buyers and seller – insurance contacts are complex and the insurance itself is an intangible product.

(*c*) Insurance pricing is — typical and unique and requires estimation before the costs are fully known.

(*d*) Social welfare – insurance by definition is a sound device and optimally should be made available to public at large without discrimination.

7.1 Insurance Act, 1938

Insurance Act, 1938 and Insurance Rule, 1939 primarily govern the conduct of insurance business in India. As per the Preamble of the Act, Insurance Act, 1938 is an act to consolidate and amend the law relating to the business of insurance. Most of the provisions of the Act are applicable to all classes of insurance business.

7.1.1 Definitions

(*i*) Life insurance business is defined in the Section 2(11) and includes the contracts of insurance upon human life, which include the granting of disability, allowances, accident benefits, annuities and superannuation allowances. This business may be linked or non-linked business or both.

(*ii*) General insurance business is defined under Section 2(6-B) that includes the marine, fire and miscellaneous insurance business whether carried on singly or in combination with one or more of them, i.e., may be linked insurance business.

(*iii*) Marine insurance business includes the business effecting the contract of insurance upon vessels of any description, including the cargo of freights and other interests. (Section 2.13A)

(*iv*) Fire insurance is the insurance, which includes the risks insured against the fire and incidental to fire. (Section 2(6A))

(*v*) Miscellaneous insurance includes the business of effecting contracts of insurance, which are not principally, or wholly of the kind or kinds included above. (Section 2.13B)

The insurer, as defined by Section 2(9) as amended by the IRDA Act, 1999 means and includes:

- An individual.
- Body of individuals unincorporated.

- Body corporate but not incorporated under the law of country.
- Anybody corporate (not being a person specified above) standing as subsidiary company within the meaning of Indian Companies Act, 1956.
- Any person who has standing contract with the underwriter, who is a member of the society of Lloyds and authorized to issue cover notes and other documents to others on their behalf in conducting the insurance business, provided they carry on business of insurance in India, or their principal place of business is domiciled in India, or established with the object of obtaining insurance business, employs a representative or maintains a place of business in India.

7.1.2 Prohibition on Conduct of Insurance Business

Section 2c of the Act prohibits persons to carry on insurance business until he is:

(*a*) A public company.

(*b*) A registered society under.

(*c*) A body corporate incorporated under the law of any country outside India not being in the nature of a private company. However, the central government is empowered to exempt any insurer or any person for the purpose of carrying on the business of granting superannuation allowances and annuities as per Section 211(c) or for the purpose of carrying general insurance business. Exempted insurer after the promulgation of IRDA Act, 1999 only Indian Insurance company can carry insurance business.

7.1.3 Licensing

Section 3 of the Act, as ammended by IRDA Act, 1999 read together with Section 3A and 3B deals with the registration, sanctioning of license and its renewal and issuance of certificate of soundness for life insurers.

Licensing Conditions

Only Indian Insurance companies to be granted licenses: Under the Act, it is mandatory that only an Indian insurance company can carry on an insurance business in India. An Indian insurance company is a company registered under the Companies Act 1956 where the aggregate foreign equity shareholding does not exceed 26 per cent and whose sole purpose is to carry on a life, general or reinsurance business.

Two-stage Licensing Process

Stage 1 – Requisition for Registration

An application has to be made to the Authority with all the prescribed disclosure norms. Some of the important items cover:

1. Promoter's background, financial strength, shareholders' agreement and reasons for entering the sector.
2. Director's background.

3. Capital structure, initial and future.
4. Financial projections for 5 years.
5. Scenario Building and Sensitivity Analysis.
6. Rural and social sector strategy.

There is no provision for appeal in the event of a second rejection. A revised application is permissible by the applicant company only after 2 years with an additional condition that this will be with a new set of promoters or for a different class of insurance business.

Stage 2 – Application for Registration

After the requisition is granted by the Authority, the applicant is required to make an application for registration. Information to be disclosed includes:

- Proof of paid-up capital of ₹ 100 crore.
- Proof of deposit.
- Marketing and distribution information. This should include information on market research, product information, distribution strategy and Details, Sales promotion, customer service.
- *Operations:* Information should cover underwriting, information technology, internal controls, personnel.
- *Investment:* Information on investment, philosophy, strategy and ground level arrangements.
- *Reinsurance:* Information on Approach and Terms.
- *Expenditure:* This should include a description of the manner in which the expenses of administration have been estimated. These expenses will have to be distinguished between first year and renewal, fixed and variable. The proposed expenses as a per cent of premium at levels of operational offices, supervisory offices and head office.

Licensing Criteria

Some of the important parameters include:

- Promoter and directors' background
- Volume of business and earning prospects
- Product profit
- Actuarial and professional expertise
- Public interest
- Promoter's financial strength
- Rural and social sector focus
- Capital structure
- Infrastructure

Other Licensing Issues

An appeal can be made to the Central Government against the decision of Authority, which shall be final. The applicant company can submit a new application only after two years with the additional condition that it has to be with a new set of promoters or for a different class of insurance business. The Authority will grant more licenses to applicants for life and health insurance than general insurance. Licenses expire on the 31st day of March each year and have to be renewed each year.

Capital Requirement and Foreign Stake

Section 6 of the Act requires that minimum paid-up equity capital required for a life insurance is ₹ 100 crore and for a reinsurer ₹ 200 crore. The capital contributed can only be in the form of equity shares as preference shares cannot be issued. The incumbent, LIC, would be required to increase its equity share capital from the existing ₹ 5 crore to ₹ 100 crore within a period of six months from the date of commencement of the IRDA Act. Also, the four GIC subsidiaries would have to increase the equity share capital to ₹ 100 crore from ₹ 40 crore are present. The GIC will not be required to bring in additional capital since its present capital base is ₹ 215 crore.

The certificate of registration of insurance business is for a period of one year only. The certificate is renewal every year. The insurance company has to apply for renewal of license by paying the requisite fee of ₹ 50,000 and along with one per cent of total gross premium written directly by insurer in India during the last financial year. This application for renewal has to be made in the month of December every year.

7.1.4 Policies – Premiums, Claims and Related Issues

Advance Payment of Premium

No insurer shall assume any risk unless and until the premium is received in advance or is guaranteed to be paid or a deposit is made in advance in the prescribed manner. This rule of advance payment of premium may be relaxed in circumstances specified in the rules framed under the Act.

Section 38 of Insurance Act, 1938 explains the procedure by which the insurance policy can be transferred to the transferee, and insurer being the transferee.

Assignment and Transfer of Insurance Policies

Section 38: (1) A transfer or assignment of a policy of life insurance, whether with or without consideration, may be made only by an endorsement upon the policy itself or by a separate instrument, signed in either case by the transferor or by the assignor or his duly authorized agent and attested by at least one witness, specifically setting forth the fact of transfer or assignment.

(2) The transfer or assignment shall be complete and effectual upon the execution of such endorsement or instrument duly attested but except where the transfer or assignment is in favour of the insurer shall not be operative as against an insurer and shall not confer upon the transferee or assignee, or his legal representative, any right to sue for the amount of such policy or the moneys secured thereby until a notice in writing of the transfer or assignment if and either the said endorsement or instrument itself or a copy thereof certified to be correct by both transferor and transferee or their duly authorised agents have been delivered to the insurer:

Provided that where the insurer maintains one or more places of business in India, such notice shall be delivered only at the place in India mentioned in the policy for the purpose or at his principal place of business in India.

(3) The date on which the notice referred to in subsection (2) is delivered to the insurer shall regulate the priority of all claims under a transfer or assignment as between persons interested in

the policy; and where there is more than one instrument of transfer or assignment, the priority of the claims under such instruments shall be governed by the order in which the notices referred to in subsection (2) are delivered.

(4) Upon the receipt of the notice referred to in subsection (2), the insurer shall record the fact of such transfer or assignment together with the date thereof and the name of the transferee or the assignee and shall, on the request of the person by whom the notice was given, or of the transferee or assignee, on payment of a fee not exceeding one rupee, grant a written acknowledgment of the receipt of such notice; and any such acknowledgment shall be conclusive evidence against the insurer that he has duly received the notice to which such acknowledgment relates.

(5) Subject to the terms and conditions of the transfer or assignment, the insurer shall, from the date of the receipt of the notice referred to in subsection (2), recognize the transferee or assignee named in the notice as the only person entitled to benefit under the policy, and such person shall subject to all liabilities and equities to which the transferor or assignor was subject at the date of the transfer or assignment and may institute any proceedings in relation to the policy without obtaining the consent of the transferor or assignor or making him a party to such proceedings.

(6) Any rights and remedies of an assignee or transferee of a policy of life insurance under an assignment or transfer affected prior to the commencement of this Act shall not be affected by the provisions of this section.

(7) Notwithstanding any law or custom having the force of law to the contrary, and assignment in favour of a person made with the condition that it shall be inoperative or that the interest shall pass to some other person on the happening of a specified event during the lifetime of the person whose life is insured, and an assignment in favour of the survivor or survivors of a number of persons shall be valid.

The *Section 39* of the Insurance Act, 1938 and amendments made thereafter deals with the provisions of nomination of a policy by the policyholder.

The holder of a policy of life insurance on his own life may nominate the person or persons to whom he wants the policy money to be paid in the event of his death. He may do so either at the time of effecting the policy or at any time before the policy matures for payment. Where the nominee is a minor, the policyholder may indicate in the prescribed manner any person to receive the money during the minority of the nominee.

Nomination by Policyholder

Section 39: (1) The holder of a policy of life insurance on his own life, may, when effecting the policy or at any time before the policy matures for payment, nominate the person or persons to whom the money secured by the policy shall be paid in the event of his death:

Provided that, where any nominee is a minor, it shall be lawful for the policyholder to appoint in the prescribed manner any person to receive the money secured by the policy in the event of his death during the minority of the nominee.

(2) Any such nomination in order to be effectual shall, unless it is incorporated in the text of the policy itself, be made by an endorsement on the policy communicated to the insurer and

registered by him in the records relating to the policy and any such nomination may at any time before the policy matures for payment be cancelled or changed by an endorsement or a further endorsement or a will, as the case may be, but unless notice in writing of any such cancellation or change has been delivered to the insurer, the insurer shall not be liable for any payment under the policy made *bona fide* by him to a nominee mentioned in the text of the policy or registered in records of the insurer.

(3) The insurer shall furnish to the policyholder a written acknowledgment of having registered a nomination or a cancellation change thereof, and may charge a fee not exceeding one rupee for registering such cancellation or change.

(4) A transfer or assignment of a policy made in accordance with Section 38 shall automatically cancel a nomination:

Provided that the assignment of a policy to the insurer who bears the rats on the policy at the time of the assignment, in consideration of a loan granted by that insurer on the security of the policy within its surrender value, or its reassignment on repayment of the loan shall not cancel a nomination, but shall affect the rights of the nominee only to the extent of the insurer's interest in the policy.

(5) Where the policy matures for payment during the lifetime of the person whose life is insured or where the nominee or, if there are more nominees than one, all the nominees die before the policy-holder or his heirs or legal representatives or the holder of a succession certificate, as the case may be.

(6) Where the nominee or, if there are more nominees than one, a nominee or nominees survive the person whose life is insured, the amount secured by the policy shall be payable to such survivor or survivors.

(7) The provisions of this section shall not apply to any policy of life insurance to which Section 6 of the Married Women's Property Act, 1874 (3 of 1874), applies or has at any time applied:

Provided that where a nomination made whether before or after the commencement of the Insurance (Amendment) Act, 1946 (VII of 1946), in favour of the wife of the person who has insured his life or of his wife and children or any of them is expressed, whether or not on the face of the policy as being made under this section, the said section 6 shall be deemed not to apply or not to have applied to the policy.

Misstatement or Concealment [S. 45]

Section 45 provides that after the expiry of two years from the date on which a policy is effected, the policy shall not be called in question by the insurer on the ground that a statement made in the proposal, or medical officer's report, or by a referee or friend of the assured, or in any other document relating to the issue of the policy, was inaccurate or false. Thus, a policy can be avoided by the insurer on the ground of a misrepresentation or suppression only within two years of the date of the policy.

Payment of Money into Court

Section 47 of the Act explains the method of payment of claim by the insurer into the Court and settlement of claim by the interference of the Court. Section 47A explains the method of payment of small amounts of claims under life insurance policy.

Section 47: (1) Wherein respect of any policy of life insurance maturing for payment an insurer is of opinion that by reason of conflicting claims to or insufficiency of proof of title to the amount secured thereby or for any other adequate reason it is impossible otherwise for the insurer to obtain a satisfactory discharge for the payment of such amount, the insurer may, apply to pay the amount into the Court within the jurisdiction of which is situated the place at which such amount is payable under the terms of the policy or otherwise.

(2) A receipt granted by the Court for any such payment shall be a satisfactory discharge to the insurer for the payment of such amount.

(3) An application for permission to make a payment into Court under this section, shall be made by a petition verified by an affidavit signed by a principal officer of the insurer setting forth the following particulars, namely:

(*a*) the name of the insured person and his address;

(*b*) if the insured person is deceased, the date and place of his death;

(*c*) the nature of the policy and the amount secured by it;

(*d*) the name and address of each claimant so far as is known to the insurer with details of every notice of claim received;

(*e*) the reasons why in the opinion of the insurer satisfactory discharge cannot be obtained for the payment of the amount; and

(*f*) the address at which the insurer may be served with notice of any proceeding relating to disposal of the amount paid into Court.

(4) An application under this section shall not be entertained by the Court if the application is made before the expiry of six months from the maturing of the policy by survival, or from the date of receipt of notice by the insurer of the death of the insured, as the case may be.

(5) If it appears to the Court that a satisfactory discharge for the payment of the amount cannot otherwise be obtained by the insurer, it shall allow the amount to be paid into Court and shall invest the amount in Government securities pending its disposal.

(6) The insurer shall transmit to the Court every notice of claim received after the making of the application under subsection (3), and any payment required by the Court as costs of the proceedings or otherwise in connection with the disposal of the amount paid into Court shall as to the cost of the application under subsection (3) be borne by the insurer and as to any other costs be in the discretion of the Court.

(7) The Court shall cause notice to be given to every ascertained claimant of the fact that the amount has been paid into Court, and shall cause notice at the cost of any claimant applying to withdraw the amount to be given to every other ascertained claimant.

(8) The Court shall decide all questions relating to the disposal of claims to the amount paid into Court.

Claims on Small Life Insurance Policies

Section 47A: (1) In the event of any dispute relating to the settlement of a claim on a policy of life insurance assuring a sum not exceeding two thousand rupees (exclusive of any profit or bonus not being a guaranteed profit or bonus) issued by an insurer in respect of insurance business transacted in India, arising between a claimant under the policy and the insurer who issued the policy or has otherwise assumed liability in respect thereof, the dispute may at the option of the claimant be referred to the Authority for decision and the Authority may, after giving an opportunity to the parties to be heard and after making such further inquires as he may think fit, decide the matter.

(2) The decision of the Authority under this subsection shall be final and shall not be called in question in any Court, and may be executed by the Court which would have been competent to decide the dispute if it had not been referred to the Authority as if it were a decree passed by that Court.

(3) These shall be charged and collected in respect of the duties of the Authority under this section such fees whether by way of percentage or otherwise as may be prescribed.

7.1.5 Appointment of Agents

Prohibition of Payment by Way of Commission or Otherwise for Procuring Business

Section 40: (1) No person shall after the expiry of six months from the commencement of this Act, pay or contract to pay any remuneration or reward whether by way of commission or otherwise for soliciting or procuring insurance business in India to any person except an insurance agent or an intermediary or insurance intermediary.

(1A) In this Section and Section 40A, 41 and 43 references to an insurance agent shall be construed as including references to an individual soliciting or procuring insurance business exclusively in the territories which immediately before the 1st November, 1956 were comprised in a Part B State notified in this behalf by the Central Government in the Official Gazette and holding a valid licence as an insurance agent under the law of that Part B State.

(2) No insurance agent shall be paid or contract to be paid by way of commission or as remuneration in any form an amount exceeding, in the case of life insurance business, forty per cent of the first year's premium payable on any policy or policies effected through him and five per cent of a renewal premium, payable on such a policy, or, in the case of business of any other class, fifteen per cent of the premium:

Provided that insurers in respect of life insurance business only may pay during the first ten years of their business to their insurance agents fifty-five per cent of the first years premium payable on any policy or policies effected through them and six per cent of the renewal premiums payable on such policies:

Provided further that nothing in this subsection shall apply in respect of any policy of life insurance issued after the 31st day of December, 1950, or in respect of any policy of general insurance issued after the commencement of the Insurance (Amendment) Act, 1950 (47 of 1950).

(2A) Save as hereinafter provided, no insurance agent or intermediary or insurance intermediary shall be paid or contract to be paid by way of commission or as remuneration in any form any amount in respect of any policy not effected through him:

Provided that where a policy of life insurance has lapsed and it cannot under the terms and conditions applicable to it be revived without further medical examination of the person whose life was insured thereby, an insurer, after giving by notice in writing to the insurance agent through whom the policy was effected if such agent continues to be an agent of the insist an opportunity to effect the revival of the policy within a time specified in the notice, being not less than one month from the date of the receipt by him of the notice, may pay to another insurance agent who effects the revival of the policy an amount calculated at a rate not exceeding half the rate of commission at which the agent through whom the policy was effected would have been paid had the policy not lapsed, on the sum payable on revival of the policy on account of arrear premiums (excluding any interest on such arrear premiums) and also on the subsequent renewal premiums payable on the policy.

(3) Nothing in this section shall prevent the payment under any contract existing prior to the 27th day of January, 1937, of gratuities or renewal commission to many person, whether an insurance agent within the meaning of this Act or not, or to his representatives after his decease in respect of insurance business effected through him before the said date.

Limitation of Expenditure on Commission

Section 40A: (I) No person shall pay or contract to pay to an insurance agent, and no insurance agent shall receive or contract to receive by way of commission or remuneration in any form in respect of any policy of life insurance issued in India by an insurer after the 31st day of December, 1950, and effected through an insurance agent, an amount exceeding:

(*a*) where the policy grants an *immediate annuity or a deferred* annuity in consideration of a single premium, or where only one premium is payable on the policy, two per cent of that premium,

(*b*) where the policy grants a deferred annuity in consideration or more than one premium, seven-and-a-half per cent of the first year's premium, and two per cent of each renewal premium payable on the policy, and

(*c*) in any other case, thirty-five per cent of the first year's premium, seven-and-a-half per cent of the second and third year's renewal premium, and thereafter five per cent of each renewal premium payable on the policy.

Provided that in a case referred to in clause (c), an insurer, during the first ten years of his business may pay to an insurance agent and an insurance agent may receive from such an insurer, forty per cent of the first year's premium payable on the policy:

Provided further that in case referred to in clause (c) where the rate of commission payable on the first year's premium is equal to or less than twenty-one per cent thereof, and the rate on the fourth and fifth year's premiums does not exceed is per cent thereof, the Life Insurance Corporation of India may pay to an insurance agent, and the insurance agent may receive from it, commission on the sixth and subsequent year's renewal premiums payable on the policy at a rate not exceeding six per cent of each renewal premium.

(2) No person shall pay or contract to pay to a special agent, and no special agent, shall receive or contract to receive, by way of commission or as remuneration in any form, in respect of any policy of life insurance issued in India by an insurer after the 31st day of December, 1950, and effected through a special agent, an amount exceeding—

(*a*) in a case referred to in clause (a) of subsection (1), one half per cent of the premium,

(*b*) in a case referred to in clause (b) of subsection (1), two per cent of the first year's premium payable on the policy and

(*c*) in a case referred to in clause (c) of subsection (1), fifteen per cent of the first year's premium payable on the policy:

Provided that in a case referred to in clause (c), an insurer, during the first ten years of his business, may pay to a special agent, and a special agent may receive from such an insurer, seventeen-and-a-half per cent of the first year's premium payable on the policy:

Provided further that in a case referred to in clause (c), where the rate of commission payable on the first year's premium is equal to or less than twenty-one per cent thereof, and the rate on the fourth and fifty year's premiums does not exceed six per cent thereof, the Life Insurance Corporation of India may pay to an insurance agent, and the insurance agent may receive from it, commission on the sixth and subsequent year's renewal premiums payable on the policy at a rate not exceeding six per cent of each renewal premium.

(3) No person shall pay or contract to pay to a special agent, and no special agent, shall receive or contract to receive, by way of commission or remuneration in any form in respect of any policy of general insurance issued in India by an insurer after the commencement of Insurance (Amendment Act), 1968, and effected through an insurance agent, an amount not exceeding fifteen per cent of the premium payable on the policy where the policy relates to fire or marine insurance or miscellaneous insurance.

(4) No person shall pay or contract to pay to a principal agent, and no principal agent shall receive or contract to receive, by way of commission or remuneration in any form, in respect of any policy of general insurance issued in India by an insurer after the commencement of the Insurance (Amendment) Act, I950, and effected through a principal agent, an amount exceeding —

(*a*) in the case referred to in clause (*a*) of subsection (3), twenty per cent of the premium payable on the policy, and

(*b*) in the case referred to in clause (*b*) of that subsection, fifteen per cent of the policy, less any commission payable to any insurance agent in respect of the said policy:

Provided that the Authority may, in such circumstances and to such extent and for such period as may be specified, authorise the payment of commission or remuneration exceeding the limits specified in this subsection to a principal agent of an insurer incorporated or domiciled elsewhere than in India, if such agent carries out and has continuously carried out in his own office duties on behalf of the insurer which would otherwise have been performed by the insurer.

(5) Without prejudice to the provisions of Section 102 in respect of a contravention of any of the provisions of the preceding subsections by an insurer, any insurance agent who contravenes the provisions of subsection (1) or subsection (3) shall be punishable with fine which may extend to one hundred rupees.

Limitation of Expenses of Management in Life Insurance Business

Section 40B: (I) Every insurer transacting life insurance business in India shall furnish to the Controller, within such time as may be prescribed, statements in the prescribed form certified by an actuary on the basis of premiums currently used by him in regard to new business in respect of mortality, rate of interest, expenses and bonus loading.

(2) After the 31st day of December, 1950, no insurer shall, in respect of life insurance business transacted by him in India, spend as expenses of management in any calendar year an amount in excess of the prescribed limits and in prescribing any such limits regard shall be had to the size and age of the insurer and the provision generally made for expenses of management in the premium rates of insurers:

Provided that where an insurer has spent as such expenses in any year an amount in excess of the amount permissible under this subsection, he shall not be deemed to have contravened the provisions of this section, if the excess amount so spent is within such limits as may be fixed in respect of the year by the Authority after consultation with the Executive Committee of the Life Insurance Council constituted under section 64F, by which the actual expenses incurred may exceed the expenses permissible under this subsection.

(3) In respect of any statement mentioned in subsection (1), the Authority may require that it shall be submitted to another actuary, appointed by the insurer for the purpose and approved by the Authority, for certification by him, whether with or without modifications.

(4) Every insurer transacting life insurance business in India shall incorporate in the revenue account:

(*a*) a certificate signed by the chairman and two directors and by the principal officer of the insurer, and an auditor's certificate, certifying that all expenses of management in respect of life insurance business transacted by the insurer in India have been fully debited in the revenue account as expenses, and

(*b*) if the insurer is carrying on any other class of insurance business in addition to life insurance business, an auditor's certificate certifying that all charges incurred in respect of his life insurance business and in respect of his business other than life insurance business have been fully debited in the respective revenue accounts.

Explanation: In this section,

(*a*) "calendar year" or "year" means, in relation to an insurer who is required to furnish returns in accordance with subsection (2) of Section 16, the period covered by the revenue account furnished by such insurer under clause (b) of that subsection;

(*b*) "expenses of management" means all charges wherever incurred whether directly or indirectly, and includes:

(*i*) commission payments of all kinds,

(*ii*) any amount of expenses capitalised,

(*iii*) in the case of an insurer having his principal place of business outside India, a proper share of head office expenses which shall not be less than such percentage as may be prescribed of the total premiums (less reinsurance) received during the year in respect of life insurance business transacted by him in India, but does not include in the case of an insurer having his principal place of business in India any share of head office expenses in respect of life insurance business transacted by him outside India.

Limitation of Expenses of Management in General Insurance Business

Section 40C: (1) After the 31st day of December, 1949, no insurer shall, in respect of any class of general insurance business transacted by him in India, spend in any calendar year as expenses of management including commission or remuneration for procuring business an amount in excess of the prescribed limits and in prescribing any such limits regard shall be had to the size and age of the insurer:

Provided that where an insurer has spend as such expenses in any year an amount in excess of the amount permissible under this subsection, he shall not be deemed to have contravened the provisions of this section, if the excess amount so spent is within such limits as may be fixed in respect of the year by the Authority after consultation with the Executive Committee of the General Insurance. Council constituted under section 64F, by which the actual expenses incurred may exceed the expenses permissible under this subsection.

(2) Every insurer as aforesaid shall incorporate in the revenue account a certificate signed by the chairman and two directors and by the principal officer of the insurer, and by an auditor certifying that all expenses of management wherever incurred, whether directly or indirectly, in respect of the business referred to in this section have been fully debited in the revenue account as expenses.

Explanation: In this section,

(*a*) "calendar year" shall have the meaning assigned to it in Section 40B;

(*b*) "expenses of management" means all charges, wherever insured whether directly or indirectly, including commission payments of all kinds and, in the case of an insurer having his principal place of business outside India, a proper share of head office expenses, which shall not be less than such percentage as may be prescribed, of his gross premium income (that is to say, the premium income without taking into account premiums or reinsurance ceded or accepted) written direct in India during the year, but in computing the expenses of management in India the following, and only the following expenses may be excluded, namely:

(*i*) in the case of an insurer having his principal place of business in India, a share of head office expenses in respect of general insurance business transacted by him outside India not exceeding such percentage of his gross direct premium written outside India as may be prescribed;

(*ii*) in the case of an insurer having his principal place of business outside India, a share of the expenses of his office in India in respect of general insurance business transacted by him outside India through his office in India, not exceeding such percentage of his gross direct premium written outside India through his office in India, as may be prescribed;

(*iii*) any expenses debited to profit and loss account relating exclusively to the management of capital, and dealings with shareholders and a proper share of managerial expenses calculated in such manner as may be prescribed; and

(*iv*) any expenses debited to claims in the revenue account in Form F of Part II of the Third Schedule;

(*c*) "insurance business transacted in India" includes insurance business, wherever effected relating to any property situate in India or to any vessel or aircraft registered in India.

Prohibition of Rebates

Section 41: (1) No person shall allow or offer to allow, either directly or indirectly, as an inducement to any person to take or renew or continue an insurance in respect of any kind of risk relating to lives or property in India, any rebate of the whole or part of the commission payable or any rebate of the premium shown on the policy, nor shall any person taking out or renewing or continuing a policy accept any rebate, except such rebate as may be allowed in accordance with the published prospectuses or tables of the insurer:

Provided that acceptance by an insurance agent of commission in connection with a policy of life insurance taken out by himself on his own life shall not be deemed to be acceptance of a rebate of premium within the meaning of this subsection if at the time of such acceptance the insurance agent satisfies the prescribed conditions establishing that he is a *bona fide* insurance agent employed by the insurer.

(2) Any person making default in complying with the provisions of this section shall be punishable with fine which may extend to five hundred rupees.

Licensing of Insurance Agents

Section 42: (1) The Authority or an officer authorised by him in this behalf shall, in the manner determined by the regulations made by it and on payment of the fee which shall not be determined by the regulations, which shall not be more than two hundred and fifty rupees, issue to any person making any application in the manner determined by the regulations, a licence to act as an insurance agent for the purpose of soliciting or procuring insurance business:

Provided that—

(*i*) in the case of an individual, he does not suffer from any of the disqualification mentioned in subsection (4); and

(*ii*) in the case of a company or firm, any of its directors or partners does not suffer from any of the said disqualifications:

Provided further that any licence issued immediately before the commencement of the Insurance Regulatory and Development Authority Act, 1999, shall be deemed to have been issued in accordance with the regulations which provide for such licence.

(2) A licence issued under this section shall entitle the holder to act as an insurance agent for any insurer.

(3) A licence issued under this section, after the commencement of the Insurance Regulatory and Development Authority Act, 1999, shall remain in force for a period of three years only from the date of issue, but shall, if the applicant being an individual does not, or being a company or firm any of its directors or partners, does not suffer from any of the disqualification mentioned in clauses (b), (c), (d), (e), (ea) and (f) of subsection (4) and the application for renewal of the licence reaches the issuing authority at least thirty days before the date on which the licence ceases to remain in force, be renewed for a period of three years at any one time on payment of the fee determined by the regulations made by the Authority which shall not be more than rupees two hundred and fifty, and an additional fee of an amount determined by the regulations not exceeding rupees one hundred by way of penalty, if the application for renewal of the licence does not reach the issuing authority at least thirty days before the date on which the licence ceases to remain in force.

(3A) No application for the renewal of a licence under this section shall be entertained if the application does not reach the issuing authority before the licence ceases to remain in force:

Provided that the Authority may, if satisfied that undue hardship would be caused otherwise, accept any application in contravention of this subsection on payment by the applicant of a penalty of seven hundred and fifty rupees.

(4) The disqualifications above referred to shall be the following:

(*a*) that the person is a minor;

(*b*) that he is found to be of unsound mind by a Court of competent jurisdiction;

(*c*) that he has been found guilty of criminal misappropriation or criminal breach of trust or cheating or forgery or an abetment of or attempt to commit any such offence by a Court of competent jurisdiction:

Provided that where at least five years have elapsed since the completion of the sentence imposed on any person in respect of any such offence, the Authority shall ordinarily declare in respect of such person that his conviction shall cease to operate as a disqualification under this clause;

(*d*) that in the course of any judicial proceeding relating to any policy of insurance of the winding up of an insurance company or in the course of an investigation of the affairs of all insurer it has then found that he has been guilty off or has knowingly participated in or connived at any fraud, dishonestly for misrepresentation against an insurer or an insured.

(*e*) that in the case of an individual, he does not possess the requisite qualifications and practical training for a period not exceeding twelve months, as may be specified by the regulations made by the Authority in this behalf;

(*f*) that in the case of a company or firm making an application under subsection (1) or subsection (3), a director or a partner or one or more of its officers or other employees so designated by it and in the case of any other person, the chief executive, by whatever name called, or one or more of his employees designated by him, do not possess the requisite qualifications and practical training and have not passed such an examination as required under clauses (e) and (f);

(*g*) that he violates the code of conduct as may be specified by the regulations made by the Authority.

(5) if it be found that an insurance agent being an individual is, or being a company or firm contains a director or partner who is suffering from any of the disqualifications mentioned in subsection (4), then, without prejudice to any other penalty to which he may be liable, the Authority shall, and if the insurance agent has knowingly contravened any of the provisions of this Act may, cancel the licence issued to the agent under this section.

(6) The Authority may issue a duplicate licence to replace a licence lost, destroyed or mutilated on payment of such fee not exceeding rupees fifty as may be determined by the regulations.

(7) Any person who acts as an insurance agent without holding a licence issued under this section to act as such shall be punishable with fine which may extend to five hundred rupees, and any insurer or any person acting on behalf of an insurer, who appoints as an insurance agent any person not licensed to act as such or transacts any insurance business in India through any such person shall be punishable with fine which may extend to one thousand rupees.

(8) Where the person contravening subsection (7) is a company or a firm, then, without prejudice to any other proceedings which may be taken against the company, or firm, every director, manager, secretary or other officer of the company, and every partner of the firm who is knowingly a party to such contravention shall be punishable with fine which may extend to five thousand rupees.

Registration of Principal Agents, Chief Agents and Special Agents

Section 42A: (1) The Authority or an officer authorised by it in this behalf shall in the prescribed manner and on payment of the prescribed fee, which shall not be more than twenty five rupees for a principal agent or a chief agent and ten rupees for a special agent, register any person who makes an application to him in the prescribed manner if,—

(*a*) in the case of an individual, he does not suffer from any of the disqualifications mentioned in subsection (4) of Section 42, or

(*b*) in the case of a company or firm, any of its directors or partners does not suffer from any of the said disqualifications,

and a certificate to Act as a principal agent, chief agent or special agent, as the case may be, for the purpose of procuring insurance business shall be issued to him.

(2) A certificate issued under this section shall entitle the holder thereof to act as a principal agent, chief agent, or special agent, as the case may be, for any insurer.

(3) A certificate issued under this section shall remain in force for a period of twelve months only from the date of issue, but shall, on application made on this behalf, be renewed from year to year on production of a certificate from the insurer concerned that the provisions of clauses (2) and (3) of Part A of the Sixth Schedule in the case of a principal agent, the provisions of clauses (2) and (4) of Part B of the said Schedule in the case of a chief agent, and the provisions of clauses (2) and (3) of Part C of the said Schedule in the case of a special agent, have been complied with, and on payment of the prescribed fee, which shall not be more than twenty five rupees, in the case of a

principal agent or a chief agent, and ten rupees in the case of a special agent, and an additional fee of the prescribed amount not exceeding five rupees by way of penalty, in cases where the application for renewal of the certificate does not reach the issuing authority before the date on which the certificate ceases to remain in force:

Provided that, where the applicant is an individual, he does not suffer from any of the disqualifications mentioned in clauses (b) to (d) of subsection (4) of Section 42 and where the applicant is a company or a firm, any of its directors or partners does not suffer from any of the said disqualifications.

(4) Where it is found that the principal agent, chief agent or special agent being an individual is, or being a company or firm contains a director or partner who is suffering from any of the disqualifications mentioned in subsection (4) of Section 42, without prejudice to any other penalty to which he may be liable, the Authority shall, and where a principal agent, chief agent or special agent has contravened any of the provisions of this Act may cancel the certificate issued under this section to such principal agent, chief agent or special agent.

(5) The authority which issued any certificate under this section may issue a duplicate certificate to replace a certificate lost, destroyed or mutilated on payment of the prescribed fee, which shall not be more than two rupees.

(6) Any person who acts as a principal agent, chief agent or special agent, without holding a certificate issued under this section to act as such, shall be punishable with fine which may extend to five hundred rupees, and any insurer or any person acting on behalf of an insurer, who appoints as a principal agent, chief agent or special agent any person not entitled to act as such or transacts any insurance business in India through any such person, shall be punishable with fine which may extend to one thousand rupees.

(7) Where the person contravening subsection (6) is a company or a firm, then, without prejudice to any other proceedings which may be taken against the company or firm, every director, manager, secretary or any other officer of the company, and every partner of the firm who is knowingly a party to such contravention shall be punishable with fine which may extend to five hundred rupees.

(8) The provisions of subsections (6) and (7) shall not take effect until the expiry of six months from the commencement of the Insurance (Amendment) Act, 1950.

(9) No insurer shall, on or after the commencement of the Insurance (Amendment) Act, 2002, appointment or transact any insurance business in India through any principal agent, chief agent or special agent.

Regulation of Employment of Principal Agents

Section 42B: (1) No insurer shall, after the expiration of seven years from the commencement of the Insurance (Amendment) Act, 1950, appoint, or transact any insurance business in India, through a principal agent.

(2) Every contract between an insurer and a principal agent shall be in writing and the terms contained in Part A of the Sixth Schedule shall be deemed to be incorporated in, and form part of, every such contract.

(3) No insurer shall, after the commencement of the Insurance (Amendment) Act, 1950 (47 of 1950), appoint any person as a principal agent except in a presidency town unless the appointment is by way of renewal of any contract subsisting at such commencement.

(4) Within sixty days of the commencement of the Insurance (Amendment) Act, 1950 (47 of 1950), every principal agent shall file with the insurer concerned a full list of insurance agents employed by him indicating the terms of the contract between the principal agent and each of such insurance agents, and, if any principal agent fails to file such a list within the period specified, any commission payable to such principal agent on premiums received from the date of expiry of the said period of sixty days until the date of the filing of the said list shall, notwithstanding anything in any contract to the contrary, cease to be so payable.

(5) A certified copy of every contract as is referred to in subsection (2) shall be furnished by the insurer to the Authority within thirty days of his entering into such contract, and intimation of any change in any such contract shall be furnished by the insurer with full particulars thereof to the Authority within thirty days of the making of any such change.

(6) If the commission due to any insurance agent in respect of any general insurance business procured by such agent is not paid by the principal agent for any reason, the insurer may pay the insurance agent the commission so due and recover the amount so paid from the principal agent concerned.

(7) Every contract as is referred to in subsection (2), subsisting at the commencement of the Insurance (Amendment) Act, 1950 (47 of 1950), shall, with respect to terms regarding remuneration, be deemed to have been so altered as to be in accordance with the provisions of subsection (4) of Section 40A.

(8) If any dispute arises as to whether a person is or was a principal agent, the matter shall be referred to the Authority, whose decision shall be final.

(9) Every insurer shall maintain a register in which the name and address of every principal agent appointed by him, the date of such appointment and the date, if any, on which the appointment ceased shall be entered.

Regulation of Employment of Chief and Special Agents

Section 42C: (1) Every contract between art insurer carrying on life insurance business and a chief agent shall be in writing, and shall specify the area (not being less in extent than a district or the equivalent thereof) for which the chief agent is appointed, and the terms contained in Part B of the Sixth Schedule shall be deemed to be incorporated in, and form part of, every such contract.

(2) No chief agent shall, either directly or through insurance agents or special agents employed by or through him, procure life insurance business for the insurer or any area outside the area for which he has been appointed or in any area for which another chief agent has been appointed or in any area in which the head office or any branch office of the insurer is operating, and neither the head office nor any branch office of the insurer shall operate in any area for which a chief agent has been appointed:

Provided that nothing in this subsection shall be deemed to prohibit the head office of an insurer which had been operating at the commencement of the Insurance (Amendment) Act, 1950;

for a period of not less than ten years before such commencement within the municipal limits of any town where the head office is situate, and a chief agent who, in pursuance of an agreement in writing, had been operating for a similar period within such limits, from continuing to operate within the said limits:

Provided further that nothing in this subsection shall be deemed to prohibit an insurance agent from procuring life insurance business in or from any area and submitting the proposals direct to the principal office of the insurer in India.

(3) Within sixty days of the commencement of the Insurance (Amendment) Act, 1950, every chief agent shall file with the insurer concerned a full list of the insurance agents employed by him, indicating the terms of the contract between the chief agent and each of such insurance agents and the business secured by each of such agents, and if any chief agent fails to file such a list within the period specified, any commission payable to such chief agent on premiums received from the date of the expiry of the said period of sixty days until the date of the filing of the said list shall, notwithstanding anything in any contract to the contrary, cease to be so payable.

(4) Every contract between an insurer carrying on life insurance business and a special agent, or between a chief agent of such insurer and a special agent, shall be in writing and the terms contained in Part C of the Sixth Schedule shall be deemed to be incorporated in, and form part of, every such contract:

Provided that the Authority may, in the case of a contract between a co-operative life insurance society as defined in clause (b) of subsection (1) of Section 95 and a co-operative society registered under the Indian Co-operative Societies Act, 1912 (2 of 1912), or under any other law for the time being in force and acting as a special agent, alter, to such extent as he thinks fit, all or any of the said terms.

(5) A certified copy of every contract as is referred to in subsection (1) or subsection (4) shall be furnished by the insurer or the chief agent to the Authority within thirty days of his entering into such contract, and intimation of any change in any such contract shall be furnished by the insurer or the chief agent with full particulars thereof to the Authority within thirty days of the making of any such change.

(6) No such contract as is referred to in subsection (1) or subsection (4) shall be entered into or renewed for a period exceeding ten years at any one time and notwithstanding the terms of any contract to the contrary, no option to renew any such contract given to any of the parties shall be enforceable without the consent of the other.

(7) Every contract between an insurer and a person acting on behalf of such insurer who, before the commencement of the Insurance (Amendment) Act, 1950), has been employing insurance agents for the purpose of life insurance business, which is subsisting on such commencement, shall terminate after the expiration of ten years from such commencement, if it does not terminate earlier:

Provided that every such contract shall be modified by the parties before the 1st day of January, 1951, to bring it into conformity with this act, and ant, such modification shall:

(*i*) as respects remuneration, whether in respect of business already procured or in respect of business to be procured thereafter, be such as may be mutually agreed upon between the parties, subject in the case of remuneration payable on business procured before such commencement, to a maximum of an overriding commission of two-and-a-half per cent plus a further commission not exceeding three-and-three quarter per cent on premiums in respect of which no commission is payable to any insurance agent;

(*ii*) be deemed to include all the terms specified in Part B or Part C of the Sixth Schedule, as the case may be:

Provided further that, in the event of any dispute as to the terms of any fresh contract, the matter shall be referred to arbitration.

(8) Any such contract as is referred to in subsection (7) which was subsisting on the 1st day of January, 1949, but has terminated or has been terminated before the commencement of the Insurance (Amendment) Act, 1950, shall be subject to the maximum limits specified in clause (i) of the proviso to subsection (7) as respects remuneration, if any, payable on business procured before the termination of the contract.

(9) Nothing in this section shall be deemed to prevent any special agent from receiving any renewal commission on policies effected through him as an insurance agent at any time before his appointment as such special agent. .

(10) If any dispute arises as to whether a person is or was a chief agent or a special agent for the purposes of this Act, the matter shall be referred to the Authority whose decision shall be final.

(11) Every insurer shall maintain a register in which the name and address of every chief agent appointed by him, the date on which the appointment was made and the date, if any, on which the appointment ceased shall be entered, and a separate register in which similar particulars relating to every special agent shall be entered, and every chief agent shall maintain a register in which similar particulars relating to every special agent appointed by him shall be entered.

Issue of Licence to Intermediary or Insurance Intermediary

Section 42D: (1) The Authority or an officer authorized by it in this behalf shall, in the manner determined by the regulations made by the Authority and on payment of the fees determined by the regulations made by the Authority, issue to any person making an application in the manner determined by the regulations, and not suffering from any of the disqualifications herein mentioned, a licence to act as an intermediary or an insurance intermediary under this Act:

Provided that,:

(*a*) in the case of an individual, he does not suffer from any of the disqualifications mentioned in subsection (4) of section 42, or

(*b*) in the case of a company or firm, any of its directors or partners does not suffer from any of the said disqualifications.

(2) A licence issued under this section shall entitle the holder thereof to act as an intermediary or insurance intermediary.

(3) A licence issued under this section shall remain in force for a period of three years only from the date of issue, but shall, if the applicant, being an individual does not, or being a company or firm any of its directors or partners does not suffer from any of the disqualifications mentioned in clauses (*b*), (*c*), (*d*), (*e*) and (*f*) of subsection (4) of section 42 and the application for renewal of licence reaches the issuing authority at least thirty days before the date on which the licence ceases to remain in force, be renewed for a period of three years at any one time on payment of the fee, determined by the regulations made by the Authority and additional fee for an amount determined by the regulations, not exceeding one hundred rupees by way of penalty, if the application for renewal of the licence does not reach the issuing authority at least thirty days before the date on which the licence ceases to remain in force.

(4) No application for the renewal of a licence under this section shall be entertained if the application does not reach the issuing authority before the licence ceases to remain in force:

Provided that the Authority may, if satisfied that undue hardship would be caused otherwise, accept any application in contravention of this subsection on payment by the application of the penalty of seven hundred and fifty rupees.

(5) The disqualifications above referred to shall be the following:

(*a*) that the person is a minor;

(*b*) that he is found to be a unsound mind by a court of competent jurisdiction;

(*c*) that he has been found guilty of criminal misappropriation or criminal breach of trust or cheating or forgery or an abetment of or attempt to commit any such offence by a court of competent jurisdiction:

Provided that, where at least five years have elapsed since the completion of the sentence imposed on any person in respect of any such offence, the Authority shall ordinarily declare in respect of such person that his conviction shall cease to operate as a disqualification under this clause;

(*d*) that in the course of any judicial proceedings relating to any policy of insurance of the winding up of an insurance company or in the course of an investigation of the affairs of an insurer it has been found that he has been guilty of or has knowingly participated in or connived at any fraud dishonestly or misrepresentation against an insurer or an insured;

(*e*) that he does not possess the requisite qualifications and practical training for a period not exceeding twelve months, as may be specified by the regulations made by the Authority in this behalf;

(*f*) that he has not passed such examinations as may be specified by the regulations made by the Authority in this behalf;

(*g*) that he violates the code of conduct as may be specified by the regulations made by the Authority.

(6) If it be found that an intermediary or an insurance intermediary suffers from any of the foregoing disqualifications, without prejudice to any other penalty to which he may be liable, the

Authority shall, and if the intermediary or an insurance intermediary has knowingly contravened any provisions of this Act may cancel the licence issued to the intermediary or insurance intermediary under this section.

(7) The Authority may issue a duplicate licence to replace a licence lost, destroyed or mutilated, on payment of such fee, as may be determined by the regulations made by the Authority.

(8) Any person who acts as an intermediary or an insurance intermediary without holding a licence issued under this section to act as such, shall be punishable with fine, and any insurer or any person who appoints as an intermediary or an insurance intermediary or any person not licensed to act as such or transacts any insurance business in India through any such person, shall be punishable with fine.

(9) Where the person contravening subsection (8) is a company or a firm, then, without prejudice to any other proceedings which may be taken against the company or firm, every director, manager, secretary or other officer of the company, and every partner of the firm who is knowingly a party to such contravention shall be punishable with fine.

Commission, Brokerage or Fee Payable to Intermediary or Insurance Intermediary

Section 42E: (1) No intermediary or insurance intermediary shall be paid or contract to be paid by way of commission, fee or as remuneration in any form, an amount exceeding thirty per cent of the premium payable as may be specified by the regulations made by the Authority, in respect of any policy or policies effected through him:

Provided that the Authority may specify different amounts payable by way of commission, fee or as remuneration to an intermediary or insurance intermediary or different classes of business of insurance.

(2) Without prejudice to the provisions contained in this Act, the Authority may, by the regulations made in this behalf, specify the requirements of capital, form of business and other conditions to act as an intermediary or insurance intermediary.

Register of Insurance Agents

Soction 43: (I) Evcry insurer and every person who acting on behalf of an Insurer employs insurance agents shall maintain a register showing the name and address of every insurance agent appointed by him and the date on which his appointment began and the date, if any, on which his appointment ceased.

7.1.6 Deposits and Investments

Section 7, 8 and 9 of the Insurance Act, 1938 deals with the deposits which are required to be made by the insurer for obtaining the license to undertake the insurance and registration of the insurer with IRD Authority.

Deposits

Section 7: (1) Every insurer shall, in respect of the insurance business carried on by him in India, deposit and keep deposited with the Reserve Bank of India in one of the offices in India of the

Bank for and on behalf of the Central Government the amount hereafter specified, either in cash or in approved securities estimated at the market value of the securities on the day of deposit, or partly in cash and partly in approved securities so estimated:

(*a*) in the case of life insurance business, a sum equivalent to one per cent of his total gross premium written direct in India in any financial year commencing after the 31st day of March, 2000, not exceeding rupees ten crore;

(*b*) in the case of general insurance business, a sum equivalent to three per cent of his total gross premium written in India, in any financial year commencing after the 31st day of March, 2000, not exceeding rupees ten crore;

(*c*) in the case of reinsurance business, a sum of rupees twenty crores

Provided that, where the business done or to be done is marine insurance only and relates exclusively to country craft or its cargo or both, the amount to be deposited under this subsection shall be one hundred thousand rupees only:

Provided further that in respect of an insurer not having a share capital and carrying on only such insurance business as in the opinion of the Central Government is not carried on ordinarily by insurers under separate policies, the Central Government may, by notification under Official Gazette, order that the provisions of this subsection shall apply to such insurer with the modification that instead of sum of rupees twenty lakh or rupees ten lakh, as the case may be, the deposit to be made by such insurer shall be such amount, being not less than one hundred and fifty thousand rupees, as may be specified in the said order.

(2) Where the insurer is an insurer specified in sub-clause (c) of clause (9) of Section 2, he shall be deemed to have complied with the provisions of this section as to deposits, if in respect of insurance business carried on by him in India under a standing contract of the nature referred to in sub-clause (c) of clause (9) of Section 2 a deposit of an amount one-and-a-half times that specified in subsection (1) has been made in the Reserve Bank of India in one of the offices in India of the Bank for and on behalf of the Central Government in cash or approved securities estimated at the market value of the securities on the day of deposit by or on behalf of the underwriters who are members of the Society of Lloyd's with whom he has his standing contract.

(3) Where the deposit to be made by an insurer not carrying on insurance business in India immediately before the commencement of the Insurance (Amendment) Act, 1968, a deposit of rupees ten lakhs shall be made before the application for registration is made, and the provision of clause (*ii*) of subsection (1A) shall apply to such insurer after his registration as they apply to an insurer specified in clause (a) of subsection (1).

(4) An insurer shall not be registered for any class of insurance business in addition to the class or classes for which is already registered until the full deposit required under subsection (1) has been made.

(5) Where an insurer who intends to become a member of a group, does not carry on all the classes of insurance business carried on by the other insurers in such group, or, where out of the several insurers who desire to form themselves into a group, any insurer does not carry on all the classes of insurance business carried on by the other insurers who desire to form themselves into

the group, such insurer may be registered for that class or those classes of insurance business which is or are carried on by the other insurers of the group or the proposed group, as the case may be, and where any application for registration is made by any such insurer, the Authority may, notwithstanding anything contained in subsection (2A) of Section 3 or subsection (4), register such insurer for one or more additional classes of insurance, if the following conditions are fulfilled, namely:

(*a*) the Authority is satisfied that registration for the proposed one or more additional classes of insurance business would qualify the insurer to become number of a group;

(*b*) agreements have been executed by all the insurers in the group or proposed group, as the case may be, and such agreements in the opinion of the Authority, satisfy the requirements of the *Explanation* to subsection (1B); and

(*c*) the insurer has, after the commencement of the Insurance (Amendment) Act, 1968, made deposit of a sum not less than the total of all the instalments of deposit which he would have been required to make after such commencement till the date of his becoming a member of the group, had he been a member of the group from such commencement.

(6) The Authority shall cancel the registration made in pursuance of the provisions of sub section (5), if the insurer referred to therein fails to become, within a period of three months from the date of such registration, a member of the group or proposed group, as the case may be, and, where such registration has been cancelled, the provisions of this Act shall apply to the insurer as if he had not been registered for the class or classes of insurance business in relation to which his registration has been cancelled.

(7) Securities already deposited with the Controller of Currency in compliance with the Indian Life Assurance Companies Act, 1912 (6 of 1912), shall be transferred by him to the Reserve Bank of India and shall, to the extent of their market value as at the date of the commencement of this Act, be deemed to be deposited under this Act, as the instalment or as part of this instalment to be made under the foregoing provisions of this section before the application for registration is made whether any such application is or is not in fact made.

(8) A deposit made in cash shall be held by the Reserve Bank of India to the credit of the insurer and shall except to the extent, if any, to which the cash has been invested in securities under subsection (9A), be returnable to the insurer in cash in any case in which under the provisions of this Act a deposit is to be returned; and any interest accruing due and collected on securities deposited under subsection (1) or subsection (2) shall be paid to the insurer, subject only to deduction of the normal commission chargeable for the realization of interest.

(9) The insurer may at any time replace any securities deposited by him under this section with the Reserve Bank of India either by cash or by other approved securities or partly by cash and partly by other approved securities, provided that such cash, or the value of such other approved securities estimated at the market rates prevailing at the time of replacement, or such cash together with such value, as the case may be, is not less than the value of the securities replaced estimated at the market rates prevailing when they were deposited.

(9A) The Reserve Bank of India shall, if so requested by the insurer,—

(*a*) sell any securities deposited by him with the Bank under this section and hold the cash realized by such sale as deposit, or

(*b*) invest in approved securities specified by the insurer the whole or any part of a deposit held by it in cash or the whole or any part of cash received by it on the sale of or on the maturing of securities deposited by the insurer, and hold the securities in which investment is so made as deposit.

and may charge the normal commission on such sale or on such investment.

(9B) where subsection (9A) applies

(*a*) if the cash realized by the sale of or on the maturing of the securities (excluding in the former case the interest accrued) falls short of the market value of the securities at the date on which they were deposited with the Bank, the insurer shall make good the deficiency by a further deposit either in cash or in approved securities estimated at the market value of the securities, on the day on which they are deposited, or partly in cash and partly in approved securities so estimated, within a period of two months from the date on which the securities matured or were sold or where the securities matured or were sold before the 21st day of March, 1940, within a period of four months from the commencement of the Insurance (Amendment) Act, 1940 (20 of 1940); and unless he does so the insurer shall be deemed to have failed to comply with the requirements of this section as to deposits; and

(*b*) if the cash realized by the sale of or on the maturity of the securities (excluding in the former case the interest accrued) exceeds the market value of the securities at the date on which they were deposited with the Bank, the Central Government may, if satisfied that the full amount required to be deposited under subsection (1) is in deposit, direct the Reserve Bank to return the excess.

(10) If any part of a deposit made under this section is used in the discharge of any liability of the insurer, the insurer shall deposit such additional sum in cash or approved securities estimated at the market value of the securities on the day of deposit, or partly in cash and partly in such securities, as will make up the amount so used. The insurer shall be deemed to have failed to comply with the requirements of subsection (1), unless the deficiency is supplied within a period of two months from the date when the deposit or any part thereof is so used for discharge of liabilities.

Reservation of Deposits

Section 8: (1) Any deposit made under Section 7 or Section 98 shall be deemed to be part of the assets of the insurer but shall not be susceptible of any assignment or charge; nor shall it be available for the discharge of any liability of the insurer other than liabilities arising out of policies of insurance issued by the insurer so long as any such liabilities remain undischarged; nor shall it be liable to attachment in execution of any decree except a decree obtained by a policyholder of the insurer in respect of a debt due upon a policy which debt the policyholder has failed to realise in any other way.

(2) Where a deposit is made in respect of life insurance business the deposit made in respect thereof shall not be available for discharge of any liability of the insurer other than liabilities arising out of policies of life insurance issued by the insurer.

Refund of Deposit

Section 9: Where an insurer has ceased to carry on in India all classes of insurance business, and his liabilities in India in respect of all classes of insurance business have been satisfied or are otherwise provided for, the court may, on the application of the insurer, order the return to the insurer of the deposit made by him under this Act.

Section 27 and 28 deals with investments by insurance companies. Following provisions have been made:

For Life Insurance

(*a*) 25% of the sum stated above in the Government Securities.

(*b*) Not less than 25% of the sum in the Government securities or other Approved securities.

[(*a*) and (*b*) put together should not be more than 50%.]

(*c*) Not less than 15% of the sum in infrastructure and social sector.

(*d*) Not less than 20% in other securities as stated in Schedule I of IRDA Regulations 2000.

(*e*) Not less than 15% in other approved investments to be governed by the prudential norms specified in the above referred Regulation.

[(*d*) and (*e*) put together should not be more than 25%.]

For Pension

(*a*) Not less than 20% in Government securities.

(*b*) And annuity business not less than 20% in Government securities or in approved Securities.

(*c*) Balance 60% in the approved investments specified in the Schedule I of IRDA Regulations 2000.

General Insurance Business

(*a*) 20% in the Central Government Securities.

(*b*) Not less than 10% State Government Securities.

[(*a*) and (*b*) class should not be more than 30%].

(*c*) 5% housing and loans to the State Government.

(*d*) Not less than 10% in infrastructure and social sector.

(*e*) Not exceeding 55% in other approved investments governed by the prudential norms including the securities specified by IRDA.

7.1.7 Management and Administration

Power to Appoint Staff

Section 33A: The Authority may appoint such staff, and at such places as it or he may consider necessary, for the scrutiny of the returns, statements and information furnished by insurers under this Act and generally to ensure the efficient performance of the functions of the Authority under this Act.

Power of Authority to Issue Directions

Section 34: (1) where the Authority is satisfied that —

(*a*) in the public interest; or

(*b*) to prevent the affairs of any insurer being conducted in a manner detrimental to the interests of the policyholders or in a manner prejudicial to the interests of the insurer; or

(*c*) generally to secure the proper management of any insurer, it is necessary to issue directions to insurers generally or to any insurer. In particular, he may, from time to time, issue such directions as he deems fit, and the insurers or the insurer, as the case may be, shall be bound to comply with such directions:

Provided that no such directions shall be issued to any insurer in particular unless such insurer has been given a reasonable opportunity of being heard.

(2) The Authority may, on representation made to him or on his own motion, modify or cancel any direction issued under subsection (1), and in so modifying or canceling any directions, may impose such conditions as he thinks fit, subject to which the modification or cancellation shall have effect.

Appointing of Managing Directors etc.

Section 34A to 34D provides the IRDA to appoint, reappoint remove the managerial and other staff and decide the renumeration payable to them.

Amendment of provisions relating to appointments of managing directors, etc., to be subject to previous approval of the Authority

Section 34A: (1) In the case of an insurer,—

(*a*) no amendment made, after the commencement of the Insurance (Amendment) Act, 1968, of any provision relating to the appointment, reappointment, termination of appointment or remuneration of a managing or whole time director, or of a manager or a chief executive officer, by whatever name called, whether that provision be contained in the insurers memorandum or articles of associations, or in an agreement entered into by him, or in any resolution passed by the insurer in general meeting or by his Board of Directors shall have effect unless approved by the Authority;

(*b*) no appointment, re appointment or termination of appointment made after the commencement of the Insurance (Amendment) Act, 1968, of a managing or whole time director, or a manager or a chief executive officer, by whatever name called, shall have effect unless such appointment, reappointment or termination of appointment is made with the previous approval of the Authority.

Explanation: For the purposes of this subsection, any provision conferring any benefit or providing any amenity or perquisite, in whatever form, whether during or after the termination of the term of office of the manager or the chief executive officer, by whatever name called or a managing or whole time director, shall be deemed to be a provision relating to his remuneration.

(2) Nothing contained in Sections 268 and 269, the proviso to subsection (3) of Section 309, Sections 310 and 311, the proviso to Section 387 and Section 388 (insofar as Section 388 makes the provisions of Sections 310 and 311 apply in relation to the manager of a company) of the Companies Act, 1956 (1 of 1956), shall apply to any matter in respect of which the approval of the Authority has to be obtained under subsection (1).

(3) No act done by a person as a managing or whole time director or a director not liable to retire by rotation or a manager or a chief executive officer, by whatever name called, shall be deemed to be invalid on the ground that it is subsequently discovered that his appointment or reappointment had not taken effect by reason of any of the provisions of this Act; but nothing in this subsection shall be construed as rendering valid any act done by such person after his appointment or reappointment has been shown to the insurer not to have had effect.

Power of Authority to Remove Managerial Persons from Office

Section 34B: (1) Where the Authority is satisfied that in the public interest or for preventing the affairs of an insurer being conducted in a manner detrimental to the interests of the policyholders or for securing the proper management of any insurer it is necessary so to do, he may, for reasons to be recorded in writing, by order, remove from office, with effect from such date as may be specified in the order, any director or the chief executive officer, by whatever name called, of the insurer.

(2) No order under subsection (1) shall be made unless the director or chief executive officer concerned has been given a reasonable opportunity of making a representation to the Authority against the proposed order:

Provided that if, in the opinion of the Controller, any delay would be detrimental to the interests of the insurer or his policyholders, he may, at the time of giving the opportunity aforesaid or at any time thereafter, by order direct that, pending the consideration of the representation aforesaid, if any, the director or, as the case may be, chief executive officer, shall not, with effect from the date of such order,:

(*a*) act as such director or chief executive officer of the insurer;

(*b*) in any way, whether directly, indirectly, be concerned with, or take part in the management of the insurer.

(3) Where any order is made in respect of a director or chief executive officer of an insurer under subsection (1), he shall cease to be a director or as the case may be chief executive officer of the insurer and shall not, in any way, whether directly or indirectly, be concerned with, or take part in, the management of any insurer for such period not exceeding five years as may be specified in the order.

(4) If any person in respect of whom an order is made by the Authority under subsection (1) or under the proviso to subsection (2) contravenes the provisions of this section, he shall be punishable with fine which may extend to two hundred and fifty rupees for each day during which such contravention continues.

(5) Where an order under subsection (1) has been made, the Authority may, by order in writing, appoint a suitable person in place of the director or chief executive officer who has been removed from his office under that subsection, with effect from such date as may be specified in the order.

(6) Any person appointed as director or chief executive officer under this section shall:

(*a*) hold office during the pleasure of the Controller and subject thereto for a period not exceeding three years or such further periods not exceeding three years at a time as the Authority may specify;

(*b*) not incur any obligation or liability by reason only of his being a director or chief executive officer or for anything done or omitted to be done in good faith in the execution of the duties of his office or in relation thereto.

(7) Notwithstanding anything contained in any law or in any contract, memorandum or articles of association, on the removal of a person from office under this section, that person shall not be entitled to claim any compensation for the loss or termination of office.

Power of Controller to Appoint Additional Directors

Section 34C: (1) If the Authority is of opinion that in the public interest or in the interests of an insurer or his policyholders, it is necessary so to do, he may, from time to time, by order in writing, appoint, with effect from such date as may be specified in the order, one or more persons to hold office as additional directors of the insurer:

Provided that the number of additional directors so appointed shall not, at any time, exceed five or one-third of the maximum strength fixed for the Board by the articles of association of the insurer, whichever is less.

(2) Any person appointed as additional director in pursuance of this section,—

(*a*) shall hold office during the pleasure of the Authority, and subject thereto for a period not exceeding three years or such further periods not exceeding three years at a time as the Authority may specify;

(*b*) shall not incur any obligation or liability by reason only of his being a director or for anything done or omitted to be done in good faith in the execution of the duties of his office or in relation thereto; and

(*c*) shall not be required to hold qualification shares of the insurer.

(3) For the purpose of reckoning any preparation of the total number of directors of the insurer, any additional director appointed under this section shall not be taken into account.

Sections 34B and 34C to Override Other Laws

Section 34D: Any appointment or removal of a director or chief executive officer in pursuance of Section 34B or Section 34C shall have effect notwithstanding anything to the contrary contained in the Companies Act, 1956 (1 of 1956), or any other law for the time being in force or in any contract or any other instrument.

Powers of Tariff Advisory Committee (TAC)

Section 64UC read together with the Insurance Rules 1939 defines the role and powers of TAC.

Power of the Advisory Committee to Regulate Rates, Advantages, etc.

Section 64UC: (1) The Advisory Committee may, from time to time and to the extent it deems expedient, control and regulate the rates, advantages, terms and conditions that may be offered by insurers in respect of any risk or any class or category of risks, the rates, advantages, terms and conditions of which, in its opinion, it is proper to control and regulate, and any such rate, advantages, terms and conditions shall be binding on all insurers:

Provided that the Authority may, permit any insurer to offer, during such period (being not more than two years but which may be extended by periods of not more than two years at a time) and subject to such conditions as may be specified by him, rates, advantages, terms or conditions different from those fixed by the Advisory Committee in respect of any particular category of risks, if he is satisfied that such insurer generally issues policies only to a restricted class of the public or under a restricted category of risks.

(2) In fixing, amending or modifying any rates, advantages, terms or conditions, relating to any risk, the Advisory Committee shall try to ensure, as far as possible, that there is no unfair discrimination between risk of essentially the same hazard, and also that consideration is given to past and prospective loss experience:

Provided that the Advisory Committee may, at its discretion, make suitable allowances for the degree of credibility to be assigned to the past experience including allowances for random fluctuations and may also, at its discretion, make suitable allowances for future fluctuations and unforeseen future contingencies including hazards of conflagration or catastrophe or both.

(3) Every decision of the Advisory Committee shall be valid only after and to the extent it is ratified by the Authority, and every such decision shall take effect from the date on which it is so ratified by the Authority, or if the Authority so orders in any case, from such earlier date as he may specify in the order.

(4) The decisions of the Advisory Committee in pursuance of the provisions of this section shall be final.

(5) Where an insurer is guilty of breach of any rate, advantage, term or condition fixed by the Advisory Committee, he shall be deemed to have contravened the provisions of this Act.

Provided that instead of proceeding against the insurer for such contravention, the Authority may, if the insurer removes the contravention by recovering the deficiency in the premium, or where it is not practicable to do so, modifies suitably or cancels the contract of insurance, compound the offence on payment to the Advisory Committee of such fine, not exceeding rupees one thousand, as he may decide in consultation with the Advisory Committee.

Transitional Provisions

Section 64UD: (1) Notwithstanding anything contained in this Part, until the names of the members of the Advisory Committee elected for the first time after the commencement of the

Insurance (Amendment) Act, 1968, are notified, the Tariff Committee of the General Insurance Council appointed under regulations made under subsection (2) of Section 64-0 as it was in force immediately before the commencement of the Insurance (Amendment) Act, 1968, and in existence on such commencement (hereafter in this Part referred to as the Tariff Committee) shall continue to function and shall be deemed to be the Advisory Committee duly elected under this Part and the Authority of Insurance shall become the Chairman of that Committee with effect from the commencement of the Insurance (Amendment) Act, 1968, and function as such, and any chairman of the Tariff Committee holding office immediately before such commencement shall cease to be the Chairman thereof from the date of such commencement but shall continue to be an ordinary member of the Advisory Committee.

Provided that the Chairperson of the Authority shall become the Chairman of the Advisory committee with effect from the commencement of the Insurance Regulatory and Development Authority Act, 1999 and function as such, and any Chairman of the Tariff Committee holding office immediately before such commencement shall cease to be the Chairman.

(2) Notwithstanding anything contained in this Part, the constitution of the Regional Councils established under Section 64P, as in force immediately before the commencement of the Insurance (Amendment) Act, 1968 (hereafter referred to as the Regional Councils), and of the Sectional Committees formed there under, existing immediately before such commencement, shall continue to be in full force and be of full effect until the regulations made by the Advisory Committee for the first time under Section 64UB come into effect and as soon as such regulations have come into effect such constitutions shall cease to have effect.

(3) Notwithstanding anything contained in this Part, until the Secretary to the Advisory Committee is nominated under subsection (2) of Section 64UA, the Secretary to the Tariff Committee holding office immediately before the commencement of the Insurance (Amendment) Act, 1968, shall function as the Secretary and shall be deemed to have been duly nominated under this Part.

(4) All rates, advantages, terms and conditions fixed by the Tariff Committee or the Regional Councils prior to the commencement of the Insurance (Amendment) Act, 1968, and in force immediately before such commencement shall continue, except to such extent as they may be altered, replaced or abolished by the Advisory Committee, to be valid and fully in force as if they were rates, advantages, terms and conditions fixed by the Advisory Committee.

Power of the Advisory Committee to Require Information, etc.

Section 64UE: (1) The Advisory Committee may require, by notice in writing, any insurer to supply to it such information or statements, periodical or *ad hoc, as* it may consider necessary to enable it to discharge its functions under this Part and every insurer shall comply with such requirements within such period as may be specified by the Advisory Committee in this behalf, failing which the insurer shall be deemed to have contravened the provisions of this Act.

(2) Any information supplied under this section shall be certified by a principal officer of the insurer or where the Advisory Committee has agreed in advance, by such other officer or officers of the insurer as the principal officer of the insurer may nominate for the purpose and if the notice so requires, also by an auditor.

(3) The Authority may, at any time, in writing, depute any subordinate of his, to make a personal inspection of the books of account, ledgers, policy registers and other books or documents of any insurer to verify the accuracy of any return or statement furnished by him under subsection (1), or to verify that full particulars have been supplied by him in respect of all policies issued by him and the insurer shall provide all facilities for such inspection, and make available to such person all the books of account, ledgers, policy registers and other books or documents of the insurer which might be needed by him for such verification and the person deputed may himself extract from out of the books and records of the insurer such information as may be needed to fill up or complete the returns required to be submitted to the Advisory Committee under this section.

(4) The Advisory Committee may, at any time, on the application of an insurer, make arrangements for the inspection of an organization which is concerned with the inspection of risks, adjustment of losses or firefighting appliances, and may, whenever necessary, advise insurers about the adequacy of the arrangements for the inspection of risks and adjustment of losses or the suitability of such appliances:

Provided that no such inspection shall be made without the written permission of the concerned organization.

Insurance Association of India

All the existing insurers, provident societies and also new entrants to join the Insurance Association of India and the Central Government, by an official notification in the Gazette will declare that all the existing insurers and provident societies are the members of the Insurance Association of India. This association is a separate entity with a common seal and perpetual succession and will have the power to acquire, hold, to sell the movable and immovable property of the association. The Insurance Association shall maintain a register of the membership and register of associate members of the Insurance Association of India. And, the names of the insurer or provident society will be removed from the register on ceasing its business of insurance. The Insurance Association of India is having two councils – Life Insurance Council and General Insurance Council.

7.1.8 Accounts and Returns (Section 10-26)

An insurer is required to keep a separate account of all receipts and payments in respect of each class of insurance, viz., Fire, Marine and miscellaneous Insurance. Every insurer is required to prepare, at the expiration of each financial year, in the prescribed forms,

(*a*) a balance sheet

(*b*) a profit and loss account

(*c*) a revenue account for each class of insurance business

These accounts are required to be audited annually by an auditor and printed and four copies to be furnished as returns to the IRDA within 6 months from the close of the financial year. Every Insurer is required to furnish to the authority a certified copy of the minutes of the proceedings of every General Meeting, within 30 days from the holding of the meeting. The Insurance Rules framed under the Act provide that the following items of information shall be maintained in respect of each class of business:

- A record of cover notes specifying the identification number, name of party, dates of commencement and expiry, type of cover granted, the amount of premium and cross-reference to the policy.
- A record of policies, which should be serially numbered, listing all policies issued, entered in chronological order, stating the number of policy, date of commencement and expiry of risk, name/s of the insured, premium received, cross reference to the relevant bank guarantee or deposit and the nature of risk granted, cross-reference to any cover note issued prior to the issue to the policy and cross-reference to any endorsement passed subsequent to the issue of the policy.
- A record of premiums showing, according to chronological order or receipt of premiums, date of receipt, the amount, and name of party from whom received and with cross-reference to policy number.
- A record of endorsements mentioning the policy number to which attached, dates of commencement and expiry of the endorsement, the type of endorsement and the additional premium charged or refund due and cross-reference to the premium register.
- A record of bank guarantees and deposits giving particulars of the party, amount and conditions of guarantee or deposits and cross-reference to the relevant policy or policies.
- A record of claims intimate mentioning name of claimant, giving reference to policy number, date of intimation of claim, interest covered, nature and cause of the loss or damage, provisional estimate of loss, amount at which settled, date of settlement of claim, recoveries from salvage or otherwise and whether surveyed. Two separate records, one relating to claims intimated and the other relating to claims paid, may be maintained if there is adequate cross-referring of information between them and if the information required under this clause is readily available from them taken together.

The rules framed under the Insurance Act, 1938 also provide that the following items of information shall be maintained for the business of the insurer as a whole.

(*i*) A register of agents.

(*ii*) A record of business procured by each agent and the amount of commission paid thereon.

(*iii*) Records of employees including field workers.

(*iv*) Cash book and disbursement book.

(*v*) A record of investments and assets.

(*vi*) Records of insurance companies with which common and facultative reinsurance arrangements of reinsurance treaties are entered into.

(*vii*) Record of facultative reinsurance ceded and accepted.

Further, the Rules provide that receipts for payments received shall be maintained in a systematic manner and documents used for assuming risk are serially numbered and field accordingly. The documents relating to claims settled, including copies of any survey of loss assessment reports, shall be maintained as follows:

(*i*) in respect of every loss or damage on which a claim of less than ₹ 5,000 has been made, for a period of three years;

(*ii*) in respect of every loss or damage on which a claim of ₹ 5,000 or more but less than rupees ₹ 20,000 has been made, for a period of five years;

(*iii*) in respect of every loss or damage on which a claim of ₹ 20,000 or more but less than rupees one lakh has been made, for a period of seven years;

(*iv*) in respect of every loss or damage on which a claim of rupees one lakh or more has been made, for a period of twelve years;

such period being counted from the date on which the claim is settled.

7.1.9 Winding up of Insurance Companies

All the existing insurers, provident societies and also new entrants to join the Insurance Association of India and the Central Government, by an official notification in the Gazette will declare that all the existing insurers and provident societies are the members of the Insurance Association of India. This association is a separate entity with a common seal and perpetual succession and will have the power to acquire, hold, to sell the movable and immovable property of the association. The Insurance Association shall maintain a register of the membership and register of associate members of. the Insurance Association of India. And, the names of the insurer of provident society will be removed from the register on ceasing its business of insurance. The Insurance Association of India is having two councils – Life Insurance Council and General Insurance Council.

Power of Central Government to Acquire Undertakings of Insurers in Certain Cases

Section 52H: (1) If, upon receipt of a report from the Authority, the Central Government is satisfied that an insurer, —

(*a*) has persistently failed to comply with —

(*i*) any direction given to him under Section 34, Section 34F or Section 34G, or

(*ii*) any order made under Sec. 34E; or

(*b*) is being managed in a manner detrimental to the public interest or to the interests of his policyholders, or shareholders,

and that —

(i) in the public interest, or

(ii) in the interest of the policyholders or shareholders of such insurer,

it is necessary to acquire the undertaking of such insurer, the Central Government may, by notified order, acquire the undertaking of such insurer (hereafter in this section and in Sections 52I, 52J and 52N and in the Eighth Schedule referred to as the acquired insurer) with effect from such date as maybe specified in the order (hereinafter in this section and in Sections 521 and 52J and in the Eighth Schedule referred to as the appointed day):

Provided that no undertaking off an insurer shall be so acquired unless such insurer has been given a reasonable opportunity of showing cause against the proposed action.

Explanation: For the purposes of this section and of Sections 52I to 52N—

(*a*) "notified order" means an order published in the official Gazette;

(*b*) "undertaking", in relation to an insurer incorporated outside India, means the undertaking of the insurer in India,

(2) Subject to the other provisions contained in this section and in Sections 52I to 52M, on the appointed day, all the assets and liabilities of the undertaking of the acquired insurer shall stand transferred to, and vest in, the Central Government.

(3) The assets and liabilities of the undertaking of the acquired insurer shall be deemed to include all rights, powers, authorities and privileges and all property, whether movable or immovable, including, in particular, cash balances, reserve funds, investments, deposits and all other interests and rights in, or arising out of, such property as may be in the possession of or held by, the acquired insurer immediately before the appointed day and all books, accounts and documents relating thereto, and shall also be deemed to include all debts, liabilities and obligations of whatever kind, then existing of the acquired insurer.

(4) Notwithstanding anything contained in subsection (2), the Central Government may, if it is satisfied that all the assets and liabilities of the undertaking of the acquired insurer should, instead of vesting in the Central Government, or continuing to so vest, vest in a corporation or company, whether established under the scheme made under Sec. 52I or not (hereafter in this section and in Section 52I to 52N and in the Eighth Schedule referred to as the acquired insurer), by order, direct that the assets and liabilities of the said undertaking, shall vest in the acquiring insurer, either on the publication of the notified order or no such other date as may be specified in this behalf in the direction.

(5) Where the undertaking of the acquired insurer vests in an acquiring insurer under subsection (4), the acquiring insurer shall, on and from the date of such vesting, be deemed to have become the transferee of the acquired insurer and all the rights and liabilities in relation to the acquired insurer shall, on and from the date of such vesting, be deemed to have been the rights and liabilities of such acquiring insurer.

(6) Unless otherwise expressly provided by or under this section or Sections 52I to 52M, all contracts, deeds, bonds, agreements, powers of attorney, grants of legal representation and other instruments of whatever nature subsisting, having effect immediately before the appointed day and to which the acquired insurer is a party or which are in favour of the acquired insurer shall be of as full force and effect against or in favour, of the Central Government or, as the case may be, the acquiring insurer, and may be enforced or acted upon as fully and effectually as of in the place of the acquired insurer the Central Government or the acquiring insurer had been a party thereto or as if they had been issued in favour of the Central Government or the acquiring insurer, as the case may be.

(7) If, on the appointed day, any suit, appeal or other proceeding, of whatever nature, is pending by or against the acquired insurer the same shall not abate, be discontinued or be, in any

way, prejudicially affected by reason of the transfer of the undertaking of the acquired insurer or of anything contained in this section or in Sections 52I to 52M, but the suit, appeal or other proceeding may be continued, prosecuted and enforced by or against the Central Government or the acquiring insurer, as the case may be.

Winding up by the Court

Section 53: (1) The Court may order the winding up in accordance with the Indian Companies Act, 1913 (7 of 1913), of any insurance company and the provisions of that Act shall, subject to the provisions of this Act apply accordingly.

(2) In additional to the grounds on which such an order may be based, the Court may order the winding up of an insurance company—

(*a*) if with the sanction of the Court previously obtained a petition in this behalf is presented by shareholders not less in number than one-tenth of the whole body of shareholders and holding not less than one-tenth of the whole share capital or by not less than fifty policyholders holding policies of life insurance that have been in force for not less than three years and are of the total value of not less than fifty thousand rupees; or

(*b*) if the Authority, who is hereby authorized to do so, applies in this behalf to the Court on any of the following grounds, namely—

(*i*) that the company has failed to deposit or to keep deposited with the Reserve Bank of India the amounts required by Section 7 or Section 98;

(*ii*) that the company having failed to comply with any requirement of this Act has continued such failure nor having contravened any provision of this Act has continued such contravention for a period of three months after notice of such failure Nor contravention has been conveyed to the company by the Authority.

(*iii*) that it appears from many returns or statements furnished under the provisions of this Act or from the results of any investigation made there under that the company is, or is deemed to be, insolvent, or

(*iv*) that the continuance of the company is prejudicial to the interest if the policyholders or to the public interest generally.

Voluntary Winding Up

Section 54: Notwithstanding anything contained in the Indian Companies Act, 1913 (7 of 1913), an insurance company shall not be wound up voluntarily except for the purpose of effecting an amalgamation or a reconstruction of the company, or on the ground that by reason of its liabilities it cannot continue its business.

Valuation of Liabilities

Section 55: (1) In the winding up of an insurance company or in the insolvency of any other insurer, the value of the assets and the liabilities of the insurer shall be ascertained in such manner and upon such basis as the liquidator or receiver in insolvency thinks fit, subject, so far as applicable, to the rule contained in the Seventh Schedule and to any directions which may be given by the Court.

(2) For the purposes of any reduction by the Court of the amount of the contracts of any insurance company, the value of the assets and liabilities of the company and all claims in respect of policies issued by it shall be ascertained in such manner and upon such basis as the Court thinks proper having regard to the rule aforesaid.

(3) The rule in the Seventh Schedule shall be of the same force and may be repealed, altered or amended as if it were a rule made in pursuance of Section 246 of the Indian Companies Act, 1913 (7 of 1913) and rules may be made under that section for the purpose of carrying into effect the provisions of this Act with respect to the winding up of insurance companies.

Application of Surplus Assets of Life Insurance Fund in Liquidation or Insolvency

Section 56: (1) In the winding up of an insurance company and in the insolvency of any other insurer the value of the assets and the liabilities of the insurer in respect of life insurance business shall be ascertained separately from the value of any other assets or any other liabilities of the insurer and no such assets shall be applied to the discharge of any liabilities other than those in respect of life insurance business except insofar as those assets exceed the liabilities in respect of life insurance business.

(2) In the winding up of an insurance company carrying on the business of life insurance or in the insolvency of any other insurer carrying on such business where any proportion of the profits of the insurer was before the commencement of the winding up or insolvency allocated to policy holders, if, when the assets and liabilities of the insurer have been ascertained, there is found to be a surplus of assets over liabilities (hereinafter referred to as a *prima facie* surplus) there shall be added to the liabilities of the insurer in respect of the life insurance business an amount equal to such proportion of the *prima facie* surplus as is equivalent to such proportion of the profits allocated to shareholders and policyholders as was allocated to policyholders during the ten years immediately preceding the commencement of the winding up and the assets of the insurer shall be deemed to exceed his liabilities only insofar as those assets exceed those liabilities after such addition:

Provided that:

(a) if in any case there has been no such allocation or if it appears to the Court that by reason of special circumstances it would be inequitable that the amount to be added to the liabilities of the insurer in respect of the life insurance business should be an amount equal to such proportion as aforesaid, the amount to be so added shall be such amount as the Court may direct, and

(*b*) for the purpose of the application of this sub section to any case where before the commencement of the winding up or insolvency a proportion of such profits as aforesaid of a branch only of the life insurance business in question has been allocated to policyholders, the value of the assets and liabilities of the insurer in respect of that branch shall be separately ascertained in like manner as the value of his assets and liabilities in respect to the life insurance business was ascertained, and the surplus so found, if any, of assets over liabilities shall, for the purpose of determining the amount to be added to:

the liabilities of the insurer in respect of the life insurance business be deemed to be the *prima facie surplus.*

Winding up of Secondary Companies

Section 57: (1) Where the insurance business or any part of the insurance business of an insurance company has been transferred to another insurance company under an arrangement in pursuance of which the first mentioned company (in this section referred to as the secondary company) or the creditors thereof has or have claims against the company to which such transfer was made (in this section referred to as the principal company) then, if the principal company is being wound up by or under the supervision of the Court, the Court shall (subject as hereinafter mentioned) order the secondary company to be wound up in conjunction with the principal company and may, by the same or any subsequent order appoint the same person to be liquidator for the two companies and make provision for such other matters as may seem to the Court necessary with a view to the companies being wound up as if they were one company.

(2) The commencement of the winding up of the principal company shall, save as otherwise ordered by the Court, be the commencement of the winding up of the secondary company.

(3) In adjusting the rights and liabilities of the members of the several companies among themselves, the Court shall have regard to the constitution of the companies and to the arrangements entered into between the companies in the same manner as the Court has regard to the rights and liabilities of different classes of contributories in the case of the winding up of a single company or as near thereto as circumstances admit.

(4) Where any company alleged to be secondary is not in process of being wound up at the same time as the principal company to which it is alleged to be secondary, the Court shall not direct the secondary company to be wound up, unless, after hearing all objections (if any) that may be urged by or on behalf of the company against its being wound up, the Court is of opinion that the company is secondary to the principal company and that the winding up of the company in conjunction with the principal company is just and equitable.

(5) An application may be made in relation to the winding up of any secondary company in conjunction with the principal company by any creditor of, or person interested in, the principal or secondary company.

(6) Where a company stands in the relation of a principal company to one insurance company and in the relation of a secondary company to some other insurance company or where there are several insurance companies standing in the relation of secondary companies to one principal company, the court may deal with any number of such companies together or in separate groups as it thinks most expedient upon the principles laid down in this section.

Schemes for Partial Winding up of Insurance Companies

Section 58: (1) If at any time it appears expedient that the affairs of an insurance company in respect of any class of business comprised in the undertaking of the Company should be wound up but that any other class of business comprised in the undertaking should continue to be carried on by the company or be transferred to another insurer, a scheme for such purposes may be prepared and submitted for confirmation of the Court in accordance with the provisions of this Act.

(2) Any scheme prepared under this section shall provide for the allocation and distribution of the assets and liabilities of the company between any classes of business affected (including the allocation of any surplus assets which may arise on the proposed winding up) for any future rights of every class of policyholders in respect of their policies and for the manner of winding up any of the affairs of the company which are proposed to be wound up and may contain provisions for altering the memorandum of the company with respect to its objects and such further provisions as may be expedient for giving effect to the scheme.

(3) The provisions of this Act relating to the valuation of liabilities of insurers in liquidation and insolvency and to the application of surplus assets of the life insurance fund in liquidation or insolvency shall apply to the winding up of any part of the affairs of a company in accordance with the scheme under this section in like manner as they apply in the winding up of an insurance company, and any scheme under this section may apply with the necessary modifications any of the provisions of the Indian Companies Act, 1913 (7 of 1913), relating to the winding up of companies.

(4) An order of the Court confirming a scheme under this section whereby the memorandum of a company is altered with respect to its objects shall as respects the alteration have effect as if it where an order confirmed under Sec. 12 of the Indian Companies Act, 1913 (7 of 1913), and the provisions of Sections 15 and 16 of that Act shall apply accordingly.

Notice of Policy Values

Section 60: In the winding up of an insurance company for the purposes of a cash distribution of the assets and in the insolvency of any other insurer the liquidator or assignee, as the case may be, in the case of all persons appearing by the books of the company or other insurer to be entitled to or interested in the policies granted by the company or other insurer shall ascertain the value of the liability of the company or other insurer to each such person and shall give notice of such value to those persons in such manner as the Court may direct and any person to whom notice is so given shall be bound by the value so ascertained unless he gives notice of his intention to dispute such value in such manner and within such time as may be specified by a rule or order of the Court.

Power of Court to Reduce Amount of Contracts of Insurance

Section 61: (1) where an insurance company is in liquidation or any other insurer is insolvent, the Court may make an order reducing the amount of the insurance contracts of the company or other insurer upon such terms and subject to such conditions as the Court thinks Just.

(2) Where a company carrying on the business of life insurance has been proved to be insolvent, the Court may if it thinks fit in place of making a winding up order reduce the amount of the insurance contracts of the company upon such terms and subject to such conditions as the Court thinks fit.

(3) Application for an order under this section may be made either by the liquidator or by or on behalf of the company or by a policyholder, or by the Authority and any person whom the Court thinks likely to be affected shall be entitled to be heard on any such application.

7.1.10 Miscellaneous Provisions

Prohibition of Rebates

No person shall allow or offer to allow as an inducement to any person to take out insurance any rebate of the whole or part of commission payable or any rebate of the premium shown in the policy. Any person making default in complying with these provisions shall be punishable with fine which may extend to five hundred rupees.

Licensing of Surveyor or Loss Assessor

A surveyor or a loss assessor must hold a valid licence, which is subject to renewal after a period of 5 years. Before admitting a claim exceeding ₹ 20,000 a general insurance company needs to obtain a report on the loss that has occurred from the surveyor or loss assessor.

Penalties

The Act has laid down penalties for contravention of the following provisions:

- Failure to maintain solvency margins.
- Failure to comply with investment norms.
- Failure to carry out rural and social sector obligations.
- Making a false statement or furnishing a false document.
- Failure to comply with the directions of the Authority.
- Failure to furnish documents, statements and returns required by the Act.

7.2 Life Insurance Corporation Act, 1956

Life insurance business in India is regulated by the provisions of the Insurance Act, 1938, Insurance Rule, 1939 and the Life Insurance Corporation Act, 1956 and rules and regulation made thereunder.

Life Insurance Corporation of India (LIC) was formed in September, 1956 by an Act of Parliament, viz , Life Insurance Corporation Act, 1956, with Capital contribution of ₹ 5 crore from the Government of India. Its main duty was to spread the message of Life Insurance in the country and mobilise peoples saving for nation-building activities. Life Insurance Corporation has also framed regulations, viz., Life Insurance Corporation (Staff) Regulation, 1960 and Life Insurance Corporation (Agents) Rules, 1972.

Section 2 (11) of the Insurance Act, 1938 defines the life insurance business as 'the business effecting contract of insurance upon human life, including any contract whereby the payment of money is assured on death (except death by accident) or the happening of any contingency dependent on human life, and any contract which is subject to payment of premiums for a term dependent on human life and shall deemed to include: *(i)* the granting of disability and double and triple indemnity accident benefits, if so, provided in the contract of insurance; *(ii)* the granting of annuities upon human life and granting of superannuation allowances and annuities payable out of any fund applicable solely to the relief and maintenance of persons engaged or who have been engaged in any particular profession, trade or employment or of the dependents of such persons'.

7.2.1 Other Definitions

(1) *"appointed day"* means the date on which the Corporation is established under section 3;

(2) *"composite insurer"* means an insurer carrying on in addition to controlled business any other kind of insurance business;

(3) *"controlled business"* means:

(*i*) in the case of any insurer specified in sub-clause (*a*) (*ii*) or sub-clause (*b*) of clause (9) of Section 2 of the Insurance Act and carrying on life insurance business:

(*a*) all his business, if he carries on no other class of insurance business;

(*b*) all the business appertaining to his life insurance business, if he carries on any other class of insurance business also;

(*c*) all his business if his certificate of registration under the Insurance Act in respect of general insurance business stands wholly cancelled for a period of more than six months on the 19th day of January, 1956.

(*ii*) in the case of any other insurer specified in clause (9) of Section 2 of the Insurance Act and carrying on life insurance business:

(*a*) all his business in India, if he carries on no other class of insurance business in India;

(*b*) all the business appertaining to his life insurance business in India, if he carries on any other class of insurance business also in India;

(*c*) all his business in India if his certificate of registration under the Insurance Act in respect of general insurance business in India stands wholly cancelled for a period of more than six months on the 19th day of January, 1956.

Explanation: An insurer is said to carry on no class of insurance business other than life insurance business, if in addition to life insurance business, he carries on only capital redemption business or annuity certain business or both; and the expression "business appertaining to his life insurance business" in sub-clause (*i*) and (*ii*) shall be construed accordingly;

(*iii*) in the case of a provident society, as defined in Section 65 of the Insurance Act, all its business;

(*iv*) in the case of the Central Government or a State Government, all life insurance business carried on by it, subject to the exceptions specified in section 44;

(4) *"Corporation"* means the Life Insurance Corporation of India established under section 3;

(5) *"Insurance Act"* means the Insurance Act, 1938 (4 of 1938);

(6) *"insurer"* means an insurer as defined in the Insurance Act who carries on life insurance business in India and includes the Government and a provident society as defined in section 65 of the Insurance Act;

(7) *"member"* means a member of the Corporation;

(8) *"prescribed"* means prescribed by rules made under this Act;

(9) *"Tribunal"* means a Tribunal constituted under section 17 and having jurisdiction in respect of any matter under the rules made under this Act;

(10) All other words and expressions used herein but not defined and defined in the Insurance Act shall have the meanings respectively assigned to them in that Act.

7.2.2 Establishment of Life Insurance Corporation of India

Establishment and Incorporation of Life Insurance Corporation of India

Section 3: (1) With effect from such date {1st September, 1956, vide Notification No. S.R.O. 1937, dated 30-8-1956, Gazette of India, Extraordinary, Pt. II, Sec. 3, p. 1799} as the Central Government may, by notification in the Official Gazette, appoint, there shall be established a Corporation called the Life Insurance Corporation of India.

(2) The Corporation shall be a body corporate having perpetual succession and a common seal with power subject to the provisions of this Act, to acquire, hold and dispose of property, and may by its name sue and be sued.

Constitution of the Corporation

Section 4: (1) The Corporation shall consist of such number of persons not exceeding fifteen as the Central Government may think fit to appoint thereto and one of them shall be appointed by the Central Government to be the Chairman thereof.

(2) Before appointing a person to be a member, the Central Government shall satisfy itself that person will have no such financial or other interest as is likely to affect prejudicially the exercise or performance by him of his functions as a member, and the Central Government shall also satisfy itself from time to time with respect to every member that he has no such interest; and any person who is, or whom the Central Government proposes to appoint and who has consented to be, a member shall, whenever required by the Central Government so to do, furnish to it such information as the Central Government considers necessary for the performance of its duties under this sub-section.

(3) A member who is in any way directly or indirectly interested in a contract made or proposed to be made by the Corporation shall as soon as possible after the relevant circumstances have come to his knowledge, disclose the nature of his interest to the Corporation and the member shall not take part in any deliberation or discussion of the Corporation with respect to that contact.

Capital of the Corporation

Section 5: (1) The original capital of the Corporation shall be five crores of rupees provided by the Central Government after due appropriation made by Parliament by law for the purpose, and the terms and conditions relating to the provision of such capital shall be such as may be determined by the Central Government.

(2) The Central Government may, on the recommendation of the Corporation, reduce the capital of the Corporation to such extent and in such manner as the Central Government may determine.

7.2.3 Functions of the Corporation

Section 6: (1) Subject, to the rules, if any, made by the Central Government in this behalf, it shall be the general duty of the Corporation to carry on life insurance business, whether in or outside India, and the Corporation shall so exercise its powers under this Act as to secure that life insurance business is developed to the best advantage of the community.

(2) Without prejudice to the generality of the provisions contained in subsection (1) but subject to the other provisions contained in this Act, the Corporation shall have power:

(*a*) to carry on capital redemption business, annuity certain business or reinsurance business insofar as such reinsurance business appertains to life insurance business;

(*b*) subject to the rules, if any, made by the Central Government in this behalf, to invest the funds of the Corporation in such manner as the Corporation may think fit and to take all such steps as may be necessary or expedient for the protection or realization of any investment; including the taking over of and administering any property offered as security for the investment until a suitable opportunity arises for its disposal;

(*c*) to acquire, hold and dispose of any property for the purpose of its business;

(*d*) to transfer the whole or any part of the life insurance business carried on outside India to any other person or persons, if in the interest of the Corporation it is expedient so to do;

(*e*) to advance or lend money upon the security of any movable property or otherwise;

(*f*) to borrow or raise any money in such manner and upon such security as the Corporation may think fit;

(*g*) to carry on either by itself or through any subsidiary any other business in any case where such other business was being carried on by a subsidiary of an insurer whose controlled business has been transferred to an vested in the Corporation under this Act;

(*h*) to carry on any other business which may seen to the Corporation to be capable of being conveniently carried on in connection with its business and calculated directly or indirectly to render profitable the business of the Corporation;

(*i*) to do all such things as may be incidental or conducive to the proper exercise of any of the powers of the Corporation.

(3) In the discharge of any of its functions, the Corporation shall act so far as may be on business principles.

7.2.4 Transfer of Existing Life Insurance Business to the Corporation

Assets and Liabilities of Existing Insurers Carrying on Controlled Business

Section 7: (1) On the appointed day, there shall be transferred to and vested in the Corporation all the assets and liabilities appertaining to the controlled business of all insurers.

(2) The assets appertaining to the controlled business of an insurer shall be deemed to include all rights and powers, and all property, whether movable or immovable, appertaining to his controlled

business, including, in particular, cash balances, reserve funds, investments, deposits and all other interests and rights in or arising out of such property as may be in the possession of the insurer and all books of account or documents relating to the controlled business of the insurer; and liabilities shall be deemed to include all debts, liabilities and obligations of whatever kind then existing and appertaining to the controlled business of the insurer.

Explanation: The expression "assets appertaining" to the controlled business of an insurer:

(*a*) in relation to a composite insurer, includes that part of the paid-up capital of the insurer or assets representing such part which has or have been allocated to the controlled business of the insurer in accordance with the rules made in this behalf;

(*b*) in relation to a Government, means the amount lying to the credit of that business on the appointed day.

(3) Where any such assets are subject to any trust referred to in subsection (6) of section 27 of the Insurance Act or to any other trust for the benefit of policyholders, the assets shall be deemed to have vested in the Corporation free from any such trust.

On 01-09-1956, all the assets and liabilities of the existing insurers were transferred to the corporation.

7.2.5 Conduct of Business

Provident, Superannuation and Other Like Funds

Section 8: (1) Where an insurer whose controlled business is to be transferred to and vested in the Corporation under section 7, has established a provident or superannuation fund or any other like fund for the benefit of his employees and constituted a trust in respect thereof (hereinafter in this section referred to as an existing trust), the moneys standing to the credit of any such fund on the appointed day, together with any other assets belonging to such fund, shall, subject to the provisions of subsection (2) stand transferred to and vest in the Corporation on the appointed day free from any such trust.

(2) Where all the employees of any such insurer do not become employees of the Corporation under section 11, the moneys and other assets belonging to any such fund as it referred to in sub-section (1), shall be apportioned between the trustees of the fund and the Corporation in the prescribed manner; and in case of any dispute regarding such apportionment, the decision of the Central Government thereon shall be final.

(3) The Corporation shall, as soon as may be after the appointed day, constitute in respect of the moneys and other assets which are transferred to and vested in it under this section, one or more trusts having objects as similar to the objects of the existing trusts as in the circumstances may be practicable.

(4) Where all the moneys and other assets belonging to an existing trust are transferred to and vested in the Corporation under this section, the trustees of such trust, except as respects things done or omitted to be done before the appointed day.

General Effect of Vesting of Controlled Business

Section 9: (1) Unless otherwise expressly provided by or under this Act, all contracts, agreements and other instruments of whatever nature subsisting or having effect immediately before the appointed day and to which an insurer whose controlled business has been transferred to and vested in the Corporation is a party or which are in favour of such insurer shall insofar as they relate to the controlled business of the insurer be of as full force and affect against or in favour of the Corporation, as the case may be, and may be enforced or acted upon as fully and effectually as if, instead of the insurer, the Corporation had been a party thereto or as if they had been entered into or issued in favour of the Corporation.

(2) If on the appointed day any suit, appeal or other legal proceeding of whatever nature is pending by or against an insurer, then, insofar as it relates to his controlled business, it shall not abate, be discontinued or be in any way prejudicially affected by reason of the transfer to the Corporation of the business of the insurer or anything done under this Act, but the suit, appeal or other proceeding may be continued prosecuted and enforced by or against the Corporation.

Provisions as to Composite Insurers

Section 10: (1) For the removal of doubts, it is hereby declared that in any case where an insurer whose controlled business has been transferred to an vested in the corporation under this Act is a composite insurer, the provisions of the preceding sections shall only apply to the extent to which any property appertains to his controlled business and to rights and powers acquired, and to debts, liabilities and obligations incurred, and to contracts, agreements and other instruments made by the insurer for the purposes of his controlled business and to legal proceedings relating to those purposes, and the provisions of those sections shall be construed accordingly.

(2) The Central Government may, by rules made in this behalf provide:

(*a*) for the determination of the question whether any property appertains to his controlled business or whether any rights, powers, debts, liabilities or obligations were acquired or incurred or any contract, agreement or other instrument was made by the insurer for the purposes of his controlled business or whether any documents relate to those purposes;

(*b*) for the allocation of the paid-up capital or assets representing such paid-up capital, as the case may be, between the controlled business of the insurer and any other business;

(*c*) for substituting for any agreements entered into by any insurer partly for the purposes of his controlled business and partly for other purposes separate agreements in the requisite terms and for any apportionments and indemnities consequent thereon;

(*d*) for the severance of leases comprising property of which part only is transferred to and vested in the Corporation by virtue of this Act and for apportionment consequent on such severance;

(*e*) for the apportionment and the making of financial adjustments with respects to any debts, liabilities of obligations incurred by any such insurer partly for the purposes of his controlled business and partly for other purposes and for any necessary variation of mortgages and encumbrances relating to such debts, liabilities or obligations;

(*f*) for the apportionment of the moneys and other assets belonging to any provident or superannuation fund or any other like fund to which the provisions of Section 8 do not apply between persons employed in connection with the controlled business of an insurer and other persons;

(*g*) for any other matters supplementary to or consequential on the matters aforesaid for which provision appears to be necessary or expedient.

(3) All rules made under this section shall be laid for not less than thirty days before both Houses of Parliament as soon as possible after they are made and shall be subject to such modifications as Parliament may make during the session in which they are so laid or the session immediately following.

(4) Where at any time before the expiration of six months from the appointed day a question has arisen under this section or under any rules made thereunder as to whether any property is or was held or used by the insurer for the purposes of his controlled business, the question shall be referred to the Tribunal for decision.

Power of Corporation to Modify Contracts of Life Insurance in Certain Cases

Section 14: The Corporation may, having regard to the financial condition on the appointed day of any insurer whose controlled business has been transferred to an vested in the Corporation, reduce the amounts of insurance under contracts of life insurance entered into by such insurer before the 19th day of January 1956, in such manner and subject to such conditions as it thinks fit:

Provided that no such reduction shall be made except in accordance with a scheme prepared by the Corporation in this behalf and approved by the Central Government.

Right of Corporation to Seek Relief in Respect of Certain Transactions of the Insurer

Section 15: (1) Where an insurer whose controlled business has been transferred to and vested in the Corporation under this Act has, at any time within five years before the 19th day of January, 1956:

(*a*) made any payment to any person without consideration;

(*b*) sold or disposed of any property of the insurer without consideration or for an inadequate consideration;

(*c*) acquired any property or rights for an excessive consideration:

(*d*) entered into or varied any agreement so as to require an excessive consideration to be paid or given by the insurer;

(*e*) entered into any other transaction of such an onerous nature as to cause a loss to, or impose a liability on, the insurer exceeding any benefit accruing to the insurer;

(*f*) if a composite insurer, transferred any property from his life department to his general department without consideration or for an inadequate consideration.

and the payment, sale, disposal, acquisition, agreement or variation thereof or other transaction or transfer was not reasonably necessary for the purpose of the controlled business of the insurer or was made with an unreasonable lack of prudence on the part of the insurer, regard being had in either case to the circumstances at the time, the Corporation may apply for relief to the Tribunal in respect of such transaction, and all parties to the transaction shall, unless the Tribunal otherwise directs, be made parties to the application.

(2) The Tribunal may make such order against any of the parties to the application as it thinks just having regard to the extent to which those parties were respectively responsible for the transaction or benefited from it and all the circumstances of the case.

(3) Where an application is made to the Tribunal under this section in respect of any transaction and the application is determined in favour of the Corporation, the Tribunal shall have exclusive jurisdiction to determine any claims outstanding in respect of the transaction.

Compensation for Acquisition of Controlled Business

Section 16: (1) Where the controlled business of an insurer has been transferred to and vested in the Corporation under this Act, compensation shall be given by the Corporation to that insurer in accordance with the principles contained in the First Schedule.

(2) The amount of the compensation to be given in accordance with the aforesaid principles shall be determined by the Corporation in the first instance, and if the amount so determined is approved by the Central Government it shall be offered to the insurer in full satisfaction of the compensation payable to him under this Act, and if, on the other hand, the amount so offered is not acceptable to the insurer he may within such time as may be prescribed for the purpose have the matter referred to the Tribunal for decision.

Constitution of Tribunals

Section 17: (1) The Central Government may for the purposes of this Act constitute one or more Tribunals and each of the Tribunals shall consist of three members appointed by the Central Government one of whom shall be a person who is, or has been, a Judge of a High Court or has been a Judge of the Supreme Court, and he shall be the Chairman thereof.

(2) A Tribunal may choose one or more persons possessing special knowledge of any matter relating to any case under inquiry to assist the Tribunal in determining any question which has to be decided by it under this Act.

(3) Every Tribunal shall have the powers of a civil court while trying a suit under the Code of Civil Procedure, 1908 (5 of 1908), in respect of the following matters:

- (*a*) summoning and enforcing the attendance of any person and examining him on oath;
- (*b*) requiring the discovery and production of documents;
- (*c*) receiving evidence on affidavits;
- (*d*) issuing commissions for the examination of witnesses or documents.

(4) Every Tribunal shall have power to regulate its own procedure and decide all matters within its competence, and may review any of its decisions in the event of there being a mistake on the face of the record or correct any arithmetic or clerical error therein.

7.2.6 Organisational Structure

Offices, Branches and Agencies

Section 18: (1) The central office of the Corporation shall be at such place as the Central Government may, by notification in the Official Gazette, specify.

(2) The Corporation shall establish a zonal office at each of the following places, namely, Bombay, Calcutta, Delhi, Kanpur and Madras, and, subject to the previous approval of the Central Government, may establish such other zonal offices as it thinks fit.

(3) The territorial limits of each zone shall be such as may be specified by the Corporation.

(4) There may be established as many divisional offices and branches in each zone as the Zonal Manager thinks fit.

Committees of the Corporation

Section 19: (1) The Corporation may entrust the general superintendence and direction of its affairs and business to an Executive Committee consisting of not more than five of its members and the Executive Committee may exercise all powers and do all such acts and things as may be delegated to it by the Corporation.

(2) The Corporation may also constitute an Investment Committee for the purpose of advising it in matters relating to the investment of its funds, and the Investment Committee shall consist of not more than seven members of whom not less than three shall be members of the Corporation and the remaining members shall be persons (whether members of the Corporation or not) who have special knowledge and experience in financial matters, particularly, matters relating to investment of funds.

(3) The Corporation may constitute such other Committees as it may think fir for the purpose of discharging such of its functions as may be delegated to them.

Managing Directors

Section 20: The Corporation may appoint one or more persons to be the Managing Director or Directors of the Corporation, and every Managing Director shall be a whole time officer of the Corporation and shall exercise such powers and perform such duties as may be entrusted or delegated to him by the Executive Committee or the Corporation.

Corporation to be Guided by the Directions of Central Government

Section 21: In the discharge of its functions under this Act, the Corporation shall be guided by such directions in matters of policy involving public interest as the Central Government may give to it in writing; and if any question arises whether a direction relates to a matter of policy involving public interest the decision of the Central Government thereon shall be final.

7.2.7 Other Important Provisions

Exclusive privilege of carrying on life insurance in India: Section 30 of the Act gives the Corporation the exclusive privilege of carrying on life insurance business in India on and from the appointed day.

Policies guaranteed by Central Government: By virtue of Section 37, the sums assured by all policies issued by the Corporation or by any insurer the liabilities under which have vested in the Corporation and all bonuses declared in respect thereof are guaranteed as to payment in cash by the Central Government.

Rule making powers of the Central Government: Section 48 empowers the Central Government to make rules to carry out the purposes of the Act. The rules may provide, *inter alia*, for:

(*i*) the terms of office and conditions of service of members;

(*ii*) the manner in which and the conditions subject to which investment may be made by the Corporation;

(*iii*) the form in which the report giving an account of the activities of the Corporation shall be prepared;

(*iv*) the conditions subject to which the Corporation may appoint employees.

Powers of the Corporation to make Regulations: Section 49 empowers the Corporation, with the previous approval of the Central Government, by notification in the Gazette of India, to make regulations for the purpose of giving effect to the provisions of the Act.

The Schedules to the Act deal with principles for determining, compensation, principles for determining the value of liabilities in certain cases and principles for determining compensation payable to chief agents.

7.2.8 Life Insurance Corporation Regulations, 1959

These regulation have been made by the Life Insurance Corporation of India in accordance with the powers vested u/s 49 of the Act subject to previous approval of Central Government. A brief summary of these regulations is given below:

Corporation shall meet atleast once in three months at a place which the Chairman may determine. Five members personally present shall be a quorum for a meeting and in the absence of quorum at a meeting, the meeting shall be adjourned to another date within a week of such meeting. If at the adjourned meeting also, the quorum is not present within half an hour from the time appointed for the meeting, the members present shall be the quorum. These provisions are similar to those given in the Companies Act, 1956. Three high powered (management) committees have been prescribed:

1. The Executive Committee
2. Investment Committee
3. Building Advisory Committee

Chairman shall be the Chief Executive of the Corporation. The Managing Directors may, with the approval of the Chairman and with prior sanction of the Corporation or any Committee of the Corporation, delegate to officers or employees the powers, authorities and discretions necessary for efficient conduct of the business of the Corporation.

The Regulations also provide that:

(*a*) all amount received on behalf of the Corporation by any officer or employee shall be credited to the appropriate Bank account of the Corporation;

(*b*) payments on behalf of the Corporation shall be made only by duly authorized officers;

(*c*) the accounts of all the offices of the Corporation shall be regularly audited by Internal Auditors;

(*d*) every office of the Corporation shall be inspected by Inspecting Officers.

7.3 General Insurance Business (Nationalization) Act, 1972

General Insurance Business was nationalized in 1972 and company by name of General Insurance Corporation of India (GIC) was formed under Companies Act, 1956 and was entrusted with the task of supervising, controlling and carrying on the business of general insurance. On the formation of the Corporation, the shares of Indian Insurance Companies vested in the Central Government stood automatically transferred to the Corporation and all the Indian Insurance Companies became subsidiaries of the Corporation. Amalgamation schemes were also framed whereby the Indian Insurance Companies were merged in one another so that ultimately there would be only four Indian companies to promote competition and also consolidate general insurance business in India.

7.3.1 Formation of GIC

GIC, under *Section 9* of the Act has an authorised capital of ₹ 75 crore into ₹ 75 lakh fully paid up shares of ₹ 100/- each. Of which, ₹ 5 crore is the initial subscribed capital of the Corporation. The Central Government could frame one or more schemes under Section 16 of the Act for merger of the companies. A copy of every scheme framed under Section 16 shall be laid before each House of Parliament.

By virtue of the provisions of Section 4 to 8 the Central Government is authorized to acquire the assets and liabilities including the shareholdings of the existing Indian Insurers on an appointed day i.e., 01-01-73. Section 7 of the Act authorised the central government to acquire the services of existing employees on the service conditions formulated by the newly established company, *viz.*, GIC.

Section 3 of the Act defines an "acquiring company" as any Indian Insurance Company and where a scheme has been framed involving the merger of one Indian Insurance Company in another or the amalgamation of two more such companies, it shall mean the Indian Insurance Company in which any other company has been merged or the company which has been formed as a result of the amalgamation.

Chapter VA of the Act contains the terms and conditions of service of officers and other employees. The company is authorized to make amendments or make rules, amend or add to the schemes which are already in existence or make new provisions or schemes for the staff of the company. All the schemes, which are newly framed or the existing schemes with amendments made thereto are to be placed before the houses of Parliament for their approval. These schemes will be operative notwithstanding anything contrary contained in any other law or any agreement, award or other instrument for the time being in force.

7.3.2 Functions of the Corporation

Section 18 of the Act describes the various functions of the GIC as follows:

"18. Functions of Corporation: (1) The functions of the Corporation shall include:

(*a*) the carrying on of any part of the general insurance business, if it thinks it desirable to do so;

(*b*) aiding, assisting and advising the acquiring companies in the matter of setting up of standards of conduct and sound practice in general insurance business and in the matter of rendering efficient service to holders of policies of general insurance;

(*c*) advising the acquiring companies in the matter of the controlling their expenses including the payment of commission and other expenses.

(*d*) advising the acquiring companies in the matter of the investment of their funds;

(*e*) issuing directions to acquiring companies in relation to the conduct of general insurance business.

(2) In issuing any directions under subsection (1), the Corporation shall keep in mind the desirability of encouraging competition amongst the acquiring companies as far as possible in order to render their services more efficient."

Section 19 defines the functions of acquiring companies:

"19. Functions of acquiring companies:

1. Subject to the rules, if any, made by the Central Government in this behalf and to its memorandum and articles of association, it shall be the duty of every acquiring company to carry on general insurance business.
2. Each acquiring company shall so function under this Act as to secure that general insurance business is developed to the best advantage of the community.
3. In the discharge of any of its functions, each acquiring company shall act so far as may be on business principles and where any directions have been issued by the Corporation shall be guided by such directions.
4. For the removal of doubts it is hereby declared that the Corporation and any acquiring company may, subject to the rules, if any, made by the Central Government in this behalf, enter into such contracts of reinsurance of reinsurance treaties as it may think fit for the protection of its interests."

7.3.3 Powers of Central Government

Section 23 of the Act empowers the Central Government is vested with the power to issue directions to the General Insurance Corporation of India and every acquiring company in the discharge of its functions and they shall be guided by such directions in regard to matters of policy involving public interest. No provision of law relating to winding up of a company shall apply to the Corporation or to an acquiring company and neither the Corporation nor any such company shall be placed in liquidation save by order of the Central Government and in such manner as it may direct.

Section 24 provides the acquiring companies, the exclusive privilege of carrying on general insurance business in India. No person shall take out or renew any policy of insurance in respect of any property in India or in shipping or vessel or aircraft registered in India with an insurer whose principal place of business is outside India save with the prior permission of the Central Government.

Under *Section 35,* the Central Government may be notification specify the application of the provisions of the Insurance Act, 1958 with such modifications as is deemed necessary to the Corporation and the acquiring companies. The Central Government is also empowered to make rules to carry out the provisions of the Act and such rules may provide for:

(*a*) manner in which the profits and other moneys received by the Corporation may be dealt with;

(*b*) the conditions subject to which the Corporation and the acquiring companies shall carry on general insurance business;

(*c*) the terms and conditions subject to which any reinsurance contract or treaties may be entered into;

(*d*) form and manner in which any notice or application may be made to the Central Government;

(*e*) the reports which may be called for by the Central Government from the Corporation and acquiring companies; and

(*f*) any other matter which is required to be or may be prescribed.

7.4 Insurance Regulatory and Development Authority Act, 1999

The Insurance Regulatory and Development Authority Act, 1999 provides for the establishment of an Authority to protect the interests of holders of insurance policies, to regulate, promote and ensure orderly growth of the insurance industry and for matters connected therewith or incidental thereto and further to amend the Insurance Act, 1938, the Life Insurance Corporation Act, 1956 and the General Insurance Business (Nationalization) Act, 1972.

The Statement of Objects and Reasons of the Act provides that the insurance industry requires a high degree of regulation. The Insurance Act, 1938 provided for the institution of the Controller of Insurance to act as a strong and powerful supervisory and regulatory authority with powers to direct, advise, caution, prohibit, investigate, inspect, prosecute, search, seize, amalgamate, authorize, register and liquidate insurance companies. However, after the nationalization of Life Insurance in 1956 and the General Insurance in 1972, the role of Controller of Insurance diminished in significance over a period of time.

7.4.1 Constitution of the Authority

Section 2(b) of the IRDA Act, 1999 defines the Authority as the Insurance Regulatory and Development Authority established under Section 3 of the Act. The Section 3 lays down the procedure for establishing the Authority. It is established by a notification by the Central Government in the Official Gazettee. The date of operation of the Authority is also notified by the Central Government by a notification. The other important characteristics of the Authority are as follows:

- It is a body corporate with perpetual succession and common seal.

- It has the powers to acquire, hold and dispose the property in its name. The property may be a movable or immovable.
- It has the powers to enter into contract in its name.
- It can sue the parties and it can be sued by the parties.
- The Central Government by notification decides the principal place of office of the Authority and the Authority has the powers to open branches or other offices as required by it.
- It consists of a Chairperson, not more than five whole time members, and not more than four part-time members. (S. 4).
- All the members are appointed by the Central Government by a notification.
- The Chairperson and members are appointed from the person of ability, integrity having the standing and experience or knowledge in life insurance or general insurance, actuarial science, finance, economics, law, accountancy, administration or any other discipline which is useful for the Authority. And preferably, the Chairperson and one of the whole time members should be experienced persons or have the knowledge in the life insurance or the general insurance or actuarial science. (S. 4).
- The term of the office of the Chairperson and the whole time members of five years and the part-time members will hold office for a period not more than the five years from the date of joining the office.
- The Chairperson will be in the office till he attains the age of sixtyfive years and the whole time member will be in the office till he attains the age of sixtytwo years (S. 5).
- The Chairperson or the whole time member or part-time member can relinquish the office by giving a notice of three months to the Central Government.
- The Central Government can remove the Chairperson, whole time member or the part-time member for the reasons of they become insolvent, physically or mentally incapable of performing duties, convicted for the moral turpitude, has acquired the financial or other interest in the insurance business, or the position of the member or the Chairperson is detrimental to the interest of the insurance or public or the policyholders. (S. 6)
- The Central Government, before removing a person from the office, has to give opportunity to the member to explain the reasons and after hearing him, if not satisfied can remove a member from service giving causes of removal.
- Any defect found in the process of appointment or any irregularity of procedures or appointment of members cannot vitiate the appointment of the member. The existence of vacancy in the body of the Authority does not affect the proceedings of the meeting of the Authority.
- The Chairperson or the members should not take any employment at least for a period of two years after they leave their positions. Under special circumstances, they can hold any office with the previous approval of the Central Government (S. 8).
- The salaries, allowance and other remunerations will be paid to the Chairperson and members as per the provisions laid down by the Central Government. The allowances and other service conditions will be prescribed by a notification.

7.4.2 Duties, Powers and Functions of the Authority

Duties

- The primary duty of the IRDA is to regulate, promote and ensure orderly growth and conduct of the insurance business and reinsurance business (S.14).
- It has to maintain proper accounts and other relevant records, prepare annual statements of accounts in such form as may be prescribed by the Central Government in consultation with the CAG.
- It has to comply with the directions of the Central Government and CAG will arrange the audit of the accounts and rectify any defects pointed by the audit conducted by it.
- The Authority has to submit the audited balance sheet and other financial statements to the Central Government and the Government will lay the reports before the houses of the Parliament.
- The Authority has to submit all the financial statements to the Central Government within nine months from the completion of the relevant financial year.
- It has the duty to scrutinise all existing and new insurance products, rates charged, terms and conditions offered and act in best interest of consumers.
- The authority is duty bound to follow the directions issued by the Central Government and report the outcome of the directions.
- Authority has the general duty to protect the interest of policyholders in matters concerning assignment, nomination, settlement of insurance claim, surrenders etc. and other terms and conditions of contract of insurance.

Powers

- The Authority has the general supervisory power of insurance industry and it has the administrative powers.
- Powers to appoint the staff and officers required to conduct the business of the Authority smoothly.
- Authority can even delegate some general or special powers by an order in writing to the Chairperson or the Members of the Authority along with conditions if it feels as necessity.
- Power to constitute committees of the members and delegate the powers to the committee.
- Power to hold and acquire movable or immovable property.
- Power to issue a certificate of registration, renew, modify, withdraw, suspend or cancel such registration to the insurer.
- Power to prepare a code of conduct to the agents, surveyors and loss assessors and other intermediaries associated with insurance business.
- Power to levy fees and other charges for carrying out the purposes of this Act.
- Power to call information from insurers inspect accounts and other documents conduct enquiries and investigate including the audit of the insurers, intermediaries' and other organizations connected with the insurance business.

- It has the power to regulate the margin of solvency and investment of funds by insurance companies.
- Power to exercise the powers sanctioned by other insurance laws of the country or by other notifications issued by the Central Government from time to time.
- It has the powers to make regulations with the consultancy of Insurance Advisory Committee in the field of finalizing the service conditions of the members regarding the meeting and transactions to be carried out by the Advisory committee in promoting the insurance business.

Functions

- Promoting and regulating the professional organizations connected with the insurance and reinsurance business.
- Promoting efficiency in the conduct of insurance business in India.
- To act as adjudicator in the settlement of disputes between the insurers, intermediaries of the insurers.
- To act as supervisory authority and regulate the functioning of Tariff Advisory Committee and various insurance companies.
- To control and regulate the rates, advantages, terms and conditions that may be offered by insurers in respect of general insurances, which are not controlled by the Tariff Advisory Committee (Non-tariff Products).
- To formulate the regulations concerning insurance in rural and social sectors.

7.4.3 Other Provisions

The Central Government has the powers under the Act to direct the Authority and grant funds under the head with sanction of the Parliament. The fund so constituted is called the Insurance Regulatory and Development Fund. This fund can be used to meet the expenses of the salaries, allowances and other remuneration of the members, officers and other employees of the Authority and to meet all other expenses required to discharge the duties and functions of the Authority. Registration fees, application frees from insurers and other intermediaries are also credited to the fund. A credit is also received u/s 7 of the Insurance Act, 1938.

The Central Government under the Act has the power to give directions to the Authority on the questions of policy of insurance business. If the central government finds that the Authority is not able to discharge the functions or perform the duties prescribed under the provisions of this Act or the Authority has defaulted in complying with the directions of the Central Government or the provisions of the Act, the financial position of the Authority is under deterrent conditions and if the Central Government feels that the Authority is working against the interest of public, can supercede the Authority and exercise its powers. This it may do by giving a notice with reasons and the authority may continue to act accordingly for a period not exceeding six months. Authority has to submit report of action taken to the Parliament. The Central Government has the power to make following rules in relations the authority:

1. The format of annual statement of accounts of the authority form and manner of submission of returns and statements and particulars are to be furnished.
2. Rules concerning the fixation of remunerations and service conditions of the staff, officers, members of the Authority.
3. To fix the allowances payable to part-time members of the Authority.
4. Any matter as may be required for by Insurance Advisory Committee.

The Act empowers the IRDA to appoint a committee by notification, to provide the advice on various insurance matters to the Authority called as Insurance Advisory Committee (IAC). This committee is established by a notification by the Authority. IAC contains not more than 25 members excluding ex-officio members to represent the various interests of commerce, industry, transport, agriculture, consumer forums, surveyors, agents, intermediaries, organizations engaged in safety and loss prevention, research bodies and employees association of insurance companies and intermediaries. The chairperson and the members of the authority are the ex-officio members the Insurance Advisory Committee. The objects of the automatically IAC shall be to advise the Authority on matters relating to the framing the regulations in relation to service conditions of the staff, conducting the transactions of various meetings and deciding the powers to be delegated etc. and any other matters required by the Authority.

The Regulatory Authority is under a duty to submit all the rules framed by it for the approval of Parliament. The provisions of other insurance laws are also applicable for the Authority, which are not in contradiction with the policy of public interest. IRDA is also generally subject to various insurance and other laws in best interest of the public.

7.4.4 IRDA Regulations

Various regulations have been framed by IRDA since its inception. These relate to licencing of insurers, regulation of intermediaries, reporting requirements, business practices, etc.

Regulations Framed under Insurance Regulatory and Development Authority Act, 1999 and the Insurance (Amendment) Act, 2002.

1. Insurance Regulatory and Development Authority (Actuarial Report and Abstract) Regulations, 2000.
2. Insurance Regulatory and Development Authority (Obligation of Insure of Rural or Social Sectors) Regulation, 2000.
3. Insurance Regulatory and Development Authority (Insurance Advertisements and Disclosure) Regulations, 2000.
4. Insurance Regulatory and Development Authority (Licensing of Insurance Agents) Regulations, 2000.
5. Insurance Regulatory and Development Authority (General Insurance – Reinsurance) Regulations, 2000.
6. Insurance Regulatory and Development Authority (Appointed Actuary) Regulations, 2000.
7. Insurance Regulatory and Development Authority (Assets, Liabilities and Solvency Margin of Insurers) Regulations, 2000.

8. Insurance Regulatory and Development Authority (Meetings) Regulations, 2000.
9. Insurance Regulatory and Development Authority (Registration of Indian Insurance Companies) Regulations, 2000.
10. Insurance Advisory Committee (Meetings) Regulations, 2000.
11. Insurance Regulatory and Development Authority (Investment) Regulations, 2000.
12. Insurance Regulatory and Development Authority (Preparation of Financial Statements and Auditor's Report of Insurance Companies) Regulations, 2002.
13. Insurance Regulatory and Development Authority (Licensing, Professional Requirements and Code of Conduct) Regulations, 2000.
14. Insurance Regulatory and Development Authority (Conditions of Service of Officers and Other Employees) Regulations, 2000.
15. Insurance Regulatory and Development Authority (Life Insurance — Reinsurance) Regulations, 2000.
16. Insurance Regulatory and Development Authority (Investment) (Amendment) Regulations, 2001.
17. Insurance Regulatory and Development Authority (Third Party Administrators – Health Services) Regulations, 2001.
18. Insurance Regulatory and Development Authority (Reinsurance Advisory Committee) Regulations, 2001.
19. Insurance Regulatory and Development Authority (Protection of Policyholders' Interest) Regulations, 2002.
20. Insurance Regulatory and Development Authority (Investment) (Amendment) Regulations, 2002.
21. Insurance Regulatory and Development Authority (Assets, Liabilities and Solvency Margin of Insurers) (Amendment) Regulations, 2002.
22. Insurance Regulatory and Development Authority (Licensing of Corporate Agents) Regulations, 2002.
23. Insurance Regulatory and Development Authority (Licensing of Insurance Agents) (Amendment) Regulations, 2002.
24. Insurance Regulatory and Development Authority (Insurance Bookers) Regulations, 2002.
25. Insurance Regulatory and Development Authority (Manner of Payment of Premium) Regulations, 2002.
26. Insurance Regulatory and Development Authority (Obligations of Insurers to Rural or Social Sectors) (Amendment) Regulations, 2002 and 2008.
27. Insurance Regulatory and Development Authority (Protection of Policyholders' Interest) (Amendment) Regulations, 2002.
28. Insurance Regulatory and Development Authority (Qualification of Actuary) Regulations, 2004.

Motor Vehicles Act, 1988

Motor Vehicles Act, 1988 provides for compulsory insurance of motor vehicles. The Act provides that no motor vehicle can be used in a public place unless there is in force in relation to vehicle a policy issued by an authorised insurer. This policy covers the insured person's liability in the event of death, bodily injury of certain persons or damage to property of third persons.

The Inland Steam Vessels Act, 1917 and the Amended Act, 1977

The Act provides that the provisions of Chapter VII of the Motors Vehicles Act, 1955 regarding insurance of mechanically propell vessels against third party risks are applicable to steam vessels. The Act maker it compulsory for the owners of operators of inland vessels to insure against legal liability of death, bodily injury or damage caused to the property of third persons and passengers.

Marine Insurance Act, 1963

Marine Insurance Act, 1963 (based on Marine Insurance Act 1906) codifies the law relating the conduct of marine insurance business in India. The provisions of the Act *inter alia* includes provisions relating to basic insurance principles (Indemnification, insurable interest, utmost good faith, subrogation and contribution, valuation, losses, warranties, return of premiums etc).

The Carriage of Goods by Sea Act, 1925

The Act defines the minimum rights, liabilities and immunities of a shipowner on loss or damage to cargo. The act deals with three aspects of a shipowners liabilities towards cargo owner:

(*i*) the circumstances when the shipowner is deemed to be liable for loss or damage to cargo unless he proves otherwise;

(*ii*) the circumstance when the shipowner is exempted from liability, i.e., when loss or damage is caused by events outside his control, e.g., perils of the seas;

(*iii*) the limits of liability of a shipowner for loss of or damage to cargo calculated in monetary terms per package or unit of cargo.

The Merchant Shipping Act, 1958

This Act also provides a certain protection to shipowners. For example, the liability of a shipowner can be limited to certain maximum sum for certain losses, provided the incident giving rise to such claim has arisen without the actual fault or privy of the shipowner.

These claims may relate to loss of life, personal injury or loss of or damage to property on land or water. The Act also confers the obligation on the shipowner to send his ship to sea in a seaworthy and safe condition.

The Bill of Lading Act, 1855

This Act defines the character of the Bill of Lading as an evidence of the contract of carriage of goods between the shipowner and the shipper, as an acknowledgement of the receipt of the goods on board the vessel and, as a document of title. The bill of lading is one of the various documents required in connection with settlement of marine cargo claims.

The Indian Ports (Major Ports) Act, 1963

This Act defines the liability of Port Trust Authorities for loss of or damage to goods whilst in their custody and prescribes time limits for filing monetary claim on, or suit against, the Port Trust Authorities.

The Indian Railways Act, 1890

The Indian Railways Act, passed in 1890 was amended in 1961 and the amendment came into force from 1st January, 1962. The Act deals with various aspects of Railway Administration. However, Chapter VII is relevant to Marine Insurance practice as it deals with the responsibility of Railway Administration as carriers.

This Chapter makes provision, *inter alia,* for the following:

(*a*) rights and liabilities of railways as carriers of goods:

(*b*) procedure for notification of claims for compensation for losses.

The Railways Claims Tribunal Act, 1987 provides for formation of tribunals to deal with claims for cargo loss, personal injuries, excess freight, etc. and prescribes procedures thereunder.

The Carriers Act, 1865

The Act defines the rights and liabilities of truck owners or operators who carry goods for public hire in respect of loss or damage to goods carried by them.

The Act also prescribes the time limit within which notice of loss or damage must be filed with the road carriers.

The Indian Post Office Act, 1898

This Act defines the liability of the Government for loss, misdelivery, delay of or damage to any postal articles in course of transmission by post.

The Carriage by Air Act, 1972

This Act gives effect to the provisions of the Warsaw Convention, 1929 and the Hague Protocol, 1955 relating to international carriage of passengers and goods by air.

The Act defines the liability of the air carrier for death of or injury to passengers and loss of or damage to registered luggage and cargo.

The Act also prescribes the maximum limits of liability for death, injury, damage etc. and also prescribes the time limits within which claims have to be filed on the air carrier.

The provisions of the Act also apply with some changes, to domestic carriage, that is, carriage within India.

Multi-modal Transportation Act, 1993

The Act provides for registration of multi-modal transport operators engaged in transportation of goods under more than one mode of transport, i.e., by rail/road and sea. The Act prescribes limits of liability of the operator, contents of documents to be issued by them, notice of loss, etc.

Workmen's Compensation Act, 1923

The Act provides for the payment by employers to their workmen of compensation for injury by accident, arising out of and in the course of employment. The object of this legislation has been stated as follows:

The growing complexity of industry in this country, with the increasing use of machinery and consequent danger to workmen, along with the comparative poverty of the workmen themselves render it advisable that they should be protected as far as possible, from hardship out of accidents.

It provides certain benefits to employees in case of accidents during employment, sickness, maternity etc.

Employees' State Insurance Act, 1948

The Employees' State Insurance Act, 1948, has been described as an Act "to provide for certain benefits to employees in cases of sickness, maternity and employment injury and to make provision for certain other matters in relation thereof "Under the Act, the Employees' State Insurance Corporation has been set up to administer the Insurance Scheme.

The Scheme is applicable to industrial employees as defined in the Act. The Act operated in certain industrial areas as notified by the Government from time to time. It is intended that the Act will be eventually extended to all industrial areas in the country. Under the scheme, a fund is maintained consisting of contributions from the employees, employers and the Government. From this fund, the following expenses are met:

(*i*) Sickness benefit, maternity benefit, disablement benefit, dependants' benefit (death) and medical treatment.

(*ii*) Establishment and maintenance of hospital, dispensaries, etc. for the benefit of the insured persons and their families.

(*iii*) Administration of the Scheme.

The Indian Stamp Act, 1899

The Indian Stamp Act requires that a policy of insurance be stamped in accordance with the schedule of rate prescribed.

The Consumer Protection Act, 1986

The Act applies to all goods and services unless specifically exempted by Central Government. The provisions of the Act are compensatory in nature.

It enshrines the following rights of the consumers:

(*i*) The right to be protected against the marketing of goods which are hazardous of life and property;

(*ii*) The right to be informed about the quality, quantity, potency, purity, standard and price of goods so as to protect the consumer against unfair trade practices;

(*iii*) The right to be heard and to be assured that consumers interest will receive due consideration at appropriate forum;

(*iv*) The right to seek redressal against unfair trade practices or unscrupulous exploitation of consumers;

(*v*) The right to consumer education.

Under Section 2(e) of the Act, the insurance is recognized as services. Chapter 32 of the Act elaborates various consumer rights.

Arbitration and Conciliation Act, 1996

Arbitration means the reference of a matter in dispute to the judgment of a person selected by the parties to the dispute. Arbitration thus is a private process of resolution of disputes and it is commonly resorted to because it is less formal, less expensive and less time-consuming than proceedings in a court of law.

An arbitration condition is incorporated in a majority of "Non-marine general insurance policies."

The main objectives of the Act, *inter alia*, are:

(*i*) To comprehensively cover international and commercial arbitration and conciliation as also domestic arbitration and conciliation;

(*ii*) To make provision for an arbitral procedure which is fair, efficient and capable of meeting the needs of the specific arbitration;

(*iii*) To provide that the arbitral tribunal gives reasons for its arbitral award;

(*iv*) To minimise the supervisory role of courts in the arbitral process;

(*v*) To permit an arbitral tribunal to use mediation, conciliation or other procedures during the arbitral proceedings to encourage settlement of disputes;

(*vi*) To provide that every final arbitral award is enforced in the same manner as if it were a decree of the court.

THE SECOND SCHEDULE
(See Section 31)

AMENDMENTS TO THE LIFE INSURANCE CORPORATION ACT, 1956 (31 of 1956)

1. In the Act, for "Controller" wherever it occurs, substitute "Authority".
2. After section 30, insert the following:

   "30A. *Exclusive privilege of Corporation to cease:* Notwithstanding anything contained in this Act, the exclusive privilege of carrying on life insurance business in India by the Corporation shall cease on and from commencement of the Insurance Regulatory and Development Authority Act, 1999 and the Corporation shall, thereafter, carry on life insurance business in India in accordance with the provisions of the Insurance Act, 1938 (4 of 1938).".

THE THIRD SCHEDULE
(See Section 32)

AMENDMENT TO THE GENERAL INSURANCE BUSINESS (NATIONALISATION) ACT, 1972 (57 of 1972)

After section 24, insert the following:

"24A. *Exclusive privilege of Corporation and acquiring companies to cease:* Notwithstanding anything contained in this Act, the exclusive privilege of the Corporation and the acquiring companies of carrying on general insurance business in India shall cease on an from the commencement of the Insurance Regulatory and Development Authority Act, 1999 and the Corporation and the acquiring companies shall, thereafter, carry on general insurance business in India in accordance with the provisions of the Insurance Act, 1938 (4 of 1938)."

Key Terms

- ❒ Licensing
- ❒ Rebate
- ❒ Registration
- ❒ Refund
- ❒ Investment
- ❒ Tariff Advisory Committee
- ❒ Assignment
- ❒ Commission
- ❒ Tribunal
- ❒ Committees
- ❒ Quorum
- ❒ Adjudicator
- ❒ Authorized Capital
- ❒ General Insurance Corporation of India
- ❒ Reinsurance
- ❒ Winding up
- ❒ Insurance Association of India
- ❒ Deposits
- ❒ Paid-up Capital
- ❒ Remuneration
- ❒ Controller
- ❒ Nomination
- ❒ Appointed Day
- ❒ Composite Insurer
- ❒ Controlled Business
- ❒ Insurance Regulatory and Development Authority
- ❒ Insurance Advisory Committee
- ❒ Acquiring Companies
- ❒ Memorandum and Articles of Association
- ❒ Subrogation

Questions for Review

1. Briefly explain the licensing procedure for insurers under the Insurance Act, 1938.
2. Write short notes on:
   (*a*) Accounts and Return
   (*b*) Advance Premium
   (*c*) Appointment of Agents/in light of the Insurance Act, 1938.

3. Enumerate the manner of investments by insurer as prescribed by the Insurance Act, 1938.
4. Discuss the various modes of winding up of insurance companies.
5. Briefly describe the functions of Life Insurance Corporation as enumerated in Life Insurance Corporation Act, 1956.
6. Write short notes on:
   (*a*) Controlled Business
   (*b*) LIC Regulations, 1959
7. Briefly describe the functions of GIC as per the provisions of General Insurance Business (Nationalization) Act, 1972.
8. Write short notes on:
   (*a*) Powers of Central Government
   (*b*) Formation of GIC

Suggested Readings

- *Bare Act – Insurance Act, 1938*
    - *Bare Act* – Life Insurance Corporation Act, 1956
    - *Bare Act* – Life Insurance Corporation Regulations, 1959.
- *Avtar Singh,* Law of Insurance, Eastern Book Company, 2004.
- *Law and Economics of Insurance,* IC87, Insurance Institute of India, Mumbai, 2003.
- *Bare Act*: General Insurance Business (Nationalization) Act, 1972.
- P.K. Gupta, *Insurance & Risk Management,* Himalaya Publishing House, Mumbai, 2004.
- Avtar Singh, *Law of Insurance,* Eastern Book Company, 2005.
- M.N. Srinivasan, *Principles of Insurance Law,* Wadwa & Company, Nagpur, 2006.

Web Resources

- *www.irdaindia*
- *www.bimaonline.com*
- *www.licindia.com*
- *www.licindia.com*

❑❑❑

CHAPTER

INSURANCE BUSINESS AND ECONOMIC ENVIRONMENT

Chapter Objectives

- The Economic Importance of Insurance
- Role of Insurance in the Economic System
- Contribution to indian economy
- Liberalisation of Insurance markets — Issues and concerns
- Accounting Principles for Preparation of Financial Statements
- Taxation Aspects of Insurance

Introduction

The primary purpose of insurance is to provide risk coverage, when the contract period extends over a long time, as in the case of life insurance, premium payments comprise of two components – one for buying risk coverage and the other towards savings. This bundling together of risk coverage and savings is peculiar to life insurance and is more common in developing countries like India. In the industrially advanced countries, this is not necessarily so and short duration life insurance contracts without a savings component are equally popular. In the developing economies because of the savings component and the long nature of the contract, life insurance has become an important instrument of mobilizing long-term funds. The savings component puts the life insurance in direct competition with other financial institutions and savings instruments.

Insurance and economic growth mutually influence each other. As the economy grows, the living standards of people increase. As a consequence, the demand for life insurance increases. As the assets of people and of business enterprises increase in the growth process, the demand for general insurance also increases. In fact, as the economy widens the demand for new types of insurance products emerges. Insurance is no longer confined to product markets; they also cover service industries. It is equally true that growth itself is facilitated by insurance. A well-developed insurance sector promotes economic growth by encouraging risk-taking.

Also insurance and more particularly life insurance is a mobilizer of long-term savings and life insurance companies are thus able to support infrastructure projects which require long-term funds. There is thus a mutually beneficial interaction between insurance and economic growth. The low income levels of the vast majority of population has been one of the factors inhibiting a faster growth of insurance in India.

As in the case of all financial institutions, insurance is an activity that needs to be regulated. This is so because the smooth functioning of business depends on the trust and confidence reposed by the customers in the solvency of the financial institutions. Insurance products are of little value to customers, if they cannot trust the company to keep its promise. The regulatory framework in relation to the insurance companies seeks to take care of three major concerns – *(a)* protection of consumers' interest, *(b)* to ensure the financial soundness of the insurance industry, and *(c)* to help the healthy growth of the insurance market.

8.1 The Economic Importance of Insurance

8.1.1 Risk Transfer

One of insurance's key roles is safeguarding the financial health of small and medium-sized enterprises. In addition to the protection provided by social security systems, private insurance cover is crucial for people to insure themselves against inability to work, set aside money for retirement or protect themselves against the loss of their assets. This is where insurance comes in as a key component in ensuring the healthy development of small and medium-sized enterprises — a fact which is of paramount importance to a country's political stability.

A sophisticated insurance sector is also important in encouraging domestic production, innovation and trade. Insurance reduces the investment risk faced by companies and the state. Many companies find it far more expensive, if not impossible, to take out a loan without purchasing the requisite insurance protection. Insured, thereby reduces the costs of raising the capital they need. This is especially important in emerging markets, as a shortage of capital is one of the major disincentives to investment. By reducing investment risk, insurance can also encourage companies to think more long term and increase their risk tolerance. A lot of investments in new production facilities and newly founded companies would never happen if every company was required to have the necessary financial means to make good every conceivable loss. While arguable, it is no exaggeration that the availability of insurance is sometimes being heralded as a factor of production in itself.

The same applies to infrastructure investments: if it weren't for insurance, a lot of infrastructure projects — such as power plants, railways or airports — would never be realised; because in the absence of sufficient financial funds to enable them to resume operations in the wake of a loss event, and without insurance, these projects would be reduced to nothing more than white elephants.

8.1.2 Information Role

Insurance plays an additional role in the economy: that of providing information. The level of insurance premiums provides an indication of existing risks and of how probable it is that a loss will occur. This helps companies make a comparison of the risk/return profiles of projects, thereby ensuring that the available resources are put to the best possible use. Insurance companies also offer consultancy services, advising on how to improve safety standards and a product's quality.

8.1.3 Capital Market Role

As well as stabilising the financial circumstances of private individuals, companies and the state, in their role as institutional investors, insurance companies contribute to the development of a well-functioning capital market thanks to the huge amount of assets they have to invest. Insurance companies receive premiums and set them aside as provisions for the payment of future claims. They proceed to invest them in the capital market, which gives them the status of major investors. From a macroeconomic point of view, the insurance market could help to mobilize national savings and narrow the investment gap of emerging economies. In emerging markets, domestic savings have not been fully mobilized despite huge funding needs arising from infrastructure projects, for example, Insurance companies as important long-term institutional investors, therefore functioning as financial intermediaries, contribute to bringing together savers and borrowers. Life insurance, in particular, can make savings available – although life insurers are themselves dependent on a functioning capital market if they are to measure up to their role in the area of risk transfer.

8.2 Contribution to Indian Economy

Insurance companies receive, without much default, a steady cash stream of premium or contributions to pension plans. Various actuary studies and models enable them to predict, relatively accurately, their expected cash outflows.

Liabilities of insurance companies being long-term or contingent in nature, liquidity is excellent and their investments are also long-term in nature.

As a combined result of all this, investments of insurance companies have been largely in bonds floated by GOI, PSUs, state governments, local bodies, corporate bodies and mortgages of long-term nature.

The insurance industry also provides crucial financial intermediary services, transferring funds from the insured to capital investment, critical for continued economic expansion and growth, simultaneously generating long-term funds for infrastructure development.

In fact, infrastructure investments are ideal for asset-liability matching for life insurance companies given their long-term liability profile. According to preliminary estimates published by the Reserve Bank of India, contribution of insurance funds to financial savings was 14.2 per cent in 2005-06, viz., 2.4 per cent of the GDP at current market prices. Development of the insurance sector is thus necessary to support continued economic transformation. Social security and pension reforms too benefit from a mature insurance industry.

Employment Generation

Life insurance industry provides increased employment opportunities. Employees in insurance sector as on 31st March, 2005 is around 2 lakhs. Many agents depend on insurance for their livelihood. No. of agents on 31st March 2004 – 15.59 lakhs. Brokers, corporate agents, training establishments provide extra employment opportunities. Many of these openings are in rural sectors. Let us have a look at global figures (Exhibit 8.1).

Exhibit – 8.1

Employment in Insurance, 2004-2008

(Annual averages, 000)

2004	764.4	604.4	29.8	1,398.6	643.3	216.8	860.1	2,258.6	47.0
2005	761.9	595.0	28.8	1,385.7	650.1	223.5	873.6	2,259.3	46.4
2006	787.4	597.4	28.0	1,412.8	659.9	230.9	890.8	2,303.7	47.8
2007	784.0	586.1	27.0	1,397.1	675.3	234.5	909.8	2,306.8	48.6
2008	804.2	569.2	28.4	1,401.8	670.1	236.9	907.0	2,308.8	49.2

Source: US Department of Labor, Bureau of Labor Statistics.

1. Establishments primarily engaged in initially underwriting insurance policies.
2. Includes claims adjusters, third-party administrators of insurance funds and other service personnel such as advisory and insurance rate-making services.
3. Includes employees of legal entities organized to provide insurance and employee benefits exclusively for the sponsor, or its employees or members. These employees are not included in the total for the insurance industry.

8.3 Role of Insurance in the Economic System

In a modern economic and financial system, the insurance sector plays three main roles. First, it provides individuals, corporations and other organizations with a mechanism for transferring some of the non-entrepreneurial risks that they face. Second, it provides a means for mobilizing long-term savings and investing them profitably in the capital market, thus indirectly stimulating the growth of the capital market itself. Third, it complements state social insurance programmes, especially in the areas of pensions, disability and health care financing.

Insurance companies provide an effective risk transfer mechanism. They can bring together a large portfolio of insurable risks where the incidence of these losses are reasonably independent of each other, and thus reduce the overall risk through portfolio diversification, i.e., the law of large numbers. In order to underwrite these risks, insurance companies must be able to price them. This means collecting credible information to allow them to estimate the frequency and severity of figure losses. In addition, the risk absorption capacity of individual insurance companies is increased dramatically through reinsurance. Reinsurance is a well-established network of risk sharing between insurance companies allowing large risk exposures to be spread not just within a national market but globally. Hence, the collective capital and risk assessment resource of the world insurance market can be drawn on to finance catastrophic losses.

Insurance companies plays a major role in mobilizing small-scale savings from across the economy, which can collectively appreciate substantially if well invested in the capital market. Insurance companies generate private sector saving in a variety of ways. First, all insurance contracts, whether life or non-life (property and casualty) insurance, give rise to some form of private saving. This arises primarily from insurance premiums being paid in advance by customers, while claims and policy settlements paid back to consumers at a later date, after covering operating and marketing costs. This time-lag between the receipt of premiums and return payments to consumers varies between different classes of insurance. Clearly, the time-lag is longer for life insurance contracts than for non-life insurance contracts, hence the accumulation of investable funds is higher. In addition, the plough back of investment returns earned on the accumulation of these invested funds by insurance companies also contributes to the total level of saving. Second, life insurance contracts, especially endowment and linked-life policies and those concerned with pension provision, have a more significant saving element.

An important aspect of the insurance risk transfer mechanism is that not only do insurance companies have access through reinsurance to a network of other insurers but also that large potential losses can be spread across domestic and international markets. Essentially, the mechanism of reinsurance is one of accessing the capital of other insurance companies. When an insurance company buys reinsurance, the premium paid is effectively a payment for the use of the capital of the reinsurer. Due to reinsurance, therefore, the capital of a national insurançe market is extended internationally since it allows domestic insurance companies access to the combined capital base of the global reinsurance market.

Economic Benefits of an Efficient Risk Transfer Mechanism

Transferring insurable risks onto efficient insurance markets has potential benefits in the following ways. When operating in competitive markets, industrial, commercial and trading enterprises have to take business risks in order to make profits. By being able to transfer some of the risks associated with these commercial and investment decisions, the decision-taking process is made less risky. Hence, decision makers faced with less uncertainty will be more prepared to undertake more adventurous and potentially more profitable activities. Insurance markets also provide protection against some of the risks associated with international trade, e.g., damage or loss of goods in transit and credit risks associated with non-payment by foreign customers. Cargo marine insurance and international credit insurance thus helps to lubricate the flow of international trade.

The risks transfer facility provided by insurance companies can be viewed in terms of the efficient use of capital. Industrial, commercial and trading enterprises would have to hold more precautionary capital to run their enterprises if there were no insurance markets. In effect, insurance companies supply contingent equity capital to industrial and commercial enterprises. This means that across the economy as a whole less equity capital is needed to support for banks in their role as financial intermediaries. One area of companies also provide some risk support for banks in their role as financial intermediaries. One area of support is the risk transfer facilities provided by credit insurance. Credit insurance is input into the supply of banking lending products. In addition, when commercial and mortgage banks have sought to increase the liquidity within their asset portfolios through the securitization of their loans, the bonds issued from this process have often been purchased by life insurance companies. Long-term liabilities, and strong cash flow positions, mean that life insurance companies are "natural" investors in the capital market. This transfer of long-term interest rate risk through loan securitizations into life insurance companies indirectly stimulates the development of the capital market.

Life insurance has historically been an important method through which individuals with relatively low incomes have been able to save and invest effectively for the longer term. By designing relatively simple life insurance and savings contracts, which can be purchased in small amounts on a regular basis, insurance companies have been able to accumulate large amounts to money from across a large proportion of population. By pooling these savings from many small investors into large accumulations of funds, insurance companies are able to invest these in a wider range of financial assets than individuals would be able to do so themselves, as well as in larger scale and more uncertain investment opportunities. This pooling benefit to individuals is not unique to life insurance. It is provided by other saving instruments, especially collective investments (CIS). In addition, because in life insurance there is a regular or contractual payment by consumers, the level and stability of personal saving may be increased, compared to what would be the case if the saving arrangement were more discretionary in nature. Life insurance companies often have active marketing strategies that encourage myopic individuals to save rather than consume. However, aggressive marketing strategies are sometimes used and this can lead to consumers purchasing inappropriate saving products. This is a negative aspect of active marketing, but these adverse effects can be minimized by a combination of statutory regulation, market self-regulation and sound corporate governance system for insurance companies and other institutional investors. Evidence exists that an active life insurance sector increases the level of long-term saving in emerging economies, not least because it provides an alternative to bank deposits for smaller investors, but also because the CIS sector does not develop until the capital market itself is relatively well developed (see Chapter 15 on Capital Markets).

Economic Benefits of the Saving and Investment Role

What are the wider economic benefits derived from the stimulation of private sector saving and its subsequent investment in the capital market? Firstly, these savings can be made available, either in the form of equity or debt capital, to manufacturing, agricultural, energy, trading or service enterprises. New companies can be set up and finance is available for existing companies to increase their level of capital expenditure in new plant, equipment etc. Moreover, particularly for life insurance, since the time horizons for investment are long-term, these savings can be tied up for a long period of time and hence can be made available for capital expenditure decisions that will only produce profits in the future. Since banks can frequently only provide short-term finance to manufacturing and other enterprises, this investment activity of life insurance complements the lending practices of the banking system because of the short-term nature of their deposits.

The long-term savings generated by life insurance companies can also be made available to help fund large-scale projects to strengthen economic infrastructure. Such infrastructure investment is especially important in emerging economies not only to underpin the growth of domestic enterprises but also to encourage foreign companies to enter the market and invest further. Other possible financial assets for insurance companies are government bonds and mortgage or mortgage-backed securities. The latter stimulate the development of the housing market.

In many OECD and emerging market economies (EMEs), governments are seeking to reform their social security or social insurance systems to reduce the current and future burden of these systems on government finances. Pressures for reform arise from a combination of factors: demographic changes, rising standards of living, and increasing public expectations. Retirement provision, health care and disability support feature as a major component of social security budgets. Through these reforms, the insurance sector and other parts of the financial services industry are increasingly being seen as potential government partners. Pension and annuity schemes, private heath insurance and accident and disability insurances are core business of insurance companies.

Insurance is of primordial importance in domestic economies and internationally. The role of insurance in the development process is difficult to access but there is some evidence that the promotion of insurance programmes might have a particularly significant impact on the level of personal saving in many developing countries.

Exhibit – 8.2

Insurance as a Percentage of GDP

	Premiums (in USD mn) 2007	*Premiums in % of GDP 2007*
America	1,417,463	7.58
North America	1,330,066	8.71
Latin America and Caribbean	87,397	2.54
Europe	1,680,693	8.03
Western Europe	1,606,324	8.85
Central and Eastern Europe	74,369	2.78
Asia	840,601	6.20
Japan and newly industrialized Asian economies	640,754	10.38
South and East Asia	176,654	3.05
Middle East and Central Asia	23,193	1.45
Africa	68,818	6.58
Oceania	53,294	4.31
World	4,060,870	7.49
Industrialized countries	3,646,523	9.05
Emerging markets	414,347	2.75
OECD	3,586,703	8.65
G7	2,852,637	9.22
EU, 15 countries	1,527,535	9.16
NAFTA	1,347,482	8.34
ASEAN	41,358	3.17

Source: Swiss Re, Economic Research & Consulting, Sigma No. 4/2007.

The economic significance of the insurance industry in a country is commonly evaluated by means of the ratio of premiums to the gross domestic products (GDP). Although this measure of insurance penetration does not give a complete picture of the insurance output because of the considerable variation in premiums rates between different countries, it has the advantage of not being influenced by currency factors. (Exhibit 8.2)

Grace and Skipper (1991) found that the income elasticity for developing countries was lower than the income elasticity for developed countries suggesting that as countries progress economically, non-life insurance becomes relatively more important.

In fact, individual country experiences are too heterogeneous to accord neatly with any very simple generalization and very little is known about the demand and supply relationship in these countries (Grace and Skipper, 1991). Some societies have achieved high levels of human development at modest levels of per capita income.

Insurance and GDP

The relationship between the insurance density and GDP is direct. Insurance density varies directly with GDP. Have a look at Exhibit 8.3.

Exhibit 8.3

International Comparison (Insurance Penetration)

Countries	*Insurance Penetration (Premiums as % of GDP-1999)*			*Insurance Penetration (Premiums as % of GDP 2000)*		
	Total	*Non-life*	*Life*	*Total*	*Non-life*	*Life*
United States	8.55	4.32	4.23	8.76	4.28	4.48
Canada	6.49	3.31	3.19	6.56	3.28	3.27
Brazil	2.01	1.66	0.35	2.11	1.75	0.36
Mexico	1.68	0.86	0.82	1.72	0.85	0.86
Chile	3.78	1.13	2.65	4.07	1.15	2.92
United Kingdom	13.35	3.05	10.30	15.78	3.07	12.71
Germany	6.52	3.55	2.96	6.54	3.55	3.00
France	8.52	2.82	5.70	9.40	2.81	6.59
Russia	2.13	1.34	0.78	2.42	1.29	1.13
Japan	11.17	2.30	8.87	10.92	2.22	8.70
South Korea	11.18	2.89	8.39	13.05	3.16	9.89
PR China	1.63	0.61	1.02	1.79	0.67	1.12
India	1.93	0.54	1.39	2.32	0.55	1.77
Malaysia	3.88	1.72	2.16	3.72	1.59	2.13
Indonesia	1.42	0.76	0.66	1.18	0.64	0.54
South Africa	16.54	2.62	13.92	16.86	2.83	14.04
Nigeria	0.95	0.88	0.07	0.66	0.53	0.13
Kenya	3.26	2.48	0.78	2.63	1.91	0.72
Australia	9.82	3.39	6.43	9.41	3.37	6.04

Source: Swiss Re, SIGMA volumes 9/2000 and 6/2001.

The statistics shows that the penetration is extremely low in India compared to our Asian partners like Japan and South Korea. This indicates a huge potential for Indian Insurance Market.

Insurance and Income Redistribution

Life insurance essential serves to transfer funds from currently employed persons via premium payments to unemployed persons, and thereby helps alleviate the problem of economic distress. Insurance proceeds on an important element in the economic well-being of dependents Government-sponsored insurance programmes strive to comprehensive achieve social goals while private programme provide attractive alternative to public welfare system.

Inflation, Business Cycles and Insurance

Inflation and business recessions directly reduces the real purchasing power and network of the people respectively. Insurance can provide a cover to these, yet the negative side is the adverse impact on the financial performance of companies.

Population Changes and Insurance

Population changes materially affects the insurance industry because of the economic consequences of changing rates of birth, death, marriage and family formation. The shifting age distribution affects the kinds and amount of insurance the people will buy.

Exhibit 8.4

STATEMENT 3

INTERNATIONAL COMPARISON OF INSURANCE DENSITY*

(In US dollar)

Country	2008**			2007**		
	Total	*Life*	*Non-life*	*Total*	*Life*	*Non-life*
Australia	3386.5	2038.0	1348.6	3000.2	1674.1	1326.1
Brazil	244.5	115.4	129.1	202.2	95.3	106.9
Canada	3170.8	1442.7	1728.0	3053.8	1386.8	1667.0
France	4131.0	2791.9	1339.2	4147.6	2928.3	1219.3
Germany	2919.2	1346.5	1572.7	2662.1	1234.1	1427.9
Netherlands	6849.5	2366;0	4483.5	6262.9	2192.4	4070.5
Russia	273.5	5.4	268.1	209.4	6.1	203.3
South Africa	870.6	707.0	163.6	878.5	719.0	159.5
Switzerland	6379.4	3551.5	2827.9	5740.7	3159.1	2581.7
United Kingdom	6857.8	5582.1	1275.7	7113.7	5730.5	1383.2
United States	4078.0	1900.6	2177.4	4086.5	1922.0	2164.4
Asian countries						
Hong Kong	3310.3	2929.6	380.8	3373.2	3031.9	341.3
Japan	3698.6	2869.5	829.2	3319.9	2583.9	736.0
Malaysia	345.4	225.9	119.5	332.1	221.5	110.6
Singapore	3179.0	2549.0	630.0	2776.0	2244.7	531.2

South Korea	1968.7	1347.7	621.0	2384.0	1656.6	727.3
Taiwan	2787.6	2281.1	499.6	2628.0	2165.7	462.3
Thailand	142.1	77.2	64.9	129.7	70.8	58.9
India ##	**47.4**	**41.2**	**6.2**	**46.6**	**40.4**	**6.2**
Bangladesh	4.4	3.3	1.1	2.9	1.9	0.9
Indonesia	29.5	20.1	9.4	30.0	20.4	9.5
Iran	58.8	4.0	54.8	49.2	3.0	46.2
Pakistan	6.8	2.8	4.0	6.5	2.6	3.9
Phillipines	25.6	16.2	9.5	23.9	15.1	8.8
PR China	105.4	71.7	33.7	69.9	44.2	25.5
Sri Lanka	32.1	12.8	19.3	24.9.	10.2	14.7
World	**633.9**	**369.7**	**264.2**	**607.7**	**358.1**	**249.6**

Source: Swiss Re, Sigma volumes 3/2008 and *312009*

* Insurance density is measured as ratio of premium (in US Dollar) to total population

** Data relates to calender year

##: data pertains to the financial year.

TABLE 2

INSURANCE PENETRATION AND DENSITY IN INDIA

Year	*Life*		*Non-Life*		*Industry*	
	Density (USD)	*Penetration (% age)*	*Density (USD)*	*Penetration (% age)*	*Density (USD)*	*Penetration (% age)*
2001	*9.1*	*2.15*	*2.4*	*0.56*	*11.5*	*2.71*
2002	*11.7*	*2.59*	*3.0*	*0.67*	*14.7*	*3.26*
2003	*12.9*	*2.26*	*3.5*	*0.62*	*16.4*	*2.88*
2004	*15.7*	*2.53*	*4.0*	*0.64*	*19.7*	*3.17*
2005	*18.3*	*2.53*	*4.4*	*0.61*	*22.7*	*3.14*
2006	*33.2*	*4.10*	*5.2*	*0.60*	*38.4*	*4.80*
2007	*40.4'*	*4.00*	*5.2*	*0.60*	*46.6*	*4.70*
2008	*41.2*	*4.00*	*6.2*	*0.60*	*47.4*	*4.60*
2009	*47.7*	*4.60*	*6.7*	*0.60*	*54.3*	*5.20*

Insurance density is measured as ratio of premium (in US Dollar) to total population.

Insurance penetration is measured as ratio of premium (in US Dollars) to GDP (in US Dollars).

Source: Swiss Re. Various Issues.

Fiscal Policy

Fiscal Policy affects an Insurance sector in the following form:

(1) Government spending

(2) Taxation

(3) Direct Controls on the business systems

(4) Moral Suasion (assistance).

8.4 Liberalization of Insurance Markets — Issues and Concerns

Opening of the insurance sector pose certain issues before every government and of course for India. Let us have a look at liberalization — its meaning and implications.

Meaning

A liberal insurance market is one in which the market, subject only to economically justifiable government restrictions, determines; who should be allowed to sell insurance, what products should be sold, how product should be sold, and the prices at which products should be sold. The first item, therefore, deals with issues such as market access and equality of competitive opportunity, including national treatment. In turn, market access issues encompass prudential regulation. Second and fourth items commonly deal with issues such as product, price, and market conduct regulation. All four items subsume competition regulation.

Preconditions for Liberalization

(*a*) Sound competition law.

(*b*) Efficient and reliable regulation.

(*c*) Phased liberalization.

(*d*) Consistency and impartiability between competitors.

(*e*) Optimum quantum of regulation.

(*f*) Efficient disclosure and dissemination of information to the society.

For developing countries, the regulation of insurance business in liberalization era possess following concerns and special interests.

(*a*) restrictions on entry, especially foreign players;

(*b*) suppression of price and product competition; and

(*c*) control of inter-industry competition from those selling similar or complementary products."

Insurance markets in countries like India inherently possess certain imperfections justifying the need for competition as well as regulation. This is attributable of the following reasons:

(*a*) Lack of knowledge on part of insureds.

(*b*) Insurance is a technical, complicated subject.

(*c*) Intensity of price discrimination is high when there is a competition.

(*d*) Externalities is cause of concern.

(*e*) Government sponsored free insurance huts, private insurance markets and thus causes imperfection.

8.5 Accounting Principles for Preparation of Financial Statements

Every insurance company is required to prepare the financial statements and make disclosures from 30th March, 2002 onwards in accordance with the guidelines of IRDA titled The Insurance

Regulatory and Development Authority (Preparation of Financial Statements and Auditors' Report of Insurance Companies) Regulations, 2002.

The formats of the financial statements applicable as per the said guidelines are:

1. For Life Insurance Business [Schedule A Part V]
   - *(a)* Revenue Account [Policyholder's Account] — Form No. A-RA
   - *(b)* Profit and Loss Account [Shareholders' Account] — Form No. A-PL
   - *(c)* Balance Sheet — Form No. A-BS
2. For General Insurance Business [Schedule B Part V]
   - *(a)* Revenue Account — Form No. B-RA
   - *(b)* Profit and Loss Account [Shareholders' Account] — Form No. B-PL
   - *(c)* Balance Sheet — Form No. B-BS

In addition, as per the guidelines, every life insurance company has to comply with the requirements of Schedule A and every general insurance company has to comply with the requirements of Schedule B. Also, the auditor's report has to be prepared in accordance with Schedule C of the guidelines.

8.6 Taxation Aspects of Insurance

Income Tax for Life Insurance Policyholders

Rebate under Sec. 80C

The following are the important income-tax provisions applicable to Life Insurance policyholders:

- An LIC policy can be taken in the name of an individual or any member of a Hindu Undivided Family (HUF).
- An individual can claim rebate on LIC premium paid on his/her life, his/her spouse, his/her children including adult children.

Under Sec. 80C of the Income Tax Act, 1961, a rebate of 20% is allowed on the life insurance premium paid by the assessee under the said act. This rebate is deductible from the total tax payable by the individual/HUF. This total amount of investment in the form of the LIC premium and other specified investment like PPF, NSC, etc. is restricted to ₹ 1,00,000/- per annum (Assessment year 2008-09).

The aforesaid sums qualify, for the purpose of this section, on the "payment" basis. Even in the case of an assessee, following mercantile system of accounting, payments, which have become due during the previous year but are outstanding on the last day of the previous year, are not eligible for deductions.

Termination of the Unit-linked Insurance Plan before Five Years

Where a member participating in the unit-linked plan terminates his participation before making contribution for a period of 5 years,. no tax deductions will be allowed in respect of contributions made in such year. Moreover, an amount equal to an aggregate of tax deductions allowed in respect of the contributions to the plan in the past years shall be deemed as tax payable by the assessee of the previous year in which he terminates his participation in the plan.

Discontinuation of the Insurance Plan before Two Years

Where a taxpayer discontinues a policy of the life insurance, before the premium for 2 years have been paid, no tax deductions will be allowed in respect of any premium paid on that policy in the year in which the policy is terminated. Further, the amount of tax deduction allowed in respect of the premium paid in respect of the policy in the year preceding that year will be deemed to be the tax payable by the assess of the year in which the policy is terminated.

In case of the single premium policy, if such policy is surrendered with two years of the date of the commencement of insurance, the amount of deduction of income tax allowed earlier shall be deemed to be the tax payable in the year of surrender.

Deduction in Respect of Pension Fund — When Available (Sec. 80CCC) (Jeevan Suraksha Policy)

- Provision of the Sec. 80CCC of the Act are applicable to all taxpayers being individuals (may be resident, or non-resident, Indian citizen or foreign citizen).
- During the previous year, the assessee has paid/deposited a sum under an annuity of the Life Insurance Corporation of India for receiving pension from the fund set up by the said corporation as approved by the Controller of Insurance.
- The aforesaid amount is paid out of the income chargeable to tax.
- Amount of the Deduction: If the aforesaid conditions are satisfied, the amount deposited or ₹ 10,000, whichever is lower, is deductible.
- The amount received by the assessee or his nominee, as pension will be taxable in the hands of the assessee or the nominee, as the case may be, in the year of the receipt.
- Rebate (with reference to the amount paid under Sec. 80CCC) will not be available under Sec. 88 to persons to whom deduction under this section has been allowed.
- Under Sec. 80 DDA, a deduction up to ₹ 20,000 per annum is allowed from the gross total income, when the contributions or deposits is made with LIC for the maintenance of a handicapped dependent.

Keyman Insurance [Sec. 37(1)]

The premium paid by the company is allowed as a 100% deductible business expenditure u/s 37(1) of the Income Tax Act.

The proceeds received by the company at the time of the maturity or death of the keyman is treated as income of the company and will be subjected to the tax.

When the company assigns policy to keyman for "No consideration" as a retirement benefit, the surrender value proceeds received by the keyman is treated as additional salary and hence tax has to be paid by the keyman.

Partnership Insurance

The insurance premium under partnership insurance on the lives of the partners is allowed as 100% business expenditure u/s 37(1) of the Act.

However, the policy proceeds on the death claims will be treated as an income of the firm and is subjected to tax.

Sum Received from Life Insurance Policy [Sec. 10(10D)]

- According to Sec. 10(10D), any sum received under a life insurance policy, including a sum allocated by the way of bonus on such policy, shall not be included in the total income of the person.
- The exemption is, however, not available in respect of such policy which is specified under Sec. 80 DDA(3) or under a keyman insurance policy.

Non-Life Insurance

Medical Insurance Premium [Sec. 80D]

- The taxpayer is an individual (may be resident, or non-resident, Indian citizen or foreign citizen) or a Hindu Undivided Family (may be resident, or non-resident).
- Insurance premium is paid by the taxpayer in accordance with the scheme framed in this behalf by the GIC of India and approved by the Central Government. The scheme is known as "Mediclaim" insurance policy.
- The aforesaid premium is paid by cheque.
- It is paid out of income chargeable to tax.
- Mediclaim policy is taken on the health of the following persons:

Taxpayer	*Insured person*
Individual	On the health of the taxpayer, on the health of the spouse dependent parents or dependent children of the tax payer.
Hindu Undivided Family	On the health of any member of the family.

- If the aforesaid conditions are satisfied, then the insurance premium paid or ₹ 15,000. whichever is lower is deductible.

Insurance Claim Received for Damage or Destruction of a Capital Asset [Sec. 45 (1A)]

- The insurance claim received on account of destruction of asset is not chargeable to tax, as "destruction" does not amount to transfer. The newly inserted subsection (1A) provides that where any person receives any money or other assets under any insurance from an insurer on account of damage to or destruction of any capital asset, as a result of flood, typhoon, hurricane, cyclone, earthquake or other convulsion of nature, riot or civil disturbance, accidental fire or explosion or because of actions by the enemy or actions taken in combating the enemy, then any profits or gains arising from receipts of such money or other assets shall be chargeable to income tax under the head "Capital Gains" and shall be deemed to be the income of such person in the previous year in which such money or other asset is received.

Insurance Premium [Sec. 36(1)(i)]

- The amount of any premium paid in respect of insurance against risk of damage or destruction of stocks or stores, used for purposes of business or profession, is allowed as deduction.

Insurance Premium Paid by a Federal Milk Co-operative Society [Sec. 36(i)(ia)]

- Insurance premium paid by the federal milk co-operative society on the lives of cattle, owned by the members of a primary milk co-operative society affiliated to it, is allowable as deduction.

Premia for Insurance on Health of Employees [Sec. 36 (i)(ib)]

- An employer can claim deduction in respect of premia paid by him by cheque for insurance on the health of his employees in accordance with the scheme framed by the General Insurance Corporation and approved by the Central Government.
- In the last budget, there was a proposal to charge service tax to the insurance premium paid by the insured. The service tax for the insurance premium was proposed to be levied at a rate of 5%. This could act as a serious impediment to the growing insurance business. However, it was later on agreed not to charge any service tax on insurance premia.

Income Tax for LIC Agents

The LIC agents can earn commission by procuring business. The commission, generally, is in nature of first year commission, renewal commission and bonus commission. The commission earned is an income, which may be taxable depending on the total income.

- If the income from all sources including LIC commission does not exceed ₹ 50,000 per annum, then one is not liable to pay income tax as it is below taxable limit.
- If the commission earned from LIC is below ₹ 60,000 per annum and if no separate books of accounts is maintained, then the entitlement for deduction is as follows:
  - *(a)* First year Commission – 50%
  - *(b)* Renewal Commission – 15%
- However, if separate bifurcation could be made then LIC agent is entitled to a flat deduction of $33^1/3$% of total commission.
- The LIC commission after claiming deduction as mentioned above will be included with other source of income for tax purposes.
- In case gross commission earned by an agent from LIC exceeds ₹ 60,000 per annum, then he cannot claim deduction referred above.

Income from other Sources [Sec. 56(2)]

As per the provisions of Sec. 56(2) of the Act, income received in the form of insurance commission is chargeable to tax under the head of "Income from other sources." Income chargeable under this head is computed in accordance with the method of accounting regularly employed by the assessee. This head of income can be evoked only if all the following conditions are met:

- There is an income;
- That income is not exempt from tax under Sec. 10 to 13A;
- That income is neither salary income, nor rental income from house property, nor income from business/profession, nor capital gains.

Tax is to be Deducted at Source from Insurance Commission [Sec. 194(D)]

- A person responsible for paying to a resident any income by the way of remuneration or reward, whether by the way of commission or otherwise, for soliciting or procuring insurance business including business relating to the continuance, renewal or revival of policies of insurance, is required to deduct income tax thereon at the rates in force (10% for the A.Y. 2002-03).
- Tax shall be deducted a the time of credit of such income to the account of the payee or the payment thereof (by whatever mode), whichever is earlier.
- No tax is required to be deducted at source if the insurance commission credited or paid during the financial year does not exceed ₹ 5,000/-.
- The person receiving insurance commission can make an application in Form No. 13 to the concerned Assessing Officer and obtain a certificate authorizing the person responsible for making payments, by the way of insurance commission, to deduct tax at a lower rate or to deduct no tax, as may be appropriate.

Taxation of Insurance Companies

Section 44 of the Income Tax Act 1961, read with first schedule of the Act deals with taxation of life Insurance business. Till 1976, Life Insurance business was taxed on the higher of Profit on investment income less expenses or Valuation surplus (excluding prior year's surplus or deficit) less 80% of bonuses declared or amounts reserved for policyholders. In the Budget of 1976 government abandoned 'higher of the two' system and adopted the annual average of the surplus disclosed by the actuarial valuation under the Insurance Act, 1938, after excluding from it any surplus or deficit included therein relating to any earlier inter-valuation period. The taxable income so determined is taxed at a flat rate of 12.5% prescribed under the first Schedule of the IT Act. This rate is not affected by the Annual Finance Acts and has remained unchanged since 1977.

Taxation of Life Insurance Companies

The Life Insurance Corporation made a formal representation in February 1974 to the government that the basis of assessment of life insurance should be simplified and in this regard the representation was referred to the Central Board of Direct Taxes (CBDT). One of the important points that emerged in the meeting of the Consultative Committee of the Ministry of Finance, held in December 1974, was that the gross valuation surplus should be the only basis for taxation and the tax should be equal to a specified percentage of a gross surplus. This change came into effect from April 1, 1977. Sec. 115B of the Income-tax Act states that:

- Where the total income of an assessee includes any profits and gains from life insurance business, the income-tax payable shall be the aggregate of the amount generated.
- The amount of income-tax calculated on the amount of profits and gains of the life insurance business included in the total income, at the rate of twelve-and-one-half per cent, and
- The amount of income-tax with which the assessee would have been chargeable had the total income of the assessee been reduced by the amount of profits and gains of the life insurance business.

"With this change in the method of taxation, two rates of tax have been introduced. A rate of 12.5 per cent on the computed profits and gains of life insurance business. The normal corporate rate on the net income in the shareholders' fund after excluding the profits from life insurance business."

Key Terms

- Insurance Density
- Liberalization
- Bottomry Contracts
- Inflation
- Insurance Density
- Macroeconomic Issues
- Respondentia
- Population
- GDP
- Fiscal Policy
- IRDA Act, 1999
- Insurance Reforms
- Malhotra Committee

Questions for Review

1. Explain the importance of insurance sector to the economy.
2. What are the necessary conditions for liberalization?
3. Trace the history of Indian Insurance industry for the period 1818-1999. What are your comments on the present state of Insurance Market?
4. Write short notes on:
   (a) Insurance Sector Reforms
   (b) Insurance Player in India
5. "From a global perspective insurance has emerged as a business risk management device to a highly sophisticated risk transfer mechanism for both individuals and corporations." Discuss.

Suggested Readings

1. D.C. Srivastava and S. Srivastava, *Indian Insurance Industry — Transition and Prospects,* New Century Publications, 2001.
2. *IRDA Annual Report,* 2001-02.

3. Spencer L. Kimbell and Herbert S. Demenberg, *Insurance, Government and Social Policy: Studies in Insurance Regulation,* The S.S. Haubner Foundation for Insurance Education, 1969.

4. Irving Pfeffer and David R. Klock, *Perspective on Insurance,* Prentice-Hall, Englewood Cliffs, 1994.

Web Resources

- www.bimaonline.com
- www.bajajallianz.com
- www.tata-aig.com
- www.hdfc.com

❑❑❑

CHAPTER

UNDERWRITING PROCESS AND METHODS

Chapter Objectives

- Underwriting Defined
- Underwriting in Life Insurance
- The Objectives and principles of Underwriting
- Underwriting in Non-life Insurance

Introduction

Underwriting as an art began in the United Kingdom since Victorian times. Where upon a group of sailors/traders began the practice to insure against the perils involved in a sea voyage, it included the insuring of the goods in transit against known perils such as piracy, weather perils and goods getting destroyed in the voyage against the payment of a pre-agreed sum by the trader(s). The practice evolved with the times and the insurance model took shape. In the early days of marine insurance, the details of a ship or cargo to be insured were described on a slip. This slip was taken to Lloyd's and the person, who was to carry the risk read the details, then signed the slip under the details of the risk. In this way, the person carrying the risk became known as the *underwriter*. The genesis of the insurance business also evolved from the United Kingdom and the first insurers were the Lloyd's industries.

9.1 Underwriting Defined

Underwriting is the prices of selecting and classifying exposures. It is directly related to rate-making or the pricing function of an insurer, because computed rates contemplate some composition of loss-producing characteristics to which they will be applied.

Underwriting is the insurance function that is responsible for assessing and classifying the degree of risk a proposed insured or group represents and making a decision concerning coverage of that risk.[1]

Underwriting includes all the activities necessary to select risks offered to the insurer in such a manner that general company objectives are fulfilled.

The person responsible for evaluation and acceptance/rejection of risks and computation of premium is called as the *underwriter*. Accordingly, the decision made by the underwriter concerning risk classification and rating is called as the *underwriting* decision. Underwriting decisions are crucial for insurers since they can make or mar an insurance company. Good underwriting helps the insurance companies in many ways. It make them financially stronger and helps secure competitive advantage. This is obvious in the sense that if risks are assessed properly, pricing will be effective and therefore the company can well compete and build up reputation.

In life insurance business, underwriting is performed by home or regional office personnel, who scrutinize applications for coverage and make decisions as to whether they will be accepted, and by agents, who produce the applications initially in the field, but these decisions may be subject to post underwriting at a higher level because the contracts are cancellable on due notice to the insured. In life insurance, agents seldom have authority to make binding underwriting decisions. In all fields of insurance, however, agency personnel usually do considerable screening of risks before submitting them to home office underwriters.

9.1.1 The Trade-off

The underwriting exercise is a trade-off between the business and survival. If the insurance company sets high standards for risk which can be undertaken, the company may loose market and consequentially, the potential premium income which can be threat to survival. If the insurance company charges too much of premium in a fashion that is become excessive, the company will loose competitive advantage. Also, if the company undertakes risk with a loose assessment in a zeal to get business, it may be dangerous because the possibility of claims may increase substantially. Hence and therefore, a proper balance is to be maintained between business and good business.

9.1.2 The Conflict

The conflict between production and underwriting are common to insurance companies. The underwriting department may have turned down business that has been previously sold by an agent, an apparent conflict of interest arises between these two areas. The problem is similar to that which exists between credit and sales in other firms, with a good sale ruined because credit is not approved. Neither the agent nor the underwriter will profit long by underwriting that is too strict or too loose. The former will choke off acceptable business and may create unnecessary expenses in cancelling business already bound by the agent, whereas the latter invites such substantial losses that the company may be forced to withdraw entirely from a given line, to the detriment of the agent.

1. Gene Stone, *Insurance Company Operations,* LOMA 2000, p. 234.

9.1.3 Guiding Principles

The two main principles of underwriting are *Adverse Selection* and *Persistency*. The underwriter must always guard himself against the adverse selection of risks. There is tendency on part of the potential insureds, those who are more likely to be affected by the happening of the adverse event, to go for insurance cover compared to ones who are well off. For example – *Ceteris Paribus*, a healthy person is less likely to go for an insurance cover than the one who becomes frequently ill. Accordingly, the potential business for the insurers would represent these class. Therefore, the underwriter should carefully appraise the inherent risk in such cases and fix the premium so as to avoid likely significant losses.

In addition, the underwriter must not offer products which the consumers cannot afford. Also the premium fixed for the insureds must be consistent enough to support the cash flow model of the insurers. The continuous renewal of policies is must to business retention. The underwriter should carefully examine the paying capacity of the potential customer before offering a product, if large number of policies are surrendered or lapsed, the company will be ruined.

9.2 The Objectives and Principles of Underwriting

The primary objective of underwriting is to see that the applicant accepted will not have a loss experience that is very different from that assumed when the rates were formulated. To this end, certain standards of selection relating to physical and moral hazards are set up when rates are calculated, and the underwriter must see that these standards are observed when a risk is accepted. For e.g., a company may decide that it will accept no fire exposures situated in areas where there is no fire department protection or will accept no one for life insurance who has had cancer within the previous five years.

When reviewing an application for property insurance for a piece of property, such as a farm, that is located where there is no fire department protection or when reviewing an application for life insurance in which the individual had cancer four and half years ago, the underwriter asks the question, "Can I make an exception for this application, or must I reject it because it does not come within the technical limitations of my instructions?" In answering this question, the underwriter visualizes what would happen to the company's loss experience if a very large number of identical risks were accepted. If the aggregate experience would be very unfavourable, the underwriter will probably reject the application.

The objectives of underwriting can be therefore expressed as follows:

1. *Product Equitable to Customer* – The underwriter should fairly assess the risk in a proposal and fix the premium justifiable to the consumer.
2. *Deliverable to the Customer* – Consumers are the final authority for buying the products. If the marketers are not able to sell so that the product becomes undeliverable, the onus is on the underwriters to carry an introspection of the various factors that caused differences between the consumers and company's expectations.
3. *Financially Feasible to the Insurance Company* — The insurers are not in the business of charity. The underwriting benefit must be reflected by the financial statements. Although, the

underwriters are not directly involved in the pricing of insurance products, yet their contribution is as vital as that of actuaries, because they operationalise the business of risk.

Most of the insurance companies formulate underwriting policy which provides the framework for underwriting decisions. It is also called as the *underwriting philosophy*. The underwriting policy specifies the line of insurance that will be written as well as prohibited exposures, the amount of coverage to be permitted on various types of exposure, the area of the country in which each line will be written, and similar restrictions. Generally, the individual who applies the underwriting rules and guidelines, called the desk underwriter, do not involve in forming the company underwriting.

The underwriting philosophy also describes in general terms how the underwriter will use reinsurance for its risk management.[2] The underwriting philosophy can be translated into *underwriting guidelines* which specify the general standards that specify which applicants are to be assigned to the risk established for each insurance product.

In life insurance, the underwriter is assisted by medical reports from the physicians that examined the applicant, by information from the agent, by an independent report (called inspection report) on the applicant prepared by an outside agency created for that purpose, and by advice from the company's own medical advisor. In property-liability insurance (as well as life insurance), the underwriter has the services of reinsurance facilities and credit departments to report on the financial standing of applicants and also can review loss histories of applicant.

Requisites of Good Underwriting

- The guiding philosophy of good underwriting is to know the risk features and factors of every risk offered for acceptance. Underwriter must determine the serious physical hazards inherent in the particular risk and the steps taken by an insured to minimize them. He should be able to visualize the risk even if he did not visit it, from the reports given and from the detailed proposal form furnished. The above presupposes that the insurer provides him with the expense needed in respect of each industry that he is asked to underwrite.
- An underwriter should be aware of the minimum risk management steps to impose by insurers in respect of each risk. He should evaluate the risk management steps a proposer on his own has implemented such as safety audit measures; staff drills to fight fires and breakdowns; investigations and remedial steps taken to prevent recurrence of fires and breakdowns etc.
- The moral hazard of the proposer in respect of housekeeping, staff relations, compliance with legal enactments, the effectiveness of corporate governance and past claims experience; and steps taken to avoid recurrence of accidents.
- The environmental issues of a proposal such as his competition, peculiarities of his particular trade or business and its vagaries must also be evaluated.
- The underwriter should be exposed to the claim occurrences of the risks that he usually accepts.

---

2. Gene Stone, *op. cit.,* p. 243.

- Familiarity with IT to extract data and information, and analytical skills to reduce problems to their bare bones is another skill that is essential in underwriting.

9.3 Underwriting in Life Insurance

Life insurance underwriting is mainly concerned with mortality. Mortality risk for an insurer is that the insured will die prior to the stipulated life. An impairment in any respect of a proposed insured's personal health, medical history, health habits, family history, occupation, or other activities that could increase that person's expected mortality risk.[3]

While underwriting risk of an individual in life insurance, following factors are generally considered by life insurance companies:

(a) Age,

(b) Sex,

(c) Height and weight,

(d) Health history (and often family health history – parents and siblings),

(e) The purpose of the insurance (such as for estate planning, or business or for family protection),

(f) Marital status and number of children,

(g) The amount of insurance the applicant already has, and any additional insurance s/he proposes to buy,

(h) Occupation (some are hazardous, and increase the rise of death),

(i) Income (to help determine suitability),

(j) Smoking or tobacco use this is an important factor, as smokers have shorter lives),

(k) Alcohol (excessive drinking seriously hurts life expectancy),

(l) Certain hobbies (e.g., race car driving, hang-gliding, piloting non-commercial aircraft), and

(m) Foreign travel (certain foreign travel is risky).

Similarly, in case of group insurance, the following factors are considered:

(a) Proposed Coverage – which includes assessment of eligibility, level of benefits which can be offered, administration of the group and the mode of payment to intermediaries.

(b) Cause of existence of the relevant group – classified on the basis of the nature of job, specific agendas etc.

(c) Size of the group – large groups are always better than small groups for obvious reasons.

(d) Nature of Group's business-based on nature of industry, cement plants and coal mines workers are more prone to respiratory/kidney problems.

(e) Geographical location of the group.

---

3. *Ibid.*

(f) Stability of the group.

(g) Attributes of group members – sex, age and work profile.

(h) Level of participation – contribution by members or else, no contribution by members.

(i) Persistency and prior experiences.

In case of renewals, the most important factor is the claims experience

Underwriters place the potential insureds in the appropriate risk class (based on various criterion) generally classified as follows:

(a) *Preferred Class:* where the happening of an adverse event or the possibility of claims is the least, i.e., the inherent risk is lesser than average risk.

(b) *Standard Class* – where the risk exposed is at par with the average risk. Most of the insured belong to this class.

(c) *Substandard Class* – where the anticipated risk is higher than the average risk. Insurance companies typically establish this risk class for proposed insureds who have permanent medical impairments or conditions, are recovering from serious illnesses or accidents, or have occupations or avocations that significantly increase their degree of risk.[4]

9.3.1 The Underwriting Process

The underwriting of life assurance is in quite a different category from other forms of personal insurances. This is because the underwriter assesses the risk at inception only. The company is then guaranteeing cover for sometimes, up to 30 years, or even throughout life. Life assurance underwriting involves looking at medical, occupational and avocation factors as well as the individual's lifestyle. In particular, the extra risk posed by AIDS has led to an increased number of questions on proposal forms, or on a separate questionnaire, about lifestyle, which are designed to identify if the proposer is likely to be in a high risk group for AIDS or HIV.

The underwriting process for life assurance involves – (1) performing field underwriting, (2) reviewing the application in the office, (3) gathering additional information, if required and (4) taking and underwriting decision. Additional information is often required by the underwriter in order to reach a decision. This can be in the form of detailed questionnaires, a report from the proposer's own doctor (Medical Attendant's Report), an examination by an independent doctor (Medical Examiner's Report) and/or specific tests.

Following steps are generally followed by underwriters:

1. Receiving Proposals/Applications

The application for insurance is the source of insurability information that the life insurance company's underwriter will evaluate first. These are generally collected by the field personnel, the agents. There are two basic parts to a typical life insurance application: (1) General Information, and (2) Medical Information.

---

4. *Ibid.*, p. 244.

The General Information section of an application asks general questions, including name, age, address, birth date, sex, income, marital status and occupation. In addition, details about the requested insurance coverage such as type of policy, amount of insurance, name and relationship of the beneficiary, other insurance that the client owns, and additional insurance applications pending as on date.

The Medical Information section of an application focuses on insured's health and asks a number of questions about health history, history of his/her family's as well. The medical section of the application is fairly extensive and must be fully completed. In addition to this, information may also gathered through a medical examination, depending on age and the face amount of coverage.

2. The Medical Report

The average medical examination (which is generally at no cost to the applicant except in case of revivals) may be conducted. Depending on the medical questions are answered, an insurance company may ask the medical doctor(s) of the client for more detail on any conditions in question. This gathering of information is practically a standardized method used with all domestic insurance companies. Life Insurance Companies generally have several sources of information about medical and financial history to assist them in the underwriting process. These include personal medical records and doctor, the Medical Information Bureau, Special Questionnaires, Inspection Reports and even Credit Records.

3. Underwriting Review

Once all of the information has been gathered, an individual from the insurance company (called an underwriter) evaluates the data. At this evaluation, the underwriter is seeking to classify the risk presented to the company. In addition, the underwriter will determine the premium for the policy based on the primary and secondary factors influencing the premium, and the premium rates the company's actuaries have set for your risk profile. As a consumer, here is the hard part to understand in getting a policy: insurance companies have different underwriting guidelines. This is why the least expensive policies are the most stringent on their guidelines. Throughout every step of the underwriting process, the life insurance agent normally provides with details, keeps abreast of where the insured stand in the process and guide and answer to the questions. Ultimately, making the underwriting process less intimidating and more manageable.

If the proposed insured presents a risk more than the risk which the insurance company is willing to cover, the application will be declined by the underwriter.

4. Policy Writing

In life insurance, the policy is usually written in a special department whose main task is to issue written contracts in accordance with instructions from the underwriting department and, because most policies are long term in nature, to keep a register of them for future reference. Insurance companies generally use automated systems which generate the computerized client record, records of payment of premium and they do verify that all the requirements of underwriting have been met.

Documents Required at the Time of Underwriting

Age Proof

Scrutiny of age is an important concern for the life insurer because old age people have high probability of dying than the younger ones and premium is calculated on the basis of age groups. Accuracy in age computation resolves hardship both to the insurer and the potential insured in the sense that the correct age avoids the company bring affected by lesser premiums or undesired risk bought or risk not bought because of fear. From the insured's perspective, it helps in charging of fair premiums and insurance availability. The proofs of age, which are generally considered are as under:

- Certified extract from municipal or other records made at the time of birth.
- Certificate of Baptism or certified extract from family Bible if it contains age or date of birth.
- Certified extract from School or College if age or date of birth is stated therein.
- Certified extract from Service Register in case of Govt. employees and employees of Quasi Govt. institutions including Public Limited Companies.
- Passport issued by the Passport Authorities in India.

Alternative Age Proofs, which are also accepted in the industry, are:

- Marriage certificate in the case of Roman Catholics issued by Roman Catholic Church.
- Certified extracts from the Service Registers of commercial Institutions or Industrial Undertakings provided it is specifically mentioned in such extracts that conclusive evidence of age was produced at the time of recruitment of the employee.
- Certificate of Birth granted by *Syedna v. Molana Badruddin Sahib of Baroda*.
- Identity Cards issued by Defence Department.
- A true copy of the University Certificate or of Matriculation/Higher Secondary Education, S.S.L. Certificate issued by a Board set up by a State/Central Government.
- Non-standard age proofs like Horoscope, Service Record where age is not verified at the time of entry, E.S.I.S, Card. Marriage Certificate in case of Muslim Proposer, Elder's Declaration, Self-declaration and Certificate by Village Panchayats are accepted subject to certain rules.

Medical Examination

Generally, at some levels and in case of endowment policies, whole life policies, the medical examination is not added for. However, if the amount of insurance is very high or the age is high or the first level examination has some adverse remarks, then the insurance company may refer the proposal for a thorough examination. Cases of pregnant women, or women with history of miscarriages or abortion are declined. Some-times, the medical examination may be waived, like in rural areas, where the facilities are not available.

After the above examinations and obtaining special reports, if required, the underwriter may accept or reject the case. Else, he is empowered to modify the sum assured, premium to be charged and manner thereof, impose conditions or provide exclusions in the policy.

In case of untrue or incorrect statement contained in the proposal, personal statement, declaration and connected documents or any material information withheld, subject to the provision of Section 45 of the Insurance Act 1938 wherever applicable, the policy shall be declared void and all claims to any benefits in virtue thereof shall cease.

After the policy is issued, the policyholder in a number of cases finds the terms not suitable to him and desires to charge them. LIC allows certain types of alterations during the lifetime of the policy. However, no alteration is permitted within one year of the commencement of the policy with some exceptions. The following alterations are allowed:

- Alteration in class or term
- Reduction in the assured
- Alteration in the mode of payment of premiums
- Alteration in the date of commencement of the policy
- Splitting up of a single policy into two or more policies
- Removal of an extra premium
- Alteration from without profit plan to with profit plan
- Alteration in name
- Correction in policies
- Settlement option of payment of assured by instalments
- Grant of accident benefit
- Grant of premium waiver benefit under CDA polices
- Alteration in currency and place of payment of policy monies.

A fee for the change or alteration in the policy is charged by the company called as the quotation fee and no additional fee is charged for giving effect to the alteration.

Special Reports

Besides the proposal form, personal statement agent's report, medical examiner's report and age proof, special medical reports may be called for, it

(*a*) The SA is very high, say ₹ 5 lakh or more

(*b*) The age at entry is very high, say, 60 years or more

(*c*) The proposer wants insurance cover under a high-risk plan.

(*d*) The normal medical examination discloses some adverse feature.

The underwriter has the right and discretion to ask for additional information through special reports, if he considers such reports necessary for a fair assessment of risk. These special reports may relate to medical condition of they may relate in income, habits, lifestyles etc. He may ask for medical reports, even if the proposal is for non-medical insurance. In the case of keyman insurance, the reports may be to establish that the life assured is indeed a key person and that the SA proposal represents fairly the value of that person and that the SA proposed represents fairly the value of that person to the enterprise.

The underwriter arrives at a decision about the acceptance of the proposal, after scrutinising the particulars available in the proposal form, personal statement, the reports of the officials and the medical reports. He may take the expert opinion of a medical referee, who is a senior doctor familiar with implications of medical history in life insurance.

The underwriter may decide to accept the proposal as a proposed at O.R. (Ordinary Rates) or on modified terms. O.R. means that the premium chargeable would be as per the standard premium tables. The modifications would be of the following kind:

(*a*) accepting for a lesser SA than proposed

(*b*) accepting for a shorter term than proposed

(*c*) accepting for a different plan than proposed

(*d*) charging a higher premia than the standard rate

(*e*) imposing a lien which reduces the insurer's liability under the policy for some time, or under some conditions.

(*f*) excluding certain specified risks the policy.

The terms under which the proposal is accepted by the underwriter, will be conveyed to the proposer. If the acceptance is as proposed and at O.R. the deposit paid along with the proposal, if adequate will be adjusted as First Premium and the risk will commence from that time. If the acceptance is on modified terms, the proposer has to agree to those modified terms. The balance of premium if any will have to be paid. If all the requirements are fulfilled by the proposer, the First Premium is adjusted and the risk commences. The First Premium is adjusted and the risk commences. The First Premium Receipt is the evidence of Commencement of risk, till the policy document is issued.

9.4 Underwriting in Non-life Insurance

The underwriting of commercial, business insurances is a much more complicated and involved task. Commercial insurances range from small shops and factories to large multinational corporations, with operations in many countries throughout the world. The degree of complexity of the underwriting required would obviously vary with the sheer size of the risk, but certain basic principles are still recognizable.

The essence of the task is that the underwriter has to evaluate the hazard associated with the risk, which is being proposed. In small cases, he may be able to do this from reading a proposal form and corresponding with the sponsor. It may be that a local inspector is asked to call and see the shop or factory for himself. In large cases this is simply impossible. Detail of the risk could not be confined to a proposal form since there is just too much information to condense, no matter how large the form may be. The insurance companies may take the help of brokers in these cases. The broker in these cases will be in a position to prepare the case for the underwriter. This may mean site inspections by the broker and the preparation of plans and reports on the relevant aspects of the risk. This documentation, which may be extremely extensive, is then passed to the underwriter and negotiation can commence on the terms, conditions, cover and price.

Several sources of information are available to the underwriter regarding the hazards of a commercial applicant for property and liability insurance:

(*a*) *Application Containing the Insurers Statements:* The basic source of underwriting information is the application, which varies for each line of insurance and for each type of coverage. The broader and more liberal the contract, usually more detailed information is required. The questions on the application are designed to give the underwriter the information needed to decide whether to accept the exposure, reject it or ask for additional information.

(*b*) *Information from the Agent or Broker:* In some line of non-life insurance, the agent may exercise his underwriting authority. For commercial insurances, the profit-sharing contracts are also entered with the agents, whereby the agent derives a special incentive if the business brought by him has resulted in a profit to the company.

(*c*) *Prior Experiences:* The past history of claims is also a source of information. In case of existing clients where the claims experience has been unfavourable, the insurance company penalizes, i.e., loads premium for new businesses or renewals of the existing ones.

(*d*) *Inspection:* Surveys are also conducted by the company's specialists/consultants to find out the accuracy of information as contained in the proposal form.

Underwriting Practices

Underwriting of non-life insurance in India is generally carried out by a department called as "new-business department." Most of the underwriting work is performed at Branch and Divisional office level, of course, in accordance with the underwriting policy and rules framed by the head office of the insurance company. The underwriting guidelines cover the following:[5]

(*a*) acceptance of normal risks irrespective of sum issued

(*b*) acceptance of normal risks upto specified sum insured

(*c*) acceptance of normal classes of business with prior approval of the controlling office (the controlling office may be head office/regional office)

(*d*) acceptance of risks with prior approval for the controlling office

(*e*) acceptance of risks subject to underwriting safeguards

(*f*) procedural matters.

The risks in fire, marine and motor insurance have generally high levels of limits of acceptance. However, in some classes of insurances, the limits are fairly low. Some of these are:[6]

(*i*) All risk insurance on jewellery etc.

(*ii*) Baggage insurance

(*iii*) Personal Accident Insurance

(*iv*) Special Contingency Insurance

5. *Practice of General Insurance,* Insurance Institute of India, p. 156.
6. *Practice of General Insurance, op. cit.,* p. 156-157.

For higher limits in these cases, the approval of controlling office is essential.

In case of fire insurance, only standard fire and special perils policy with the permitted "Add-on" covers if any, can be issued premiums and specified by Tariff Advisory Committee.

- Unless otherwise specifically provided for policy (ies) covering Buildings and/or contents shall show blockwise separate amount on *(i)* Building *(ii)* Machinery and Accessories *(iii)* Stock and Stock-in-process and *(iv)* Furniture and other contents.
- It is permissible to exclude Storm, Tempest, Flood and Inundation group of perils and or Riot, Strike, Malicious and Terrorism Damage perils at inception of the Policy by deleting the relevant perils from the Policy. The deletion should apply for the entire policy in one complex/compound/location covering the entire interest of the insured under one or more policy(ies) without any option for the selection. Reduction in premium rates for such deletion(s) may be allowed as shown under the relevant sections of the Tariff. When these perils are deleted from the scope of the policy, the general exclusions shall include these perils.

Any risk, which has not been provided for by TAC is referred to the Committee for rating. Provisional rate of ₹ 2.50 per mile is charged in such cases for covering the risks under Standard Fire and Special Perils Policy. No discounts and/or agency commission is be allowed on this rate. For add-on covers, additional rates provided in Section VIII is to be charged.

Rates shown under the tariffs are minimum rates. Insurers may charge rates higher than those given under the tariff.

The risks above the normal kind of risks are normally declined by the insurance companies. Otherwise, they are accepted by changing a higher premium and imposing restrictive conditions, clauses and warranties. For example, risks in ammunition, explosive, fireworks, celluloid, match factories etc. In a fire policy, special perils can be accepted subject to the inspection of risk. Similarly, for consequential loss policy, the audit of accounts is a must.

In case of marine insurance, the declined risks may be billion, currency over specified limits, quit in secondhand drums against leakage's, secondhand machinery against breakage etc. The age of the cargo carrying vessel is an important factor in marine insurance underwriting.

In motor insurance, acceptance of comprehensive risk is subject to the specified year of the manufacture/assembly of the vehicle. An underwriter before acceptance of risk may conduct an inspection of the vehicle. Similarly, military disposal vehicles can be covered by Act only, risks comprehensive insurance on imported cars is allowed subject to incorporation of an excess clause.[7]

Underwriting experience of various insurance players is given in Annexure 9A and 9B.

---

7. *Practice of General Insurance, op. cit.,* p. 159.

Annexure 9A

UNDERWRITING EXPERIENCE AND PROFITS OF PUBLIC SECTOR COMPANIES

(Rs. Lakh)

	New India		Oriental		National		United		Total	
	2008-09	2007-08	2008-09	2007-08	2008-09	2007-08	2008-09	2007-08	2008-09	2007-08
Net Premium	550031	491428	323510	287868	365363	318798	351041	288066	1589946	1386159
Incurred Claims (Net)	467187	417748	305719	260222	339367	283884	251505	250628	1363778	1212481
	84.94%	85.01 %	94.50%	90.40%	92.88%	89.05%	71.65%	87.00%	85.78%	87.47%
Commission, Expenses Of Management	201583	147834	111546	95496	116454	110159	123084	104916	552667	458406
	36.65%	30.08%	34.48%	33.17%	31.87%	34.55%	35.06%	36.42%	34.76%	33.07%
Increase In Reserve For Unexpired Risk	25101	10285	16830	244	23127	16945	31131	17857	96189	45331
	4.56%	2.09%	5.20%	0.08%	6.33%	5.32%	8.87%	6.20%	6.05%	3.27%
Underwriting Profitiloss	(143840)	(84439)	(110586)	(68095)	(113585)	(92190)	(54679)	(85335)	(422690)	(330059)
	-27.40%	-17 55%	-36.06%	-23.67%	-33.19%	-30.5'%	-17.09%	-31.58%	-28.30%	-24.62%
Gross Investment Income	167686	234619	99562	114315	103962	118092	108767	157725	479978	624751
Other Income Less Other Outgo	5876	1966	2182	(1986)	(3731)	(8696)	(3797)	(6576)	529	(15292)
Profit Before Tax	29723	152146	(8842)	44235	(13354)	172(,6	50291	65814	57818	279400
Income Tax Deducted At Source And Provision For Tax	7308	12033	(3576)	43305	1567	863	2686	2651	7985	58851
Net Profit After Tax	**22415**	**140113**	**(5266)**	**930**	**(14921)**	**1634:1**	**47605**	**63162**	**49833**	**220548**

Note: Figure in bracket negative amounts.

Statement 9B

UNDERWRITING EXPERIENCE AND PROFITS OF PUBLIC SECTOR COMPANIES

(Rs. Lakh)

Particulars	Royal Sundaram		Bajaj Allianz		Tata AIG		Reliance		IFFCO Tokio		ICICI-Lombard		Cholamandalam		HDFC CHUBB		Future total Generali		Uni-versal Sompo		Total			
	2008-09	2007-08	2008-09	2007-08	2008-09	2007-08	2008-09	2007-08	2008-09	2007-08	2008-09	2007-08	2008-09	2007-08	2008-09	2007-08	2008-09	2007-08	2008-09	2007-08				
Net Premium	66831	53306	200658	###	58749	52801	139956	133745	88568	73775	211641	177977	43414	32113	19477	16758	12745	184	1795	(43)	6117	1242	851199	715871
CLAIMS INCURRED Inett	41235	29915	135992	94570	35567	24771	107366	75068	6S502	50474	168454	122832	27578	15565	1448.	11417	6054	58	241	0	1200	289	607967	424631
	61.70%	55.93%	67.77%	53.98%	60.54%	46.91%	76.71%	56.13%	78.47%	68.42%	79.59%	69.02%	63.52%	48.47%	74.39%	68.49%	47.56%	31.41%	13.42%	-0.26%	19.62%	23.16%	71.42%	59.32%
Commission. Expenses Of Management	25161	19060	62261	50072	28867	22971	50989	48341	23639	19711	60300	42480	13595	10946	8717	6953	9142	1934	2823	726	1869	5333	292694	223178
	37.65%	35.75%	31.03%	28.57%	49.14%	43.50%	36.43%	36.14%	26.69%	26.72%	28.49%	23.86%	31.31%	34.09%	44.75%	41.52%	71.73%	1052.68%	157.22%	-1705.14%	30.56%	429.48%	34.39%	31.18%
Increase In Reserve For Unexpired Risk	7026	8723	11532	33711	0	7417	1070	37741	5275	9808	14282	21258	4877	7227	1529	1753	7064	312	1882	1	4402	1520	60459	127951
	10.51%	16.36%	5.75%	19.24%	0.00%	14.05%	0.76%	28.22%	5.96%	13.29%	6.75%	11.94%	11.23%	22.51%	7.85%	10.46%	55.42%	170.04%	104.84%	-1.74%	71.96%	122.38%	7.10%	17.87%
Underwriting profit/loss	(6591)	(4291)	(9126)	(3098)	(5686)	(2357)	(19468)	(27406)	(9849)	(6219)	(31388)	(8573)	(2636)	(1626)	(5259)	(3430)	(9514)	(2121)	(3151)	(769)	(1354)	158991	(109921)	(59890)
	-11.02%	-9.62%	-4.83%	-2.19%	-9.68%	-5.19%	-14.02%	-28.55%	-11.82%	-9.72%	-15.90%	-5.47%	-6.84%	-6.53%	-25.03%	-18.53%	-167.46%	1647.72%	3623.82%	1776.26%	-12.87%	2123.20%	-13.90%	-10.19%
Gross Investment Income	7557	4802	21475	18649	7172	5035	14650	10411	10541	7354	36574	22448	3851	2643	2695	1440	1174	542	1763	881	902	765	109120	74205
Other Income Less Other Outgo	8	-34	2628	1240	(536)	14	(199)	711	(0)	50	(5159)	(852)	(30)	37	42	313	(155)	(123)	(32)	(151)	(78)	(597)	(4109)	1204
PROOT Before TAX	973	477	14977	16790	950	2692	(5017)	(16284)	692	1188	27	13022	1185	1054	(2521)	(1677)	(8496)	(1701)	(1419)	(39)	(529)	(5732)	(4910)	15519
Income Tax Deducted At Source And Provision For Tax	407	6	5461	6228	526	1075	215	271	442	470	(2335)	2735	486	330	53	23	37	8	20	(9)	(139)	44	5216	11136
Let PROFIT AFTERTAX	566	471	9516	10562	424	1617	(5232)	(16555)	250	716	2362	10287	699	724	(2575)	(1700)	(8533)	(1709)	(1439)	(30)	(390)	(5775)	(10126)	4383

Note : Figure in brackets indicate negative amounts

Source : IDRA Reports

Key Terms

- Adverse Selection
- Underwriting Philosophy
- Comprehensive Risks
- Persistency
- Claims Experience

Questions for Review

1. Define underwriting. Briefly explain the trade-off and conflict in underwriting business.
2. Explain the process of underwriting in life and non-life insurance business.
3. Comment on the various underwriting practices in India.

Suggested Readings

1. *Practice of General Insurance,* IC02, Insurance Institute of India, Mumbai, 1999.
2. Genes Stone, *Insurer Company, Operations,* LOMA 2000.
3. Vaughan & Vaughan, *Essentials of Risk Management and Insurance,* John Wiley & Sons, 2002.

Web Resources

- www.life-insurance-underwriting.org
- www.insuranceinform.org
- www.insuremagic.com

❑❑❑

CHAPTER

RATING OF INSURANCE PRODUCTS

Chapter Objectives

- Fundamentals of Insurance Pricing
- Pricing Objectives
- Types of Rating
- Other Rating Consideration
- Rating in Life Insurance
- Life Insurance vs. Non-life Insurance Pricing
- Rate Making Entities
- Rate Making in General Insurance

Introduction

Pricing of Insurance products is mysterious to most of the people. It is different from the pricing of tangible where you can figure out the cost of inputs. Also, in other services, the cost of providing them can be estimated with some judgement. Insurance is the business of buying risk. Therefore, most people think in terms of what they paid for buying a risk cover and what they paid for the cover. When an insurers sells a policy, it has no way of knowing what will be the realised cost of the policy because it depends upon whether or not the policy buyer has losses and, if so, how many and how large they are. Of course, this is the reason that different people are charged different prices for policies providing the same kinds and amounts of insurance.

10.1 Fundamentals of Insurance Pricing

Pricing of insurance products is typical in the sense that in insurance transactions, the sales price (i.e., the premium) is collected before stipulated services, namely claim payments, are duly provided. "Two collary are usually drawn: *(a)* insurance pricing is rather a delicate actuarial exercise; and thus *(b)* technical reserves must be built up to represent the liabilities towards policyholders to ensure that the inherent promises to them do not become failed promises. These reserves are then invested on financial markets and placed under the supervision of the relevant regulatory authority. This is precisely why insurance firms are usually viewed as fulfilling an important financial intermediary function."[1]

"A fundamental principle of insurance pricing is that if insurers are to sell coverage willingly, they must receive premiums that:

(1) are sufficient to fund their expected claim costs and administrative costs and

(2) provide an expected profit to compensate for the cost of obtaining the capital necessary to support the sale of coverage."[2]

The premium level that is just sufficient to fund the insurer's expected cost and provide insurance company owners with a fair return on their invested capital is known as the fair premium.

Actuaries generally calculate the base premium on the basis of expected claims distribution using principle of equivalence (P = ps) such that:

$$P = E(S) + k + R$$

Where E(S) represents the mathematical expectation of claims, k denotes ongoing company running costs, while R is a risk premium which allows for coverage of unforeseen deviations in the claims amount to be paid, but still provides the company with "normal" profits, i.e., this standard pricing mechanism relies upon the so-called "law of large numbers". Within a large, diversified and homogeneous underwriting portfolio, the claims burden should converge towards its expected value.

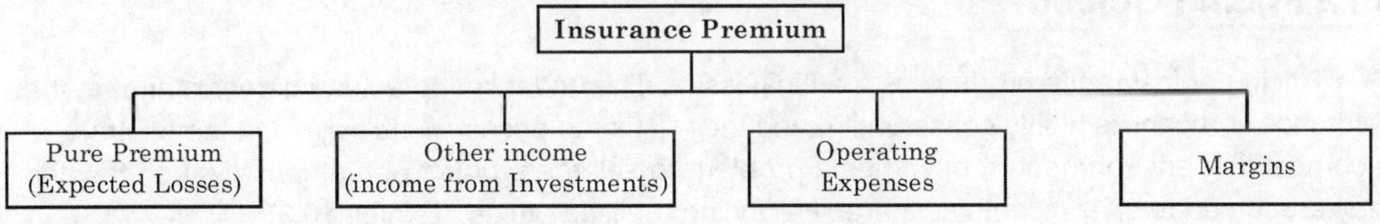

Exhibit 10.1

Pure Premium

It is the most important component of the insurance premiums. Based on actuarial calculations, it includes the amount needed to cover expected losses and loss adjustment expenses.

1. Briyo and Varenne, *Insurance from Underwriting to Derivatives,* John Wiley & Sons Ltd., 2001, p. 6.
2. Harrington and Niehaus, *Insurance and Risk Management,* McGraw-Hill, p. 115.

Operating Expenses

Operating Expenses include the sales commission and other marketing costs, taxes, and the cost of handling claims. The size of this component of premium varies from one line to another, largely dependent upon the extent and variety of policyholder services that the insurer provides.

Margin and Other Incomes

It includes an allowance for: *(a)* contingencies, and *(b)* underwriting gain or profit. Contingency funds are needed to meet unexpected increase in the number or size of benefit payments and underwriting gains are needed to provide funds for financing growth and expansion.

Rating Terminology

- Insurance prices are called as *Premiums*. Premiums are based on rates and rates are based on per unit of exposure.
- The term *rate* is used synonymous with premium in the insurance business. It is the price per unit of insurance.
- *Exposure unit* are quantitative units used in insurance pricing.
- *Loading* refers to the amount that must be added to the pure premium for other expenses, profit and margin for contingencies.

Exhibit 10.2

Kind of Insurance	*Exposure Unit*
Automobile	Automobile insured (IEV)
Fire	₹ per 100
Liability (Products)	₹ per 1,000
Worker's Compensation	₹ per 100
Life	₹ per 1,000

10.2 Pricing Objectives

Pricing of insurance products is a critical issue. The underwriting/actuarial department in the insurance company is highly conservative and tries to fix the prices *all-inclusive*. On the contrary, in a competitive environment, it becomes a problem to sell the product at mathematical prices and they are forced to offer incentives thereby reducing realised prices. [Exhibit 10.3]

Exhibit 10.3

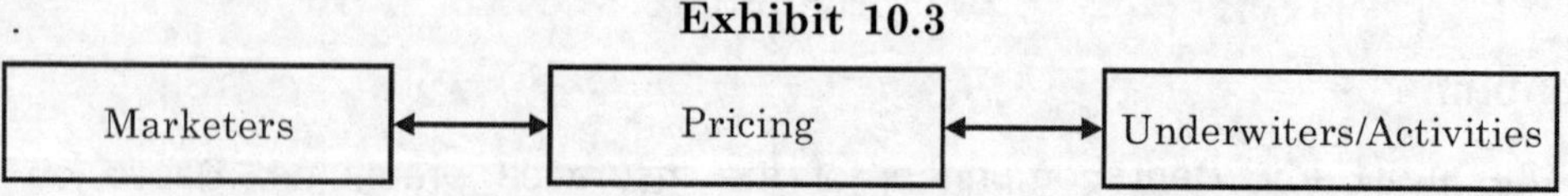

The non-life insurance business in India is substantially regulated. Tariff Advisory Committee (TAC) constituted under the Insurance Act 1938, controls and regulates the rates, advantages, terms and conditions that may be offered by insurers in respect of General Insurance Business relating to Fire, Marine (Hull), Motor, Engineering and Workmen Compensation. All other products are non-tariff. These rates are also called as statutory standards. In addition to these regulations, the pricing of insurance products must achieve the following general objectives:

(a) *Adequacy*: The rate must be adequate to generate the premium income the insurer needs to pay its claims and expenses. In addition, the insurers' income must be adequate to assure fair rate of return to the investors of funds. Also, they are sufficient to finance continuing growth and expansion.

Rating is matter of regulation by IRDA whose objective is to protect the interests of the policyholders and the shareholders. This means that the rates must be adequate enough to meet all future losses and expenses in the time and to pay a fair return on the capital employed by the shareholders for this risk-taking business. If the rates are not adequate, an insurer may become insolvent causing total loss to the policyholders' fund as well as the shareholders' fund; and cause total loss of public faith and confidence in insurance industry.

However, in insurance business, rate adequacy measurement is really complicated because of the simple reason that insurer does not know the actual costs at the time of selling the policy. Price is estimated on loss forecasting process based on statistical methods. The premium is collected in advance in view of law of large numbers (projected); and expected claim costs and other expenses. If the insurer fails to achieve the targeted number or volume of business and if the actual claim costs, especially catastrophic losses, are more than the statistically projected or forecasted loss, price collected may not be sufficient to pay all claims and expenses during the policy period. As a result, policyholders, shareholders, third party claimants and other beneficiaries may be financially harmed. This is the major concern for the regulatory authority all over the globe.[3]

(b) *Reasonableness:* The rates must not be so excessive that allows insurance companies to earn abnormal gains. There is no recipe for reasonableness, but what the insurance company can justify to the potential buyers in a free market condition is considered as reasonable.

(c) *Fairness:* The rates must not be "unfairly discriminatory". The insurance rates must be fair and must discriminate among the buyers fairly. Since the rates must vary with classifications as principle, they must not create unrest among the group of buyers. In other words, the rates must not be same for hetro-groups and must not be different for homo-groups.

(d) *Simplicity, Consistency and Flexibility:* The rating system must be simple to understand and inexpensive to use. The rate must not change frequently under circumstances warrant (responsiveness to changes in the number of expected claims and losses). There should not be any rate-cutting at the cost of shareholders' fund or other policyholders' fund. For example, if inflation causes increase in medical expenses reimbursement or payment in more automobile repair claims, the corresponding Mediclaim insurance premium or Motor OD premium need to be enhanced.

(e) *Encouragement of loss control measures:* The insurer's rating policy should encourage loss-control activities that may reduce both loss frequency and severity. With proper risk

---

3. R.C. Guria, Rating the Risks Right, IRDA Journal, September, 2006.

inspection and risk analysis, the insurer may find out the weaknesses of loss prevention measures and guide the insured accordingly to improve the arrangements so that frequency and severity can be reduced; and accordingly fire rates can be also reduced. In this regard Hazop Study, Fault Tree Analysis or Dow Index Analysis; and regular risk identification analysis deserve special mention. Also, the pricing mechanism should encourage the reduction of losses.

(*f*) *Availability of Insurance to the larger section of the society:* Because of the unreasonable prices, certain sections of the society find it difficult to obtain coverage easily at a reasonable price. So, to ensure availability of insurance products for larger section of the society as per their affordability, the insurers must have ability for proper loss forecasting; and stable, simple and transparent pricing system. Insurance business cannot be run in today's global market only with business objectives regardless of social objectives and regulatory objectives.

10.3 Types of Rating

Insurance rating assesses the cost of the insurance product. Depending upon the type of rating, the price to the buyer may be – *(a)* entirely different from the one paid by another, *(b)* same as that paid by other customers or *(c)* similar to that paid by others, but more or less than the amount for one reason or another. There are basically three recognized rate-making methods:

- Judgment rating
- Class rating
- Merit rating
    - Schedule rating
    - Experience rating
    - Retrospective rating

10.3.1 Judgment Rating

It is used when the risk proposed to be bought is so unusual that little or no statistical information about similar risk is available. Each exposure is individually evaluated, and the rate is determined largely by the underwriter's judgment. Such cases are not unusual to the insurers when the loss exposures are so diverse that a class rate cannot be calculated, or when credible loss statistics are not available. When the judgment rating is used, each premium is unique and is based on the opinion of the person making it. It is widely used in ocean marine insurance and in some lines of inland marine insurance.

10.3.2 Class Rating

Class rates are the most common rate in insurance business. Insured risks are classified on the basis of one or several important features and all that belong to the same class are subject to the same rate per unit of exposure. The rate charged reflects the claims experience for the class as a whole. It is based on the assumption that future losses to insured will be determined largely by the same set of factors. This type of rating is also termed as manual rating because the various classifications and the respective rates are in the form of printing manuals.

Life insurance is one of the line where class rates are used, viz., rates based on age, gender, healthiness, smoking and drinking habits etc. Class rating is also used for homeowners' insurance, automobile insurance, workers' compensation and health insurance. The twin considerations in class rating are:

- *How many different classifications and rates should there be?*
- *How many characteristics of the covered risks should class rating take into account?*

These two go together because the number of classifications depend upon the number of rating factors that are considered; the more the factors, the more the classifications. Following aspects are taken into considerations for Class Rating:

- ❑ Risk grouping/classification
- ❑ Homogeneous Group in respect of the following aspects
    - Nature of occupancy (Trading/Manufacturing)
    - Properties of materials (flammability, reactivity, toxicity, flash point etc.)
    - Properties of products
    - Nature and height of constructions
    - Process hazard (reaction operation, boiling point, flash point, ignition point etc.)
    - Plant/Process. (types, maintenance etc.)
    - Protection Systems and Appliances
- ❑ Credible Data Bank for Proper Statistical Analysis and Technical Justification
- ❑ Probability Distribution of Loss for the particular class of risk
- ❑ Law of large numbers
- ❑ Reinsurance rate

The class rate may be determined by dividing the amount of incurred losses and loss adjustment expenses by the number of exposure units. Incurred losses include all losses paid during the accounting period, plus amounts held as reserves for the future payment of losses that have already occurred during the same period. Loss adjustment expenses are the expenses incurred by the company in adjusting losses during the same accounting period.

Another technique could be to compare the actual loss ratio with the expected loss ratio, and the rate is adjusted accordingly. The actual loss ratio is the ratio of incurred losses and loss adjustment expenses to earned premiums. The expected loss ratio is the percentage of the premiums that is expected to be used to pay losses.

When rates are based on just a few factors, many other characteristics of each exposure are ignored. Number of rating classes is dilemma for the rate-maker. The greater the number of classes, the more the factors that can be taken into account and therefore the more similar risks in any given class will be. On the other hand, increasing the number of classes reduces the number of insured in each one. Law of large number tell that the greater the number of exposures in each class, the more reliable the prediction of future losses will be. Hence, there are reasons for having so many classes and also for having a few. Increasing the number of classes causes the risks in each class to be more nearly alike, but reducing the number of classes causes the rates to be based on a larger body of data and to be more reliable.

Some Essential Considerations of Class Rating

(*a*) **Homogeneity of Group:** The homogeneity of the class must be established with respect to nature of property, frequency and severity of loss faced by the homogeneous group.

(*b*) **Statistical Analysis for Estimated Claim Costs:** To arrive at fair premium depends on Statistical Analysis consisting of Measure of Central Tendency, Dispersion, Analysis of Probability Distribution and Variance Analysis.

10.3.3 Merit Rating

Merit rating is a modification of the class rating. It modifies the class rate of a particular class insured based on individual loss experience. It is based on the assumption that the loss experience of a particular insured will differ substantially from the loss experience of the other insured. In doing so, it reflects the extent to which a specific risk differs from the others in the same class. The various types of merit-rating plans are:

Schedule Rating

Under this plan, each exposure is individually rated. In calculation of schedule rates, the first step is to examine the risk (the person or object insured) in order to identify the features that are likely to cause losses or to prevent them. Then the risk is compared with the average or standard risk of its type. Finally deductions are made from the standard rate, for this risk's desirable features and additions are made for its undesirable features, the resultant rate is rate that is tailored made to reflect the characteristics of risk for which it is used. The scheduled rating system (for a building) takes into account the following major factors:

- Occupancy
- Construction
- Location
- Protection
- Maintenance
- Exposures
- Housekeeping and Maintenance
- Loss Prevention or Control Measures
- Management outlook and attitude for loss prevention/control measures

The various additions to and subtractions from the basic rate are based upon the judgment of the person who develop the overall scheduled rating system and important feature of this system is that it identifies the factors entering into an insured's rate.

Experience Rating

This type of rating modifies the class rate on the basis of claim experience of a particular exposure. The actual losses for a period generally of two or three years is compared with the average risks in the same class. The rate is reduced if the risk has a better record than the average, it is increased if the record is worst than average. Experience rating is used only for large risks, viz., large enough to have many losses each year reflecting a trend. Experience Rating is general restricted to large customers paying large amount of premium for different classes of business for reasonable long period. Hence, this type of rating is generally limited to larger firms that generate a sufficiently high volume of premiums and more credible experience. This type of rating may be applied to Workmen's Compensation Insurance, Liability Insurance or Group Mediclaim Insurance safely as it is being followed in other countries, which have been in deregulation for a pretty long time.

Retrospective Rating

Contrary to experience rating retrospective rating modifies the insurance cost on the basis of current experience. This is generally done by making a provision in the policy contract that final rates will be determined *retrospectively*. Generally, a range indication maximum and minimum is specified and the final premium is determined after the policy expires and depends upon the amount of losses incurred during the year. If the losses are very small, the insured will pay the minimum premium otherwise if they are very large the insured will be charged the maximum premium. Usually, the premium lies between maximum and minimum premium. Retrospective rating increases the insured's incentive to control losses, because the pay-off in premium savings can be substantial. It is generally applied to large liability and workers' compensation policies. Retrospective Rating is widely used in USA for Workmen's Compensation Policy, General Liability Policy, Auto Liability Policy, Property damage and Burglary policy for large firms.

Principally, rating will be made on risk process and cost of particular risk but not on subsidy from other funds. If proper rating method is followed by Indian insurers, fire insurance premium will get reduced substantially effecting greater market penetration, and higher productivity and efficiency.

The root of the success and survival of insurance industry lies in its skill and capability to rate the risks right. Freedom to fix price for the risk gives the real strength of the foundation and autonomy of the Industry. In the tariff free regime, Indian insurance companies will be put to real test of their ability and capacity for autonomy.

10.4 Other Rating Consideration

Apart from the above rating philosophy, there may be special conditions and rates applied to certain cases.

10.4.1 Pricing and Deductible

A deductible is voluntarily accepted by an insured to bear the first part of the amount of any claim at a figure higher than the standard excess impacts the rating of the product sold to the particular client. In a package or mega policy, deductibles are arranged separately for material damage insurance or at a combined figure with the associated business interruption insurance in each case with or without an aggregate limit. The use of deductible is on the rise nowadays because of mainly two factors – (*i*) capacity of the insured to bear loss (self-insurance), and (*ii*) saving of insurance cost. So if the price of product is not competitive and commensurate with the nature of risk, insurer may opt for higher deductible and increase his capacity of self-insurance. While deciding discount on deductible, the insurer takes into consideration the size of the deductible and the insured's past loss experience apart from the basis selected by the application of the insured.

10.4.2 Pricing and Warranties

As price of a product depends on its quality and specification, the price of a promise in an insurance contract depends on the nature and number of conditions/warranties and exclusions. But there are certain limitation, e.g., in the Fire policy, there are thirteen exclusions and fifteen conditions. If any of these conditions or exclusions is removed, price can be reduced accordingly, provided the insurer has got some past loss experience and fair idea of loss forecasting for such type of product. Now, a question arises as to whether an insurer can charge premium nine times the normal premium for cover for a particular class of risk without any of the nine standard exclusions applicable for standard product for that class of risk. It is neither prudent nor permissible under regulatory norms, as such pricing of a specially customized product for a particular client on his offer may not be supported by technical analysis of appropriate statistical data of past loss; and loss forecasting of the specially designed product different from the standard product based on past experience and filed with IRDA under the requirement of "File and Use".

Pricing and IRDA Requirements

- Design and rating of products must be on sound and prudent underwriting basis.
- All literature relating to the product should be in simple language for easy understanding by the public.
- The insurance product should comply with the requirements of the IRDA (Protection of Policyholders' Interests) Regulations 2002.
- Insurers should use similar wordings for describing the same cover.
- The pricing of products should be based on support of appropriate data and technical justification.
- Margins built into rates shall be consistent with the experience of the insurer in respect of commission, expenses of management, contingencies and profit.
- Insurer should confirm that it has taken necessary steps to ensure that competition will not lead to unprincipled rate cutting and other improper methods.

Risk Inspection and Risk Identification by Line Underwriters: This has to be ensured while applying internal guide rates for the small and simple risks as they are doing now while applying tariff. In this regard, the underwriters may look into the following aspects especially over and above the guidelines prescribed in the underwriting policy of the company for arriving at merit rating or experienced rating as mentioned above.

1. Risk Inspection Report
2. Risk Analysis and Loss Control Measures
3. Risk Classification
4. FEA Arrangements Review
5. Security Measures Review
6. Class of Construction (1, 11, Open, Other)
7. Statement of House Keeping and Hazards
8. Process Control (manual, electric, electronic)
9. Market Trend and Expected Claim Costs
10. Special Characteristics of particular risks
11. Loss Experienced as per Data bank of the client
12. Reference to Guide Rates
13. Provisions for good features
14. Discount or loading for bad risks as inspection report

In addition, the underwriting policy must specify the guidelines as to how the risks are to be identified, analyzed and evaluated for application of proper guide rates by the line underwriters for the small and simple risks to be underwritten by them to maintain uniformity and standard in implementation of underwriting policy and its control all over the country. The said policy must also prescribe the basis, ways and means of scheduled rating or merit rating as the case may be.

10.5 Rating in Life Insurance

The process of rate making in life insurance involve the logical steps of risk classification, pricing using mortality tables and adjustments.

Method of Risk Classification in Life Insurance

The two methods commonly employed in the classification of risks are:

(*a*) ***Judgment Method:*** The underwriter studies all the features of the life to be insured and on the basis of analysis of various factors takes a decision. Under this method, the company depend upon the combined judgment of those in the medical actuarial and other areas who are qualified for the work to make underwriting decisions. The judgment method of rating functions effectively when is only one unfavorable factor to consider whether the decisions to be made is simply whether to accept the proposed insured at standard rates or to reject him or her entirely. However, situations where multiple factors are involved or a proper substandard classification is needed, then this method cannot be efficiently applied.

(*b*) ***Numerical Rating:*** In this method, a large number of factors, which influence mortality, are taken in account. For various factors, debits (additions) or credits (subtractions) are made to the scores. The numerical ratings vary from company to company — 75 to 500 Illustratively, as rating increases, the quality of risk diminishes. A rating in the range of

75-125 is generally considered as standard and *over and above 125 substandard.* An underwriter has to take into account the nature and combined effects of extra risks, e.g., impairments jointly causing additional extra risks. In these cases some additions are made to the arrived rates calculated independently.

In pricing of life insurance products, the main factors used in rating are (*a*) mortality, (*b*) expenses, and (*c*) interest. The first step to rate is to identify the risk class.

Mortality Tables are prepared on the basis of study of assured lives for a period of time, usually a to 5 years. At every age, deaths take place. These are tabulated showing rate of dying and rate of surviving (complementary probability) for every year.

A typical mortality table would appear like this:

Exhibit 10.4
1961-64 OM Table

Age at the beginning of the year	*No. of living at the beginning of the year*	*No. of death during during the year*	*Yearly probability of death*	*Yearly probability of surviving*
1	*2*	*3*	*4*	*5*
35	9,78,217	1410	00144	99856
36	9,77,807	1535	00157	99894
37	9,76,272	1679	00172	99828
38	9,74,593	1842	00189	99811
39	9,72,751	2633	00209	99791
40	9,70718	2242	00231	99769
41	9,68,476	2479	00256	99744
42	9,65,997	2743	00284	99716
43	9,63,254	3044	00316	99384
44	9,60,210	3370	00351	99633
45	9,56,840	3732	00390	99610

This table shows that the chance of dying at the age of 35 is .00144, it increases to .00390 at the age of 45. The last column shows the probability of survival. These probabilities of death and survival are made for use of arriving at the *mathematical value* of the risk for lives belonging to a group whose experience may be expected to more or less compare favorably with the mortality table. If it happens, one can say that the premiums charged are adequate to meet the risk involved. In other words mortality experience is satisfactory.

Treatment of Substandard Life Insurance Risks

The three broad classifications of substandard risks are:

(*a*) ***Increasing Extra Risk:*** This category reflects the extra mortality risks caused due to impairments with the increase in age. Persons with extra weight are likely to have blood pressure or heart problems, as they grow older.

(*b*) ***Constant Extra Risk:*** This group reflects the lives with hazard that remain constant through life. These hazards do not create variations in mortality as such, e.g., permanent total disablement — lost of limbs.

(c) ***Decreasing Extra Risk:*** These lives represent cases where the extra risk decreases with passage of risk since the consideration of proposal. A person who has just been operated for a problem becomes normal over a time period. At the time of proposal, the risk was substandard, but with passage of time, it has become a simple risk.

The popular methods of treating substandard risk are:

(a) ***Increase in Premium:*** Increase in normal premium (multiple table extra) is the most common method adopted by the insurance companies for treatment of substandard risks. Under this method, premiums can be treated as follows:

(*i*) the proposer's age is increased by a few years (e.g., 3-5 years) which results in increases in premium or

(*ii*) a special mortality table is developed for each substandard classification that reflects the experience of each and asset of gross premium is computed for the classification.

(*b*) ***Flat Extra Premium:*** In situation where the extra risk is expected is constant, a flat extra premium may be changed. The policy remains standard one for all purposes including dividends and non-forfeiture values.

(*c*) ***Other Method:*** The other methods of refund are:

(*i*) Limited death benefit equal to refund of premium if death occurs in the earlier years.

(*ii*) A lien (contingent debt) may be created as the policy such that upon the assured dies in the lien period, the lien amount shall be deducted from sum payable under the policy.

(*iii*) A proposal may be declined by the insurer if there is increasing extra risk.

(*iv*) Restrictive clauses may be imposed as exclusions under the policy.

(*v*) The insurance cover may be reduced by amount and/or time or the plan may be changed.

(*vi*) Another option from insurance company is to defer the cover till the extra risk is over.

Calculation of Premium

In calculating premium, the following variables are considered:

(*i*) Term and Plan

(*ii*) Riders

(*iii*) Extras

(*iv*) Sum Assured

(*v*) Mode of payment

The rates of premium are quoted per thousand for various age groups. The table rates are then multiplied by the sum assured to arrive at a base premium. Then to the base premium, the addition or dedications are made. Consider the following example:

Example 2

Sum proposed	₹ 50,0000
Cover	Moneyback Policy
Term	35 years
Table Rates	₹ 27,00 per thousand
Adjustment Rate for High SI	+ ₹ 1.60 per thousand
Double Accident Benefit (DAB)	1%
Mode of Per cent	Semi-Annual

Calculation

Tabular Premium (₹ 5,00,000 × 27/1000)	13,500
Adjustment Benefit for large SI (₹ 5,00,000 × 1.60/1000)	800
Annual Premium	14,300
DAB Extra (1%)	1430
Total Price	15,730
Sem-annual Premium (15730/2)	₹ 7865

Example 2

Plan	Whole life
Sum-assured	₹ 1,00,000
Riders	DAB
Health Extra	5%
Age	31
Premium Payments	35 years
Tabular Premium (Whole Life, Premium Payments 35)	₹ 29.40
Adjustment for Large Sum Assured ₹ 1.5	₹ 1.60
Adjustment for quarterly mode	Nil
Total	**31.00**
Annual Premium (31.00 × 100)	₹ 3,100
Health Extra (5%)	₹ 155.00
Total Annual Premium (including extra)	₹ 3255.00
Quarterly Instalment Premium	₹ 813.75

10.6 Life Insurance vs. Non-life Insurance Pricing

Pricing of life Insurance products is simpler and life insurance rates are more stable and precise. In life insurance, the main factors used for determining the premium rates are: *(a)* Mortality, *(b)* expenses and (c) interest. The insurers from time to time including the IRDA Annual Reports also publish the mortality statistics. In non-life insurance, the insurers make estimates of the claims cost based on past experience, which are subject to review from time to time. The factors considered when pricing general insurance products are: *(a)* Claims cost, *(b)* business acquisition cost, *(c)* management expenses, *(d)* margin for fluctuations in claims experience and *(e)* a reasonable profit. Accordingly, the life insurance and non-life insurance pricing can be distinguished as follows:

10.7 Rate-making Entities

The individual insurers or professional rate making organisations may determine insurance rates. However, actuaries are generally involved in the rate-making process.

Professional Rate-making Organizations

Professional rate-making organizations are the specialists that perform the rating work for the insurance companies. The reason for existence of such organizations is that many companies do not have the sufficient data of their own. By working together and pooling their premium and loss data, they can develop a more reliable rating information. Co-operative rate-making is also suitable for smaller companies.

Actuaries

Actuaries are the specialists in the mathematics of insurance, who carry out the prime responsibility of the rate-making process either working in companies or otherwise. They make financial sense of the future by applying mathematical models to problems of insurance and finance. Actuaries are experts who perform actuarial analysis of insurance rates, rating procedures, rating plans, and schedules of insurance companies. These are professionals who are experienced in reviewing and analysing insurance operations, reserves and underwriting procedures and provide technical assistance regarding actuarial matters to policy examiners and other technical staff. They perform the following functions:

(*a*) Developing new forms of insurance to meet the changing needs of consumers.

(*b*) Determining the reserves needed to meet the future obligations.

(*c*) Analysing the expenses and earnings and providing database for distribution of surpluses.

(*d*) Conducting research studies on claims experiences, projecting future claims and earnings.

(*e*) Communicating with the company officials, agents, policyholders, and regulatory authorities about company policies and practices.

Qualified actuaries are in great demand in India with few qualified ones available. It is considered to be one of the best career options. One must have a professional qualification from the Actuarial Society of India or such institutions abroad. The actuarial profession in the world is about 150 years old. In 1848, the Institute of Actuaries was established in London. The Actuarial Society of India was established in Bombay in 1944. In exercise of the powers conferred by clause (zd) of subsection (2) of Section 114A of the Insurance Act, 1938 (4 of 1938), the Insurance Regulatory and Development Authority, in consultation with the Insurance Advisory Committee has made certain regulations regarding Actuaries. According to the guidelines, an insurer registered to carry on insurance business in India shall, subject to sub-regulation (2), appoint an actuary who shall be known as the Appointed Actuary for the purpose of the Act. A person shall be eligible to be appointed as an appointed actuary for an insurer if he or she shall be —

(*a*) Ordinary resident in India.

(*b*) A fellow member of the Actuarial Society of India.

(*c*) An Employee of the life insurer, in case of life insurance business.

(*d*) An Employee of the insurer or a consulting actuary, in case of general insurance business.

(*e*) A person who has not committed any breach of professional misconduct.

(*f*) A person against whom no disciplinary action by the Actuarial Society of India or any other actuarial body is pending.

(*g*) Not an appointed actuary of another insurer.

(*h*) A person who possesses a Certificate of Practice issued by the Actuarial Society of India; and

(*i*) Not over the age of seventy years.

Every insurer shall seek the approval of the Authority for the appointment of appointed actuary, submitting the application in form IRDA-AA-1. The text of the IRDA guidelines concerning actuaries are given in Annexure 10A.

10.8 Rate Making in General Insurance

In general insurance, apart from the normal rating procedures, the rates may be regulated for certain classes of products. Tariff Advisory Committee, to certain extent, controls the prices on some specific classes of insurances.

'Tariff' is defined as *fixed rate* on which a product or service is offered to customer. In tariff or regulated market condition, either price or features of an offering or both are fixed and monitored by some regulator in market.

10.8.1 Tariff Advisory Committee

In 1896, Bombay Association of fire was established, under the close supervision of fire office committee in UK. In 1905, this association was replaced by *Fire Insurance Association* with offices at Bombay, Calcutta, Delhi and Madras. Bombay Association of Fire initiated the regulation of rates, term and conditions and they were adopted by the Fire Insurance Association. The Insurance Association of India with membership of all insurers adopted the structure pertaining to rates, terms and conditions determined by Tariff committee under the control of the *Tariff Advisory Council.*

Later, *Tarif Advisory Committee* (TAC) was formed by another amendment to the insurance Act replacing the Tariff committee. TAC is a statutory body under the insurance Act, 1938. The IRDA Act, 1999, along with the resultant modifications to the Insurance Act have reconfirmed the regulatory role of TAC.

Section 64V of Insurance Act, 1938 defines TAC as a body that controls and regulates the rates, terms and advantages of general Insurance business in India.

10.8.2 What is a Tariff Rate?

Tax fixes the tariffs regarding the general insurance product. "A tariff is merely a schedule of premium rates and policy terms and conditions applicable to risks in a class of business". A tariff rate in the Indian context is the minimum rates to be charged for a tariff cover with a prescribed wording: a reduced rate charged amounts to a breach of tariff provision. When all the insurance companies operating in a market follow tariff system of pricing, the market is said to be tariffed market, viz., the Indian General Insurance Market. Under such a system, insurers have no choice of product and price differentiation. Tariff system leaves very little scope for competition among the insurance companies. Product differentiation is absent. The insurers can compete on the basis of customer services instead of competing on price and product differentiation. *Tariff rate is the price of a general insurance product.* In Life Insurance, premium is the price. Tariff rates prescribed by IRDA should be followed by all General Insurance Companies.

10.8.3 Basic General Insurance Product Pricing Structure

- Claims cost
- Management cost
- Business acquisition cost
- Margins and reasonable profits.

10.8.4 Objectives of Maintaining System of Tariffs

- Ensuring the long-term financial stability of Insurance enterprises.
- Facilitating classification of risks according to their special characteristics.
- To provide rates for various insurance products.
- To prevent uneconomic competition by containing predatory rate war which could lead to chaos bankruptcy and loss of credibility of the market.
- Maintaining Market Stability
- To ensure that rates and terms are equitable and non-discriminatory.
- To ensure a moderate competition.
- Making rate setting more scientific and base it on systematic analysis.

10.8.5 Why Detariffing?

Initially tariffs were introduced to protect the customer's interest. But for insurance companies, tariff system leaves very little scope for competition. Since the liberalization of insurance sector, many companies (General Insurance) have entered in the market. It is also a known fact that when sellers are more, the customer will usually end up with a fair deal.

Moreover all the companies that are in general insurance business have big plan for future. It can be expected that they will always play safe. Finally, we have a watchdog (IRDA) which can award a red card to the erring plays. In the present scenario, market should move towards a free rate regime according to transparent plan. Marketing every one subject to tariff is not a desirable long-term solution. Privatization and tariff cannot go hand in hand and hence the shift from tariff to detariff regime. In due course of shifting from tariffing to detariffing regime, the rates would fall in line with international trends. This process should be encouraged.

Detariffing and Its Impact on India

The final phase of the detariff process is likely to provide opportunities for the following:

- expanded and enhanced cover;
- customized cover for a specific exposure or peril;
- cover on a first-loss basis; and
- CAT perils-only cover.

Annexure 10 A

THE GAZETTE OF INDIA: EXTRAORDINARY

[PART III — SEC. 4]

INSURANCE REGULATORY AND DEVELOPMENT AUTHORITY,

NEW DELHI

NOTIFICATION

New Delhi, 14th July, 2000

Insurance Regulatory and Development Authority (Appointed Actuary) Regulations, 2000

F.No.IRDA/Reg./7/2000 —

In exercise of the powers conferred by clause (zd) of subsection (2) of Section 114A of the Insurance Act, 1938 (4 of 1938), the Insurance Regulatory and Development Authority, in consultation with the Insurance Advisory Committee, hereby makes the following regulations, namely:

1. Short title and commencement: (1) These regulations may be called the Insurance Regulatory and Development Authority (Appointed Actuary) Regulations, 2000.

(2) They shall come into force from the date of their publication in the *Official Gazette.*

2. Definitions: (1) In these regulations, unless the context otherwise requires —

(a) "Act" means the Insurance Act, 1938 (4 of 1938);

(b) "Actuarial Society of India" means Actuarial Society of India registered under Societies Registration Act 1860; (21 of 1860);

(c) "Appointed Actuary" means an actuary mentioned in Regulation 3 below;

(d) "Authority" means the Insurance Regulatory and Development Authority established under subsection (1) of Section 3 of the Insurance Regulatory and Development Authority Act, 1999 (41 of 1999);

(e) "Professional Standard" means the standard of practice specified, with the concurrence of the Authority, by the Actuarial Society of India by issue of guidance notes to its members.

(2) All words and expressions used herein and not defined herein but defined in the Insurance Act, 1938 (4 of 1938), or in the Insurance Regulatory and Development Authority Act, 1999 (41 of 1999), shall have the meanings respectively assigned to them in those Acts.

3. Procedure for Appointment of an Appointed Actuary: (1) An insurer registered to carry on insurance business in India shall, subject to sub-regulation (2), appoint an actuary, who shall be known as the 'Appointed Actuary' for the purposes of the Act.

(2) A person shall be eligible to be appointed as an appointed actuary for an insurer, if he or she shall be —

(i) ordinarily resident in India;

(ii) a Fellow Member of the Actuarial Society of India;

(iii) an employee of the life insurer, in case of life insurance business;

(iv) an employee of the insurer or a consulting actuary, in case of general insurance business;

(iv) a person who has not committed any breach of professional conduct;

(v) a person against whom no disciplinary action by the Actuarial Society of India or any other actuarial professional body is pending;

(vi) not an appointed actuary of another insurer;

(vii) a person who possesses a Certificate of Practice issued by the Actuarial Society of India; and

(viii) not over the age of seventy years.

(3) An insurer shall seek the approval of the Authority for the appointment of appointed actuary, submitting the application in Form IRDA-AA-1.

(4) The Authority shall, within thirty days from the date of receipt of application, either accept or reject the same:

Provided that before rejecting the application, the Authority shall give an opportunity of being heard to the insurer.

(5) If an insurer does not receive approval within thirty days of the receipt of such application by the Authority, the insurer shall deem that the approval has been granted by the Authority.

(6) An insurer, who is unable to appoint an appointed actuary in accordance with sub-regulation (2), shall make an application to the Authority in writing for relaxation of one or more conditions mentioned in sub-regulation 2.

(7) The Authority shall, on receipt of the application referred to in sub-regulation (6), communicate its decision to the insurer within thirty days of receipt of such application.

(8) The appointment of an appointed actuary shall take effect from the date of approval by the Authority.

4. Effect of rejection of the application: The insurer shall, within four weeks of rejection of the application referred to under regulation 3, apply to the Authority for the appointment of a person other than the one rejected by it under regulation 3 as an appointed actuary, for the purposes of these regulations.

5. Life Insurer not to carry on business of insurance without an appointed actuary: A life insurer shall not carry on business of insurance without an appointed actuary.

6. Cessation of Appointment of Appointed Actuary: (1) An appointed actuary shall cease to be so, if he or she has been given notice of withdrawal of approval by the Authority on the following grounds:

(a) that he or she ceases to be eligible in accordance with sub-regulation (2) of regulation (3), or;

(b) that he or she has, in the opinion of the Authority, failed to perform adequately and properly the duties and obligations of an appointed actuary under these regulations.

(2) The Authority shall give an appointed actuary a reasonable opportunity of being heard, if he or she has been given a notice of withdrawal of approval by it.

(3) If a person ceases to be an appointed actuary of an insurer otherwise than on the grounds mentioned in sub-regulation (1), the insurer and the appointed actuary shall intimate the Authority the reasons therefor within fifteen days of such a cessation.

7. Powers of Appointed Actuary: (1) An appointed actuary shall have access to all information or documents in possession, or under control, of the insurer if such access is necessary for the proper and effective performance of the functions and duties of the appointed actuary.

(2) The appointed actuary may seek any information for the purpose of sub-regulation (1) of this regulation from any officer or employee of the insurer.

(3) The appointed actuary shall be entitled —

(a) to attend all meetings of the management including the directors of the insurer;

(b) to speak and discuss on any matter, at such meeting,—

(i) that relates to the actuarial advice given to the directors;

(ii) that may affect the solvency of the insurer;

(iii) that may affect the ability of the insurer to meet the reasonable expectations of policyholders; or

(iv) on which actuarial advice is necessary;

(c) to attend, —

(i) any meeting of the shareholders or the policyholders of the insurer; or

(ii) any other meeting of members of the insurer at which the insurer's annual accounts or financial statements are to be considered or at which any matter in connection with the appointed actuary's duties is discussed.

8. Duties and obligations: In particular and without prejudice to the generality of the foregoing matters, and in the interests of the insurance industry and the policyholders, the duties and obligations of an appointed actuary of an insurer shall include:

(a) rendering actuarial advice to the management of the insurer, in particular in the areas of product design and pricing, insurance contract wording, investments and reinsurance;

(b) ensuring the solvency of the insurer at all times;

(c) complying with the provisions of the Section 64 V of the Act in regard to certification of the assets and liabilities that have been valued in the manner required under the said section;

(d) complying with the provisions of the Section 64 VA of the Act in regard to maintenance of required solvency margin in the manner required under the said section;

(e) drawing the attention of management of the insurer, to any matter on which he or she thinks that action is required to be taken by the insurer to avoid —

(i) any contravention of the Act; or

(ii) prejudice to the interests of policyholders;

(f) complying with the Authority's directions from time to time;

(g) in the case of the insurer carrying on life insurance business,—

(i) to certify the actuarial report and abstract and other returns as required under section 13 of the Act;

(ii) to comply with the provisions of Section 21 of the Act in regard to further information required by the Authority;

(iii) to comply with the provisions of Section 40-B of the Act in regard to the bases of premium;

(iv) to comply with the provisions of the Section 112 of the Act in regard to recommendation of interim bonus or bonuses payable by life insurer to policyholders whose policies mature for payment by reason of death or otherwise during the inter-valuation period;

(v) to ensure that all the requisite records have been made available to him or her for the purpose of conducting actuarial valuation of liabilities and assets of the insurer;

(vi) to ensure that the premium rates of the insurance products are fair;

(vii) to certify that the mathematical reserves have been determined taking into account the guidance notes issued by the Actuarial Society of India and any directions given by the Authority;

(viii) to ensure that the policyholders' reasonable expectations have been considered in the matter of valuation of liabilities and distribution of surplus to the participating policyholders who are entitled for a share of surplus;

(ix) to submit the actuarial advice in the interests of the insurance industry and the policyholders;

(h) in the case of the insurer carrying on general insurance business to ensure, —

(i) that the rates are fair in respect of those contracts that are governed by the insurer's in-house tariff;

(ii) that the actuarial principles, in the determination of liabilities, have been used in the calculation of reserves for incurred but not reported claims (IBNR) and other reserves where actuarial advice is sought by the Authority;

(iii) informing the Authority in writing of his or her opinion, within a reasonable time, whether,—

(a) the insurer has contravened the Act or any other Acts;

(b) the contravention is of such a nature that it may affect significantly the interests of the owners or beneficiaries of policies issued by the insurer;

(c) the directors of the insurer have failed to take such action as is reasonably necessary to enable him to exercise his or her duties and obligations under this regulation; or

(d) an officer or employee of the insurer has engaged in conduct calculated to prevent him or her from exercising his or her duties and obligations under this regulation.

9. Absolute Privilege of Appointed Actuary: (1) An appointed actuary shall enjoy absolute privilege to make any statement, oral or written, for the purpose of the performance of his functions as appointed actuary. This is in addition to any other privilege conferred upon an appointed actuary under any other Regulations.

(2) Any provision of the letter of appointment of the appointed actuary, which restricts or prevents his duties, obligations and privileges under these regulations, shall be of no effect.

10. Applicability to reinsurance business: These regulations shall apply to reinsurers carrying on reinsurance business in India.

Form IRDA-AA-1

Particulars of Appointed Actuary

1. Name of Insurer:
2. Name of Actuary:
3. Residential Address with telephone number: [Residential addresses during the last five years have to be furnished].
4. Official Address with telephone number:
5. Date of Appointment:
6. Date and Place of Birth.
7. Annual Remuneration and Fringe Benefits.
8. Shareholding (in per cent of shareholding) in the Indian Insurance Company (for which the applicant is the Appointed Actuary) and also in the promoter's companies, if any.
9. Professional Qualifications:
10. Working Experience (give also particulars of previous experience as Appointed Actuary in India or elsewhere).
11. Achievements and special positions held presently or previously.
12. Names, countries of incorporation, addresses and principal activities of any other firms or companies in which the applicant was a director, partner, proprietor or an employee.
13. Particulars of any criminal conviction for offences in India or elsewhere:
14. Has the applicant been adjudicated bankrupt during the last ten years? If so, give details:
15. Has the applicant been disciplined by any professional bodies or any insurance regulator? If so give details:

❑❑❑

UNIT III
LIFE INSURANCE

LIFE INSURANCE — CONCEPTUAL FRAMEWORK

CHAPTER

Chapter Objectives

- Life Insurance: Meaning and Definition
- Features Of Life Insurance
- Nature Of Insurance
- Benefits Of Life Insurance
- Life Insurance Players in India
- Life Insurance Demand and Outlook

Introduction

Life Insurance, usually referred to as 'life assurance' insures the insured against the happening of certain event, i.e., death through the time when it may happen is uncertain. The life insurance contract can be described as 'contingent contracts' because the loss of life cannot be compensated and only a specified sum of money is paid if the insured dies. In addition to this, life insurance is considered a better way of making investment along with the benefits of protection against the risks of death.

11.1 Life Insurance: Meaning and Definition

Section 2 of the Indian Insurance Act, 1938 has defined life insurance as: "Life Insurance business is the business of effecting contracts upon human life."

A life insurance contract may be defined as 'a contract whereby the insurer, in consideration of a premium paid either in lump sum or in periodic instalments, undertakes to pay an annuity or a certain sum of money, either on the death of the insured or on the expiry of a certain number of years.'

In simple words, it may be defined as 'a contract whereby the insurance company, in consideration of periodical premium, agrees to pay a certain amount either on the death or on the maturity of the policy, whichever is earlier.'

J.H. Maggee has defined life insurance in the following words: The life insurance contract embodies an agreement, in which, broadly stated, the insurer undertakes to pay a stipulated sum upon the death of the insured, or at some designated time to a designated beneficiary.

As such, under life insurance, the sum assured under policy is paid to the insured if policy matures during his lifetime and to his nominees in case of death. The premium may be paid in lump sum or in monthly, quarterly, half-yearly or yearly instalments.

11.2 Features of Life Insurance

1. Like other contracts of insurance, the life insurance contract is also the outcome of an offer made by the insured and its acceptance by the insurer. Usually, contract of life insurance is made in writing.
2. The insurance company agrees to pay a certain sum of money either on the death of the insured or on the maturity of the policy, whichever is earlier.
3. The insured is under obligation to pay periodically the amount of payment till the death of insured or expiry of the period of policy, whichever is earlier.
4. The contract of life insurance is not a contract of indemnity because the loss caused by the death cannot be calculated in money terms, nor is money any compensation for loss of one's life.
5. Insurable interest must be present in the person insured at the time when the policy is taken in case of life insurance, which may or may not be present at the time of insured's death.
6. Life insurance extends the hand of protection to those who are left supportless and helps financially in case of death of the insured. It is also considered to be the best alternative for making savings.
7. Life insurance covers under scope certain other risks which are connected with the human life in addition to the risk of death. For example, in case of total and permanent disability or the living death, temporary disability and medical expenses, compulsory retirement or the economic death risks, etc., have also been covered under the purview of life insurance these days.
8. It relieves the insured from the sword of Damocles, i.e., various risks and uncertainties which may occur before and after the death of the insured.

11.3 Nature of Insurance

On the basis of present-day economic environment, there are few basic needs for which life insurance is needed. The life insurance is concerned with the hazards that stand across the life of every person that is dying prematurely leaving dependent and that of living to old age without visible means of support.

(a) **Family Protection.** To protect the families from the economic hardships after the death of the bread-winner member of the family.

(b) **Investment of Savings.** Savings provide the new source of income when permanent earning stops and Life Assurance provide an immediate source of income for one's family on the death of an insured person prematurely.

(c) **Additional Way of Earnings.** It provides an insured additional earning by way of bonus and interest credited by the Life Insurance Corporation.

(d) **Helpful at the Time of Cessation of Earnings.** Life Assurance is needed because when one ceases to earn money, insurer provides certain sum of money to the insured as per various terms of policies.

So, the fundamental principle of life insurance is to save a person from uncertainties like premature death, old age, etc.

11.4 Benefits of Life Insurance

The following are the advantages of Life Insurance:

1. Superior Saving Plan: Unlike any other savings plan, a life insurance policy affords full protection against risk of death. In the event of death of a policyholder, the insurance company makes available the full sum assured to the policyholders' near and dear ones. In comparison, any other savings plan would amount to the total savings accumulated till date. If the death occurs prematurely, such savings can be much lesser than the sum assured. Evidently, the potential financial loss to the family of the policyholder is sizable.

2. Encourage Saving Habits: Life Insurance encourages saving habits. Long-term savings can be made in a painless manner because of the easy instalment facility built into the scheme. The insured person can pay premiums through monthly, quarterly, half-yearly or yearly instalments. The salary saving scheme, popularly known as SSS; provides a convenient method of paying premium each month through deduction from one's salary. The employer is authorized by the employee to deduct the insurance premium monthly and remit to the Life Insurance Corporation. The Salary Saving Scheme (SSS) can be introduced in any institution or organization subject to specified terms and conditions laid down by insurer.

3. Suitable for Raising Loans: Life Insurance policy can be given as security to raise a loan even for commercial purposes also. The loan can be raised without any delay on safe security of the policy. Even after an initial period payments if the policyholder finds it difficult to continue with the payment of premium, he can surrender the policy for a surrender value amount with the Life Insurance Corporation.

4. Easy Settlement Protection Against Creditors: The maturity value of Life Insurance policy can be protected against the claims of the creditors of the life assured by valid assignment of a policy. The policyholder can nominate a person to whom the policy money would be payable in event of his death.

5. Tax Relief: The Income Tax relief is available for amounts paid by way of premium for life insurance subject to the income tax rates in force. Assesses can avail themselves of provisions in the law for tax relief. In this manner, the assured is required to pay lower premium for his insurance than he would have to pay otherwise. Under Section 80C of the Income Tax Act, 1956, the premium paid is allowed as a deduction from Gross Total Income (GTI). Contribution to pension plans qualifies for deduction under section 80CCC. Also 100% of the premium paid is deductible as expenditure from business income. When these benefits are factored in, it is found that most policies offer returns that are comparable/or even better than other saving modes such as PPF, NSC etc. Moreover, the cost of insurance is a very negligible.

6. Estate Duty: Life Insurance ensures the definite sum of money after the death of the insured without resorting to sale of assets at a loss on realization. So, it is the best way of making provision for payment of Estate Duty.

7. Economic Protection: Life Insurance provides economic protection to the family members of the insured in case of his untimely death who might be the sole bread-earner of the family. It reduces the sufferings of the families on happening of a contingent event. It is considered to be the most effective device for providing family security.

8. Investment Element: In Life Insurance, the insured is required to pay the premium. The premium is a kind of investment. The premium is returned to the insured along with additional bonus amount after the expiry of the period of contract.

9. Helpful to the Government: Life Insurance provides long-term funds to the government for different development schemes. This helps the government to develop infrastructure to develop infrastructure and serve the society.

10. Money when Needed: A suitable insurance plan or a combination of different plans can be taken out as life insurance to meet the specific needs that are likely to arise in future, such as children's education, start-in-life or marriage provision, etc. Alternatively, policy money can be so arranged to be made available at the time of one's retirement from service to be used for any specific purpose, such as for the purchase of plot, house or for other investments. Loans are also granted to the policyholders, subject to certain conditions, for house building or for purchase of flats, etc.

11. Ready Marketability and Suitability for Quick Borrowing: A life insurance policy can, after a certain time period (generally three years), be surrendered for a cash value. The policy is also acceptable as a security for a commercial loan, for example, a student loan. It is particularly advisable for housing loans when an acceptable LIC policy may also cause the lending institution to give loan at lower interest rates.

12. Disability and Accidental Death Benefits: Death is not the only hazard that is insured; many policies also include disability benefits. Typically, these provide for waiver of future premiums and payment of monthly instalments spread over certain time period. Many policies can also provide for an extra sum to be paid (typically equal to the sum assured) if death occurs as a result of accident.

11.5 Life Insurance Players in India

The year 2000 was a defining movement in the history of Indian Insurance Industry. For the first time, the sector was opened up to private companies. Now, we find a number of private insurance companies entered into the Indian insurance market. If the FDI is raised from 26% to 49%, the number will be multiplied. Following are the private players in the life insurance sector in India.

1. Bajaj Allianz Life Insurance Company Limited
2. Birla Sun Life Insurance Co. Ltd.
3. HDFC Standard Life Insurance Co. Ltd.
4. ICICI Prudential Life Insurance Co. Ltd.
5. ING Vysya Life Insurance Co. Ltd.
6. Max New York Life Insurance Co. Ltd.
7. Met Life Insurance Co. Pvt. Ltd.
8. Kotak Mahindra Old Mutual Life Insurance Limited
9. SBI Mutual Life Insurance Limited
10. Tata AIG Life Insurance Co. Ltd.
11. Reliance Life Insurance Co. Ltd.
12. Aviva Life Insurance Co. Pvt. Ltd.
13. Sahara Life Insurance Co. Ltd.
14. Shriram Life Insurance Co. Ltd.
15. Bharti Life Insurance Co. Ltd.
16. Future Generali Life Insurance Co. Ltd.
17. IDBI Fortis Life Insurance Company Ltd.
18. Canara HSBC Oriental Bank of Commerce Life Insurance Company Ltd.
19. Aegon Religare Life Insurance Company Ltd.
20. DLF Pramerica Life Insurance Company Ltd.
21. Star Union Dai-ichi Life Insurance Company Ltd.
22. India First Life Insurance Company Ltd.

11.6 Life Insurance Demand and Outlook

Life insurance sector has started acquiring new shapes with newer innovations in the post liberalization era. Big brands like Birla, Tata, ICICI, HDFC etc. have tied up with foreign partners. The life insurance has been the baby of LIC of India, primarily because of its monopoly till privatization. Even though the growth has been impressive over years, yet the penetration is pretty low. Let us have a look at the life insurance average index. The number of policies sold is very low viz., 13.2 per 100 persons compared to the Asian counterparts like Malaysia and Japan where it is 37.0 and 201.4 respectively.

The life insurance premium as a percentage of GDP is very low and which is expected in improve in coming years indicating a vast potential for the players.

The expected demand as per research studies show a vast potential to the extent of 650 million estimated for 2005. The key reasons for the optimistic outlook can be described on two accounts:

From the Viewpoint of Investment

1. The life insurance sector has demonstrated in the past, its commitment to provide a steady and secured return compared to other forms of investments.
2. The life insurance premiums offer tax incentives, which have been continuing since long. However, Kelkar Committee recommendations have posed a threat. Yet these have not been implemented.
3. The life investments have proved least risk options compared to stock markets where investors in one form or other have burned hands including the UTI fiasco.

From Social Angle

1. The change in lifestyle and attitudes, shift to nuclear family system have urged the need for insurance.
2. The increasing literacy rate has resulted in channeling of financial resource from savings to financial assets.
3. The life insurance covers can be used as collateral security for obtaining loans, which positively affected the demand for life products.
4. The young population ratio is the highest in India, which is likely to drive the demand for insurance.

From Macroeconomic Angle

1. The average annual percentage growth of GDP is approximately 5% (Exhibit 11B).
2. The infant mortality rate is improving, viz., 61.467 deaths/1000 live births compared to past (Exhibit 11B).
3. The middle class is expanding and its per capita income is growing.
4. The percentage of financial assets in household savings is growing, viz., in 2000-01 it was 11% of the total household savings of 20.9%.

In addition to above, the private players and, also, LIC are coming out with new and innovative products which are likely to attract the potential customers.

Exhibit 11.1
Life Business Development by Region

Real growth rates	*Growth rate 2007*	*Annual average growth rate 1997-2006*
Region		
World	5.3%	4.3%
Industrialized countries	4.6%	3.8%
North America	5.3%	3.8%
Western Europe	5.5%	6.9%

Japan and newly industrialized Asian economies	1.8%	0.3%
Oceania	7.9%	1.6%
Emerging markets	13.1%	13.5%
South and East Asia	16.8%	19.3%
Latin America and Caribbean	11.4%	10.4%
Central and Eastern Europe	17.0%	7.6%
Africa	3.4%	7.5%
Middle East and Central Asia	8.7%	5.8%

Exhibit 11.2
Life insurance growth, penetration and density by region

	Premiums (in USD mn) 2007	*Real growth 2007*	*Share of world market (in %) 2007*	*Premiums in % of GDP 2007*	*Premiums per capita (in USD) 2007*
America	659,759	6.1	27.57	3.53	732.3
North America	623,950	5.8	26.07	4.09	1,869.3
Latin America and Caribbean	35,809	11.4	1.50	1.04	63.1
Europe	1,035,942	5.6	43.29	5.00	1,222.6
Western Europe	1,017,881	5.5	42.53	5.68	2,014.0
Central and Eastern Europe	18,062	17.0	0.75	0.68	55.5
Asia	623,469	4.3	26.05	4.61	156.7
Japan and newly industrialized Asian economies	493,567	1.8	20.62	8.02	2,331.6
South and East Asia	124,136	16.8	5.19	2.15	35.9
Middle East and Central Asia	5,766	8.7	0.24	0.36	18.7
Oceania	35,807	7.9	1.50	3.42	1,071.4
Africa	38,111	3.4	1.59	3.08	39.6
World	2,393,089	5.4	100.00	4.41	358.1
Industrialized countries	2,174,313	4.7	90.86	5.42	2,142.6
Emerging markets	218,776	13.1	9.14	1.45	38.4
OECD	2,105,446	4.2	87.98	5.10	1,738.7
G7	1,681,968	3.7	70.28	5.51	2,304.5
EU, 15 countries	975,158	5.6	40.75	5.94	2,376.1
NAFTA	631,603	5.8	26.39	3.91	1,434.4
ASEAN	26,988	16.7	1.13	2.16	53.8

Source: Swiss Re, Economic Research & Consulting, Sigma No. 4/2007

Key Terms

- ❒ Insurance Coverage Index
- ❒ Life Fund
- ❒ Technical Account
- ❒ Sum Assured
- ❒ Revenue Account
- ❒ Shareholder's Account

Questions for Review

1. Enumerate the advantages of life insurance to individuals.
2. Evaluate the performance of life insurance sector in the pre and post-liberalization period.

Suggested Readings

1. G.R. Desai, *Life Insurance in India — Its History and Dimensions of Growth,* Macmillan India Ltd., 1973.
2. *Insurance Business Environment,* Insurance Institute of India, Mumbai.
3. IRDA Annual Report 2001-02.
4. R.M. Ray, *Life Insurance in India,* Indian Institute of Public Administration, New Delhi, 1982.
5. S.R. Chawla, *Attitude Towards Life Insurance Cover,* NCAER, New Delhi, 1979.
6. *Tryst with Trust — A History of Life Insurance*, Life Insurance Corporation of India, 1991.

Web Resources

- www.licindia.com
- www.myiris.com
- www.best-life-insurance-online.com
- www.irdaindia.org

❑❑❑

LIFE CONTRACTS AND RATING

CHAPTER

Chapter Objectives

- Basic Components of a Life Insurance Contract
- Other Policy Provisions
- Basic procedure for issuing a life insurance policy
- Alterations
- Issue of Duplicate Policy
- Nomination
- Assignment
- Lapse and Revivals
- Policy Loans
- Foreclosure
- Married Women's Property (MWP) Act Policies
- Method of Risk Classification in life insurance
- Treatment of Sub-Standard Life Insurance Risks
- Calculation of Premium

Introduction

Life Insurance document is the evidence of insurance contact between the insurer and insured that has to last for a relatively long period. These contracts are generally standardised with condition and exceptions. However, the policy document is the physical evidence of various alterations or modifications in the contract.

12.1 Basic Components of a Life Insurance Contract

A life insurance policy expresses the terms of contract between the insurer and the insured. The policy document should reveal: (*i*) the definition of the risk covered, (*ii*) the duration of the risk, (*iii*) the premium, and (*iv*) the amount of insurance (Ref. Law of Insurance Macgillvary). The policy, however, states rights and privileges of the insured person and his obligations as well. The policy documents will have standardised and printed conditions. Any variation will be provided by suitable endorsements placed on the policy. The life policy contains the following details:

(*a*) **'Heading'** contains the name and address of the Insurer. This also indicate the jurisdiction in cases of legal disputes and also the address where any notices can be served by the Insured against the company.

(*b*) **'Preamble'** states the intention of the parties to the contract in brief and general terms. It introduces both the parties. The receipt of the proposal and declaration as well as the first premium from the proposer are acknowledged. The statement and declarations contained in the proposal and personal statement are stated to be the basis of the agreement.

(*c*) **'Operative Clause'** mentions the mutual responsibilities and obligations of both the parties as follows:

(*1*) In consideration of payment of the first premium and subsequent premiums as and when they fall due (the payment of premiums is made a condition precedent for performance of the contract by the insurer).

(*2*) The insurer agrees to pay the benefits secured under the policy including bonus in respect of participating policies.

(*3*) On receipt of proof satisfactory to the company—

(*i*) the happening of event on which the benefits are payable.

(*ii*) the title of the person claiming payment.

(*iii*) age of the life assured, if not already admitted.

(*d*) **'Proviso'** contains two stipulations: (*a*) the conditions and privileges printed on the back of the policy shall be deemed to be a part of the policy and (*b*) every endorsement placed evidencing alterations etc., shall be deemed to be part of the policy.

(*e*) **'Schedule'** contains details of the particular contract. The details can be classified as follows:

(*i*) *Identifying the policyholder:* policy number, date of commencement, date of proposal, name and address of the proposer and life assured.

(*ii*) *Scope of Cover:* plan and term of insurance, sum assured, date of maturity, events on the happening of which the benefits become payable, any additional benefits like accident benefit.

(*iii*) *To whom the sum assured is payable:* specific information and also name of nominee.

(*iv*) *Premium:* the instalment premium, due dates, mode of payment of premium, period during which premiums are payable, dates on last premium.

(*v*) *Age:* age of the life assured and whether the same has been admitted.

(*vi*) Space for any special provisions.

(*f*) **'Attestation':** the policy should be stamped and then signed by an authorized official of the company.

(g) **'Conditions and Privileges':** these are usually printed on the back of the Policy Document and can be classified into following groups:

(*i*) *Conditions:* These explain the nature of the contract: like proof of age here mention is made that premium is calculated on the basis of age and if age has already not been admitted and subsequently proved to be higher than stated, the company reserves to modify any terms of the contract.

- *Forfeiture in certain events:* Three events under which the benefits secured under the policy can be forfeited, viz., (1) non-payment or premiums subject to non-forfeiture privilege, (2) in the event of any condition being contravened and (3) in case there has been untrue or incorrect statements regarding material facts subject to Section 45 of insurance contract.
- *Suicide:* This condition stipulates that in the event of death due to suicide within one year from the commencement of risk, the policy shall be void.
- *Other restrictive clauses:* Certain clauses like extra premiums charged for temporary periods, lien clause, excluding certain risks like accident and disability benefits to physically handicapped persons, pregnancy clauses, etc.,
- *Assignment and Nomination:* This condition merely stipulates that notice of assignment or nomination should be submitted for registration with the insurance company and in registering the notice, the company does not accept any responsibility or express any opinion as to its validity or legal effect.

(*ii*) *Privileges:* Certain privileges are allowed under the policy. For example, in payment of premiums — days of grace allowed (both in the event of death and when the policy is in force during the days of grace), full sum assured will be paid subject to deduction of overdue premiums. This privilege also stipulates that in the event of death when the policy is in full force for the full sum assured, the unpaid premium, if any, due before the next policy anniversary will be deducted from the claim amount.

- *Revival of discontinued policies:* A policy lapses if the premium due is not paid before the expiry of the days of grace. Subsequently, the policy can be revived subject to certain conditions, which may vary from company to company. These conditions for revival of a lapsed policy are stated in this privilege.
- *Non-forfeiture regulations:* As per Insurance Act, 1938 a life insurance policy whereunder premiums have been paid for a continuous period of three years cannot wholly lapse by will have to acquire some value. This privilege is referred to as 'Non-forfeiture' regulation. The method of calculation of such value will have to be incorporated in the policy.

12.2 Other Policy Provisions

Apart from the various conditions and privileges mentioned above, the provisions are made in the provision by way of clauses. Some of these are stated below:

(a) Ownership Clause: till the owner' is alive, he has all contracted right under the policy.

(b) Entirety Clause: the policy documents and ansurances form the entire part of the contract.

(c) Reinstatement Revival Clause: which empower the policyholder to reinstate (revive) of premium but object to some conditions.

(d) Policy Loan Clause: which allows the insured to take a cash loan on the policy subject to condltion.

(e) Dividend Clause: which allows the insurer to pay dividend on participating poliers.

(f) Waiver of premium: where the insured becomes totally disabled (permanent/partial/total disablement). Also called as disability benefit.

(g) Accident benefit: which allows the insurer to pay benefit over and above the normal benefit (in case of death/disablement) occurring due to accident.

(h) Guaranteed Surrender Value Clause: which shows the cash value receivable if the policy is surrendered. It may also indicate the former for calculation.

12.3 Basic Procedure for Issuing a Life Insurance Policy

Insurance is a contract as discussed earlier. Therefore, the process of life insurance starts with the proposal made by the prospective insured (called as the proposer) in a standard application form issued by insurance companies generally made available by agents. Once the policy has been selected, the proposer has to provide information about income, age and health. If there is a need for medical examination, the report of the medical examiner is sent to the insurance company confidentially. The agent or the development officer generally does a first level underwriting and a report thereon is sent to the company. This report provides information about the financial position and need and adequacy of insurance for the proposer. It also contains the information gathered by the agent/development officer from his personal sources or inquiries made on the basis of the information furnished by the proposer. Thereafter, the documents are scrutinized from various angles particularly age, financial condition and health status.

Age Proof

Scrutiny of age is an important concern for the life insurer because old age people have high probability of dying than the younger ones and premium is calculated on the basis of age groups. Accuracy in age computation resolves hardship both to the insurer and the potential insured in the sense that that correct age avoids the company being affected by lesser premiums or undesired risk bought or risk not bought because of fear. From the insured's perspective, it helps in charging of fair premiums and insurance availability. The proofs of age, which are generally considered are as under:

- Certified extract from municipal or other records made at the time of birth.
- Certificate of Baptism or certified extract from family Bible if it contains age or date of birth.

- Certified extract from School or College if age or date of birth is stated therein.
- Certified extract from Service Register in case of Govt. employees and employees of Quasi-Govt. institutions including Public Limited Companies and
- Passport issued by the Passport Authorities in India.

Alternative Age Proofs, which are also accepted in the industry, are:

- Marriage certificate in the case of Roman Catholics issued by Roman Catholic Church.
- Certified extracts from the Service Registers of Commercial Institutions or Industrial Undertakings provided it is specifically mentioned in such extracts that conclusive evidence of age was produced at the time of recruitment of the employee.
- Certificate of Birth granted by *Syedna v. Molana Badruddin Sahib of Baroda*.
- Identity Cards issued by Defence Department.
- A true copy of the University Certificate or of Matriculation/Higher Secondary Education, S.S.L. Certificate issued by a Board set up by a State/Central Government.
- Non-standard age proofs like Horoscope, Service Record where age is not verified at the time of entry, E.S.I.S. Card, Marriage Certificate in case of Muslim Proposer, Elder's Declaration, Self-declaration and Certificate by Village Panchayats are accepted subject to certain rules.

Medical Examination

Generally, at some levels and in case of endowment policies, whole life policies, the medical examination is not asked for. However, if the amount of insurance is very high or the age is high or the first level examination has some adverse remarks, then the insurance company may refer the proposal for a thorough examination. Cases of pregnant women, or women with history of miscarriages or abortion are declined. Sometimes, the medical examination may be waived, like in rural areas, where the facilities are not available.

After the above examinations and obtaining special reports, if required, the underwriter may accept or reject the case. Else, he is empowered to modify the sum assured, premium to be charged and manner thereof, impose conditions or provide exclusions in the policy.

In case of untrue or incorrect statement contained in the proposal, personal statement, declaration and connected documents or any material information withheld, subject to the provision of Section 45 of the Insurance Act 1938, wherever applicable, the policy shall be declared void and all claims to any benefits in virtue thereof shall cease.

After the policy is issued, the policyholder in a number of cases finds the terms not suitable to him and desires to change them. LIC allows certain types of alterations during the lifetime of the policy. However, no alteration is permitted within one year of the commencement of the policy with some exceptions. The following alterations are allowed —

- Alteration in class or term
- Reduction in the sum assured
- Alteration in the mode of payment of premiums

- Alteration in the date of commencement of the policy
- Splitting up of a single policy into two or more policies
- Removal of an extra premium
- Alteration from without profit plan to with profit plan
- Alternation in name
- Correction in policies
- Settlement option of payment of sum assured by instalments
- Grant of accident benefit
- Grant of premium waiver benefit under CDA policies
- Alteration in currency and place of payment of policy moneys.

A fee for the change or alteration in the policy is charged by the company called as the quotation fee and no additional fee is charged for giving effect to the alteration.

12.4 Alterations

The policy document embodies the terms of the contract. These terms continue to operate throughout the currency of the policy unless modified by mutual consent of the parties to the contract, viz., the policyholder and the insurer. Situations may arise where the policyholder may desire alterations in the terms of the contract to suit changed circumstances. For example, the policyholder may find it difficult to continue the payment of premiums for the original SA and may like to reduce the SA or he may ask for change of mode of payment of premium.

The types of alterations for which requests are normally made are:

(*a*) Alteration in plan or term

(*b*) Reduction in SA

(*c*) Change in mode of payment of premium

(*d*) Alteration in name

(*e*) Change of the nominee

(*f*) Removal of an extra premium

(*g*) Splitting up of policy into two or more policies

(*h*) Alteration from without profit to with profit plan or *vice versa*

(*i*) Grant of accident benefit

(*j*) Settlement option of payment of SA by instalments

(*k*) Grant of premium waiver benefit

(*l*) Correction in policies (generally soon after commencement)

Alterations are considered if the policy is in force for the full SA. Alterations are not normally allowed in the first year of the policy, unless they be by way of correction or changes which do not affect the basic insurance contract, like change in addresses, change in nominations, etc.

While considering the request for alterations, the insurer tries to ensure that there is no "adverse selection" against the insurer. That is, the risk should not increase after alteration. Increased SA, increasing the term, change form endowment to anticipated endowment plan, are alterations that increase risk. For this reason, alterations are generally not allowed if they involve change:

(*a*) to a longer term

(*b*) extended the premium paying period

(*c*) from one plan of insurance to another that represents increased risk

Some alterations are made by suitable endorsements on the policy itself. A fresh policy document may be issued if the alterations are of a substantial nature. This will happen, for example, if the policy has to be split into two or more policies incorporating the desired alterations.

A fee is usually charged to effect alterations except in certain cases such as correction of mistakes. No fee is charged for alteration of frequency of mode of payment from quarterly to yearly or half-yearly mode because such an alteration reduces the administrative work in servicing the policy. The fee is partly meant to cover expenses and partly to discourage frequency in alterations.

12.5 Issue of Duplicate Policy

A duplicate policy confers on its owner the same rights and privileges as the original policy. The following are the requirements for issuing a duplicate policy:

1. Insertion of an advertisement at the policyholder's cost in one English daily newspaper having wide circulation in the State where the loss is reported to have occurred. A copy of the newspaper in which the advertisement appeared should be sent to the servicing office one month after its appearance. If no objection has been lodged with LIC regarding the policy in question, a duplicate policy will be issued after complying further requirements, i.e., Indemnity Bond and payment of charges for preparing duplicate policy and stamp fee.
2. However, the requirement of advertisement and Indemnity Bond may be dispensed with or modified in certain circumstances as given below:
   - loss of policy by theft
   - destruction of policy by fire
   - loss of policy while in custody of an office of government
   - mutilated or damaged policy
   - policy in torn and a part of it is missing
   - policy partially destroyed by white ants.

The need to have a duplicate policy also arises at the time of receiving Maturity Amount or Death Claim, to obtain Surrender Value/Loan and to obtain a Duplicate Policy in other cases.

12.6 Nomination

Nomination is the process of identifying a person to receive the policy money in the event of the depth of the policyholder. Nomination can be done at the inception of the policy by providing details of nominee in the proposal form. However, if the nomination is not given at the beginning, the policyholder can give it at a later date. This nomination has to be effected by giving notice in a prescribed form to the insurer and getting it endorsed on Policy Bond. Change of Nomination can be done by the policyholder any time during the term of the policy and any number of times. For this, the policyholder has to give a notice in a prescribed form to the insurer and get it endorsed at the back of the policy.

Further, nomination can be removed any time by the policyholder without giving prior notice to the nominee. Nomination can be done only by a policyholder, who is a major, and on a policy on his own life. Under Nomination, the nominee gets only the right to receive the policy money in the event of the death of the policyholder. Nomination does not pass on the property in the policy. If Nominee dies when the policyholder is still surviving then the nomination would be ineffective. Nomination has no effect if the policyholder is surviving. If nominee dies after the death of the policyholder but before receiving policy money, then also nomination becomes ineffective and only the Legal Heirs of the policyholder can claim money. In the case of children's policies, nomination is not done until the child becomes a major. Nomination is governed by Section 39 of Insurance Act 1938.

The nominee is statutorily recognised as a payee who can give a valid discharge to the Corporation for the payment of policy moneys. Nomination will be incorporated in the text of the policy at the time of its issue. After the policy is prepared and issued and if no Nomination has been incorporated, the assured can ordinarily affect the nomination only by an endorsement on the policy itself. A nomination made in this manner is required to be notified to the Corporation and registered by it in its records. A nomination is not required to be stamped. Any change or cancellation of nomination should be given in writing only by the Life Assured. Nomination under Joint Life Policy can only be a joint nomination. Nomination in favour of a stranger cannot be made as there is no insurable interest and moral hazard may be involved.

Nomination in favour of wife and children as a class is not valid. Specific names of the existing wife and children should be mentioned. Where nomination is made in favour of successive nominees, i.e., nominee "A" failing him to nominee "B" failing whom nominee "C", the nomination in favour of one individual in the order mentioned will be considered. Where the nominee is a minor, an appointee has to be appointed to receive the monies in the event of the assured's death during the minority of the nominee. No nomination can be made under a policy financed from HUF funds. In the case of first endorsement of nomination, the date of registration of nomination will be the date of receipt of the policy by the servicing office and in case of any other nomination or cancellation or change thereof, the date of receipt of the policy and/or of notice whichever is later, will be the date of registration.

12.7 Assignment

Assignment is a means whereby the beneficial interest, right and title under a policy gets transferred from Assignor to Assignee. 'Assignor' is the policyholder who transfers the title, and 'Assignee' is the person who derives the title from the Assignor. Assignment can be made only after acquiring the policy. Assignment can be done only for consideration — for money or money's worth or goods, moral and meritorious consideration, like love and affection. Assignment can be made by mere endorsement on the policy or by a separate duly stamped Deed. Assignment can be done by the Proposer, Policyholder or the Absolute Assignee. Assignor must be a major, and must have an absolute right over the policy. Assignment must be in writing and the Assignor's signature along with a Wwtness is a must. Notice of Assignment should be submitted to the insurer. There are two types of assignments:

1. *Conditional Assignment* whereby the assignor and the assignee may agree that on the happening of a specified event which does not depend on the will of the assignor, the assignment will be suspended or revoked wholly or in part. Conditional Assignment is usually effected for consideration of natural love and affection.
2. *Absolute Assignment* whereby all the rights, title and interest which the assignor has in the policy passes on to the assignee without reversion to the assignor or his estate in any event. Absolute Assignment is usually effected for valuable consideration.

On assigning the policy, the Assignor loses his right over the policy and the Assignee gets the right and becomes the owner of the policy. The Assignee can further reassign the policy and he also has a right to sue under the policy. A valid assignment once made cannot be cancelled. It can be done only by another valid assignment. In all the cases, assignment automatically cancels an earlier nomination. However, when the policy is assigned to the insurer say for loan, nomination gets affected and it does not get cancelled. Under Conditional Assignment, if the Conditional Assignee dies, the benefit under the policy goes back to the life assured if surviving. Otherwise, the benefit goes to Policyholder's Nominee. Under Absolute Assignment, if the Absolute Assignee dies, the benefits under the policy go to the Legal Heirs of the Assignee. Assignment is governed by Section 38 of Insurance Act, 1938.

An assignment has an effect of directly transferring the rights of the transferor in respect of the property transferred. Immediately on execution of an assignment of the Policy of life assurance the assignor forgoes all his rights, title and interest in the Policy to the assignee. The premium/loan interest notices etc. in such cases will be sent to the assignee. In case the assignment is made in favour of public bodies, institutions, trust etc., premium notices/receipt will be addressed to the official who has been designated by the institutions as a person to receive such notice.

An assignment of a life insurance policy once validly executed, cannot be cancelled or rendered in effectual by the assignor. Scoring of such assignments or super scribing words like 'cancelled' on such assignment does not annul the assignment. And the only way to cancel such assignment would be to get it reassigned by the assignee in favour of the assignor.

Reassignment

An assignee may during the currency of the policy reassign the interest in the policy to the previous assignor, such reassignment will have the effect of cancelling the assignment and the interest title of the policy revert to the previous assignor.

12.8 Lapse and Revivals

Where the premium is not paid on the due date or within the days of grace, the policy lapses but it can be revived at any time during the remaining period of the policy, subject to medical evidence and arrears of premium along with interest thereon at the applicable rate. If the policy has lapsed within 3 years of the date of commencement, it is not entitled to any claims' concession, except days of grace, usually 30 days. As per IRDA guidelines details, all those policies which have lapsed is required to be submitted within stipulated time to IRDA.

Revivals

If the premium under a policy is not paid within the days of grace, the policy lapses. Revival is a fresh contract wherein the insurer can impose fresh terms and conditions. In case of LIC, a lapsed policy can be revived within 5 years from the date of first unpaid premium. A policy can be revived under the following types of revival:

1. Ordinary Revival

If a revival of the policy is effected within 6 months from the due of first unpaid premium, no personal statement regarding health is required and the policy is revived on collection of delayed premium plus interest. The rate of interest to be charged for such delayed premium will depend on the date of commencement of the policy.

2. Revival on Non-medical Basis

For revival of the policy on non-medical basis, the amount to be revived should not exceed the prescribed limit for non-medical assurance taken by the life assured.

3. Revival on Medical Basis

If a policy cannot be revived under ordinary revival or revival on non-medical basis, it can be revived with medical requirements. The medical requirements will depend upon the amount to be revived.

4. The Other Schemes for Revival are:

- Special Revival Scheme
- Revival by instalment
- Loan-cum-revival
- Survival Benefit-cum-revival

Special Revival Scheme: If the policy was in force for at least 6 months and has not acquired surrender value, the policy may be revived where the original date of the policy is shifted by the period for which the policy was in force. A fresh policy was will have to be issued for the age as on that date. The arrears of premiums will be a nominal amount. The cost of the preparation of the policy will have to be borne by the policyholder.

Revival by Instalment: The policyholder, in that case, can pay arrears of premium by suitable instalments, which should be paid alongwith regular premiums. *The unpaid instalments of premiums are treated as a debt/charge against the policy.*

Loan-cum-Revival: If the lapsation period is long, the arrears of premiums could be a very substantial amount, the insurer offers a Loan-cum-Revival scheme, provided the policy has acquired surrender value, notionally on the date of revival.

12.9 Policy Loans

Most of the insurance companies give privilege to the policyholder to obtain loans on certain policies subject to certain rules. The policyholder has to apply for a loan in a prescribed form and submit the Policy Bond along with the form duly completed. The loan amount is calculated depending on the Surrender Value (SV) that the policy would have acquired, and approximately 85% of the Surrender Value are given as loan. Loans can also be perceived as riders offered by some private insurance companies. Rate of interest charged on loans taken on insurance policies varies from company to company and from time to time. A policyholder can repay the loan amount either in part or in full, any time during the term of the policy. For LIC, the minimum repayment should be ₹ 50 and thereafter in multiples of ₹ 10. If the loan amount is not repaid during the term of the policy or early claim, the amount of loan plus interest, if any, will be deducted from the claim money payable and the balance amount will be paid to the claimant. In case of LIC, if the interest is not paid regularly every half year, then the interest is calculated on compound interest basis. If the premiums are not paid regularly, that is, if the policy is not kept in force, there is a possibility that the loan amount along with accrued interest exceeds the surrender value. At that stage, foreclosure action is taken on the policy.

Generally, plans for Children or special plans like Jeevan Griha and Deferred Annuity/Pension Plans as well as Moneyback Plans etc. are not eligible for loans. The requirement for granting a loan are as under:

(*a*) Application for loan with an endorsement of terms and conditions of the loan is being placed on the policy.

(*b*) Policy to be assigned absolutely in favour of the Corporation.

(*c*) A receipt for the loan amount.

In case of LIC, the maximum loan amount available under the policy is 90% of the Surrender Value of the policy (85% in case of paid-up policies) including cash value of bonus. The minimum period for which a loan can be granted is six months from the date of its payment. If repayment of loan is desired within this period, the interest for the minimum period of six months will have to be paid. In case the policy becomes a claim either by maturity or death within six months from the date of loan, interest will be charged only upto the date of maturity/death.

12.10 Foreclosure

Foreclosure means the writing off the policy before its actual maturity. If the balance in the Individual Policyholders' Account falls below minimum stipulated amount, the company may at any time foreclose and terminate the policy. When a loan is granted under a policy, the life assured has an option to pay the interest or allow it to accumulate to be adjusted from the policy moneys payable when end, the claim arises. This is possible only if the premiums are paid regularly and the policy remains in full force. If the insured defaults in the payment of premium and the surrender values are in adequate to meet the arrears of loan and interest, to service the principal loan and accumulated interest foreclosure may be adopted by the insurer.

1. Before taking a foreclosure action, the policyholder is requested to pay the arrears of loan interest. If he continues default, the policy is foreclosed, policy and surrendered to loan. The balance surrender value after adjusting the principal loan and outstanding loan interest paid to the policyholder. However, a foreclosed policy may be reinstated.
2. It is possible to reinstate a foreclosed policy, if desired by the party, provided
   - if the outstanding loan interest with accumulated interest thereon is paid unto date, and
   - a satisfactory evidence of continued good health is provided:
3. The reinstatement of a foreclosed policy is not allowed if the balance surrender value has been paid to the policyholder because it is presumed that policyholder had accepted the foreclosure action.
4. Nomination ceases if there is foreclosure. If life assured dies before payment of the balance surrender value, the amount is not payable to the nominee, but only to the legal heirs of the decreased assured.

12.11 Married Women's Property (MWP) Act Policies

A Married Women's Property Act policy constitutes a trust in favour of the wife and for children and no separate assignment is necessary. The beneficiaries are fully protected from creditors except to the extent of any interest in the policy retained by the assured.

Section 5: Married Woman May Effect Policy of Insurance

Any married woman may effect a policy of insurance on her own behalf and independently of her husband; and the same and all benefit thereof, if expressed on the face of it to be so effected, shall ensure as her separate property, and the contract evidenced by such policy shall be as valid as if made with an unmarried woman.

Section 6: Insurance by Husband for Benefit of Wife

(1) A policy of insurance effected by any married man on his own life, and expressed on the face of it to be for the benefit of his wife, or of his wife and children, or any of them, shall ensure and be deemed to be a trust for the benefit of his wife, or of his wife and children, or any of them, according to the interest so expressed, and shall not, so long as any object of the trust remains, be subject to the control of the husband, or to his creditors, or form part of his estate.

When the sum secured by the policy becomes payable, it shall, unless special trustees are duly appointed to receive and hold the same, be paid to the Official Trustee of the [State] in which the office at which the insurance was effected is situate, and shall be received and held by him upon the trusts expressed in the policy, or such of them as are then existing.

And in reference to such sum he shall stand in the same position in all respects as if he had been duly appointed trustee thereof by a High Court, under Act No. XVII of 1864 to constitute an office of Official Trustee.

Nothing herein contained shall operate to destroy or impede the right of any creditor to be paid out of the proceeds of any policy of assurance which may have been effected with intent to defraud creditors.

(2) Notwithstanding anything contained in Section 2, the provisions of subsection (1) shall apply in the case of any policy of insurance such as is referred to therein which is effected-

(*a*) by any Hindu, Muhammadan, Sikh or Jain—

(*i*) in Madras, after the thirty-first day of December, 1913, or

(*ii*) in any other territory to which this Act extended immediately before the commencement of the Married Women's Property (Extension) Act 1959, after the first day of April, 1923, or

(*iii*) in any territory to which this Act extends on and from the commencement of the Married Women's Property (Extension) Act, 1959, on or after such commencement;

(*b*) by a Buddhist in any territory to which this Act extends, on or after the commencement of the Married Women's Property (Extension) Act, 1959:

Provided that nothing herein contained shall affect any right or liability which has accrued or been Incurred under any decree of a competent court passed:

(i) before the first day of April, 1923, in any case to which sub-clause (i) or sub-clause (ii) of clause (a) applies; or

(ii) before the commencement of the Married Women's Property (Extension) Act, 1959 (61 of 1959), in any case to which sub-clause (iii) of clause (a) or clause (b) applies.]

When taking a policy, the proposal form filled in by married women in slightly different from the normal proposal forms. A policy can be taken under the married women's property act. The act provides that married women may take a policy on her life or on the life of her husband exclusively for her owns benefit. In the case of single women proponent, sometimes a question is asked enquiring the status of the women — married or to be married, in order to determine the special risk incidental to child birth. The proposal ends with the declaration to be signed by the proponent and the life proposed. While filling the form, if the beneficiary is absolute, signature of beneficiary is required in all cases. If life to be assured has not attained 18 years of age, a parent's or guardian's signature is required. Following documents are generally required:

- Age proof certificate
- Full medical report.
- Duly completed and signed proposal form.
- Family history record.
- If non-standard age proof, policyholders have to submit extra annexures signed by the proposer.
- Duly filled in agent's confidential report.
- Moral hazard report for sum proposed over ₹ 0.1 million. In all non-medical (general), cases, MHR is necessary irrespective of the sum assured.
- In case of married women, if the age proof contains the maiden name, a declaration giving her maiden name by way of a separate letter duly signed is a must.

A supplementary statement has to be made when the applicant is a Woman which includes the following particulars:

- *Name:* If married, state full maiden name.
- Husband's name and occupation
- How much assurance does he carry and in whose favour
- Document pertaining to property owned by the person
- Statement pertaining to annual income of the individual
- Statement stating dependents supported by the policyholder

The policy issued under this act must be on the life of a married man, and taken out by himself which therefore precludes the joint life policies or Children's Deferred Assurance policies under the act.

The proposer who appoints the trustee may reserve the power to revoke the appointment of trustee and appoint another. Also, no loan can be granted under this policy unless the proposer had while appointing the trustees, specifically authorized the trustees to obtain loan on the policy. The trustees also cannot surrender the policy.

12.12 Method of Risk Classification in Life Insurance

The two methods commonly employed in the classification of risks are:

(*a*) ***Judgment Method:*** The underwriter studies all the features of the life to be insured and on the basis of analysis of various factors takes a decision. Under this method, the company depend upon the combined judgement of those in the medical, actuarial, and other areas who are qualified for this work to make underwriting decisions. The judgment method of rating functions effectively when there is only one unfavorable factor to consider whether the decisions to be made is simply whether to accept the proposed insured at standard rates or to reject him or her entirely. However, situations where multiple factors are involved or a proper substandard classification is needed, then this method can not be efficiently applied.

(*b*) ***Numerical Rating:*** In this method, a large number of factors, which influence mortality, are taken in account. For various factors, debits (additions) or credits (subtractions) are made to the scores. The numerical ratings vary from company to company — 75 to 500. Illustratively, as rating increases, the quality of risk diminishes. A rating in the range of 75-125 is generally considered as standard and *over and above 125 as substandard.* An underwriter has to take into account the nature and combined effects of extra risks, e.g., impairments jointly causing additional extra risks. In these cases, some additions are made to the arrived rates calculated independently.

12.13 Factors Affecting the Pricing of Life Insurance Products

Life insurance is an institution which convert uncertainty into certainty. It is not humanly possible to prevent the occurrence of an event (peril) insured against. But the uncertainty of financial loss suffered by a few, because of the happening of the events, can be eliminated and/or reduced to a great extent, by the distribution of a large number of people. Thus, instead of being borne by one, the loss can be distributed equally among all persons facing the risk. Every one of the group of people makes a contribution to a common fund. The measure of this common contribution is called premium.

The premium to be charged under a life insurance policy depends on three factors:

(a) Rate of mortality

(b) Rate of interest

(c) Operational expenses

(a) Mortality Rate and Premium: The establishment of any plan of insuring against death requires some means of giving mathematical values to the probabilities of death. This can be accomplished thorough the mortality statistics, i.e., mortality rate. Mortality tables are presentations of such data organised in a form to be usable in estimating the course of future death. The cost of insurance coverage (i.e., premium) is calculated simply by multiplying the sum assured and the value of mortality at a particular age. This is called natural premium.

For example, if at the age of 30, mortality rate is 0.00117, it means that out of a group of 1, 00,000 persons all aged 30 years, 11% are expected to die before they reach age 31. If all these persons wish to take a policy of ₹ 1 lakh for a term of one year, then the premium will be ₹ 117.

(b) Rate of Interest and Premium: The second factor which affects premium is interest. In the simplest insurance contracts, the premium is paid in a lump sum when the policy is issued. But the claim payments are made over time, (say after a certain number of years). Insurers invest the premium amount collected in different investment areas and earn interest. This interest is reflected in the calculation of premium. In other words, the premium reflects the time value of money.

The insurance company assumes a certain rate of interest based on its experience, while computing the rates of premium. The premium calculated based on the combination of both mortality rates and interest factor is called **Net Premium.**

Consider the previous example, at the end of the year, 117 persons will claim the sum assured, i.e., insurance company need 117 lakh at the end of the year. In case of natural premium, i.e., if the insurance company only consider the mortality rate, the y collect 117 lakh rupees from all 1 lakh people. If the insurance company earns 6% interest, then they have to collect only 110.38 lakh (117/1.06) from 1 lakh people. This, the premium charged per person will be ₹ 110.38.

(c) Expenses and Premium: The third factor which goes into the computation of premiums is the expense factor. There are two types of expenses: *(i)* Premium related expenses such as agent's commission, renewal expenses *(ii)* Policy related expenses are added to the net premium to calculate the final premium. This is called **Gross Premium** or **Office Premium.** Process of adding these expenses to the net premium is called loading.

12.4 Treatment of Sub-standard Life Insurance Risks

The three broad classifications of substandard risks are:

(*a*) ***Increasing Extra Risk:*** This category reflects the extra mortality risks caused due to impairments with the increase in age. Persons with extra weight are likely to have blood pressure or heart problems, as they grow older.

(*b*) ***Constant Extra Risk:*** This group reflects the lives with hazard that remain constant through life. These hazards do not create variations in mortality as such, e.g., permanent total disablement-lost of limbs.

(*c*) ***Decreasing Extra Risk:*** These lives represent cases where the extra risk decreases with passage of risk since the consideration of proposal. A person who has just been operated for a problem becomes normal over a time period. At the time of proposal the risk was substandard, but with passage of time, it has become a simple risk.

The popular methods of treating substandard risk are:

(*a*) ***Increase in Premium:*** Increase in normal premium (multiple table extra) is the most common method adopted by the insurance companies for treatment of substandard risks. Under this method, premiums can be treated as follows:

(*i*) the proposer's age is increased by a few years (e.g., 3-5 years) which results in increase in premium or

(*ii*) a special mortality table is developed for each substandard classification that reflects the experience of each and a set of gross premium is computed for the classification.

(*b*) ***Flat Extra Premium:*** In situation where the extra risk is expected be constant, a flat extra premium may be changed. The policy remains a standard one for all purposes including dividends and non-forfeiture values.

(*c*) ***Other Methods:*** The other methods of refund are:

(*i*) Limited death benefit equal to refund of premium if death occurs in the earlier years.

(*ii*) A lien (contingent debt) may be created an the policy such that upon the assured dies in the lien period, the lien amount shall be deducted from sum payable under the policy.

(*iii*) A proposal may be declined by the insurer if there is increasing extra risk.

(*iv*) Restrictive clauses may be imposed as exclusions under the policy.

(*v*) The insurance cover may be reduced by amount and/or time or the plan may be changed.

(*vi*) Another option from insurance company is to defer the cover till the extra risk is over.

12.15 Calculation of Premium

In calculating premium, the following variable are considered:

(*i*) Term and Plan

(*ii*) Riders

(*iii*) Extras

(*iv*) Sum Assured

(*v*) Mode of payment

The rates of premium are quoted per thousand for various age groups. The table rates are then multiplied by the sum assured to arrive at a base premium. Then to the base premium, the addition or dedications are made. Consider the following example:

Example 1

Sum proposed	**₹ 50,0000**
Cover	Moneyback Policy
Age (near birthday)	30
Term	35 years
Table Rates	₹ 27.00 per thousand
Adjustment Rate for High SI	+ ₹ 1.60 per thousand
Double Accident Benefit (DAB)	1%
Mode of Payment	Semi-annual
Calculation	
Tabular Premium (₹ 5,00,000 × 27/1000)	13,500
Adjustment Benefit for Large SI (₹ 5,00,000 × 1.60/1000)	800
Annual Premium	14,300
DAB Extra (1%)	1430
Total Price	15,730
Semi-annual Premium (15730/2)	₹ 7865

Example 2

Plan	Whole life
Sum Assured	₹ 1,00,000
Riders	DAB
Health Extra	5%
Age	31
Premium Payments	35 years
Tabular Premium (Whole life, Premium Payments 35)	₹ 29.40
Adjustment for Large Sum Assured ₹ 1.50	₹ 1.60
Adjustment for Quarterly Mode	Nil
Total	**31.00**
Annual Premium (31.00 × 100)	₹ 3,100
Health Extra (5%)	₹ 155.00
Total Annual Premium (including extra)	₹ 3255.00
Quarterly Instalment Premium	₹ 813.75

Key Terms

- Preamble
- Attestation
- Forfeiture
- Privileges
- Exclusions
- Foreclosure
- Mortality Rate
- Schedule
- Conditions
- Suicide
- Alterations
- Assignment
- Sub-standard Risk

Questions for Review

1. Write short notes on:
   (*a*) Conditions and Priviledges in Life Contract
   (*b*) Issue of Duplicate Policy
   (*c*) Married Women Property Act Policies
2. Can a life insurance policy once issued be altered? If yes, how and on what basis?
3. Distinguish between:
   (*a*) Nomination and Assignment
   (*b*) Surrender and Foreclosure
4. Distinguish between 'Lapsed Policy' and 'Policy in Force'. What is the name of the process that alters a policy status from 'lapse' into 'in force'? Explain this process in detail.
5. What are the basic components of a life insurance contract?
6. Explain the procedure of issuing a life insurance policy.
7. Why proof of age is an important concern for all life insurers? How an insurance company can verify the age proof?
8. Describe the provisions of a suicide clause in a life insurance policy. What protections does it provide to the insurer?
9. What do you mean by policy loan provision? When can a loan be given under a policy? How is loan amount determined?
10. How risks are classified in life insurance? What are the various methods of treatment of substandard risks?
11. What are the different methods of rating?
12. Explain the factors affecting the pricing of life insurance products.
13. Write short notes on:
    (*a*) Mortality Rate
    (*b*) Medical Examination

14. Assuming that you are an underwriter, explain how will you treat the different classes of Sun-standard risks?
15. Distinguish between:
    (*a*) Standard Life and Substandard Life.
    (*b*) Judgment Rating and Class Rating.

Suggested Readings

- S.L. Kane, *Principles of Life Insurance,* Himalaya Publishing House, Mumbai, 2003.
- *Practice of Life Assurance,* IC02, Insurance Institute of India, Mumbai, 2003.
- *Practice of Life Assurance,* IC02, Insurance Institute of India, Mumbai.
- Robert I. Mehr, *Life Insurance — Theory and Practice,* Business Publications Inc., 1977.
- T.S. Mann, *Law and Practice of Life Insurance in India,* Deep and Deep, 1987.
- S.S. Huebner, Kenneth Block Jr. and Robert S. Clive, *Life and Health Insurance,* Pearson Edu., 2002.

❑❑❑

LIFE POLICIES AND MANAGEMENT

CHAPTER

Chapter Objectives

- Approaches to Valuation
- Types of Policies
- Term Life Policies
- Whole Life Insurance Policies
- Endowment Insurance Policies
- Annuities
- Policies Based on Other Classifications

Introduction

Life Insurance cover is needed by individuals for various purposes. The choice for a life insurance plan depends upon the need level of the individuals. These needs include the family protection, old age survival for self and dependents, needs for consequences of disability/ mishappenings, diminution in the value of assets due to depreciation, inflation and other macro-economic factors. The amount that would be sufficient to satisfy the needs as mentioned and support any dependants for as long as they are in need of support can be estimated by some approaches discussed in following paragraphs.

13.1 Approaches to Valuation

Human Life Value Approach

The concept of Human Life Value (HLV) helps us to arrive at a fairly estimated insurance needs for an earning individual who has to manage day-to-day maintenance, well-being of all his dependents and also has to provide for financial, security in future to these dependents in case of his premature death, through a life insurance cover. The life cover purchased by the income earner is a substitute for the income stream, which may be discontinued on account of disability or an early death. Disability is presumed to be a total and permanent disability making the individual incapable of earning an income.

Economic Value

In terms of physical composition, the worth of a human body is nothing but from a earning capacity perspective, it may be millions of rupees. This earning power does not create any economic value unless its benefits are derived by a person or organization. Therefore, a human life has an economic value when monetary value is derived during its existence.

In general, the family of an earning individual is completely dependent on him for subsistence, for other comforts and amenities. Family's economic security is protected till the family head is able to continue the flow of income stream as a result of his productive efforts. Out of his present earnings, he also saves for creation of an estate in future to arrange for economic security to his dependents. This potential estate has also to be added to the present economic gain the family is getting. Thus, HLV of an individual is the economic value to his family.

$$H = (E - M) \times an \quad \text{where is } N$$

where H = Human Life Value

E = Earnings per annum

M = Charge for Maintenance + Tax Liability + Life Insurance Premium

an = Annuity Factor at a given rate of discount

N = The Working Period (Retirement age – Present age).

Multiple Approach

This method is a simpler approach leading to a rough estimate. According to this approach, the HLV is equal to a given multiple of current income. The resulting sum, when invested, is designed to produce an income similar to that earned at present. For example, if it were expected that the available interest rate would be 5.5 per cent, then a multiple of around 10 times current salary would be invested (that is 5.5% × 10 = 55% of current salary). This approach is based on the assumption that every human being's efforts are directed towards fulfillment of basic physiological needs. The popular need hierarchy theory of Maslow suggests that physiological needs, safety needs and belongingness and love needs get the priority over esteem needs, self-actualizing needs and aesthetic needs. An earning individual has to provide for livelihood and well-being of the family members dependent on him. The requirement for an individual in terms of various funds are: Adjustment fund, Clean-up fund, Education fund, Marriage fund, Spouse fund, Mortgage Redemption fund, Retirement fund etc.

Capital Retention Approach

This method is similar to the need analysis approach. A minimum capital is assumed to be preserved for distribution to the legal heirs after the death of the individuals for their (heirs') survival.

13.2 Types of Policies

The two basic elements in a life insurance cover are: (*a*) death cover and (*b*) risk cover. The insurance plans that provide only the death covers, i.e., the benefits are paid on the death of the insured person are called as *Term Assurance Plans,* else, the plans under which the benefits are paid on the survival of the insured within a specified period are called as *Pure Endowment Plans.* All types of insurance covers are a mix of these basic elementary plans.

Classification based on Time

(*a*) *Whole life :* Whole term, Limited term, Convertible

(*b*) *Term plans :* Limited, Convertible, Renewable

(*c*) *Endowment plans :* Pure, Joint, Double, Anticipated

Classification based on Premium Payment

(*a*) Single premium policies

(*b*) Level premium policies

Classification based on Claim Payment

(*a*) Fixed sum policies

(*b*) Annuity policies

Classification based on Number of Persons Assured

(*a*) Single life

(*b*) Multiple life

Classification based on Participation in Profit

(*a*) With Profit Policies

(*b*) Without Profit Policies

In addition to above, there may be various categories of policies depends upon the riders attached or a specific purpose of the cover, e.g., children education policy, marriage policy *etc.*

13.3 Term Life Policies

This is simplest and the cheapest form of life insurance policy sold in the market today. The term insurance provides for life insurance protection for the selected term (period of years) only. In case the person (whose life is insured) dies during the term, the benefits are payable under the policy and in case of his survival till the end of the selected term the policy normally expires without any benefit becoming payable. Term insurance may be regarded as temporary insurance and is more nearly comparable with 'Property and casualty insurance' contract than the other forms of life insurance contracts.

For example, if a person insures his life under a 5 years term insurance contract, the insurer does not have any obligation to pay anything unless the person dies before the expiry of the 5-year term. All the premiums paid by the insured are considered to be fully earned by the insurer at the end of the term and the policy has no further value. Because of its nature, the premium for term insurance contracts is relatively low. Term insurance policies are also sold with convertibility, renewability or re-entry guarantees/options.

Convertibility is an option by which the policyholder can get his term insurance contract converted to some other type of life insurance contract before the expiry of the selected term without the need for additional medical examination.

Renewability is an option by which the policyholder can renew the contract for a further period of years without the need for fresh medical examination.

Re-entry option is one whereby a policyholder can continue the policy at the end of the selected term for a further period at a low rate of premium if he establishes his insurability to the satisfaction of the insurer, which commonly is affected by way of fresh medical examinations. If the potential insured cannot prove his insurability, he may get the cover at loaded prices, i.e., by payment of extra premium.

Terminal Illness Benefit

Terminal illness is a condition where the medical practitioner attending to the life of the assured and a medical examiner duly authorized by the insurance company are of the opinion that the assured is likely to die as a result of the illness within a period of 6 months. Some insurers include an additional benefit under term insurance plans and provide for along with the basic benefits. Another type of covers may be where the insurer provide for a part of the sum assured upon the life assured getting afflicted by a terminal illness. The practice this terminal benefits is not very common. Based on the level of coverage, the term insurance policies can be classified into the following types:

1. Level benefit term insurance
   (*a*) Level premium
   (*b*) Increasing (stepped) premium
2. Decreasing benefit term insurance
   (*a*) Mortgage redemption
   (*b*) Payer benefit rider
3. Increasing benefit term insurance
   (*a*) Constant growth
   (*b*) Index linked

Level benefit term insurance policies are those, where the coverage remains constant throughout the term of the insurance policy. The premium payable under the policy may be constant throughout the term or increasing every year with the increase in the insured's age.

Increasing benefit term insurance contracts are those whereunder the insurance coverage under the contract keeps on increasing periodically over the term. It can either increase at a pre-determined rate or may be index linked.

For example, a term insurance policy for a face value of ₹ 100,000 can start with a coverage for the face value for the first 5 years, can increased by 50% every five years, *viz.*, to ₹ 150,000 during the period from 6th to the 10th years, to ₹ 200,000 from the 11th to 15th years and so on. On the other hand, the insurance coverage under the policy can be linked to an external index like consumer price index or industrial production index and can increase alongwith the index.

Decreasing benefit term insurance policies are those under which the insurance coverage keeps decreasing with the passage of time and the most common among this type of policies is the Mortgage redemption insurance contracts. Here, the insurance policy is linked to a debt availed with the insurance coverage being equal to the outstanding loan at any point of time. As and when the loan is rapid in instalments, the insurance coverage is reduced and becomes nil on liquidation of the loan. The payer benefit term insurance is mostly sold as rider (added benefit) to the insurance policies on the lives of minors or dependants. It provides for waiver of payment of premium under the insurance policy on the life of a dependant, upon the death of the parent or guardian on whose life the rider is issued. Hence, the coverage is equal to the total balance of premium instalments due under the policy of the dependent, which decreases, with the payment of each instalment of premium.

13.4 Whole Life Insurance Policies

Whole life insurance policies are intended to provide life insurance protection over the lifetime of the assured. The essence of whole life insurance is that it provides for payment of the assured amount upon the insured's death regardless of when it occurs. Under whole life policies, the payment of the assured sum is a certainty in contrast to the term insurance contracts and obviously, the time of payment of the assured sum is an uncertainty.

Whole life policies can be either participating type or non-participating type. *Participating type policies* are those which are entitled to a share in the distributable surplus (profits) of the life insurance company, whereby the cash value of the policy can goes up, with the announcement of bonus/dividends. *Non-participating policies* have the benefit remaining the same throughout the life of the policy.

There can be the following types of whole life policies:

1. Ordinary whole life insurance
2. Limited payment whole life insurance
3. Convertible whole life insurance
4. Increasing whole life insurance

Ordinary Whole Life

These are plain vanilla type whole life policies, where the insured keeps paying the premium throughout his life and the benefits assured under the policy are payable to the beneficiaries upon the death of the life insured. Here again, based on the mortality assumptions used by the insurers, a certain maximum age is fixed, on survival of the life insured to that age, the policy will be treated as matured and the benefits assured under the policy will be paid to the policyholder in cancellation of the policy.

Limited Payment Life Policies

Here, though the benefits assured under the policy are payable only on the death of the life insured, the premium payment liability can be fixed at the option of the policyholder. He can choose at the outset the number of years he would like to pay the premium and based on that the quantum of premium payable under the policy is determined. Thereafter the premium has to be paid for the chosen term or till death of the insured, whichever is earlier. On completion of the chosen premium payment term, no further premium needs to be paid and the benefits assured under the policy will (including bonus/dividend declared after the premium paying term, if any) will be paid upon the death of the insure.

Convertible Whole Life Insurance

As the name suggests, these are whole life insurance policies with an option to the policyholder to convert them into endowment insurance policy at the expiry of a certain number of years, say 5 years. These are helpful to those people who have a need for a higher sum of insurance but temporarily cannot afford the premium for such a sum under endowment plan.

Increasing Whole Life Insurance Policy

As we have seen in case of term insurance policies, the cover under the whole life policies can also be subjected to a regular increase at a pre-determined level or linked to an external index. Thus the life insured can be provided with an insurance protection commensurate with the inflation level or increased needs.

Special Provision : Most of the insurers provide for payment of the benefits to the life insured himself on his reaching an advanced age, say 85 or 90. Also under plain vanilla Whole Life Policies, even though the conditions stipulate that the premium should be paid for life, insurers normally stop requiring payment of premium on the life insured reaching a selected advanced age, say 75 or 80.

The savings component that builds up in these policies arises because of the level premium system. In assessing the premium for the cover, the actuary has to estimate the expected investment return that will be achieved on the unused premium that builds up in the early years. This figure is always a conservative one to ensure that the premium charged generates sufficient funds to meet the losses when they arise. In practice, the actual return is usually higher and the surplus that accumulates is passes back to the policyholders by way of bonuses. The accumulated bonuses are paid, in addition to the sum insured, when the policy death benefit is paid.

It is possible for the full cost of insurance to be met by one single premium, instead of annual (or more frequent) premiums.

The benefits of whole of life policies include the capacity to terminate and cash in the policy; that is, they have a surrender value, and the capacity to borrow up to 90 per cent of that cash value at very competitive interest rates. Many insurers also allow the facility of advancing premium payable from the cash value of the policy described above. Hence, as the cash value accumulates, it is possible to 'skip' a premium payment; the policy will only lapse once the unpaid premiums (plus interest) exceed the cash value.

One variant of whole life assurance contracts is that which provides for payment of a fixed sum of money on the life insured surviving periodic intervals of time from commencement of the policy.

One such policy can typically provide for payment of say 10% of the original any time, the policy provides for payment of full sum insured without deduction of the survival benefit instalments. This kind of policy is called an anticipated whole life insurance policy.

This takes care of two different needs that a client may face, viz., providing for the dependants of the insured in case of death and at the same time taking care of the intermittent financial needs of the client himself. This provides for family protection as well as liquidity for the breadwinner.

13.5 Endowment Insurance Policies

Unlike whole life, an endowment life insurance policy is designed primarily to provide a living benefit and only secondarily to provide life insurance. Therefore, it is more of an investment than a whole life policy. Endowment life insurance pays the face value of the policy either at the insured certain age or after a number of years of premium payment.

Endowment life insurance is a method of accumulating capital for a specific purpose and protecting the savings programme. Many investors use endowment life insurance to fund anticipated financial needs, such as college education or retirement.

Premium for an endowment life policy is much higher than those for a whole life policy. Endowment policies are of various types of which a few are described as follows:

(*a*) *Pure Endowment:* Where the sum assured is payable to policyholders either on survival or death within the endowment period.

(*b*) *Joint Endowment:* Where the policy covers the risk on two or more lives under the single policy.

(*c*) *Marriage Endowment:* Where the policy is designed to meet the marriage financing needs of the family member of the policyholder.

Similarly, we have covers like education, children deferred endowment, double cover, triple cover, anticipated endowment policies *etc.*

(*i*) *Endowment Assurance Policy (with or without profits):* The face value of the policy will be paid either on death of the insured during the period of insurance or on maturity if the insured survives up to the end of the term.

(*ii*) *Bhavishya Jeevan Policy (with profits):* This is an Endowment Assurance under which premiums during the first five years will be very high and from the sixth year it will be scaled down to almostone-third of the original premium. This is suitable to professionals with a limited going to the Gulf for employment.

(*iii*) *Jeevan Mitra (Double Cover or Triple Cover)*: This is a *withprofit* Endowment Assurance with risk coverage to the extent of twice or thrice the face value of the policy. On maturity, the face value of the policy is paid.

(*iv*) *Jeevan Griha (Double Cover or Triple Cover) :* This is a low cost, *without profit* Endowment Assurance. Risk coverage will be twice or thrice the face value of the policy. The face value of the policy is paid in maturity. This plan is most suitable as collateral security for housing loans.

(*v*) *New Jana Raksha (with profits):* This is an Endowment Plan suitable for people in Rural Areas. After payment of at least two years' premiums, risk is covered for the next 3 years *even if premiums are not paid.* Agriculurists who depend on the vagaries of nature find this policy very attractive.

(*vi*) *Jeeven Shree (without profits but with guaranteed addition):* This is an Endowment Assurance, with limited premium paying period, suitable to the *Top End* of the society. The minimum sum assured under this policy is ₹ 5 lakh. The LIC of India allows Keyman Insurance under this plan only.

(*vii*) *Asha Deep II (with profits)*: This is basically an Endowment Assurance plan with a rider to cover four serious illnesses, viz., cancer, paralytic stroke leading to permanent disability, kidney failure (both kidneys) and cardiac bypass surgery. In case the insured is affected by any one of the above conditions in any year except the first year of the policy, LIC of India: *(a)* pays 50% of the sum assured immediately, *(b)* waives payment of all further premiums, *(c)* pays an annuity of 10% of sum assured till date of maturity and *(d)* pays the balance of 50% of Sum Assured on death or on maturity with bonus.

Marriage Endowment or Education Annuity (with-profits): This is an Endowment Assurance, *no immediate payment is made.* Payment in lump sum (in case of Marriage Endowment) and payment in half-yearly instalments spread over a period of 5 years (in case of Education Annuity) are arranged on/from date of maturity only. Several benefits are available on maturity.

Money Back Plans **:** These are all basically Endowment Assurance Policies. But the face value of the policy is paid in installments on survival of the insured at the end of fixed terms during the period of insurance, the balance of the face value of the policy being made available on maturity. In case of death during the period of insurance, the total sum assured (without deducting any survival benefits already paid) will be made available to the beneficiaries. For example, under a 20-year Moneyback Policy, on survival of the insured at the end of the 5th year, 10th year and 15th year of the policy, 20% of sum assured is paid on each occasion. These are called Survival Benefits. The balance of 60% of sum assured along with bonus is paid on maturity. In case of death of the insured any time during the 20-year period, full sum assured along with accrued bonus is paid without deducting any survival benefits already paid.

Moneyback (20 years, 25 years), Jeevan Surabi, Jeevan Sanchay are all different types of Money Back Plan. Jeevan Sneha is a special type of Moneyback Plan designed for females. For children also, LIC of India offers a separate Moneyback Policy.

Special Plans

(*i*) *For children:* LIC of India has designed several products for children. Children Deferred Assurance Plans, New Children Deferred Assurance Plan, Jeevan Balya, Jeevan Kishore, Children's Moneyback Plan, etc. For girls specially, Jeevan Sukanya is offered.

(*ii*) *For the benefit of disabled children:* Parents can take either Jeevan Aadhar or Jeevan Vishwas Policies. In respect of both the policies, exemption from Income Tax is available up to an annual premium of ₹ 20,000 subject to certain conditions.

(*iii*) Jeevan Aadhar is limited payment whole life policy on the life of the parent. On the death of the parent, 20% of the face value of the policy is immediately paid and the balance of 80% will be converted into annuity payable monthly to the disabled child.

(*iv*) Jeevan Vishwas is an Endowment Policy. Weather on the death of the parent or on maturity of the policy, benefits similar to the Jeevan Aadhar Policy are available to the disabled child.

Medical Benefits

LIC has designed a policy by the name *Jeevan Asha* II.

This is an Endowment Assurance with a medical benefit rider. 2% of the face value of the policy is paid every two years (at the option of the insured) to enable the policy owner to have regular medical check-ups. The first such payment is made after three years. Twice during the period of insurance, LIC reimburses expenses up to for 20% to 50% of face value of the policy minor or major surgeries. On death, the full sum assured is paid. On maturity of the policy, sum assured less any payments made during the period of insurance is paid.

Joint Life Policies

These are also a kind of Endowment Insurance Products:

(*a*) Jeevan Saathi is a Joint Life Assurance for husband and wife. During the period of insurance, on death of one life, the insurer pays the face value of the policy but subsequently risk coverage continues on the second life till the date of maturity. Premiums payable from the date of death of first life are waived. On maturity or on death of second life, if earlier, face value of the policy is paid.

(*b*) Jeevan Saritha is also a Joint Life Assurance for husband and wife but provides benefit of joint life and last survivorship annuity also apart from lump sum payment on death or maturity.

13.6 Annuities

Annuity Policies

Annuity is a contract that provides an income for a specified period of time.

Annuity schemes are those wherein policyholders regular contributions over a period of time (or a one-time contribution) accumulate to form a corpus with the insurer. The corpus is used to yield a regular income that is paid to policyholders until death starting from the desired retirement age. Some annuity schemes have the option to pay the survivors a lump sum amount upon the death of insured in addition to the regular income while the insured is alive.

For example: Jeevan Dhara and Jeevan Akshay plans currently offer a guaranteed return of 12.5% and 10% respectively in addition to life cover.

Life insurance contracts in simple form are different from the annuity contracts in the sense that the insurer pays in the even of the death of insured in a life insurance contract, while in an annuity contract the insurer stops paying upon the death of the insured.

Annuities are of the following types:

- **Immediate:** An immediate annuity provides income for a guaranteed period of time. Payments begin within one year of purchase. Income payments can either be for life, for a specified number of years or a combination of both.
- **Deferred:** In the case of a deferred annuity, the payments to the annuitant start after a certain deferment period. A deferred annuity is made with either a single purchase payment (Single Premium Deferred Annuity) or several purchase payments over time (Flexible Premium Deferred Annuity). A deferred annuity can be converted into a stream of income at any time after 12 months.
- **Fixed:** A fixed annuity assures minimum rate of return.
- **Variable:** A variable annuity offers a variety of investment fund account portfolios, including growth-oriented portfolios that can help you keep up with inflation. Variable annuity values and income payments may vary based on the underlying performance of the selected portfolio.

Benefits of Annuities

- Helps accumulate long-term savings.
- Helps maximize income in retirement
- Provides lifetime of regular income source
- Tax benefits u/s 88 of the Income Tax Act, 1961
- Benefits the beneficiary on the death of the annuitant.

However, there is a cost involved if the insured wants to get out of the annuity before a certain specified time.

Options in Annuity

Single life annuity: The annuitant receives income payments for the rest of his/her life.

Single life with period certain: The annuitant receives income for the rest of his or her life. If the annuitant dies before receiving a specific number of payment (period certain), the beneficiary will receive income for the remainder of the period; thus, a minimum number of payments are guaranteed.

Joint and Survivor: The annuitant and the designated joint annuitant will receive income for the rest of their lives. Upon the death of the annuitant, payments would continue to the joint annuitant at a percentage of the original level as selected by the annuitant at the time the income option was chosen.

Joint and survivor with period certain: The annuitant and the designated joint annuitant will receive income for the rest of their lives. If the annuitant and his or her joint annuitant die before a specific number of payments, the beneficiary will receive income for the remainder of the period certain.

13.7 Policies Based on Other Classifications

13.7.1 Premium Payment

The following important policies are issued by the Corporation on the basis of premium payment.

(i) Single Premium Policy: Single Premium Policy is useful to those who desire to provide the whole premium in one instalment at the time of taking the policy. Single Premium Policy becomes matured on the assured's death or on his attainment of selected term whichever occurs earlier.

(ii) Level Premium Policy: Unlike single premium policy, under this policy premiums are payable on a regular basis for a selected term or till prior death. It is useful to those persons having regular earnings. Premium is lesser as compared to a single premium policy. The sum assured becomes payable if the assured reaches a particular age or on the assured's death whichever is earlier.

13.7.2 Number of Persons Assured

Policies on the basis of Number of Persons assured are:

(i) Single Life Policies: This policy is designed on the basis of number of persons assured. Single Life Policy covers the risk on one individual. It may be issued on one's own life or on another's life. The policy amount is payable to the insured on attaining a selected term or on the death of the life assured whichever is earlier.

(ii) Multiple Life Policies: Multiple Life Policies is a policy issued on the basis of the number of persons assured. The Multiple Life Policies may be joint Life Policies or last Survivorship Policies. Unlike Single Life Policy, Joint Life Policy covers the risks of more than two individuals. The sum assured is payable at the time of maturity or on the event of the death of the first assured whichever is earlier. This policy is useful to partners of a firm or on the lives of husband and wife of a family. Under Last Survivorship Policy, the sum assured shall be payable at the death of last survivor or on the attaining a selected term if earlier.

13.7.3 Participation in Profits

Participating policies refers to the policies, which are entitled for getting the benefit of bonus. Bonus is the share of the profit of the insurance company earned during a particular financial year. Policies issued on the basis of participation in profits are discussed below:

(i) With Profit Policies (or) Participating Policies: With Profit policies are also termed as Participating Policies. Unlike Non-participating Policies, Participating policyholders are entitled to get the share of profits or bonus or benefits or paid up facilities as per the terms and conditions of the Corporation. The sum assured with profits shall become payable to the insured at the end of the maturity or in the event of death if earlier.

(ii) Without Profit Policies (or) Non-participating Policies: Under this policy, Sum assured will become payable without any paid-up facilities to the insured at the end of the selected term or on the death of life assured if earlier.

Key Terms

- Economic Value
- Accident and Disability
- Whole Life Policies
- Endowment Policies
- Term Assurance
- Annuities
- Moneyback Policies
- Single Life Policies
- Life Annuity
- Multiple Life Policies
- Participating Policies
- Non-participating Policies
- Single Premium Policy
- Level Premium Policy
- Last Survivorship Policy

Questions for Review

1. Explain the various approaches to valuation of human life for deciding the appropriate risk cover.
2. Discuss the various types of annuity plans.
3. Write short notes on:
   (a) Whole Life Plans
   (b) Moneyback Policies
   (c) Marriage Endowment policy
4. Classify life insurance policies based on the mode of payment of premium.
5. Define Endowment Policy. How does it differ from a Whole Life Policy? Is it possible to convert a whole life policy into an endowment policy? If yes, explain how.
6. What are the various kinds of endowment policies?

Suggested Readings

1. S.L. Kane, *Principles of Life Insurance,* Himalaya Publishing House, Mumbai, 2003.
2. *Practice of Life Assurance,* IC02, Insurance Institute of India, 2003.

Web Resources

- www.licindia.com
- www.insurance.yahoo.com

❑❑❑

UNIT IV
NON-LIFE INSURANCE

INTRODUCTION TO GENERAL INSURANCE

Chapter Objectives

- Historical Framework of general Insurance in India
- Industry Structure
- GIC — Organisation and Working
- Performance Statistics (1992-93 to 2000-01)
- Issue of Insurance Policies
- Rating Procedures
- Claim Settlements

Introduction

General Insurance in India has seen various phases. The Industrial Revolution in the West and the consequent growth of sea-faring trade and commerce in the 17th century and finally the British occupation. General Insurance sector in India dates back to 1850, when Tritron Insurance Company, for general insurance was incorporated in 1907, The Indian Mercantile Insurance Co. Ltd. was set up to transact all classes of general insurance business. Insurance Act was passed in 1928 but it was subsequently reviewed and comphrensive legislation was enacted in 1938. In 1957, General Insurance Council, a wing of the Insurance Association of India, framed a code of conduct for ensuring fair conduct and sound business practices. In 1968, the Insurance Act, 1938 was amended to regulate investments and set minimum solvency margin and the Tariff Advisory Committee set up. Management of Non-Life insurers was taken over by the Central Government in 1971 as a prelude to nationalisation. General Insurance business was nationalized with effect from 1.1.1973 by the General Insurance Business (Nationalisation) Act, 1972. Last few years have witnessed a spurt growth in the general insurance business in India. Of this motor insurance has proved to be the most unprofitable business and is cause of concern to most of the insurers.

14.1 Historical Framework of general Insurance in India

The introduction of general insurance in India is attributable to the Industrial Revolution in the West and the consequent growth of sea-faring trade and commerce in the 17th century. It came to India as a legacy of British occupation. British and other foreign insurance companies through their agencies in India transacted this business.

General Insurance sector in India dates back to 1850, when Tritron Insurance Company, for general insurance was incorporated in 1907. The Indian Mercantile Insurance Co. Ltd. was set up to transact all classes of general insurance business. Insurance Act was passed in 1928 but it was subsequently reviewed and comprehensive legislation was enacted in 1938. In 1957, General Insurance Council, a wing of the Insurance Association of India, framed a code of conduct for ensuring fair conduct and sound business practices. In 1968, the Insurance Act, 1938 was amended to regulate investments and set minimum solvency margin and the Tariff Advisory Committee was set up.

Management of Non-life insurers was taken over by the Central Government in 1971 as a prelude to nationalization. General Insurance business was nationalized with effect from 1.1.1973 by the General Insurance Business (Nationalization) Act, 1972.

Prior to 1973, General Insurance was urban-centric, catering mainly to the needs of organized trade and Industry. 107 insurers including branches of foreign companies operating the country were amalgamated. GIC was incorporated as a company in 1972 and it commenced business on January 1, 1973. The Government of India subscribed to the capital of GIC. GIC, in turn subscribed to the capital of four companies. All the four companies are government companies registered under the Companies Act. These are:

- National Insurance Company. Ltd.
- New India Assurance Company. Ltd.
- Oriental Fire and General Insurance Company. Ltd.
- United India Insurance Company. Ltd.

"The main objectives of nationalization were to ensure the development of the general insurance business in sympathy with the best of interest and advantage to the community. Further, these companies were required to promote competition in the economy and to prevent the concentration of wealth and growth of monopoly. They were supposed to spread their activities over geographical area, innovate new products as per the requirements of different segments of population and also meet social objectives through formulating policies for weaker sections of society."

These subsidiaries carry out the entire major portion of the general insurance business in the country and surrender 20% of it to GIC through the obligatory reinsurance premium on a quota share basis. However, certain new players have also ventured into the general insurance business.

- Tata AIG General Insurance Co. Ltd.
- Bajaj Allianz General Insurance Co. Ltd.

- Reliance General Insurance Co. Ltd.
- Royal Sundaram General Insurance Co. Ltd.
- IFFCO-TOKIO General Insurance Co. Ltd.
- ICICI Lombard General Insurance Co. Ltd.

14.2 Industry Structure

Presently, GIC is the leader in General Insurance business and is under the Ministry of Finance. Of course, it has to and is accountable to IRDA. As per the IRDA guidelines, every insurance company has to report on specific matters to IRDA within a time schedule. The current and emerging structure of the industry is given is Exhibit 14.1 and 14.2.

Exhibit 14.1

CURRENT STRUCTURE OF THE INDUSTRY

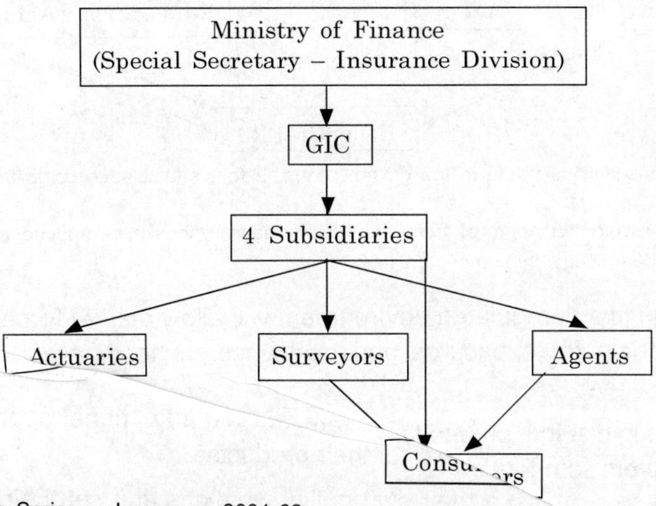

Source: The ET Knowledge Series ~ Insurance 2001-02.

In addition to IRDA, GIC along with its subsidiaries will be required to report to Ministry of Finance also. The professionalism will be strengthened both in the public and private sector, viz., actuaries who were and present consultants to the insurance companies are expected to be employed with the respective organization. With an increase in competition in the industry, mergers and acquisitions will become common phenomenon. Also, newer distribution channels are likely to bring a sweeping change in the product efficiency and customer-oriented strategies of insurance companies.

14.2.1 Issues in General Insurance Business

Strengths/Opportunities

- The intense competition brought about by deregulation has encouraged the industry to innovate in all areas; from underwriting, marketing, policy holder servicing to record keeping

- Aggressive marketing strategies by private sector insurers will buy consumer awareness of risk and expand the markets for products

Exhibit 14.2

EMERGING STRUCTURE OF THE INDUSTRY

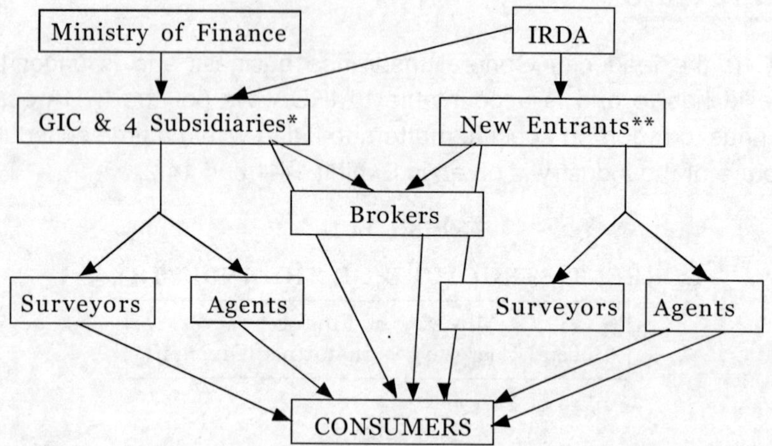

* Depending on recommendations made to the government, the four subsidiaries could be merged or made independent bodies.

** New entrants would require an approval from the RBI if they are banks or finance companies.

Source: The ET Knowledge Series Insurance 2001-02.

- Competition in a deregulated environment will allow market forces to set premiums that are appropriate for exposures and push insurers to differentiate their products and services.
- Innovations in distribution and improvements in market penetration will follow public and private insurers compete to market their products
- Allowing insurers to issue their own policy wordings and set their own rates will enable underwriters to tailor products to meet client needs.
- The existence of stringent licensing requirements ensure that only adequately capitalized and professionally managed companies are eligible to carry out insurance and reinsurance.
- The Insurance Regulatory Development Authority of India's (RDA) emphasis on quarterly reporting/monitoring of insurer solvency will enhance capital adequacy and transparency.
- Licensed brokers are very much part of the intermediary structure and only those with adequate capital, professional experience and expertise will be licensed by IRDA.

Weaknesses/Challenges

- Premiums rates will remain under pressure due to intense competition on the more profitable lines.
- Falling premium income — without a corresponding reduction in clams — is likely to drive down profits.

- Reinsurance is likely to cost more as treaty reinsurers reduce ceding commissions to compensate for the lower rates following deregulation.
- Public and private sector insurer's greater reliance on their investment portfolios to generate sufficient income and gains for net profits would subject them to the volatility of the financial markets.
- Private insurers need to raise more capital, otherwise growth could be constrained since reliance on reinsurance for capital relief is not always viable or available.
- Traditional distribution channels, especially tied agents, need to be improved to match the new product offerings.
- There is general lack of transparency as financial and operational data for insurers are not readily available as none of India's insurers are directly listed on stock exchanges.
- Like all developing economies on a fast track, the shortage of trained insurance professionals and technicians at all levels cannot be recommended in the short term.
- Natural catastrophes will always be present the Indian sub-continent is vulnerable to cyclones, floods, hurricanes and earthquakes, and until there is a national capacity (similar to the terrorism pool) to manage losses, dependence on overseas reinsurers will continue.

14.2.2 Detariffing

India's general insurance industry has undergone detariffing in three phases:

= 1994 — marine cargo, personal accident, health, banker's liability and aviation

= 2005 — 06-marine hull segment

= 2007 — fire, engineering and motor own damage (OD). However, the detariffing did not immediately allow for free pricing. Instead, insurers were required to follow the "file and use" method, whereby they were expected to file a charter of proposed rates, which was than approved by IRDA.

The restrictions on price discounts during the initial periods were intended to ensure orderly price adjustments. They were removed in January 2008. The only segment that remains under a tariff regime is the third party motor business, although there has been a large upward revision in this area's premium rates by regulators in recent times. Moreover, commercial third party motor business, which has traditionally contributed to adverse claims ratios, has been moved to a common pool, resulting in loss sharing.

14.3 GIC — Organization and Working

General Insurance Corporation of India came into picture with the nationalization of the general insurance sector by promulgating the General Insurance Business (Nationalization) Act, 1972 and four subsidiaries were formed. As per Section 18 of the said Act, the GIC has to perform the following functions.

The functions of the Corporation are stated in Section 18 to be:

(*a*) the carrying on of any part of the general insurance business if it thinks it desirable to do so;

(*b*) aiding, assisting and advising the companies in the matter of setting up standards of conduct and sound practice in general insurance business and in rendering efficient service to policyholders;

(*c*) advising the companies in the matter of controlling their expenses and investment of funds; and

(*d*) issuing directions to companies in relation to the conduct of general insurance business.

Organization

Exhibit 14.3

Current Structure of GIC Ministry of Finance Insurance Division GIC

Subsidiaries	*Subsidiaries*	*Foreign Joint*	*In India*	*Abroad*	*Ventures*
National Insurance Co. Ltd. (Kolkata)	New India Assurance Co. Ltd. (Mumbai)	Oriental Insurance Co. Ltd. (Delhi)	United India Insurance Co. Ltd. (Chennai)	Kenindia Assurance Co. Ltd. (Nairobi)	Others
India International Pvt. Ltd. (Singapore)		New India International Ltd. (UK)			Others

Source: The ET Knowledge Series Insurance 2001-02.

The current structure of GIC is given in Exhibit 14.3. There is a likely possibility that the four subsidiaries of GIC be made independent. Government entities and GIC would come under the joint purview of Ministry of Finance and the IRDA (Exhibit 14.4) This may be a better step in light of competition in the industry.

The performance of GIC and its subsidiaries for the financial years 1998-99 to 2000-01 are given in Table 14.4.

14.4 Performance Statistics (1992-93 to 2000-01)

As said earlier, the General Insurance business was nationalized in 1972. After this period, the sector grew gradually with many new developments. Till 1992-93, the growth was overall good. Net premium income registering 14.57%.

However, the claim ratio rose sharply from 50.8% to 68.7% during 1972-73 to 1992-93 primarily due to motor insurance losses.

Higher yields has also resulted in a sharp increase in investment income.

Let us have a look at statistics of the recent past, viz., period from 1996-97 to 1999-2000.

Table 14.2

Industry Performance: Post-nationalization Period up to 1993

	1972-73	1979-80	1984-85	1990-91	1991-92	1992-93
Net Premium Income	222	481	1,191	2,742	3,450	3,868
Net Claims Payable	113	296	795	1,898	2,303	2,839
Net Commission, Expenses of Management & Other Charges	68	121	287	652	802	908
Unexpired Risk Reserve	23	49	97	311	422	240
Underwriting Profit/Loss	18	15	12	– 118	– 77	– 119
Interest, Dividend & Rents	21	87	245	603	808	915
Other Income (Net)	– 0.7	– 7	6	– 3	– 62	17
Profit Before Tax	38	92	264	482	669	779
Profit Before Tax (excluding dividend from subsidiary companies.)	38	78	235	445	613	723
Tax Provision	21	49	107	148	241	276
Net Profit	14	43	157	334	428	503
Net Profit (excluding dividend from subsidiary companiess.)	14	29	129	298	372	447
Capital & Reserve (including Reserve for Unexpired Risk and Investment Reserve)	239	620	1,427	3,403	4,275	4,965
Capital & Free Reserves	99	315	695	1791	2,242	2,602

Source: The Malhotra Committee Report 1993.

The performance of the general insurance sector in the said period has been impressive. The statistics shows that capital and funds have grown from ₹ 8,501 crore in 1996-97 to ₹ 133,694 crore implying a growth rate of almost double.

Table 14.3

(Figure in Millions of ₹)

Particulars	*1990-91*	*1996/97*	*1997/98*	*1998/99*	*1999/00*
Capital & Funds	34024	85,011	100,492	118,819	133,694
To Assets	66808	187576	215,720	245,572	279,202
Gross Direct Premium	29130	73,479	80,856	91,575	99,822
Net Premium Income	27424	67,331	73,571	84,025	93,634
Investment Income & Profit Less Outgo	5,998	17,203	20,077	21,536	24,917
Profit Before Tax	4815	10,919	16,236	14,670	11,526

Source: www.interlinkre.com

The net premium income has also registered a CAGR of 27% (approx.) during the period 1990-91 to 1999-200. Investment in the industry have also increased by 16.52 times (during the period 1996-97 to 2000-01), viz., ₹ 1,447 crores to ₹ 23,849 crore.

Also, the ratio of Net Premium income to Gross Premium has gone up from 91.67% in 1996-97 to 95.36% (1999-2000). The figures are likely to improve further because of growing competition and enhanced focus on cost optimisation.

Distribution of Gross Direct Premium

Exhibit 14.6

GROSS DIRECT PREMIUM INCOME IN INDIA

	TOTAL (₹ Crore)		Market Share (In per cent)	
Company	2007-08	2008-09	2007-08	2008-09
National	4007.23	4279.90	14.40	14.10
New India	5276.92	5508.83	18.97	18.15
Oriental	3808.14	3964.25	13.69	13.06
United	3739.56	4277.77	13.44	14.09
Sub-Total	**16831.85**	**18030.75**	**60.49**	**59.41**
Royal Sundaram	694.41	803.36	2.50	2.65
Reliance	1946.42	1914.88	7.00	6.31
Iffco. T okio	1128.15	1374.06	4.05	4.53
Tata AIG	782.64	823.92	2.81.	2.71
ICICI Lombard	3307.12	3402.04	11.89	11.21
Bajaj Allianz	2379.92	2619.29	8.55	8.63
Cholamandalam	522.34	685.44	1.88	2.26
HDFC Ergo	220.60	339.21	0.79	1.12
Future Generali	9.81	186.49	0.04	0.61
Universal Sompo	0.48	30.14	0.00	0.10
Shriram	–	113.76	–	0.37
Bharti Axa	–	28.50	–	0.09
Raheja aBE	–	–	–	–
Sub-Total	**10991.89**	**12321.09**	**39.51**	**40.59**
Grand Total	**27823.74**	**30351.84**	**100.00**	**100.00**

Note: '–' I indicates not in operation

The Motor business continued to be the largest general insurance segment, although its share in the total non-life premium declined marginally in 2008-09 to 43.94 per cent from 45.59 per cent in 2007-08.

PREMIUM (WITHIN INDIA) UNDERWRITTEN BY NON-LIFE INSURERS - SEGMENT-WISE

(₹ Crore)

Segment	2007-08	2008-09
Fire	3459	3383
	(12.43)	(11.14)
Marine	1799	1957
	(6.47)	(6.45)

Motor	12685	13336
	(45.59)	(43.94)
Health	4894	6088
	(17.59)	(20.06)
Others	4986	5588
	(17.92)	(18.41)
Total Premium	**27824**	**30352**
	(100)	**(100)**

Note: Figure in brackets indicates market share (in percent)

The premium collection in Health surged further to ls.6088 crore in 2008-09 from ₹ 4894 crore of 2007-08, registering a growth of 24.40 per cent. This led to an increase in its share to the total premium to 20.06 per cent in 2008-09 from 17.59 per cent in 2007-08 and 13:33 per cent in 2006-07. The growth in the health segment was higher than the average general industry growth.

The Fire segment witnessed a decline in premium collection in absolute terms as well as in terms of its market share in 2008-09 from the previous year. Under Fire insurance, the total premium underwritten in 2008. 09 was ₹ 3383 crore (₹ 3459 crore in 2007-08), resulting into a fall in its market share to 11.14 per cent from 12.43 per cent in 2007-08.

Exhibit 14.7

Equity Share Capital of Non-Life Insurance Companies (As on 31st March)

(₹ *CRORE*)

Name of the Insurer	*As on 31st March 2008*	*Infusion During 2008-09*	*As on 31st March 2009*	*Foreign Promoter*	*Indian Promoter*	*FDI (per cent)*
Non life insurers						
Royal Sundaram Alliance Insurance Co. Ltd.	170.00	40.00	210.00	54.60	155.40	26.00
Reliance General Insurance Co. Ltd.	107.15	5.93	113.08	0.00	113.08	0.00
Bajaj Allianz General Insurance Co.Ltd	110.23	0.00	110.23	28.66	81.57	26.00
IFFCO. TOKIO General Insurance Co.Ltd	220.00	27.00	247.00	64.22	182.78	26.00
TAT A AIG General Insurance Co. Ltd.	225.00	75.00	300.00	/ 8.DO	222.00	26.00
ICICI Lombard General Insurance Co.Ltd	377.36	25.78	403.14	104.39	298.74	25.90
HDFC ERGO General Insurance Co.Ltd	150.00	50.00	200.00	52.00	148.00	26.00
Cholamandalam MS General Insurance Co. Ltd.	141.96	0.00	141.96	36.91	105.05	26.00
Future Generlai Insurance Co.Ltd.	150.00	40.25	190.25	4B.51	m.74	25.50

Universal Sompo Insurance Co.Ltd.	150.00	0.00	150.00	39.00	111.00	26.00
Bharti AXA General Insurance Company Ltd.			162.58	36.13	126.45	22.22
Shriram General Insurance Company Ltd .			105.00	27.30	77.70	26.00
Raheja OBE General Insurance Co. Ltd.			200.00	52.00	148.00	26.00
Sub Total (Private Sector)	1801.70	263.96	2533.23	621.72	1911.51	24.54
United India Insurance Co. Ltd.	150.00	0.00	150.00	0.00	150.00	0.00
The New India Assurance Co. Ltd.	200.00	0.00	200.00	'0.00	200.00	0.00
The Oriental Insurance Co.Ltd.	100.00	0.00	100.00	0.00	100.00	0.00
National Insurance Co. Ltd.	100.00	0.00	100.00	0.00	100.00	0.00
Sub TotallPublic Sector)	550.00	0.00	550.00	0.00	550.00	0.00
Total (Non Life)	2351.70	263.96	3083.23	621.72	241.51	20.16
Export Credit Guarantee Corporation.	900.00	0.00	900.00	0.00	900.00	0.00
Agriculture Insurance Company of India.	200.00	0.00	200.00	0.00	200.00	0.00
Star Health & Allied Insurance Co. Ltd.	108.60	0.70	109.30	27.98	81.32	25.60
Apollo DKV Insurance Co.Ltd.	100.55	6.82	107.37	26.91	80.46	25.06
Generellnsurance Corporation of India	430.00	0.00	430.00	0.00	430.00	0.00
GRAND TOTAL	**16387.27**	**6228.10**	**23082.95**	**5031.12**	**18051.83**	**21.80**

* started operation during 2008-09

14.5 Issue of Insurance Policies

Insurance being a contract, requires the offer and acceptance as its main essentials. In case of general insurance, the proposal form (printed and standardized) for respective class of insurance is to be submitted by the insurer to the insurance company. However, in case of marine cargo insurance, it is not customary to use a proposal form, rather sometimes a questionnaire is used. In some cases of large industrial fire risks, the proposal form is not used because of the inspection carried out earlier before the acceptance of risk. The proposal form generally contains *inter alia* information about the profile of the proposer, the past and previous insurance, loss experiences etc. In some cases of insurance, special questions are also asked to further explore the attributes of the risk proposed to be bought.

What is General Insurance?

Insurance other than 'Life Insurance' falls under the category of General Insurance. General Insurance comprises of insurance of property against fire, burglary etc, personal insurance such as

Accident and Health Insurance, and liability insurance which covers legal liabilities. There are also other covers such as Errors and Omissions insurance for professionals, credit insurance etc.

Non-life insurance companies have products that cover property against fire and allied perils, flood, storm, inundation, earthquake and so on. There are products that cover property against burglary, theft etc. The non-life companies also offer policies covering machinery against breakdown, there are policies that cover the hull of ships and so on. A Marine Cargo policy covers goods in transit including by sea, air and road. Further, insurance of motor vehicles against damages and theft forms a major chunk of non-life insurance business.

In respect of insurance of property, it is important that the cover is taken for the actual value of the property to avoid being imposed a penalty should there be a claim. Where a property is undervalued for the purposes of insurance, the insured will have to bear a rateable proportion of the loss. For instance if the value of a property is ₹ 100 and it is insured for ₹ 50/-, in the event of a loss to the extent of say ₹ 50/-, the maximum claim amount payable would be ₹ 25/- (50% of the loss being borne by the insured for underinsuring the property by 50%). This concept is quite often not understood by most insureds.

Personal insurance covers include policies for Accident, Health etc. Products offering Personal Accident cover are benefit policies. Health insurance covers offered by non-life insurers are mainly hospitalization covers either on reimbursement or cashless basis. The cashless service is offered through Third Party Administrators who have arrangements with various service providers, i.e., hospitals. The Third Party Administrators also provide service for reimbursement claims. Sometimes, the insurers themselves process reimbursement claims.

Accident and health insurance policies are available for individuals as well as groups. A group could be a group of employees of an organization or holders of credit cards or depositholders in a bank etc. Normally when a group is covered, insurers offer group discounts.

Liability insurance covers such as Motor Third Party Liability Insurance, Workmen's Compensation Policy etc offer cover against legal liabilities that may arise under the respective statutes—Motor Vehicles Act, The Workmen's Compensation Act etc. Some of the covers such as the foregoing (Motor Third Party and Workmen's Compensation policy) are compulsory by statute. Liability Insurance not compulsory by statute is also gaining popularity these days. Many industries insure against Public liability. There are liability covers available for products as well.

There are general insurance products that are in the nature of package policies offering a combination of the covers mentioned above. For instance, there are package policies available for householders, shopkeepers and also for professionals such as doctors, chartered accountants etc. Apart from offering standard covers, insurers also offer customized or tailor-made ones.

Suitable general Insurance covers are necessary for every family. It is important to protect one's property, which one might have acquired from one's hard earned income. A loss or damage to one's property can leave one shattered. Losses created by catastrophes such as the tsunami, earthquakes, cyclones etc. have left many homeless and penniless. Such losses can be devastating but insurance could help mitigate them. Property can be covered, so also the people against Personal Accident. A Health Insurance policy can provide financial relief to a person undergoing medical treatment whether due to a disease or an injury.

Most general insurance covers are annual contracts. However, there are few products that are long-term. It is important for proposers to read and understand the terms and conditions of a policy before they enter into an insurance contract. The proposal form needs to be filled in completely and correctly by a proposer to ensure that the cover is adequate and the right one.

Underwriting has been discussed in detail in Chapter 24. So, once it is decided that the risk shall be bought and the consideration is received, the *cover notes* are generally issued in advance of policy. A cover note is a sufficient evidence of an insurance cover. Cover notes are sometimes issued pending negotiations or rate fixation. In case of motor insurance, *certificate of insurance* is issued.

The policy document is a formal one, evidencing the contract of insurance. When the contract is in the purview of TAC, the wordings should be exactly on the same pattern as prescribed. The main parts of a standard insurance policy are – heading, recital clause, insuring clause, schedule, authentication, conditions and warranties etc. The special clauses in an insurance policy can be inserted by attachments known as endorsements. Whenever the insurance polices are interpreted, these are to be in whole and in their usual sense. Insurance policies generally expire at the end of one year and must be renewed immediately. It is not obligatory on part of the insurer to send notice to the insured, but as a business practice they do inform him.

General insurance or non-life insurance policies, including automobile and homeowners policies, provide payments depending on the loss from a particular financial event. General insurance typically comprises any insurance that is not determined to be *life insurance.* It is called property and casualty insurance in the US and Non-life Insurance in Continental Europe. In the UK, General insurance is broadly divided into three areas; *personal lines, commercial lines* and *London market.* In India, general; insurance is classfied as Fire, Marine and miscellaneous insurances.

Some examples of Non-life Insurance Policies are:

Commercial

Fire Policies

- Fire Consequential Loss
- Fire Insurance
- Consequential Loss (Fire) Insurance Policy (Bajaj Allianz)

Liabilities

- Medical Establishment
- Product Liability
- Public Liability — Act
- Public Liability — Industrial Risks

Travel

- Globetrotter Overseas Corporate Travel Insurance(ICICI Lombard)

Engineering

- Advance Loss of Profits
- Boiler & Pressure Plant
- Civil Engineering Completed Risk
- Contractor's All Risks

- Contractor's Plant & Machinery
- Deterioration of Stocks
- Erection All Risks
- Industrial All Risks
- Machinery Insurance Policy
- Machinery Loss of Profit

Guarantee Insurance

- Fidelity Guarantee Insurance
- Fidelity Guarantee Policy (Bajaj Allianz)
- Guarantee-Missing Documents
- Business Credit Shield (New India Indemnity Assurance)

Motor

- Commercial Vehicles

Miscellaneous

- Banker's Indemnity
- Burglary Insurance
- Electronic Equipment Policy
- Jewellers' Block
- LPG Dealers
- Money Insurance
- Office Umbrella
- Shopkeepers' Policy
- Special Contingency
- Business Guard Sanjeevini (Tata-AIG)
- Business Guard Jyothi (Tata-AIG)
- Trade Protector (IFFCO Tokio)
- Merchant's Cover (ICICI Lombard)

Marine

- Marine Insurance

Generic

Personal Accident

- Bhagyasree Child Welfare
- Janata Personal Accident
- Personal Accident
- Traffic Accident Policy
- NRI Accident Insurance Policy
- Rajarajeswari Mahila Kalyan
- Executive Guard (Tata-AIG)
- Family Guard (Tata-AIG)
- Personal Accident (Bajaj Allianz)
- Personal Accident (IFFCO Tokio)
- Personal Accident (Cholamandalam)
- Accident Shield (Royal Sundaram)
- Personal Accident (ICICI Lombard)

Health

- Mediclaim
- For Retired Persons
- Hospital Cash Daily Allowance Policy (Bajaj Allianz)
- Critical Illness (Bajaj Allianz)
- Health Guard (Bajaj Allianz)
- Health Shield (Royal Sundaram)

Motor

- Motor Car Insurance
- Two-wheeler Insurance

Property

- All Risks Insurance
- Burglary Insurance
- Sampoorna Suraksha Bima
- Burglary Insurance (Bajaj-Allianz)
- Domestic Appliances Policy
- Electronic Equipment Insurance
- Fire Policy — Home
- Householder's Package Policy
- Pedal Cycle Policy
- Plate Glass Insurance
- Transit Insurance
- TV Policy
- Householder's Insurance (Bajaj Allianz)
- Home Secure (Tata-AIG)
- Office Package Insurance (Bajaj Allianz)
- Money Insurance (Bajaj Allianz)
- Plate Glass Insurance (Bajaj Allianz)
- Home & Family Protector (IFFCO Tokio)
- Standard Fire & Special Perils (IFFCO Tokio)
- Burglary & House Breaking (IFFCO Tokio)
- Home Shield (Royal Sundaram)
- Home Insurance (ICICI Lombard)

Liabilities' Insurance

- Directors' & Officer's Liability
- Employers' Liability
- Golfers' & Sportsmen
- Pets (Dog Insurance)
- Professional Indemnity
- Public Liability
- Public Liability (Bajaj Allianz)
- Professional Indemnity (ICICI Lombard)

Gun Insurance

- Gun Insurance

Travel

- Baggage Insurance Policy (withdrawn)
- Standard Overseas Mediclaim Policy
- Overseas Mediclaim Policy
- Suhana Safar
- Travel Companion (Bajaj-Allianz)
- Travel Guard (Tata-AIG)
- Travel Shield (Royal Sundaram)
- Travel protector (IFFCO Tokio)
- Globetrotter Overseas Individual Travel Insurance (ICICI Lombard)

14.6 Rating Procedures

The rates for various classes of general insurance are based on the risk classes and associated hazards. The rates for various insurance products are prescribed on the basis of experiences and attributes of the subject-matter of insurance. In case of fire insurance, the parameters for classification of risks are occupancy of the premises (residential places, commercial places, industrial/manufacturing premises, exposure to heating, lighting, ignition manufacturing processes), types and ingredients of construction etc. In case of motor vehicles, the classification is done on the basis of manufacturing design, use and value. The prices of various subject-matter of insurance are subject to discrimination based on the risk and loss exposures.

The Tariff Advisory Committee (TAC) has prescribed the rates for various products relating to Fire, Marine (Hull), Motor, Engineering and Workmen Compensation Insurance. TAC prescribes the minimum rates, loading for various hazards and incentives for risk improvements for various classes of insurance. Other than these classes, the rates are market-determined. However, the rate which a company charges for insurance products, as a general rule should not be less than the base minimum actuarial calculation and cover for expenses.

Hazards

In case of fire insurance, the main physical hazards are – construction, occupancy, nature of flooring (applicable to buildings), process of manufacture, situation etc. In case of marine insurance, these are – the life of the vessel, voyage route, loading/unloading conditions, the warehousing facilities, nature and value of stocks, packing methodology etc. In case of motor vehicles, age, nature, type of the vehicle, the concession of the vehicle and use of the vehicle are important hazards. Similarly, in case of fidelity insurance, the accounting and control systems, the method of check and supervision etc. are important. In case of burglary insurance, the value of the article, the circumstances, the location etc. are important physical hazards.

The moral hazards may be dishonesty, carelessness (no worry insurance company will pay), deliberately inflated losses, economic conditions etc.

All hazards associated with a given proposal are assessed and rates are fixed accordingly. In case the risk is high, the proposal is declined or *warranties may be imposed*. A survey of the insurable property is generally carried out by the agent or the Ist/IInd level underwriter. The limits on the claims may be *excess* or *franchisee*. The motto behind fixing these limits is to restrict the small claims and the total amount of claims. When the loss exceeds the excess limit, full amount is paid under the franchisee clause and the Blanca is paid under the excess clause.

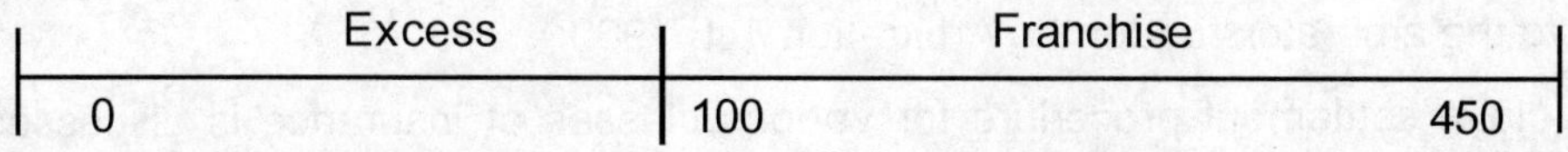

Excess		Franchise	
0	100		450

If the claim made is 90, nothing shall be paid. If the claim is 300, then 200 will be paid.

Premiums

The premiums in case of non-life insurance are generally on an annual basis. If the insurance cover is for less than 12 months, special scales *short scales* may be used as prescribed for various products. If the consideration for the premium totally or partially fails without fraud or otherwise on part of the assured or his agents, then the premiums shall be accordingly returned (Sec. 84 of the Insurance Act, 1938). Premium is refunded only when the policy provides for it. The premium conventionally has to be received in advance with the proposal. The policy comes into force only when the premium is actually received.

14.7 Claim Settlements

All insurance contracts are based on the information provided by the insured in the proposal form. The proper settlement of claim essentially requires a thorough knowledge of the various legal aspects, practices and procedures etc. The insurance company is known by its efficiency in claims settlement. The correctness of the information furnished in the proposal form is verified at the time of a claim, when physical inspection of the property is done. In case of any misrepresentation, it would be the prerogative of the Insurance Company to avoid a claim, or avoid the policy itself, or pay a claim for a reduced amount. Therefore, the proposal form initiated at the time of buying insurance plays an important role as it affects the consequential claims under the policy contract. The claim settlement generally involves the following procedure:

1. *Notice of Loss:* The loss or damage should be reported to the insurer immediately within the time-frame of the policy conditions. Immediate notice of loss allows the insurer to investigate the loss early and protect its interests.
2. *Claim Form:* On receipt of claim intimation, the insurer will forward a claim form. Claim forms vary with classes of insurance. Claim forms usually contain information such as time of loss, cause of loss, place and extent of loss, circumstances when loss took place etc. apart from the general information about the claimant. The claimant has to submit the completed claim form along with an estimate of the loss to the insurer. It is preferable to submit an itemised estimate with separate values.
3. *Scrutinisation:* The claim made by the insured shall be scrutinized for: *(a)* policy in force at the time of loss, *(b)* coverage of the policy, *(c)* subject-matter of the insurance, *(d)* adequacy of the notice of loss etc.
4. *Investigation and Assessment:* The insurer will arrange for inspection of the damaged items to assess the loss. In case of major losses, specialist-licensed surveyor/loss assessors are deputed. The insured has to provide the required documents to substantiate the extent of loss. In case the cause of loss is not established, it is for the insured to prove that the loss or damage has occurred due to an insured peril.
5. *Settlement and Arbitration:* On agreement of claim amount between the insured and the insurer, the claim is settled. Otherwise, in case of dispute, the matter is generally referred to the arbitrators under the Arbitration Act, 1960.

The claim settlement procedure for various classes of insurance is discussed in detail in Chapter 38.

Key Terms

- ❐ Claim Ratio
- ❐ Technical Reserves
- ❐ Sectoral Investments
- ❐ Reserve for unexpired risks
- ❐ Gross Direct Premium
- ❐ Miscellaneous Insurance
- ❐ Revenue Account
- ❐ Cover Note

- Arbitration
- Certificate of Insurance
- Excess
- Settlement
- TAC
- Franchisee

Questions for Review

1. Briefly trace the performance of General Insurance Industry from Nationalization to Privatization.
2. Compare the performance of various subsidiaries of GIC for the financial year 2000-01 to 2001-02.
3. List the insurance products regulated by Tariff Advisory Committee.
4. Briefly explain the claim settlement process in case of general insurances.

Suggested Readings

1. *Practice of General Insurance,* Insurance Institute of India, Mumbai, 1997.
2. P. Periasamy, *Principles and Practice of Insurance,* Himalaya Publishing House, 2003.
3. IRDA Annual Report 2001-02.
4. *Practice of General Insurance,* ICII, Insurance Institute of India, Mumbai, 1999.
5. S.S. Heubner *et al., Property and Liability Insurance,* Prentice-Hall, 1982.
6. Irving Pfeffer and Others, *Perspectives on Insurance,* Prentice-Hall, 1974.

Web Resources

- www.bimaguru.com
- www.irdaindia.org
- www.insure.com
- www.bimaonline.com
- www.indutr-magic.com

❑❑❑

FIRE INSURANCE

Chapter Objectives

- Fire Insurance Contracts
- Fire Insurance Proposals
- Fire Insurance Coverages
- Special Coverages
- Fire Underwriting & Rating
- Fire Insurance Claims
- Progress of Fire Insurance
- Fire Reinurance – An Illustration

Introduction

Fire Insurance is a profitable product to most of the insurance companies. Contract of fire insurance is a contract of indemnity provided to the insured by the insurer to indemnify him against the loss of property by or incidental to fire and or lighting, explosion etc. The contract of fire insurance has three peculiar features – (a) It is personal in nature, (b) Cause of fire is immaterial and (c) Covers losses as a whole.

Acceptance of fire insurance proposals is governed by regulations of Tariff Advisory Committee All India Fire Tariff. A fire insurance proposal generally requires the information on the details of property insured, risk inspection report, warranties etc.

The fire insurance policy has been nomenclatured Section II of the All India Fire Tariff as Standard Fire and Special Perils Policy.

The tariff Advisory Committee has prescribed three types of fire coverages viz., Policy A, Policy B and Policy C. In addition there are special cover ages like Reinstatement Value Polices, Stock Policies, Consequential Loss Policies etc.

Fire insurance claims settlement is a comprehensive procedure requires the scrutiny of fire policy, its extensions and schedule attached. The usual process involves basic verification of the property subject to loss, scrutiny of the coverage of perils, allotment of Claim Number, Issue of Claim Form, Appointment of Surveyor, submission of investigation Report and Discharge Voucher and final payment.

The extent of indemnity depends upon the value of property insured, consequential loss, expenses on rework and debris removal etc. In the case of valued policies, the valuations is placed on the subject matter of the policy, except in case of fraud or mistake, conclusively establishes the sum required for the purpose of full indemnity in case of total loss. In case of unvalued policies the value is generally determined according to the intrinsic value or the market value on the date the fire occurred.

15.1 Fire Insurance Contracts

Section 2(6A) of Insurance Act, 1938 defines "Fire insurance business" as "the business of effecting, otherwise than incidentally, to some other class of insurance business, contracts of insurance against loss by incidental to fire or other occurrence customarily included among the risks insured against in fire insurance policies."

The contract of fire insurance is similar to other contracts and comes into being when a person seeking insurance protection enters into a contract with the insurer to indemnify him against the loss of property by or incidental to fire and or lightning, explosion etc. There is no statutory enactment for regulation of fire business in India akin to Marine insurance which is governed by the Indian Marine Insurance Act, 1963.

15.1.1 Features of a Fire Insurance Contract

(*a*) *It is personal in nature:* It does not ensure the safety of the insured property. Its purpose is to see that the insured does not suffer loss by reason of his interest in the insured property. So, it is personal in nature in the sense that it involves the payment of money if the loss occurs.

(*b*) *Cause of fire is immaterial:* The insurer irrespective of the cause of fire will reimburse the loss due to fire. The doctrine of *causa proxima* applied unless there is a suspicion of fraud or wilful act or otherwise falling outside the scope of the contract.

(*c*) *Indivisibility:* The fire insurance contract covers the fire losses in whole and generally indivisible unless specifically provided by the contract.

15.1.2 Application of Insurance Principles to Fire Insurance

Insurable Interest

Ownership is a conclusive evidence of an insurable interest. Where the property is charged or mortgaged to a financier as security, the financier acquires insurable interest. The insurable interest in fire insurance must exist at the time of cover, continue throughout its currency and should exist at the time of loss. In case the subject-matter of insurance is transferred, the policy does not transfer automatically, it must be agreed by the insurer and endorsed on the policy document.

Indemnity

The indemnity for loss or damage suffered is the reinstatement or the market value. In case of property, market value or the reinstatement value is used. However, stocks are valued on the basis of market value. The sum insured should always represent the true value of the property.

Utmost Good Faith

The insured is bound to disclose all material facts to the insurer, which have a bearing on the contract. If the subject-matter of insurance is materially altered, the insured should give notice the insurer immediately. The guiding principle states that the insured should assume as if uninsured all times and accordingly is bound to take care of the insured property always.

Subrogation and Contribution

The insurers are entitled to subrogation rights when they have indemnified the losses to the insured and can proceed to recover the losses from third parties. In case the property has been insured from more than one insurer, the rateable proportion shall apply in the event of claims.

15.2 Fire Insurance Proposals

Acceptance of fire insurance proposals is governed by regulations of Tariff Advisory Committee All India Fire Tariff. A fire insurance proposal generally requires the following information:

Proposer's Details

- Name and address including phone, fax no. and e-mail address.
- Business and its nature of the proposer.
- Paid-up capital of the proposer's enterprise.
- Names of various parties having insurable interest.
- Location of risk to be covered and insurance period.
- Whether the fire insurance was declined by other insurers or accepted subject to special conditions in respect of given proposal.
- Claims experience.

Coverage

- Inclusion of flood, cyclone, type of perils and inclusion/deletion of riot, strike, malicious damage, Terrorism.
- Coverage of plinth and foundation to be covered along with the building.
- Whether add-on covers required.

Details of Property

- Type of property — commercial/residential.
- If shop whether hazardous goods (as per list) are stored; if so, whether the stock value exceeds 5% of the total stock value.
- If warehouse/godown (not located in a manufacturing unit), details of the goods stored.
- If industrial/manufacturing unit details of goods manufactured and capacity utilization.
- Utilities
- Height of building
- Age of building
- Fire Protection devices
- Construction material details.

Declaration is normally required as to the authentication of information furnished.

Risk Inspection Report

Risk Inspection Report is generally prepared to arrive at a correct risk assessment and rate the proposal. The risk inspection generaly covers the following:

- Generic Information
- Process of Manufacturing/Provision
- Fire Protection Mechanism
- Moral Hazards
- Claims Experience
- Conclusion and Comments.
- Lightning, Heating and Power
- Exposure Details
- Management and Supervision of proposed risk
- Sum Insured and PML — Adequacy and Efficiency
- Risk Improvement Measures

Section 64VB of the Insurance Act requires that no risk can be assumed unless and until the full premium is received in advance.

15.2.1 Warranties

Class of Construction

"Warranted that the buildings are not of Kachcha construction consisting of walls and/or roofs of wooden planks/thatched leaves and/or grass/hay of any kind/bamboo/plastic cloth/asphalt cloth/ canvas/tarpaulin and the like."

Fea Warranty

"Warranted that Fire Extinguishing Appliances in respect of which discount is given shall conform to the Tariff Advisory Committee regulations and shall be maintained in efficient working condition at all times and an annual maintenance contract with an external agency shall be in force at all times throughout the currency of this policy."

Apart from warranties which are not in printed form, the other ones are typed in policy. Special clauses, extensions, etc. (if applicable) are also attached and referred to in the Schedule.

15.3 Fire Insurance Coverages

15.3.1 Standard Fire Policy

The fire insurance policy has been nomenclatured Section II of the All India Fire Tariff as Standard Fire and Special Perils Policy. The standard risks covered, add-on covers, exclusions, conditions as prescribed by the tariff are described as follows:

Standard Risks

Fire

Destruction or damage to the property insured by its own fermentation, natural heating or spontaneous combustion or its undergoing any heating or drying process cannot be treated as damage due to fire. For e.g., paints or chemicals in a factory undergoing heat treatment and consequently damaged by fire is not covered. Further, bring of property insured by order of any Public Authority is excluded from the scope of cover.

Lightning

Lightning may result in fire damage or other types of damage, such as a roof broken by a falling chimney struck by lightning or cracks in a building due to a lightning strike. Both fire and other types of damages caused by lightning are covered by the policy.

Explosion/Implosion

Explosion is defined as a sudden, violent burst with a loud report. An explosion is caused inside a vessel when the pressure within the vessel exceeds the atmospheric pressure acting externally on its surface. An explosion may cause fire damage or concussion damage. An implosion means bursting inward or collapses. This takes place when the external pressure exceeds the internal pressure. This policy, however, does not cover destruction or damage caused to the boilers (other than domestic boilers), economisers or other vessels in which steam is generated and machinery or apparatus subject to centrifugal force by its own explosion/implosion. These risks can be covered in a Boiler and Pressure Plant Insurance Policy, which is specially designed to handle these risks.

Aircraft Damage

The loss or damage to the property (by fire or otherwise) directly caused by aircraft and other aerial devices and/or articles dropped there from is covered. However, destruction or damage resulting from pressure waves caused by aircraft travelling at supersonic speed is excluded from the scope of the policy.

Riot, Strike, Malicious and Terrorism Damage

The act of any person taking part along with others in any disturbance of public peace (other than war, invasion, mutiny, civil commotion etc.) is construed to be a riot, strike or a terrorist activity. Any loss or physical damage to the property insured directly caused by such activity or by the action of any lawful authorities in suppressing such disturbance or minimizing its consequences is covered. Further the wilful act of any striker or locked out worker, in connection with a strike or a lockout, or the action of any lawful authority in suppressing such act, resulting in visible physical damage by external means, is also covered. Malicious act would mean an act with malicious intent but excluding omission of any kind by any person, resulting in visible physical damage to the insured property, whether or not the act is committed in the course of disturbance of public peace or not. Burglary, housebreaking, theft or larceny does not constitute a malicious act for the purpose of this cover. Total or partial cessation of work or the retarding or interruption or cessation of any process or operations; or, permanent dispossession resulting from confiscation, commandeering, requisition or destruction by order of the Government or any lawfully constituted authority; or permanent or temporary dispossession of any building or plant or unit or machinery resulting from the unlawful occupation by any person of the same or prevention of access to the same, are not covered.

Storm, Cyclone, Typhoon, Tempest, Hurricane, Tornado, Flood and Inundation

Storm, Cyclone, Typhoon, Tempest, Tornado and Hurricane are all various types of violent natural disturbances that are accompanied by thunder or strong winds or heavy rainfall. Flood or Inundation occurs when the water rises to an abnormal level. Flood or inundation should not only be understood in the common sense of the terms, i.e., flood in river or lakes, but also accumulation of water due to choked drains would be deemed to be flood.

Impact Damage

Impact by any Rail/Road vehicle or animal by direct contact with the insured property is covered. However, such vehicles or animals should not belong to or owned by the insured or any occupier of the premises or their employees while acting in the course of their employment.

Subsidence and Landslide Including Rockslide

Destruction or damage caused by Subsidence of part of the site on which the property stands or Landslide/Rockslide is covered. While Subsidence means sinking of land or building to a lower level, Landslide means sliding down of land usually on a hill. However, normal cracking, settlement or bedding down of new structures; settlement or movement of made up ground; coastal or river erosion; defective design or workmanship or use of defective materials; and demolition, construction, structural alterations or repair of any property or groundworks or excavations, are not covered.

Bursting and/or Overflowing of Water Tanks, Apparatus and Pipes

Loss or damage to property by water or otherwise on account of bursting or accidental overflowing of water tanks, apparatus and pipes is covered.

Missile Testing Operations

Destruction or damage due to impact or otherwise from trajectory/projectiles in connection with missile testing operations by the insured or anyone else, is covered.

Leakage from Automatic Sprinkler Installations

Damage caused by water accidentally discharged or leaked out from automatic sprinkler installations in the insured's premises is covered. However, such destruction or damage caused by repairs or alterations to the buildings or premises; repairs removal or extension of the sprinkler installation; and defects in construction known to the insured, are not covered.

Bush Fire

This covers damage caused by burning, whether accidental or otherwise, of bush and jungles and the clearing of lands by fire, but excluding destruction or damage caused by Forest Fire.

The policy may be extended to cover earth quake, fire and shock; deterioration of stock in the cold storages following power failure as a result of insured peril, additional expenditure involved in removal of debris, architect, consulting engineers' fee over and above the amount covered by the policy, forest fire, spontaneous combustion and impact damage due to own vehicles. In case of a partial loss, Insurance Company shall effect payment for repairs and replacement. In case of policy with reinstatement value clause, cost of reinstatement will be paid on completion of reinstatement subject to overall limit of the sum insured. Insurance company may at its option, also repair or replace the affected property instead of paying for the cost of restoration.

Exclusions

This policy does not cover:

1. 5 per cent of each and every claim resulting from lightning/storm/tempest/flood/inundation/subsidence and landslide including rockslide covered under the policy.
2. Loss destruction or damage caused by war, invasion, act of foreign enemy hostilities or war-like operations (whether war is declared or not), civil war, mutiny, civil commotion assuming the proportions of or amounting to a popular rising, military rising, rebellion, revolution, insurrection or military or usurped power.
3. Loss, destruction or damage directly or indirectly caused to the property insured by:
    - Ionizing radiations or contamination by radioactivity from any nuclear fuel or from any nuclear waste from the combustion of nuclear fuel.
    - The radioactive toxic, explosives or other hazardous properties of any explosive nuclear assembly or nuclear component thereof.
4. Loss, destruction or damage caused to the insured property by pollution or contamination excluding:
    - Pollution or contamination which itself results from a peril hereby insured against.
    - Any peril hereby insured against which itself results from pollution or contamination.
5. Loss, destruction or damage directly to solution or unset precious stones curios, works of art for an amount exceeding ₹ 10,000, manuscripts plans, drawings, securities, obligations or documents of any kind stamps, coins or paper money, cheques, books of accounts or other business books, computer systems, records, explosives unless otherwise expressly stated in the policy.

6. Loss, destruction or damage to the stocks in cold storage premises caused by change of temperature.
7. Loss, destruction or damage to any electrical and/or electronic machine, apparatus, fixture or fitting (excluding fans and electrical wiring in dwellings) arising from or occasioned by overrunning, excessive pressure, shortcircuiting, arcing, self-heating, or leakage of electricity, from whatever cause (lightning included).
8. Expenses necessarily incurred on: (*i*) Architect's surveyor's and consulting engineer's fees and (*ii*) Debris removal by the insured following a loss, destruction or damage to the property insured by an insured peril in excess of 3 per cent and 1 per cent of the claim amount, respectively.
9. Loss of earnings, loss by delay, loss of market or other consequential or indirect loss or damage or any kind or description whatsoever.

The clauses covered above are subject to the normal general conditions of the insurance company.

Add-on Covers

The insurers can issue the standard fire policy as per the New Fire Tariff along with added benefits at the option of the policyholders by charging additional premium. These added benefits or add-on covers are as follows:

- Architect's, surveyor's and consulting engineer's fees (in excess of 3 per cent claim amount).
- Debris removal (in excess of 1 per cent of claim amount).
- Deterioration of stocks in cold storage premises due to power failure following damage due to an insured peril.
- Forest fire.
- Impact damage due to insured's own vehicles, forklifts and the like and articles dropped therefrom.
- Spontaneous combustion.
- Omission to insure additions, alterations or extensions.
- Earthquake (fire and shock) as per minimum rates and excess applicable as specified in the Tariff.

In respect of the above add-on covers. The insurance company will compulsorily deduct 5 per cent of each claim before paying the claim proceeds to the insured.

The standard policies exclude certain perils from the scope of cover. The main reasons for the exclusions are:

(*i*) To restrict the cover to normal coverage required by the typical or average insured. Personal Accident Policy which provides for the agreed benefits to be paid under certain specified contingencies, does not cover medical expenses, which can be included on payment of an additional premium. Similarly, Workmen's Compensation Policy indemnifies the insured against his liability at law to his direct employees, and provides for the Insured's legal liability to employees of sub-contractor to be included by payment of premium at a tariff rate on the wages payable to workmen of subcontractor. Similarly, policy can be extended to cover medical expenses, and the diseases specified in Part III of the Schedule C on payment of an additional premium.

(*ii*) To exclude loss which are of an extraordinary or catastrophic nature, e.g., the earthquake peril for locations involving storage of materials, and industrial/manufacturing risks. In view of concentration of material, property involving huge sum insured, perils of earthquake, and/or flood etc. could cause losses which might assume proportion of a catastrophe. While for residences, offices, shops and for tiny sector, etc., these perils (of earthquake and flood, etc.) are offered as in-built perils, as for these risks, perils of earthquake and flood may not cause catastrophic losses.

(*iii*) To precisely define and clarify the scope of cover. For example, to prevent disputes in the event of a loss which is akin to fire but is not within the meaning of the policy, spontaneous combustion is excluded under fire policy.

(*iv*) To exclude risks which may be accepted after obtaining more underwriting information or arranging inspection, e.g., flood risk in fire insurance, pollution cover under public liability policy, and cover for exports under Product's Liability Policy.

(*v*) To exclude losses which are convertible under other policies. This eliminates duplication of coverage. For example, the general public liability policy excludes liability arising out of the use of Motor Vehicle, because a Motor Third Party Policy is available. Similarly, Plate Glass Policy does not cover loss of or damage by fire, which can be covered separately under a Fire Insurance Policy.

(*vi*) To exclude risks which cause losses of high degree of frequency, e.g. the risks of larceny under Burglary (Business Premises) Policy, and shortages, which are discovered at periodic stock taking.

(*vii*) To exclude loss which are caused intentionally, e.g., suicide under personal accident policies.

(*viii*) To exclude losses, which are inevitable, e.g., wear and tear and depreciation under motor policies and 'inherent vice' under marine cargo policies.

(*ix*) To exclude losses which are commercially uninsurable, e.g., war and nuclear risks.

(*x*) The standard policies may also exclude certain classes of property from the coverage. For example, the fire policy excludes certain classes of property, e.g., documents, coins, paper money, books of account, unless expressly stated in the policy. The intention is to ascertain the existence of such property and, if necessary to include certain classes of property in the coverage subject to special terms and conditions. Similarly curios, works of art, paintings can be covered after obtaining valuation report, from the Director of Museum and stamps collection can be covered on production of valuation certificate from Philatelic Society.

15.3.2 Standard Policy Coverages

The Tariff Advisory Committee has prescribed three types of fire coverages, viz., Policy A, Policy B and Policy C.

Policy A

Fire Policy A covers the following perils — (*i*) fire, (*ii*) lightning, (*iii*) explosion/implosion, (*iv*) impact damage, (*v*) aircraft damage, (*vi*) riot, strike and malicious and terrorist damage, (*vii*) storm, cyclone, tempest, hurricane, tornado, flood and inundation, (*viii*) earthquake, (*ix*) subsidence and landslide (including rockslide).

Only Policy A can be issued to cover artisans workshops, bio-gas plants, village and cottage industries, tiny sector or small-scale industries.

Policy B

Fire Policy B covers the perils — (*i*) fire, (*ii*) lightning, (*iii*) explosion/implosion, (*iv*) impact damage, (*v*) aircraft damage, (*vi*) riot, strike and malicious and terrorist damage. (The cover is similar to Policy C).

The tariff permits exclusion of riot, strike and malicious and terrorist damage perils, with specified reduction in the premium rate under the policy.

Policy C

Fire Policy (Policy 'C') is issued to cover industrial/manufacturing risks and storage risk and covers — (*i*) fire, (*ii*) lightning, (*iii*) explosion/implosion, (*iv*) impact damage, (*v*) riot, strike and malicious and terrorist damage.

The riot, strike and malicious and terrorist damage perils can be excluded on specific request with an agreed reduction in the premium rate.

The fire policy C may be extended to cover special perils on payment of extra premium. These special perils are:

(*a*) Spontaneous combustion

(*b*) Earthquake (shock and fire)

(*c*) Storm, tempest, flood and inundation

(*d*) Subsidence and landslide

(*e*) Accident leakage or contamination of oil

(*f*) Spoilage of stock/machinery due to interruption of process of manufacture by insured perils

(*g*) Deterioration of stocks due to power failure following damage to premises of Public Power Stations

(*h*) Bursting/overflowing of water tanks, apparatus and pipes

(*i*) Sprinkler leakage

(*j*) Bush or forest fire

(*k*) Subterranean fire

(*l*) Missile testing operations cover.

Fire Policy A and B (Simple Risks): Fire Policy A and B are issued in respect of dwellings, offices, hotels and shops, educational institutions, etc.

15.4 Special Coverages

Apart from standard coverages, fire policy may also be issued to meet the specific requirements of clients. Some of these are:

(*a*) Reinstatement Value Polices

(*b*) Stock Policies

(*c*) Consequential Loss Policies.

15.4.1 Reinstatement Value Policies

In this policy, attaching the Reinstatement Value Clause of the fire policy modifies the basis of settlement of claims. Under the latter policy, losses are settled on the basis of market value of the property on the date of fire. This value, which takes into account depreciation, wear and tear, etc. will not be found adequate by the insured who desires to replace the property by a new one of the same kind, type of capacity. *This policy is issued in respect of building, plant, machinery, furniture and fixtures, fittings etc.*

Under the policy, the insurers pay, not the depreciated value (*i.e.* market value) but *the cost of replacement of the damaged property by new property of the same kind*. The advantages are obvious — during inflationary periods the new reinstatement value is far higher than the depreciated value. The sum insured is required to reflect the new replacement value and not the market value as under the normal fire policy. The reinstatement value clause of the policy places liability on the insured to complete the reinstatement work within 12 months of the loss/damage. Else, the claim will be settled on the basis of normal indemnity (market value). Also of the cost of reinstatement > Sum Insured, the rateable proportion applies.

15.4.2 Policies for Stocks

There are three types of policies for stocks.

Floater Policies

Stocks at various locations can be covered under one sum insured by floater policies, since these policies take care of frequent changes in sum insured at various locations.

These policies may be issued to cover stocks in one amount situated in a more than one specified building situated: (1) within the limits of one city/town/village, (2) more than one city/village/town but upto 50 locations, and (3) for more than 50 locations in various cities/towns/villages. The Floating policies are not issued in respect of immovable property nor are they issued to Transport Contractors and Clearing and Forwarding Agents.

Floating policies for risks situated within the limits of one city/town/village may be issued by charging 25% loading over and above the highest rate applicable to any one risk. 50% loading over and above the highest rate applicable to any one risk is charged under policies covering upto 50 locations in more than one city town/village.

The maximum sum insured at any one location should not be more than 10% of the total sum insured. It is essential that the insured should have a good internal audit and accounting procedure under which total amount of risk and locations can, if required, be established. The condition of average is applied to the limit of sum insured at each location, and also to the total sum insured under the policy.

A policy issued to cover in one amount, more than 50 locations in various cities/towns/villages is subject to the undernoted regulations:

Total sum insured in respect of all locations should not be less than ₹ 3 crore.

The maximum sum insured at any one location should not be more than 10% of the total sum insured.

The address of the locations should be declared to the company, at the inception, and changes advised as and when they occur. However, when locations cannot be identified or change is very frequent, the requirement of specifying address of locations is relaxed, but the number of unspecified locations should not exceed 10% the total number of locations, or 20 locations whichever is lower.

The insured should have a good internal audit and accounting procedure to establish total amount at risk and locations at a particular time.

The pro-rata conditions of average is applied to the limit of sum insured at each location and also to the total sum insured under the policy.

Declaration Policies

Declaration policies are useful to businesses, which face frequent fluctuations in stock quantity or value. Insurance companies can issue these policies subject to the following conditions:

- The minimum sum insured is ₹ 1 crore.
- Monthly declarations based on the average of the highest value at risk on each day or highest value on any day of the month are to be submitted by the insured to the insurer.
- Reduction in sum insured is not allowed under the policy.
- The insured cannot claim refund of premium on adjustment based on the declarations in excess of 50 per cent of the total premiums.
- The basis of value for declaration shall be the market value prior to the loss or as otherwise agreed to between the insurance company and the insured.

Exclusions

Declaration policies cannot be issued in respect of insurance required for a short period stocks undergoing process and stocks at railway sidings. Also, these policies are not sanctioned to:

(a) Transport contractors and Forwarding and clearing agents *(b)* in respect of stock-in-process *(c)* insurances for short period.

Advantages

1. The premium is limited to the actual amount of risk irrespective of the sum insured.
2. The liability of the insurer is concurrent under the policy.
3. Provision for adjustment of premium is an incentive to the insured to effect cover for the maximum amount.

Example

Assume that the sum insured is ₹ 1,00,00,000 and the rate per mille is ₹ 1.20. The insured is liable to pay a provisional premium of ₹ 12,000. Now, if the aggregate of monthly declarations comes out to be ₹ 13,20,00,000. The average monthly declaration value will be ₹ 1,10,00,000 (₹ 13,20,00,000/12). Accordingly, the premium on the policy will be ₹ 13,200 (₹ 1,10,00,000 × 1.20). The additional premium to be borne by the insured will be ₹ 1,200.

Floater Declaration Policies

These policies combine the features of the floater and declaration policies. All rules relating to Floater Policies and Declaration Policies shall apply here except:

- The minimum premium retention of the insurance company shall be 80 per cent of the annual premium.
- Minimum sum insured is ₹ 2 crore.

15.4.3 Consequential Loss Policies

Coverage and Suitability

This policy is suitable for business establishments and corporate for whom business interruption would mean heavy monetary loss in view of huge fixed costs. Fire consequential loss policy provides cover for expenses and increased cost of working as a result of business interruption following a loss covered by the fire policy. Insurance cover can be taken for the maximum period of the anticipated interruption in the event of loss. In addition, the supplier's and the customer's premises on which the business is dependent, cost of auditors fee (required to submit the monetary claim) can also be insured.

Because of the business interruption following a loss, there may be a reduction in turnover and this may affect the anticipated gross profit. Fixed costs are to be incurred immaterial of the production activity. Consequential loss policy covers reduction in gross profit due to business interruption. The additional expenditure necessarily incurred for avoiding or reducing the fall in turnover during the interruption period is covered under this policy. Also, there are overhead expenses of running the business such as salaries, wages, taxes, interest etc. which continue to be incurred inspite of the interruption of the production.

Premium

Premium chargeable depends on the type of industry/business, the anticipated gross profit, indemnity period chosen and additional covers required. Refund of premium (not exceeding 50%) can be claimed based on the actual gross profit figures as per the audited balance sheet after the expiry of the policy.

Basic fire policy to cover the assets at the business premises is a prerequisite. For claiming benefits under this policy, the *loss* should first be admitted under the fire policy. Amount of gross profit required to be insured, the indemnity period, details of the business premises to be covered and additional covers required shall be provided in the proposal form.

Advantage

In case of major fire loss, the business operations get interrupted resulting in reduced turnover and eventually in loss of profits. It is a well-known fact that fixed or standing charges have to be incurred immaterial whether there has been any production or not. All these are not covered by the normal fire policy. It is here that the consequential loss policy comes into force. Thus, for overall protection to the business and its profitability, consequential policy is necessary in addition to the fire insurance policy.

15.5 Fire Underwriting and Rating

15.5.1 Rate Fixation in Fire Insurance

The rate of fire insurance is prescribed by All India Fire Tariff. Insurers may charge rate higher than the tariff rates. The computation of rate is done in the following manner:

(*a*) Base rates are arrived for the class of property.

(*b*) Reduction in rates is allowed for deletion of STFI and/or RSMTD perils, if opted not to be included.

(*c*) Extra tariff is added for Hazardous Assets.

(*d*) Discount is allowed for claims experience.

(*e*) Further discount is allowed for betterment of risks.

The rates of insurance generally depend upon the nature of physical hazards, classification of risks, loss experience and nature of risks. Following considerations are taken into account while fixing premiums:

- Premium rating depends on the type of occupancy — whether industrial or otherwise.
- All property located in an industrial complex will be charged on rate depending on the product(s) made.
- Facilities outside industrial complexes will be rated depending on the nature of occupancy at individual location.
- Storage areas will be rated based on the hazardous nature of goods held.
- Additional premium is charged to include “Add-on” covers.

- Discount in premium is given based on past claims history and fire protection facilities provided at the premises.
- The insured can also opt out riot, strike, malicious and terrorism damage covers and flood group and perils for reduction in premium.

The risks are classified as simple risks, Industrial/Manufacturing risks, Utilities, Storage risks, Tank farms/Gasholders' Risks (Section III-VII of the tariff).

15.5.2 Fire Insurance Documents

Proposal Form

The proposal form contains the following information:

- Details of the proposer — location details, nature and location of risk, nature of business, financial performance, claims history, existing insurances etc.
- Type of coverage — inclusions and exclusions opted for
- Details of subject-matter of insurance
- Sum Insured — computation basis and basis of indemnity
- Insured Declaration/Authentication
- Risk inspection Report

Cover Note

A cover note is issued pending issue of policy. It contains the following information:

- Proposer details
- Sum Insured
- Details of risk covered
- Details of premium
- Date of issue and validity
- Date of commencement and expiry of cover
- Authentication
- Warranties and clauses

Policy Document

The fire policy must follow the format prescribed by the tariff. It contains all the information as contained in the cover note as mentioned above. In addition, it contains the endorsement and alterations made to the policy.

15.5.3 Cancellation of Policies

If insurance is cancelled at the option of insured, the retention of premium shall be at short period scale. Else if the insurance is cancelled by the insurer, the insurer refunds the premium on pro-rata basis.

If the policy is cancelled on account of:

- an order by a local authority/state/central government
- a building is completed when it was in course of construction

- demolition
- the premium is refunded on pro-rata basis.

15.5.4 Mid-term Cover

Mid-term cover are not granted for STFI and/or RSMTD perils. Whenever they are granted, the following conditions apply:

- Insurers must receive a specific advice from the insured accompanied by payment of additional premium.
- Cover shall commence 15 days after the receipt of premium.
- Premium rates prescribed in the Tariff are charged on short period scale basis on full sum insured for the balance period, i.e., upto the expiry of the policy.

Mid-term increase in sum insured is also allowed on pro-rata basis.

15.5.5 Claims Experience Discount

Claims experience discount is the discount offered on the basis of favorable claims experience. This discount may be offered on all policies covering the Insured's interest on the principle of one risk-one rate or of the preceding three policy periods.

This discount is applicable to risks rateable under Sections IV, V, VI and VII of the All India Fire Tariff.

Discounts (%)	*Incurred Claims Ratio*
15	Upto 5%
10	Above 5% and upto 10%
5	Above 10% and upto 15%

15.5.6 FEA Discount

Fire Extinguishing Appliances discount is offered for risk improvement as per the following conditions:

- Firc Extinguishing system shall be erected and tested as per the regulations of the TAC.
- Certificate from Professionals/Professional Agencies confirming the efficiency of the system and its compliance with the Rules shall be submitted by the insured to insurer at stipulated times.
- The installation of the system shall be maintained in efficient working order at all times and annual maintenance contract with an approved external agency shall be in force.

	Type of Installation	*Discount %*
(*a*)	Hand Appliances & Trailer Pumps/Fire Engines	2.5
(*b*)	Hand Appliances & Hydrant System	5
(*c*)	Hand Appliances & Sprinkler/Fixed Water Spray System	7.5
(*d*)	Hand Appliances + Hydrant System & Sprinkler/Fixed Water Spray System	10

Source: Fire and Conequential Loss Insurance, IC57, Insurance Institute of India, Mumbai.

The above discounts are non-cumulative and are unaffected by the presence of hand appliances.

15.6 Fire Insurance Claims

15.6.1 Fire Claims Procedure

Fire insurance claims settlement is a comprehensive procedure requires the scrutiny of fire policy, its extensions and schedule attached. The onus of proof in a fire claim is that of insured and the insurer has to verify whether the *causa proxima* was a covered peril or not. Following procedure is generally followed after receipt of a claim notice from the insured:

Basic Verification

On receipt of intimation of a claim, the first step is to verify that:

- Whether the policy is in force (affective).
- The perils covered under the policy include cause of loss.
- The property affected and location involved are both covered as per the policy schedule.
- The interest involved is the same as referred to in the policy.

Allotment of Claim Number

If the above conditions are satisfied, then the claim is registered by the insurer and a claim number (unique) is allotted, which is to be used as reference for any future correspondence regarding the claim.

Issue of Claim Form

After the registration of the claim, a claim form is issued to the insured for completion and return. The following information is required by a claim form:

- Name of the insured, policy number and address.
- Date, time, cause and circumstances of fire or occurrence of insured peril.
- Details of damage property.
- Sound value of the property at the time of fire. Where the insurance consists of several items, a declaration is required for the value of each item under which the claim is made.
- Amount claimed after deduction of salvage value.
- Situation and occupancy of premises in which the fire occurred.
- Capacity in which the insured claims, whether as owner or mortgagee or the like.
- Any other person(s) interested in the damage property.
- If any other insurance on such property was in force.

A claim settlement procedures is devoted to:

- Determine the amount of loss.
- Determine the method of settlement applicable.

- Explain the decision on claim to relevant parties.
- Notify the claimant in accordance with policy guidelines and code of practice.
- Complete the claim documentation.
- Payment and related formalities.

Appointment of Surveyor

In case the amount of claim made is small, the claim is simple and straightforward and is usually investigated by the official of the insuring company and processed and settled on the basis of investigation report and claim form. But if the loss is expected to be large, then independent loss surveyors and loss assessors are appointed to carry out a detailed investigation of the loss. These surveyors should have a license, to act as loss surveyors, issued by the Controller of Insurance. The surveyor is furnished with all the information and documents which help him determining the amount of loss and subsequently the liability of the insurance company.

Investigation Report and Discharge Voucher

The report of the loss surveyor and a discharge voucher is sent to the assured for his consent and signature and return. The receipt of such voucher duly signed by the assured initiates the insurers to send the cheque with an amount of the claim. The discharge voucher is to be signed by all the persons whose name appears in the policy document, and the cheque is drawn in favor of all the parties as mentioned in the policy. When the insurance is on coinsurance basis, the surveyor is appointed by the leading insurer where the losses involved are large and reinsurance arrangement provide for the 'cash loss settlements'. If the loss amount exceeds the pre-agreed figure, the insurers are entitled to recover the reinsurers' share immediately on payment of loss to the insured.

Where a difference arises regarding the quantum of compensation, the condition 11 of the Fire Policies 'A' and 'B' and condition 13 of Standard Fire Policies 'C' are invoked and the case is then referred to arbitrators appointed by the parties.

Disputes arises when the insurer repudiates the liability by stating that the loss is not covered under the terms and conditions of the policy or there has been a misrepresentation or fraud on the part of the insured or there has been a breach of warranty. The disputes may also concern the amount of indemnification as assessed by the insurer *vis-a-vis* as required by the insured. The insured in such cases can go to consumer redressal forums or the parties by mutual agreement can appoint an arbitrator or the insured can move the Court of law, directly or if not satisfied with the decision of the arbitrator or the consumer forum, as the case may be.

On the happening of any loss or damage to any of the property insured by this policy, the insurer may:

- Take the possession of the building or the premises where the loss of damage has taken place;
- Take possession or required to be delivered to it any property of the insured in the building or on the premises at the time of the loss or damage as per policy condition;
- Keep in possession of any such property and examine, sort, arrange, remove or otherwise deal with the same and

- Sell any such property or dispose off the same for the account of the concerned.

In case of assignment, the insurer may be required to make payments to other than the insured, who claims to be entitled to the payment under the policy, after producing necessary documents which may include:

- Probate of the deceased's will
- Letter of administration
- Certificate of appointment in case of appointment of a trustee in bankruptcy.

15.6.2 Extent of Indemnity

Indemnity is determined by the following:

- The value of the subject-matter of the insurance affected which depends upon the following parameters:
  - The value at the time of loss
  - The value at the place of loss
  - The real or intrinsic value excluding any sentimental value
  - Prospective profit or other consequential and indirect losses are excluded
- The sum insured under the policy for the affected property.
- The extent of insurable interest of the assured in the property on which the insurance policy is affected.
- Value of salvage.
- Application of pro-rata average.
- Deduction for any excess, if any.
- The contribution condition in cases where more than one insurance policy covers the same property.
- All rights and remedies arising out of the loss passes to insurers by subrogation.
- In case of successive losses, the sum insured under the policy will be reduced by the amount of the loss paid and the reduced sum insured is the sum insured for subsequent losses.

15.6.3Valuation Under Valued Policies

In the case of valued policies, the valuation is placed on the subject-matter of the policy, except in case of fraud or mistake, conclusively establishes the sum required for the purpose of full indemnity in case of total loss. In such cases, the insured does not need to prove the amount of loss that has taken place and on his proving of total loss he is entitled to recover the full amount even though the practical result may be to give more than true indemnity. In the cases of partial loss, where the subject-matter is not destroyed but only damaged, the insured being entitled to indemnity only, cannot recover more then the amount of damage sustained by him. In such cases it is immaterial whether the policy is valued, because what is actually valued is the subject-matter of insurance and not the amount of loss.

15.6.4 Valuation Under Unvalued Policies

In case of unvalued policies, the amount of insurance specified in the policy does not necessarily represent the true measure of indemnity. In such cases, it is generally determined according to the intrinsic value or the market value on the date the fire occurred.

Where the insured has limited insurable interest, he is precluded from recovering more than the value of his interest in the subject-matter of insurance. Otherwise principle of indemnity and good faith would be violated.

- The form of the policy enables the assured to recover the full amount.
- he insured, at the time of insuring, intends to insure the whole value of the subject-matter for the purpose of covering not merely his own limited interest but also the interest of all other persons who are interested in the subject-matter.
- There is no law which prohibits the insured from recovering the full amount.

15.7 Progress of Fire Insurance

Fire insurance is its present form has evolved after the incident of "Great Fire" which destroyed various buildings and inherent assets in the year 1966 and it lasted for many days. The first fire policy came in 1967. The fire insurance also developed during the industrial revolution.

The fire insurance was in nascent stage in India till liberalization even though, the fire insurance commercially developed in British times. Some of the early companies included Sun Insurance, Royal Ex?? Assurance, Phoenix Assurance during 17-9-1790 period. GIC was nationalized in 1972 and since then its four subsidiaries were having monopoly till 1999.

The share of business of GIC and its subsidiaries in 1972 was more than 75% of the total premium collected. It rose to around ₹ 180 crore with monopoly of GIC and its subsidiaries in 1981. The fire insurance business has recorded a substantial rise thereafter *viz.,* the group direct premium in 1987 was around ₹ 425 crore which went up to ₹ 1219.38 crores in 1993-94 and ₹ 2390 crore in 1999-2000 (Exhibit 15.1).

FIRE INSURANCE STATISTICS

Exhibit 15.1: Business Generated (Gross Direct Premium)

Companies	*1993-94*	*1994-95*	*1995-96*	*1996-97*	*1997-98*	*1998-99*	*1999-2000*
GIC	160.39	180.35	204.60	226.56	246.99	263.03	295.00
NIC	221.82	224.63	292.71	319.56	339.37	374.49	418.41
OIC	210.85	234.80	287.39	316.74	354.64	362.69	421.43
NIAC	361.14	416.03	500.65	482.33	567.28	581.89	726.77
UII	265.19	294.66	347.79	397.72	425.85	464.47	529.27
Total	**1219.39**	**1350.47**	**1633.14**	**1742.91**	**1934.13**	**2046.57**	**2390.88**

Profits (₹ in crore)

Companies	*1993-94*	*1994-95*	*1995-96*	*1996-97*	*1997-98*	*1998-99*	*1999-2000*
GIC	39.12	28.02	14.43	57.32	86.43	89.48	91.62
NIC	39.39	12.35	15.43	46.30	89.09	61.16	90.42

OIC	44.25	45.26	-2.47	34.14	101.63	88.36	52.13
NIAC	57.49	52.74	65.89	98.08	153.17	165.68	134.29
UII	67.79	79.13	38.18	91.71	113.28	134.60	172.65
Total	**248.04**	**217.50**	**131.46**	**327.55**	**543.60**	**539.28**	**541.11**

15.7.1 Profitability Before Privatisation

Fire insurance has been a profitable business for the India insurers. The profit (operating) earned by GIC in the year 1999-2000 was 31.00% of Gross Direct Premium Income and that of UTI was 32.62%. Both the companies have been outperformers. During the period 1993-94 to 1999-2000, there were no instances of losses except one in 1995-96 when OIC incurred a marginal loss. (Exhibit 15.2)

Exhibit 15.2: Profit %age

Companies	*1993-94*	*1994-95*	*1995-96*	*1996-97*	*1997-98*	*1998-99*	*1999-2000*
GIC	24.39%	15.54%	7.05%	25.30%	34.99%	34.02%	31.06%
NIC	17.76%	5.50%	5.27%	14.49%	26.25%	16.33%	21.61%
OIC	20.99%	19.28%	-0.86%	10.78%	28.66%	24.36%	12.37%
NIAC	15.92%	12.68%	13.16%	20.33%	27.00%	28.47%	18.48%
UII	25.56%	26.85%	10.98%	23.06%	26.60%	28.98%	32.62%

15.7.2 Post-liberalization Progress

Premium Income

After privatisation, especially in the year 2000-01, the fire premium dipped slightly and afterward started growing at a fast rate. During this time many private companies ventured into the fire insurance business significant among them are Reliance General Insurance, IFFbo-Tokio and Bajajk Allianz, Royalk Sundaram took a quantum leap in the year 2002-03 and declined afterwards. As per the figures of 2004-05, the prominent among the private players was ICICI Lombard (Exhibit 15C).

The income of the public sector companies also witnessed a growth immediately after privatisation till 2002-03 and it declined afterwards. This is attributable to the aggressive marketing strategies and new product offerrings by the private players.

Exhibit 15.3: Fire Insurance (Gross Direct Premium Income)

Fire Insurance Statistics

Business Generated(Gross Direct Premium - ₹ in crores)

Companies	*1993-94*	*1994-95*	*1995-96*	*1996-97*	*1997-98*	*1998-99*	*1999-2000*
GIC	160.39	180.35	204.60	226.56	246.99	263.03	295.00
NIC	221.82	224.63	292.71	319.56	339.37	374.49	418.41
OIC	210.85	234.80	287.39	316.74	354.64	362.69	421.43
NIAC	361.14	416.03	500.65	482.33	567.28	581.89	726.77
UII	265.19	294.66	347.79	397.72	425.85	464.47	529.27
Total	**1219.39**	**1350.47**	**1633.14**	**1742.91**	**1934.13**	**2046.57**	**2390.88**

Profits(₹ in Crores)

Companies	*1993-94*	*1994-95*	*1995-96*	*1996-97*	*1997-98*	*1998-99*	*1999-2000*
GIC	39.12	28.02	14.43	57.32	86.43	89.48	91.62
NIC	39.39	12.35	15.43	46.30	89.09	61.16	90.42
OIC	44.25	45.26	-2.47	34.14	101.63	88.36	52.13
NIAC	57.49	52.74	65.89	98.08	153.17	165.68	134.29
UII	67.79	79.13	38.18	91.71	113.28	134.60	172.65
Total	**248.04**	**217.50**	**131.46**	**327.55**	**543.60**	**539.28**	**541.11**
Profit %age							
GIC	24.39%	15.54%	7.05%	25.30%	34.99%	34.02%	31.06%
NIC	17.76%	5.50%	5.27%	14.49%	26.25%	16.33%	21.61%
OIC	20.99%	19.28%	-0.86%	10.78%	28.66%	24.36%	12.37%
NIAC	15.92%	12.68%	13.16%	20.33%	27.00%	28.47%	18.48%
UII	25.56%	26.85%	10.98%	23.06%	26.60%	28.98%	32.62%

Exhibit 15.4 Fire Insurance (Gross Direct Premium Income)

Company	2000-01	2001-02	2002-03	2003-04	2004-05	2005-06	2006-07	2007-08	2008-09
National	460.87	491.83	507.85	515.77	537.64	483.94	492.52	380.72	393.59
New India	760.29	859.89	867.46	775.2	788.88	839.63	909.98	743.43	773.33
Oriental	485.03	521.67	532.64	524	493.95	546.89	540.07	478.2	440.65
United India	606.03	635.89	604.18	631.32	590.91	645.48	664.34	524.3	570.8
ECGC*	-	-	39.16	-	-	-	-	-	-
GIC*/Others**	-	-	55.42	-	-	-	-	3.51	29.85
Royal Sundaram	-	17.9	103.52	50.53	63.01	91.74	98.39	68.87	48.84
Reliance	-	45.84	49.91	46.36	53.58	47.76	145.88	143.27	136.84
IFFCO-Tokio	-	36.15	123.75	142.88	172.78	236.29	291.02	215.17	195.28
TATA AIG	-	19.36	60.64	78.44	83.71	116.27	136.95	129.77	144.76
ICICI Lombard	-	10.98	5.32	239.46	277.45	308.47	393.83	471.35	283.02
Bajaj Allianz	-	27.88	-	120.29	219.42	351.4	370.31	273.49	253.06
Cholamandalam	-	-	-	25.44	47.78	72.83	77.98	68.3	53.84
HDFC-Chubb	-	-	-	0.36	1.81	6.81	11.1	12.83	58.79
Total	**2312.22**	**2667.39**	**2949.85**	**3150.05**	**3330.92**	**3747.51**	**4132.37**	**3513.21**	**3382.65**

***Others include Future Generali and Universal Sompo*

Market Shares

The monopoly of the public players was seriously hit after privitisation. It is evident from Table 15.5 that the shares of public sector companies is declining and that of private players is picking up. In 2004-05, the share of private players was 27.60% which is remarkable. (Exhibit 15D)

Exhibit 15.5: Market Share

Public Co. Shares	100.00%	94.07%	85.16%	77.66%	72.39%	67.14%	63.09%	60.53%
Private Co. Shares	0.00%	5.93%	14.84%	22.34%	27.61%	32.86%	36.91%	39.47%

Growth Rates

Fire insurance business has been growing but at an erratic rate. The year 2001-02 saw a negative growth rate when the insurance sector was opened for pubic players. The Compounded Average Growth rate for the eleven-year period from 1993-94 to 2008-09 is around 7.04% which is satisfactory when compared to other counterparts in the developing countries of the world.

Exhibit 15.6: Fire Insurance

Years	*1993-94*	*1994-95*	*1995-96*	*1996-97*	*1997-98*	*1998-99*	*1999-2000*	*2000-01*
Gross Direct Premium	1219.39	1350.47	1633.14	1742.91	1934.13	2046.57	2390.88	2312.22
Annual Growth Rate		10.75%	20.93%	6.72%	10.97%	5.81%	16.82%	-3.29%
Years	*2001-02*	*2002-03*	*2003-04*	*2004-05*	*2005-06*	*2006-07*	*2007-08*	*2008-09*
Gross Direct Premium	2667.39	2949.85	3150.05	3330.92	3747.51	4132.37	3513.21	3382.65
Annual Growth Rate	15.36%	10.59%	6.79%	5.74%	12.51%	10.27%	-14.98%	-3.72%
Compounded Average Growth Rate			7.04%					

Exhibit 15.7: Fire Insurance

(Opearting Profits — ₹ Crore

Company	*2003-04*	*2004-05*	*2005-06*	*2006-07*	*2007-08*
National	197.43	138.69	27.22	123.32	21.28
New India	294.77	230.83	19.57	233.02	283.36
Oriental	161.63	138.69	51.61	144.98	-16.77
United India	233.46	184.77	115.74	2.83	97.13
ECGC*	-	-	-	-	-
GIC*/Others**					-12.10
Royal Sundaram	9.23	7.24	11.53	18.81	6.38
Reliance	6.00	7.34	7.93	35.77	24.44
IFFCO-Tokio	15.66	28.15	36.97	46.00	14.99
TATA AIG	19.63	17.93	22.49	28.08	24.93
ICICI Lombard	38.31	52.35	48.13	73.85	18.05
Bajaj Allianz	22.52	47.24	46.91	79.21	71.92
Cholamandalam	0.40	1.79	-0.70	17.90	19.50
HDFC-Chubb	-0.54	-0.27	-0.66	1.64	2.24
Total	**998.5**	**854.75**	**386.74**	**805.41**	**555.35**

15.8 Fire Reinurance – An Illustration

Reinsurance of fire business in India is primarily headed by GIC in accordance with the IRDA guidelines. The obligatory session (20% quota share) is compulsorily needed to GIC and rest is dealt by treaties. The quota cession is retained in India itself to protect drainage of foreign exchange. The treaties take into account the sum insured and probable maximum loss. This requires classification of risk as illustrated below:

Non-risk Booked Risks: Smaller risks having sum insured less than ₹ 5 crores, which are not normally entered into the risk register maintained for the purpose-retention is 100% in India and reinsurance is affected using excess of loss cover.

Booked Risks: Medium Risks – Sum insured > ₹ 5 crore and PML < ₹. 26 crore.

The risks are entered in the register and are termed as Risk Booked. The underwriting of medium-sized risks is as under:

Obligatory	20.00%
Net Account	45.00%
Market fire pool	30.00%
Companies. Fire surplus treaty	0.5.00%
Total	**100.00%**

The Indian market retention for Medium Size Risks is 95%.

Listed Risks: All risks having a PML greater than ₹ 26 crore are classified as listed risks.

Key Terms

- ❒ Reinsurance
- ❒ Surplus
- ❒ Treaty
- ❒ Reinsurance Arrangements
- ❒ TAC
- ❒ AIFT
- ❒ Gross Direct Premium
- ❒ Operating Profit
- ❒ Valued Policy
- ❒ Inspection Report
- ❒ Adjustment
- ❒ Surveyor
- ❒ Consequential Loss
- ❒ Floater Policies
- ❒ Facultatives
- ❒ Risk Register
- ❒ Obligatory Cessions
- ❒ FEA Discount
- ❒ Pro-rata Basis
- ❒ Shot-period Scale
- ❒ Underwriting Experience
- ❒ CAGR
- ❒ Discharge Voucher
- ❒ Unvalued Policy
- ❒ Claim Register
- ❒ Add-on — Cover
- ❒ Declaration Policies
- ❒ Reinstatement Value Policies

Questions for Review

1. Give an example of how fire exposure worth ₹ 5000 crores would be reinsurance using various arrangement.
2. Briefly explain the steps in filing and settlement of fire claims.
3. What are the rights of the insurer, once a claim is admitted under the fire policy?

4. Write short notes on:
   (*a*) Arbitration
   (*b*) Limited Insurable Interest.
5. Briefly comment on the progress of Fire Insurance in India.
6. What major changes have took place in the fire insurance business segment after privatisation?
7. Briefly explain the various underwriting considerations in fire insurance business.
8. Discuss the importance of "depreciation factor" in fire insurance loss assessment.
9. Explain how basis rate are arrived at under the Consequential Loss (Fire) cover?
10. Define fire insurance. Explain the important features of a standard fire policy.
11. Write short notes on:
    (*a*) Fire Extinguishing Appliance Discount
    (*b*) Dual Basis of Wages Insurance
    (*c*) Debris Removal Clause.
12. Distinguish between:
    (*a*) Standard Fire Policy and Reinstatement Value Policy
    (*b*) Floater and Declaration Policies
    (*c*) Originating Factors vs. Contributory Factors

Suggested Readings

1. Irving Pfeffer and David, R., Klock, *Perspectives on Insurance,* Prentice Hall, Englewood Ciffs, 1974.
2. *Fire and Consequential Loss Insurance,* Insurance Institute of India, Mumbai, 2004.
3. Fire *and Consequential Loss Insurance,* IC 57, Insurance Institute of India, Mumbai 2001.
4. *IRDA Annual Report 2001-02.*
5. *Insurance Law Manual,* Taxmann, 2001.
6. *All India Fire Tariff prescribed by Tariff Advisory Committee.*
7. IRDA Reports.
8. Articles on Insurance.
9. CAG Reports.
10. Gupta, P.K., Insurance and Risk Management, Himalaya Publishing House, Mumbai, 2004.

Web Resources

- www.globalreinsurance.com
- www.reinsurance.org
- www.re-world.com

❑❑❑

MARINE INSURANCE

Chapter Objectives

- History of Marine Insurance
- Marine Insurance – Definition and Types
- Nature of Marine Insurance Contract
- Marine Insurance Policies
- Marine Insurance Policy Conditions
- Special Marine Covers
- Cargo Underwriting
- Hull Underwriting
- Marine Losses
- Settlement of Claims
- Marine Cargo Losses and Frauds
- Marine Stock Throughout Policy

Introduction

Insurance on the risks of transportation of goods is one of the oldest and most vital forms of insurance. The value of goods shipped by business firms each year cost millions of rupees. These goods are exposed to damage or loss from numerous transportation perils. The goods can be protected by ocean marine and inland marine contracts. Ocean marine insurance provides protection for goods transported over water. All types of ocean-going vessels and their cargo can be insured by ocean marine contracts, the legal liability of shipowners and cargo owners can also be insured. Inland marine insurance provides protection for goods shipped on land. It includes insurance on imports and exports, domestic shipments, and means of transportation such as bridges and tunnels. In addition, inland marine insurance can be used to insure fine art, jewellery, fur and other properties.

16.1 History of Marine Insurance

Ocean marine insurance is one of the earliest forms of insurance. Commerce by ship was well established in the Mediterranean Sea, 2000 years before the birth of Christ. The Babylonians, Phoenicians, Greeks and Romans were great sea traders. Coincident with the development of this trade, insurance transactions emerged as distinct commercial agreements. *Bottomary* was a transaction protecting an owner from financial loss if his ship was destroyed. The bottomary loan was an early forerunner of ocean marine insurance. On the other hand, some elements of the modern insurance transaction were missing. Actuarial science was not practiced, although the Phoenicians were noted mathematicians, so premiums were probably not based on mathematical estimates but on intuition. Today, judgmental estimates remain the basis of marine underwriting. The early sea traders and moneylenders also lacked a highly developed body of law like that providing the environment for the modern insurance transaction.

Respondentia loans were comparable to bottomary loans, the difference being the subject of the loan. Otherwise, the transaction was comparable. A merchant, placing cargo on a ship, would take out a loan using the cargo as collateral. The moneylender, for a premium in addition to the regular interest charged, agreed to forgive the loan if the cargo were lost. Again, modern ocean marine cargo insurance is very similar to the respondentia loan.

Evidences of marine insurance contract are found in Mediterranean voyages. The literature of 1400 also indicates the charging of prime for marine insurance policies. The law of Wishky (1300), the Ordinance of Barcelona (1435) and the Guidon de la Mar (1600) provide evidence of marine insurance development in Europe. In 1779, the underinites at Lloyds adopted a uniform marine insurance contract which is a common form of policy in use today.

During the period 1720-1820, the companies like London Association and Royal Exchange Association enjoyed major marine insurance market share.

In 1909, the Marine Insurance (Gambling Policies) Act was adopted and the modest pattern of British regulation was set as it is in substance today.

Major international markets for marine includes UK, US, Europe, Japan, etc. The most dominated UK Marine Insurance market includes players like Lloyds, mutual association and affiliates of non-UK based insurance companies.

16.2 Marine Insurance – Definition and Types

A contract of marine insurance is an agreement whereby the insurer undertakes to indemnify the assured in a manner and to the extent thereby agreed, against marine losses, that is, the losses incidental to marine adventure. Marine insurance cover gives financial protection from total loss or partial damage of seagoing ships and cargoes. In return for the payment of a premium, the underwriter of a marine risk or 'line' insures the shipowner, ship-charterer or merchant, for part or the whole value of a ship or cargo. Freight charges paid in advance may be insured by the ship-owner. Each type of marine insurance requires an assessment of the nature, size are value of the risk and the underwriter calculate his premium according to the quality of the ship or cargo and the destination and route of the voyage at risk. Marine insurance contracts are amongst the least charging and most familiar of all types of risk business. *There is a marine adventure when any insurable property is exposed to marine perils.* Marine perils also known as perils of the seas, means the perils consequent on, or incidental to, the navigation of the sea or the perils of the seas, such as fire, war perils, pirates, rovers, thieves, captures, jettisons, barratry and any other perils which are either of the like kind or may be designed by the policy. Marine Insurance business means the business of effecting contracts of insurance upon vessels of any description, including cargoes, freights and other interests which may be legally insured minor in relation to such vessels, cargoes and freights, oods, wares, merchandise and property of whatever description insured for any transit by land or water or both, and whether or not including warehouse risks or similar risks in addition or as incidental to such transit and includes any other risks customarily included among the risks insured against in marine insurance policies. The two broad categories of marine insurance are – ocean marine insurance and inland marine insurance.

16.2.1 Ocean Marine Insurance

Ocean marine insurance is one of the forms of transportation insurance. The ocean marine contracts are incredibly complex, reflecting basic marine law, trade customs, and court interpretations of the various policy provisions. Ocean marine insurance can be divided into four basic classes to reflect the various insurable interests:

Hull Insurance covers physical damage to the ship or vessel. It is similar to collision insurance that covers physical damage to a automobile caused by collision. Hull insurance is always written with a deductible. In addition, it contains a collision liability clause that covers the owner's legal liability if the ship collides with another vessel or damages its cargo. However, the running down clause does not cover legal liability on that vessel arising out of injury or death to other persons, damage to piers and docks, and personal injury and death of crew members.

Cargo Insurance covers the shipper of the goods if the goods are damaged or lost. The policy can be written to cover a single shipment. If regular shipments are made, an open-cargo policy can be used that insures the goods automatically when a shipment is made. The shipper is required to report periodically the number of shipments that are made. The open-cargo policy has no expiration date and remains in force until it is cancelled.

Protection and Indemnity (P&I) Insurance is usually written as a separate contract that provides comprehensive liability insurance for property damage or bodily injury to third parties. P&I insurance protects the shipowner for damage caused by the ship to piers, docks and harbour installations, damage to the ship's cargo, illness or injury to the passengers or crew, and fines and penalties.

Freight Insurance indemnifies the shipowner for the loss of earnings if the goods are damaged or lost and are not delivered.

Ocean marine insurance has certain fundamental concepts:

Covered Perils: An ocean marine policy provides broad coverage for certain specified perils, including perils of the sea, such as damage or loss from bad weather, high waves, collision, sinking, and stranding. Other covered perils include loss from fire, enemies, pirates, thieves, jettison (throwing goods overboard to save the ship), barratry (fraud by the master or crew at the expense of the ship or cargo owners), and similar perils. Ocean marine insurance can also be written on an "all-risks" basis. All unexpected and fortuitous losses are covered except those losses specifically excluded. Common exclusions are losses due to delay, war, inherent vice (tendency of certain types of property to decompose), and strikes, riots, or civil commotion.

Particular Average: In marine insurance, the word 'average' refers to a partial loss. A particular average is a loss that falls entirely on a particular interest, as contrasted with a general average, a loss that falls on all parties to the voyage. Under the free of particular average clause (FPA), partial losses are not covered unless the loss is caused by certain perils, such as stranding, sinking, burning or collision of the vessel. The FPA clause can be written with franchise deductible, where the franchise amount is stated as a percentage of the insured property. Thus, an FPA clause of 3% means that a covered loss under 3% falls entirely on the insured; if the loss is 3% or more, the insurer pays the loss in full.

General Average: A general average is a loss incurred for the common good and consequently is shared by all parties to the venture. Each party must pay its share of the loss based on the proportion that its interest bears to the total value in the venture. Four conditions must be satisfied to have a general average loss:

- *Necessary:* The sacrifice is necessary to protect all interests in the venture — ship, cargo, and freight.
- *Voluntary:* The sacrifice must be voluntary.
- *Successful:* The effort must be successful. At least part of the value must be saved.
- *Free from Fault:* Any party that claims a general average contribution from other interests in the voyage must be free from fault with respect to the risk that threatens the venture.

Sue and Labour: Under this, the insured is required to do everything possible to save and preserve the goods in case of loss. The insured who fails to do this has violated a policy condition, hence loses the rights of recovery.

Abandonment: In ocean marine insurance, two types of total losses are recognized: actual and constructive. Actual total loss occurs when the property is completely destroyed. Constructive total loss occurs when, even though the ship or other subject-matter of insurance is not totally destroyed, it would cost more to restore it than it is worth. The ship may be abandoned to the insurer and the insured collects the full amount of the policy. The salvage then belongs to the insurer, who is usually in a better position to dispose of it than the insured because the insurer deals with salvage companies all over the world and is experienced in such matters.

Warehouse to Warehouse: Under the terms of the warehouse to warehouse clause, such protection as is afforded under the insuring agreement extends from the time the goods leave the warehouse of the shipper, even if it is located far inland, until they reach the warehouse of the consignee.

Coinsurance: although an ocean marine policy does not contain a specific coinsurance clause, losses are settled as if there is a 100 per cent coinsurance clause. An ocean marine policy is a valued contract, by which the face amount is paid if a total loss occurs. If the insurance carried does not equal the full value of the goods at the time of loss, the insured must share in the loss.

Warranties: There are two types of warranties in marine insurance: express and implied. Express warranties are written into the contract and become a condition of the coverage relating to potential causes of an insured event. And can be of the type free of capture and seizure warranty (FC&S), strike, riot and civil commotion (SR&CC), delay warranty and trading warranty. Implied warranties are not written into the policy but become a part of it by custom. Breach of warranty in marine insurance voids the coverage, even if the breach is immaterial to the risk. It can be of types of seaworthiness, deviation and legality.

16.2.3 Inland Marine Insurance

Inland marine insurance grew out of ocean marine insurance. Ocean marine insurance first covered property from the point of embarkation to the place where the goods landed. As commerce and trade developed, the goods had to be shipped over land as well. Inland marine insurance developed in the 1920s to cover property being transported over land, means of transportation such as bridges and tunnels, and property of a mobile nature.

Commercial property that can be insured by inland marine contracts can be conveniently classified into five categories:

- Domestic Goods in Transit.
- *Property Held by Bailees:* Bailees are legally liable for damage to customer's property only if they or their employees are negligent.
- *Mobile Equipment and Property:* Inland marine property floaters can be used to cover property that is frequently moved from one location to another.
- *Property of Certain Dealers:* Certain "block" policies are used to insure dealers. Most policies provide coverage on an "all-risks" basis.
- *Means of Transportation and Communication:* This refers to property at a fixed location that is used in transportation or communication.

For purposes of regulation, inland marine contracts are classified into two categories; *filed forms* and *non-filed forms.* With filed forms, the policy forms and rates are filed with the State Insurance Department. Filed forms are typically used in situations where there are a large number of potential insurers and the loss exposures are reasonably homogeneous. In contrast, non-filed forms refer to policy forms and rates that are not filed with the State Insurance Department. Non-filed forms are used in situations where the insured has specialized or unique needs, the number of potential insureds is relatively small, and the loss exposures are diverse.

16.3 Nature of Marine Insurance Contract

Marine insurance contract being a contract should first satisfy the essential elements of a valid contract. In addition, it should satisfy the insurance principles as applicable to marine insurance. Further, there are specific provisions given in the Marine Insurance Act, 1973.

The essential elements of a marine insurance contract from the perspective of Indian Contract Act *inter alia* includes:

(*a*) *Offer* – in the form of proposal.

(*b*) *Acceptance* – issue of a cover note/policy.

(*c*) *Consideration* – premium payable on the policy

Insurance Principles Applied to Marine Business

Utmost Good Faith

The insured is bound to disclose all material facts to the insurer before the contract is entered into.

Example

If an equipment is transported and insurance cover was obtained as such implying as is a new one and actually the equipment is one which has been renovated, the insurer may cancel the contract as it was a concealment of fact.

However, if there is certain information, which reduces the exposure, to the insurer or which the insurer is bound to have known or waived *suo moto*, the contract is valid.

If the insurance is affected through a broker or agent, it is the duty of agent/broker to disclose all material facts. These facts not only include the communicated facts but also (by principal) facts in his knowledge. He must also know every circumstance in ordinary course of business and as communicated by his principal. All representations (material fact/fact/expectations or belief) must be communicated to the insular before obtaining the cover.

Insurable Interest

The insured may not have insurable interest at the time of contract, but he must have a reasonable expectation of acquiring it and it must exist at the time of loss. As per the provisions of the Marine Insurance Act, 1963, "every person has an insurable interest who is interested in a maritime adventure". The insurable interest may be:

(*a*) *Defeasible:* which is brought to an end by during the tenure of the voyage by occurrence of an event other than maritime perils. For example — cessation of insurable interest of the seller upon the transfer of title to the buyer.

(*b*) *Contingent:* which attaches during the tenure of the voyage on the happening of the contingent event. For example, when the goods are sold on FOB terms to the buyer, when the goods are loaded on the vessel, the seller's interest terminates, but if the goods are returned by the buyer, the interest again attaches for the seller.

It is essentially required that something must exist feasible which may be exposed to marine perils and there must be some legal or justified relationship which imply a benefit to the holder by its preservation and the insured is affected by its damage/loss/detention or occurrence of a liability in connection thereof.

Marine Insurance Act provides that in the event of "lost or not lost" clauses in marine insurance contract, the assured may recover the loss even though at that moment he has not acquired any interest because of ignorance. However, if the insured was aware of loss and the insurer was not informed, the claim may be denied on the grounds of violation of utmost good faith.

Nowadays, cargo and hull policy forms have disformed with "lost or not lost" clauses. But some ICC clauses provide that if the insured property suffers loss/damage before assured acquires interest, he is protected by the policy condition if any only if risk is transferred to him. In case of PPI (Policy Proof of Interest) policies, the underwriter may dispene with evidence of insurable interest. However, no action is tonable against them if claim is denied. Insurer has insurable interest in respect of risk underwritten which entitles him to get it reinsured.

In case of freight, the cargo owner has insurable interest in freight advanced.

Indemnity

Section 3 of the Act says that indemnity is "in the manner and to the extent thereby agreed". The indemnity depends on the contract. In case of valued policies, the measure of indemnity is the agreed value. However, in case of unvalued policies, unless provided, the indemnity has to be calculated as per the provisions of the Section 18 of the Marine Insurance Act, 1963. Indemnity valuation is difficult because values of cargo keeps on changing and its value increase the more and more it gets closer to destination. Another method of indemnity valuation is:

CIF Value of Goods

+ Allowance (%) for overheads

+ Allowance (%) for profit.

Subrogation

The insurer on the payment of claims for losses which may be partial or total, is subrogated to all the rights and remedies of the assured in respect of the subject-matter insured. In case of total loss, insurer is entitled to take over the interest of assured in toto. In case of partial loss, the insurer has not such rights. His rights are limited to the idemnity made. A letter of subrogation is generally taken from the insureds when claims are paid, in situations where the recovery is possible from third parties. If under recovery from third parties, a value greater than insured value is recovered, assured is entitled to proceeds, subject to reimbursement of claim amount due to insurers.

Contribution

When for the same subject-matter of marine insurance, there are more than one policy such that sums insured exceed the indemnity allowed by the act, the assured shall be deemed to be cover insured and rateable proportion shall apply to such cases. If the insured has recovered more than indemnity value, the excess amount shall be held in trust by him.

Warranties

Warranties, common to marine insurance contracts are the promises by the insured that something shall be done or a certain state of affairs exist or do not exist. The logical reason for imposing warranties by the insurers is to safeguard their interest from hazards and they can avoid liability in case of breach. Warranties may be:

Expressed: appearing in the policy, e.g., warranties relating to packing, shipping time period, survey/inspection etc. In case of hull insurance, express warranties include:

1. *Trading Warranty:* area of operation.
2. *Disbursement Warranty:* employment or use of the vessel for specific trade or traders.
3. *Registration/Licencing Warranty:* for the vessels engaged in fishing or sailing activities.

Proximate Cause: The liability of insurers in limited to insured perils. If it is established that insured perils was the remote cause that resulted in damage/loss, the claim may be denied by the insurer.

16.4 Marine Insurance Policies

Marine insurance policies cover risks associated with transshipments of goods like:

1. Transit of heavy goods such as rail engines by shipping vessels or
2. Consignment of diamonds sent by post or
3. Movement of household goods by rail/road/air.
4. Risks vary with the type of business transacted whether it is by importers, exporters or trading house.
5. Some form of life and transit risks is still undertaken by Indian Posts & Telegraphs Dept.

Salient Features

- The striking features of Marine Insurance policies is that they are issued on 'agreed value basis'.
- The values agreed may include all expenses incurred or to be incurred and some amount of profit margins as well. As such the valuation of the consignment is important and it should be based on supporting evidence.

A marine insurance policy:

(*a*) Must be signed by or on behalf of insurer.

(*b*) May be executed and issued to insured after the conclusion of the contract.

(*c*) Must *inter alia* include — the description of insured, subject-matter of insurance, sum insured, insurer description, period of enforcement, covered perils, exclusion etc.

(*d*) If the subject-matter of the insurance is in general terms, the policy relates to insurable interest.

(*e*) If the insurers are more than one, the joint policy represents separate contract with the respective insurers.

(*f*) A marine insurance policy must be authenticated by the issuer (insurer).

The contracts can be supply of goods on:

1. Ex-factory/godown/warehouse basis.
2. FOB basis (free on board-values arrived at, may include sale price, packing and incidentals, insurance and freight for local transit until goods are placed on the ocean-going vessel).
3. FOR (values until placed on railway wagon as in the case of FOB).
4. C&F (cost and freight values as in CIF, except the insurance costs).

CIF (cost insurance and freight would be sale price and incidental charges, insurance charges from warehouse to warehouse basis or any other point of delivery and all freight charges).

Types of Policies

There are different types of marine policies known by different names according to the manner of their execution or the risk they cover.

The major classification of marine insurance policies is:

(*a*) Policies covering damage/loss to ship/vessel/carrier hull, risk during repairs/construction, transfer risk, fleet cover.

(*b*) Policies providing cover against loss/damage to cargo particular average, general average.

(*c*) Policies protecting against third party liabilities — collision, protection against damage/loss, pollution cover, etc.

(*d*) Policies covering loss of freight etc.

Accordingly, the following popular covers are discussed here:

Voyage Policy

The voyage policy is issued to cover up a specific transit from a particular point to another. The cover ceases upon the carrier reaching the town of destination. In all the policies, the scope of cover can be:

(*i*) *Basic cover:* Basic cover is described in ICC-C clause.

(*ii*) *Wider cover:* Wider cover is described by ICC-B.

(*iii*) *All Risks cover:* All risks cover by ICC-A.

(*iv*) All risks cover does not pay all losses.

(*v*) All risks cover can be extended against 'Delay start up' or 'Consequential Loss due to Marine delays' or 'Advance loss of profits' risks.

(*vi*) While the basic policy document contains general conditions, the scope of cover and exceptions and special exclusions are attached by separate clauses known as Institute Cargo Clauses (ICC).

Extensions of Voyage Policy

(*i*) *FOB risks cover:* The road/rail transit risks can be extended until the goods are placed on board of the ocean-going vessel, which may involve country craft/lighter risks also.

(*ii*) *Sellers' contingency risks:* FOB cover can further be extended against 'Sellers' contingency risks'.

(*iii*) *Warehouse to warehouse basis*: The policy covers all risks right from the moment the goods are dispatched from the supplier's warehouse till they reach the buyers' warehouse.

Annual Policy

If a business involves regular dispatch of goods throughout the year, and the quantity can be reasonably estimated in advance, an annual policy can be obtained on the basis of estimated annual dispatches. Premiums collected in advance will be adjusted at the end of the year. In case of annual policies, the previous year's turnover and the estimated increase during the current year is the basis for fixing sum insured for annual policy.

Declaration Policy

An alternative to annual policy is declaration policy. A policy can be obtained for any specific amount so that every dispatch to be insured for transit risks can be declared as agreed to and accounted until the sum insured is exhausted. The policy can be extended for a further sum. In case of declaration policies, one has to take a policy equivalent to 3 months' estimated dispatches, which can be extended any number of times. All the dispatches should be declared without exception as per terms agreed to.

Special Declaration

If sum insured selected is more than ₹ 2 crore, a special declaration policy can be obtained for which volume discount in premium is allowed. The annual dispatches should be reasonably estimated and the policy taken. However, the sum can be extended for a couple of times in extraordinary cases of genuine reasons. In case of special declaration policies, the minimum sum insured should be ₹ 2 crore and the policies should be for sums equivalent to estimated annual dispatches. The declarations can be made at an agreed period (even after a loss). As the entire premium has to be paid in advance, volume discounts are offered.

Open Cover

It is a memorandum of agreement by which the insured will set out the terms of cover and rates of premium for one-year transaction of Marine dispatches. The open cover is not a policy and it is not negotiable. A Certificate of insurance is issued for each declaration duly stamped for appropriate value and the Certificate will be negotiable.

Duty Policy

A deviation in Marine Insurance is to issue custom duty payable for imports by the same Marine Policy though there may not be any transit risks involved. In case of CIF contracts, the exporter to the extent of CIF values would have arranged the Insurance only. Custom Duty payable, if any, would be the responsibility of the importers and they can separately obtain Custom Duty policy on 'standalone basis'.

Another special feature of custom duty policy is that it is a pure indemnity policy and the insured is paid the exact amount of loss of custom duty as a result of loss or damage to the consignment. The policy should be obtained before the vessel reaches the port of destination. Duty policy can be obtained much after dispatch of goods but before the vessel reaches the port of discharge.

Increased Value Policy

Increased value if goods imported are damaged in transit and such goods can be procured locally at prices higher than the CIF + custom duty, the increased value policy covers such difference in value. This is purely an indemnity policy and for the benefit of the insured only and cannot be assigned to others. The policy should be obtained before the overseas vessel reaches the port of destination.

Marine Delays (Marine LOP)

In case of new project where equipment has to be procured indigenously or by imports, any loss or damage to the equipment during transit may involve ordering of fresh equipment which leads to delay in completion of the project, commencement of production and thereby loss of profits. The Financial institutions who are interested in timely completion of the project for their debt servicing, would like this risk covered by an Insurance contract and the Marine (cargo) insurance policy can be extended against what are known as 'consequential loss due to Marine delays' or simply — Delay start up.

Marine Policy as a Part of Builders Risk (Marine-cum-Erection)

In case of Marine-cum-Erection Insurance policy, Marine risks are followed by storage risks, erection and testing. In the standard Marine (cargo) policy, the cover ceases after the goods are delivered at the site of erection. In a project site, it is not possible to examine any internal damage to the consignment and such losses don't surface till the time of erection. If any damage were found at the time of erection attributable to transit risks, the marine policy and erection policy bear 50% each of the cost of damage. This is possible only if both Marine policy and erection policy is taken from the same insurers.

Nature of Marine Policies

- Marine policies, except increased policies, are freely assignable. Marine policy document is a fundamental requirement for discounting invoices with local bankers without waiting for the importer to receive the overseas shipments and pay the invoices.
- Even for sale contract on FOB basis when the insurable interest ceases (the goods are placed overboard by the seller) by a notional extension of principle of insurable interest, the risk can be covered by 'Sellers' Contingency Policy'.
- Consignments sold without the support of a 'letter of credit' can also be insured for importer default to pay by "Export Credit Guarantee Corporation of India".

But for the Marine insurance policies, the trade, industry and commerce would not have developed to the present levels of turnovers anywhere in the world. A manufacturer can export their produce with confidence as their dispatches have the support of Marine insurance policies, and they can also discount their bills with local bankers without waiting for the bills being paid by the overseas importers after they receive the goods which may take months by ocean transit. Marine Insurance Policy is one of the important documents besides Invoice and Bill of Lading.

While there is no Tariff rate of premium and the insurers can charge any rate depending upon the nature of goods, the mode of transshipment, type of package, the voyage route and the past claims experience. However, extended covers like SRCC and war risks (for overseas cargo) risks are governed by special regulations and the premiums collected will be credited to the Central Government.

Shipping vessels are listed according to their age, drought weight and their classification by GIC for approval. Full details of every shipping vessel built anywhere in the world would be available in 'Lloyds Register' (issued by Lloyds of London). Minimum standards are fixed. Any vessel falling short of these standards will attract loading of premium. Service Tax and Stamp duty is always collected from the insured separately along with premiums.

Except in the case of increased value policies, no formal proposal form eliciting insurance history, claims history or matters relating to physical or moral hazards, which are common in all other policies, is called for. However, simple details of the property in transit, type of packing, mode of transport and values are to be provided in Marine Questionnaire form. The reason being that all Marine Insurance policies (cargo) are easily assignable to any one and one should have insurable interest at the time of a claim and not necessarily at the time of insurance. The policy is assigned by simply endorsing the policy on its reverse.

Open cover is a memorandum of agreement between the two parties and it is not negotiable. Increased value policy is obtained to take care of market fluctuation of prices and it can be obtained much after dispatch of goods but before the vessel reaches the port of discharge. A completed proposal form is required in this case.

16.5 Marine Insurance Policy Conditions

The standard form of marine insurance cover includes standard policy conditions known as clauses which are attached to the policy document. These clauses define the time period, scope and coverage of the marine policy. In case of international trade and transit, the clauses drafted by the technical and clauses committee of the Institute of London underwriters are adopted globally to maintain uniformity. Therefore, these are popularly nomenclatured as "INSTITUTE..... CLAUSES". In case of exclusive inland transit, the clauses drafted by Tariff Advisory Committee (TAC) are used by the insurers. These are called as Inland Transit Risk Clauses.

16.5.1 Insurance Cargo Clauses (ICC)

ICC has three set of clauses A, B and C which have grouped the various elements risks covered, exclusions, claims settlement procedure, loss minimization, etc.

ICC(C)

It covers loss of or damage to the subject-matter insured, "reasonably attributable to":

(*i*) Fire or explosion.

(*ii*) Vessel of craft being stranded, grounded, sunk or cap-sized.

(*iii*) Overturning or derailment of land conveyance.

(*iv*) Collision or contact of vessel, craft or conveyance with any external object other than water.

(*v*) Discharge of **cargo** at a port of distress.

It also covers loss or of damage to the subject-matter insured caused by:

(*i*) General average sacrifice.

(*ii*) Jettison.

"C" clauses provide major casualty coverage during the land, air or sea transit.

Liability under both to blame collection clause of the contract of affreightment.

ICC(B)

It provide all the cover that is available under the "C" clauses, but in addition cover is given for loss or of damage to the subject-matter insured "reasonably attributable to":

(*i*) Earthquake, volcanic eruption or lightening.

The insurance also covers loss of or damage to the subject-matter caused by:

(*i*) Washing overboard.

(*ii*) Entry of sea, lake or river water into the vessel, craft, hold, conveyance, container, liftvan or place of storage.

(*iii*) Total loss of any package lost overboard or dripped while loading on to or unloading from vessel or craft.

The "B" clauses provide significant additional coverage; wet damage from sea, lake or river water and accidents in loading and discharging, but there is no coverage for theft, shortage and non-delivery.

ICC(A)

Provide coverage for all risks of loss or damage to the subject-matter insured. The words "all risks" should be understood in the context of the "A" clause to cover "fortuitous loss", but not "loss that occurs inevitably."

Principle Exclusions

(*i*) *Wilful Misconduct of the Assured:* Even if the loss is proximately caused by an insured peril it is excluded if it is attributable to the wilful misconduct (deliberate damage) of the Assured.

(*ii*) Ordinary leakage, ordinary loss in weight or volume or ordinary wear and tear. Examples of losses excluded within this category would include evaporation, natural shrinkage.

(*iii*) Inadequate sufficiency or unsuitability of packing or preparation of packing of the subject-matter insured it is the duly of the insured if act as if uninsured. Clearly if goods are sent insufficiently packed to withstand the normal handling anticipated during transit, then any loss that arises therefrom should not be for insurers to pay.

(*iv*) Inherent vice or nature of the subject-matter insured examples of excluded loss would include blowing of the tins containing foodstuffs or spontaneous combustion of a cargo liable to self-heating.

(v) *Delay:* The insurer is not responsible for any loss, damage or expense proximately caused by delay although the delay can be caused by a peril insured against. Losses through delay could include loss of market or deterioration in respect of perishable goods which would not be recoverable even if the cause of the delay was peril insured such as a collision.

(vi) *Insolvency or Financial Default of Carriers:* This exclusion clause was introduced to discourage Assureds from shipping their goods on vessels whose owners, managers, charterers or operators might be in financial distress. In practice, the clause would exclude all types of claims for recovery and forwarding of goods arising from the abandonment of an insured voyage where the proximate cause was the financial distress of one of the aforementioned parties.

(vii) *Unseaworthiness and Unfitness Exclusion:* This only applies where the assured or their agents are privy to this information prior to loading.

(viii) *War and Strikes, Riots and Civil Commotions:* These risks are excluded under A, B and C clauses but can be written back into the policy.

Duration of Cover

Duration of risk starts from the moment the good, leave the warehouse or other place of storage at the place named in the policy to commence transit.

Termination of Contract of Carriage Clause

If the contract of carriage is terminated at a post or place other than the policy destination, or the transit in otherwise terminated before the delivery of goods, then the insurance terminates automatically.

16.5.2 Institute War Clauses (Air Cargo) *(Excluding Sendings by Post)*

Risks Covered

1. This insurance covers, except as provided in Clause 2 below, loss of or damage to the subject-matter insured caused by:
   - war civil, war revolution, rebellion, insurrection, or civil strife arising therefrom, or any hostile act by or against a belligerent power.
   - capture seizure arrest restraint or detainment, arising from risks covered under 1.1 above, and the consequences thereof or any attempt thereat.
   - derelict mines torpedoes bombs or other derelict weapons of war.

Exclusions

2. In no case shall this insurance cover:
   - loss damage or expense attributable to wilful misconduct of the Assured.
   - ordinary leakage, ordinary loss in weight or volume, or ordinary and tear of the subject-matter insured.
   - loss damage or expense caused by insufficiency or unsuitability of packing or preparation of the subject-matter insured (for the purpose of this Clause 2.3 "packing"

shall be deemed to include stowage in a container or liftvan but only when such stowage is carried out prior to attachment of this insurance or by the Assured or their servants).

- loss damage or expense caused by inherent vice or nature of the subject-matter insured.
- loss damage or expense arising from unfitness or aircraft conveyance container or liftvan for the safe carriage of the subject-matter insured, where the Assured or their servants are privy to such unfitness at the time the subject-matter insured is loaded therein.
- loss damage or expense proximately caused by delay, even though the delay be caused by a risk insured against.
- loss, damage or expense arising from insolvency or financial default of the owners, managers, charterers or operators of the aircraft.
- any claim based upon loss of or frustration of the voyage or adventure.
- loss damage or expense arising from any hostile use of any weapon of war employing atomic or nuclear fission and/or fusion or other like reaction or radioactive force or matter.

Duration of cover is similar to that in ICC (A), (B) and (C) but it is more restricted.

16.5.3 Institute Strikes Clauses (Cargo)

Risks Covered

1. This insurance covers, except as provided in Clauses 3 and 4 below, loss of or damage to the subject-matter insured caused by:
   - strikers, locked-out workmen, or persons taking part in labour disturbances, riots or civil commotions.
   - any terrorist or any person acting from a political motive.
2. This insurance covers general average and salvage charges, adjusted or determined according to the contract of affreightment and/or the governing law and practice, incurred to avoid or in connection with the avoidance of loss from a risk covered under these clauses.

Exclusions

3. In no case shall this insurance cover:
   - loss, damage or expense attributable to wilful misconduct of the Assured.
   - ordinary leakage, ordinary loss in weight or volume, or ordinary wear and tear of the subject-matter insured.
   - loss, damage or expense caused by insufficiency or unsuitability of packing or preparation of the subject-matter insured (for the purpose of this Clause 3.3. "packing" shall be deemed to include stowage in a container or liftvan but only when such stowage is carried out prior to attachment of this insurance or by the Assured or their servants).

- loss, damage or expense caused by inherent vice or nature of the subject-matter insured.
- loss, damage or expense proximately caused by delay, even though the delay be caused by a risk insured against (except expenses payable under Clause 2 above).
- loss, damage or expense arising from insolvency or financial default of the owners, managers, charterers or operators of the vessel.
- loss, damage or expense arising from the absence shortage or withholding or labour of any description whatsoever resulting from any strike, lockout, labour disturbance, riot or civil commotion.
- any claim based upon loss of or frustration of the voyage or adventure.
- loss, damage or expense arising from the use of any weapon of war employing atomic or nuclear fission and/or fusion or other like reaction or radioactive force of matter.
- loss, damage or expense caused by war civil, war revolution, rebellion, insurrection, or civil strife arising therefrom, or any hostile act by or against a belligerent power.

4. In no case shall this insurance cover loss damage or expense arising from:
    - unseaworthiness of vessel or craft,
    - unfitness of vessel craft conveyance container or liftvan for the safe carriage of the subject-matter insured.

    where the Assured or their servants are privy to such unseaworthiness or unfitness, at the time the subject-matter insured is loaded wherein.

Duration

5. This insurance attaches from the time the goods leave the warehouse or place of storage at the place named herein for the commencement of the transit, continues during the ordinary course of transit and terminates either:
    - on delivery to the Consignees' or other final warehouse or place of storage at the destination named herein,
    - on delivery to any other warehouse or place of storage, whether prior to or at the destination named herein, which the Assured elect to use either:
        - for storage other than in the ordinary course of transit or
        - for allocation or distribution, or
        - on the expiry of 60 days after completion of discharge overside of the goods hereby insured from the overseas vessel at the final port of discharge, whichever shall first occur.

25.5.4 Other Incidental Clauses and Warranties

Pair or Set Clause

A provision in many property and inland marine policies that the insurer is not liable for the total value of a set of items if only one item has been lost, damaged or destroyed. The loss settlement is based on the proportion that the lost or damaged part bears to the total value of the set.

Cutting Clause

A provision that damage portion should be out off and the balance utilized.

Label Clause

That the goods are properly labelled. It generally limits the liability of the insurer to the Court of repacking and relabelling the affected good.

Garbling Clause

It provides that the insurer will pay the cost of garbling which reduces further loss.

16.5.5 Inland Transit Clauses

Clause A

Covers all risks except the general exclusions as in case of ICC.

Clause B

It is a basic cover which insures for physical loss/damage to subject-matter insured caused by:

(*a*) fire, lightning, breakage of bridges

(*b*) collision, everturning of carrying vehicle

(*c*) derailment or accidents of like nature to the carrying railway wagon/vehicle.

Clause C

It covers physical loss/damage to the subject-matter insured caused by:

(*i*) fire (*ii*) lightning.

Duration of Cover

Starts with loading of goods into wagon/carrier for commencement of transit and continues during transit including customary shipments and ends with the goods are unloaded at destination railway station or destination point (i.e., transit is by road).

16.5.6 Institute Time Clauses – Hull

The various hull clauses are classified into 26 broad categories as given below:

Category	**A**	**–**	**Risks Covered and Risks Excluded**
Clause No.	6	–	Perils
Clause No.	7	–	Pollution Hazard
Clause No.	11	–	General Average and Salvage
Clause No.	14	–	New for Old
Clause No.	15	–	Bottom Treatment
Clause No.	16	–	Wages and Maintenance

Clause No.	17	–	Agency Commission
Clause No.	23	–	War Exclusion
Clause No.	24	–	Strikes Exclusion
Clause No.	25	–	Malicious Acts Exclusion
Clause No.	26	–	Nuclear Exclusion
Category	**B**	**–**	**Amount Payable**
Clause No.	12	–	Deductible
Clause No.	18	–	Unrepaired Damage
Clause No.	19	–	Constructive Total Loss
Clause No.	13	–	Duty of Assured (Sue & Labour)
Category	**C**	**–**	**Collision Liability**
Clause No.	8	–	3/4th Collision Liability
Clause No.	9	–	Sistership
Category	**D**	**–**	**Claims Procedure**
Clause No.	10	–	Notice of Claim and Tenders
Category	**E**	**–**	**Warranties**
Clause No.	1	–	Navigation
Clause No.	3	–	Breach of Warranty
Clause No.	21	–	Disbursements Warranty
Category	**F**	**–**	**Miscellaneous**
Clause No.	2	–	Continuation
Clause No.	4	–	Termination
Clause No.	5	–	Assignment
Clause No.	20	–	Freight Waiver
Clause No.	22	–	Returns for Lay Up and Cancellation.

The provision in the aforesaid clauses is similar to the various institute clauses discussed earlier.

16.6 Special Marine Covers

Special Declaration Policy

This is basically an open policy of 12 months' duration and such policies are issued to concerns having estimated annual turnover of ₹ 2 crore or above. All transits upto the sum insured are covered without any exception and total value of goods in **transit** are required to be declared at least once in a quarter in the form of a certified statement. Final premium is adjusted (downward only) on the basis of actual annual turnover of goods covered. Mid-term increase in sum insured is also permissible twice during a year. Since the insurer get a sizable premium at the inception, they grant cash discount (called turnover discount) ranging from 20% to 50% on the premium.

Multi-transit/Stock Throughout Policies

A Marine Policy terminates if during the **transit** the goods come into the control of the assured for storage other than in ordinary course of **transit,** allocation or redistribution. Subsequent transits are considered separate. Multi-**transit'** policies ensure continuous cover even in case of such exigencies. Irrespective of the number of **transit** the cover stays operative. Storage periods which may or may not include some processing can also be covered.

Package Policy for Plantation Owners (Tea, Coffee, Rubber, Cardamon)

Cover commences from the collection point of green/raw/plucked plantation, continues during storage and various stages of processing in the factory, subsequent **transit** to anywhere in the world including further storage at intermediate and final destination godowns and terminates on delivery to the final customer.

Package Policy for Exporters

Exporters having DEEC certificates under DES can have this package policy which covers import of raw materials from overseas, storage, processing and export to overseas customers.

Duly Insurance Policy

Importers may take out insurance policy to cover the additional value of goods resulting due to payment of customs duty.

Sellers Contingency Policy

In almost all exports where credit is allowed by the seller to the buyer and the goods are not exported on CIF basis, responsibility for the goods passes to the buyer when the goods are loaded on to the overseas vessel but ownership does not change until the buyer accepts the goods and relative documents. Thus, if the seller is allowing credit to the buyer and has shipped goods on FOB terms.

16.7 Cargo Underwriting

Cargo underwriting needs a careful assessment of the various factors which are considered in arriving at a decision to accept/reject risk, acceptance of risk subject to conditions and premium to be charged.

No standardized proposal form and procedure for cargo underwriting exists. The onus is on the proposer to disclose all factors material to the risk and correspondingly the underwriter has to make all inquiries in detail relating to a risk. These are:

(*a*) Name and address of the proposer and his business or trade.

(*b*) Name and address of the bankers involved and Letter of Credit number if the transaction is under documentary credit.

(*c*) Subject-matter to be insured.

(*d*) Type of packing and its authentication.

(*e*) Value of the interest to be insured and the sum to be insured.

(*f*) An analysis or break-up of the sum insured components of the sum insured individually ascertained and summed up.

(*g*) Whether the proposer has declared the entire transit for insurance or is the insurance proposed in respect of a part of the whole transit.

(*h*) Description of the "voyage" including transshipments, if any, and details of interior or land transits.

(*i*) Name of the carrying vessel or shipping line for transit.

(*j*) Other term and conditions of insurance

Underwriting Factors – Cargo Risks

1. The Vessel

One of the important consideration in cargo risk rating is the carrying vessel. As per ICC clauses, the carrying vessel must comply with the classification standards by recognized bodies.

The clauses stipulate that the rates agreed for insurance apply to cargoes carried on mechanically self-propelled vessels, or those constructed by steel, or classified by one of the recognized societies. This helps to restrict agreed rates on an Open Cover to apply only to goods carried on vessels complying with the standard requirements of the Institute Classification Clause. Cargoes not complying with Classification Clause are subject to additional premium.

GIC has a special scheme of approving vessels for vessels engaged in exports business. Under the scheme, the vessel is approved for a particular voyage only as long as the ship remains in the same ownership and is not given out to any charter. Similar system is applicable to vessels engaged in import cargoes to Indian ports. Normal rates of premium are charged on such approved vessels.

2. The Voyage of Transit

ICC cover is from "Warehouse to Warehouse" which includes land transit by rail or road from the time the goods leave the warehouse to the port of shipment. It also includes air carriage in some areas as specified in the cover. Under the Transit Clause of the ICC, no cover is provided during any period before transit actually commences.

If cargo is by inland transit by rail/road from destination port to consignee's warehouse or to an alternative place for storage or for allocation of for distribution, the underwriters must consider the nature of such interior transits in terms of distances from ports and methods of conveyance employed.

3. The Nature of Cargo to be Insured

The nature of the product or commodity insured from the point of view of susceptibility to damage through various causes is a vital consideration for an underwriter to be taken into account. ICC(A) covers all risks of loss or damage to the subject-matter of insurance. Underwriting must ascertain what is accidental, fortuitous, and unexpected and also natural, ordinary and usual in its nature (normal/obvious), with regard to particular circumstances. Nature of goods must be ascertained with respect to various perils.

Losses arising from careless handling, improper stowage, theft, pilferage, non-delivery etc., (extraneous perils) are provided in the ICC(B) and ICC(C) must be able to visualize such extraneous risks.

4. Packing

Packing ensures that the goods reach destination in the same perfect condition in which they were when they left the shipper's premises. Packing is an important factor in risk improvement as it helps in preventing cargo losses. Insufficient, adequate, improper unsuitable and defective packing increases physical hazards and severity of losses.

As per ICC clauses, "In no case shall this insurance cover loss, damage or expense caused by insufficiency or unsuitability, of packing or preparation of the subject-matter insured ("packing" shall be deemed to include stowage in a container or liftvan, but only when such stowage is carried out prior to attachment of this insurance by the assured).

Following factors are usually considered in packing:

- Strength of the packing material
- Weight of the package unit
- Package unit mobility–handling and costs
- Nature of goods packed
- Hazards and perils of transit.

5. Type of Cover

Underwriting involves determination of appropriate cover based on various factors including characteristic of a given vessel or voyage or the nature of cargo and packing. A common set of risk factors are specified by ICC(A), CBI and (C).

ICC(C) risks provide the base rate and additions are made for risk added by ICC(B) and ICC(A) and further additional covers

16.8 Hull Underwriting

A proposal form is submitted by the shipowner which starts the process of underwriting. On the basis of proposal form, the various perils and hazards associated with the hull are ascertained.

A. Technical details of the vessel:

(*a*) Type of the vessel

(*b*) Construction of the vessel (wood, fibreglass, steel etc.)

(*c*) Name of the builders and place where builts

(*d*) Age of the vessel (year of manufacture)

(*e*) Tonnage (GRT and DWT)

(*f*) Dimensions

(*g*) Whether the vessel is equipped with: (*i*) twin screws, (*ii*) double bottom and (*iii*) collision bulkhead

(*h*) Method of propulsion and particulars of engine/machinery

(*i*) Particulars of fire extinguishing equipment

(*j*) Value of the vessel, cargo usually carried, records of ownership and management

(*k*) Claims experience.

If the physical hazards are detected the insurer may insist on a pre-insurance survey, imposition of warranties, limiting the scope of the cover, imposing adequate excess to be born eby the assured and loading of premium and putting additional terms and conditions. Else, the proposal will be rejected for moral hazards.

In India, all ocean-going vessels beyond a certain value are rated by the Tariff Advisory Committee (TAC). A Technical Assistance Group (Hull) consisting of experienced persons dealing in hull insurance is appointed by TAC. For vessels falling under the category of ocean-going vessels, the insurers have to approach TAC for rating. The rating as well as the terms and conditions of insurance will depend on the experience of the underwriter. TAC has laid down Tariffs in respect of following risks:

- Fishing vessels
- Sailing vessels
- Inland vessels
- Dredgers

Hull Rating

Various factors are considered by the underwriters to calculate a rate for the hull risk. In calculating the rate of premium to be charged, the hull risk is divided into two parts: (*i*) the total loss element of risk and (*ii*) average loss element (termed as "ex. T.L."). Accordingly, it is customary to agree a separate rate for each part of the risk and to combine these to arrive at the overall rate that will appear in the policy and called the "Slip Rate". The total loss rate is taken as the current market rate for total loss. It is a rate per cent applied to the insured value of the vessel and is thus conditioned by the value factor of the ship. The ex. T.L. is determined by the size of the ship. It is a fixed amount say ₹ 35 multiplied by the Dead Weight Tonnage (DWT) of the vessel or the Gross Register Tonnage (GRT).

The Total Loss Rate for the vessel is fixed after considering various factors like the age of the vessel, type, value, claims history, world total loss experience of that type of ship, ownership and management factors, special nature of trade etc. The "ex. T.L. premium" takes into account factors like the size of the vessel and the degree of its sophistication, trading limits, fleet record etc.

All the premiums are clubbed and the resultant premium divided by the insured value (IV) which is translated into a single rate called as slip rate.

Example

Line	–	SAFE SHIPPING LINE
Vessel	–	M.V. "OCEAN MASTER"
Year built	–	2004
GRT	–	10,000
Insured Value	–	₹ 15,00,00,000
Type	–	General cargo carrier
Trading	–	Worldwide, subject to Institute Warranties
Total Loss Rate	–	0.75%
Rate for "other than Total loss" (ex. T.L.)	–	₹ 50/- per GRT
Deductible	–	₹ 6,00,000

Calculation of Premium

(A) Total Loss Premium @ ₹ 0.75% on ₹ 15,00,00,000 = ₹ 11,25,000

(B) Ex. T.L. Premium @ ₹ 50 per GRT, i.e., 50 × 10,000 = ₹ 5,00,000

(A) + (B) = Total Premium = ₹ 15,25,000

"Slip Rate" is expressed as: $\frac{16,25,000 \times 100}{15,00,000} = 1.083$

Base Premium is calculated by applying the slip rate to the IV of the vessel.

Hull Rating (Renewals)

The Joint Hull Committee in London is responsible for the structure of the Joint Hull formula, which is a basis recommended for rating renewal insurances in respect of ships insured in the London market. In India, the rating of ocean-going vessels in a fleet on renewal is done by TAC based on the "Indian Hull Understanding". The application forms should be submitted to the TAC within 60 days of the renewal date of the fleet with the full claims statistics available of both paid and outstanding claims. The committee determines the renewal rates on the basis of:

(*a*) The category of the fleet based on the total sum insured under Hull and Machinery interests.

(*b*) Fleet experience, i.e., net premiums and losses paid and outstanding for a stated period.

Normally, claims experience of past four years and current year are considered.

16.9 Marine Losses

Marine losses under the marine policy are defined in the Marine Insurance Act, 1963. These may be of following types:

1.	Total Loss	–		Actual or Constructive
2.	Partial Loss	–	(*a*)	Particular Average
			(*b*)	General Average
3.	Expenses	–	(*a*)	Sue and Labour Charges
			(*b*)	Particular Charges
			(*c*)	Salvage Charges

4. Extra charges which include fees of surveys, sale of property etc.

Actual Total Loss

Section 57(1) of the Marine Insurance Act, 1963 defines actual total loss as the loss where the subject-matter insured is destroyed, or so damaged as to cease to be a thing of the kind insured, or where the assured is irretrievably deprived thereof.

Section 58 of the Act provides that if no news has been received after the lapse of a reasonable period, it is presumed to be an actual total loss on account of a marine peril.

Constructive Total Loss

Section 60(1) defines a constructive total loss as the loss when the subject-matter is reasonably abandoned because either:

(*a*) actual total loss appears unavoidable, or

(*b*) to prevent actual total loss requires expenditure exceeding the saved value.

Section 60(2) in addition, provides that there is a constructive total loss when the insured is deprived of the subject-matter and,

(*a*) it is unlikely that he can recover it, or

(*b*) the cost of recovery would exceed its value when recovered.

Therefore, a constructive total loss would occur if the cost of repairing the damage would exceed the value of the ship when repaired.

The cost of repairs is ascertained on the basis of estimates prepared by the insurers' surveyors and those representing the shipowners.

Section 60(2)(iii) provides that there is constructive total loss of goods where the cost of repairing the damage and forwarding the goods to their destination would exceed their value on arrival. The latter cost would include such charges as landing, drying, and warehousing, reshipping and onward carriage to the port of destination.

Section 61 of the Act states "where there is a constructive total loss the assured may either treat the loss as a partial loss, or abandon the subject-matter insured to the insurer and treat the loss as if it were an actual total loss."

Section 56 of the Act provides that any loss other than a total loss is a partial loss.

Section 64(1) defines a particular average loss as the partial loss of the subject-matter insured, caused by a peril insured against, and which is not a general average loss.

Particular average, therefore implies a fortuitous partial loss caused by a an insured peril. Examples of particular average include damage to the ship by stranding, running a ground, collision or damage to the cargo by fire, sea water etc.

General average loss defined in Section 66(1) of the Act as "a loss caused by or directly consequential on a general average act. It includes a general average expenditure as well as a general average sacrifice."

Section 66(2) provides that "There is a general average act where any extraordinary sacrifice or expenditure is voluntarily and reasonably made or incurred in time of peril for the purpose of preserving the property imperilled in the common adventure."

Particular Charges

Section 64(2) of Marine Insurance Act, 1963 defines particular charges as expenses incurred by or on behalf of the assured for the safety or preservation of the subject-matter insured. They are expenses other than general average and salvage charges.

Sue and Labour Clause

This clauses enforces common law duty of the assured and his agents to act at all times, though uninsured, and to take such measures as may be reasonable for the purpose of averting or minimizing loss or damage which is covered by the insurance.

Examples of the sue and labour charges are:

(*i*) Hides damaged by sea water; reconditioning expenses at an intermediate port to prevent aggravation of damage are sue and labour charges.

(*ii*) Due to a maritime casualty, a ship puts into a port of refuge for repairs which would take some weeks. The cost of extra fodder fed to the live cattle insured against 'All Risks' during the period of repairs is sue and labour charge.

(*iii*) The additional cost of forwarding cargo from a port of refuge to earn the freight payable on delivery at destination is recoverable, if, in the absence of such cost, a claim could result for a total loss on freight.

Extra Charge

Survey fees are payable only if the loss is payable under the policy.

Salvage Charges

Section 65 of Marine Insurance Act defines salvage charges as the charges that are recoverable under maritime law by a salvor independently of marine contract.

Average Adjusters

Average adjuster adjust the general average losses. He has specialized knowledge and also the parties' reputation for strict impartiality which ensure that his findings are acceptable to all concerned. The adjuster's fees are allowed in general average calculation.

16.10 Settlement of Claims

Marine insurance claims are of two broad types — marine hull and marine cargo. Both are dealt separately in the following sections.

16.10.1 Marine Hull

Types of Marine Hull Claims

Marine Hulls are divided into three groups, viz.:

(*a*) Ocean-going vessels and other vessels rated exclusively by the Tariff Advisory Committee.

(*b*) Vessels insured under Builder's Risk Policies, Ship Repairer's Liability Policies, Ship Breaking Policies and the Charterer's Liability Policies.

(*c*) All the vessels and/or operations of which rates have been provided in Marine Hull Manual under specific Tariffs or otherwise and all other vessels/operations not covered by (*a*) and (*b*) above.

The types of hull claims are:

- Total Loss/Constructive Total Loss;
- Particular Average/Particular Charges i.e., Partial Losses/Expenses;
- Salvage and Salvage Charges–either Salvage Awards or Salvage under contract;
- General Average;
- Collision Liability;
- Liability and Non-liability Claims (such as wreck removal) falling under the P&I section for the policy where such cover is granted;
- Sue and Labour charges;
- Personal Accident Claims for crew covered under Sailing/Fishing Vessels Tariffs.

Following claims are generally considered for reference to professional Average Adjusters:

(1) All claims falling under Category 1.1 "A" unless the claim involved is straightforward and also for a nominal amount.

(2) (*a*) GA or GA/PA claims on vessels under Category 1.1 "C".

(*b*) Collision Liability claims requiring cross liability adjustment in respect of risk falling under Category 1.1 "B" and "C".

Procedures of Claims Settlement

Following considerations are important while deciding on *ocean-going vessels*:

(*a*) nature and quantum of claims likely to arise under this category;

(*b*) likelihood of occurrence of loss in distant foreign waters;

(*c*) involvement of laws and practices of foreign jurisdictions, and

(*d*) involvement of foreign professional and/or firms like surveyors, repair yards, adjusters, solicitors, arbitrators, courts, etc.

The current system of processing these claims in accordance with the international practices and these practices are likely to continue except insofar as the provisions of the Indian Statutes are concerned.

Sundry Hulls (including Sailing vessels, Fishing vessels, Inland vessels etc.).

Following procedure is generally adopted for claim settlement:

- A Licensed Surveyor is appointed in all cases of Partial Losses/Expenses. Also Licensed Surveyor are appointed in case of TL/CTL only where the vessel or its wreck, of reasonable value is available for inspection or making reasonable attempt to salvage.
- On receipt of loss intimation a letter is written "on *without prejudice basis"* to the insured advising about the appointment of Surveyor and/or investigator requesting the insured to render full co-operation to the Surveyor/Investigator appointed and to return the claim form duly completed and signed.
- Notice of Abandonment of the vessel/wreck in writing is a prerequisite for a constructive Total Loss Claim. Practically speaking, insurers decline *prima facie* acceptance of the Notice of Abandonment. However, insurer's refusal to accept abandonment does not legally prejudice the insured's claim for a CTL once the Notice of Abandonment has been issued by the insured and received by the insurer. Notwithstanding this the insurer generally refuse acceptance of abandonment of the wreck till the probable liabilities attaching to the wreck (Port and other dues, statutory requirement of wreck removal in case of vessel sunk in navigate channel, etc.) are reasonably estimated as considered.
- Total loss claim is settled on the basis of the statements and documents, as also the investigator's/Surveyor's report as the case may be if the circumstances are found to be reasonably acceptable. As per the Marine Insurance Act, following acceptance of a claim for total loss of a vessel, the insurers become entitled to the wreck or the proceeds thereof, if any. However, before enforcing such entitlement, the insurers ascertain whether or not any liability, statutory or otherwise, is reasonably likely to attach to such wreck or proceeds thereof.
- Since Marine Hull Policy is issued for a composite sum insured, representing the aggregate values of Hull and Machinery and showing Hull or Machinery values separately in the policy being prohibited, no claim for total or Constructive Total Loss is considered for settlement on the basis of and on account of either Hull or Machinery value alone.
- In case of partial loss, surveyors are duty bound to achieve assessment net of salvage, if any because it is difficult and very often not economical for the underwriters to get involved in salvage take-over and disposal. However, where this is not possible, arrangements are made to take over the salvage from the insured before the settlement of the claim and disposed accordingly.
- Claims occurring in foreign waters are generally dealt with in the same manner as in the case of Ocean-going vessels.

Documents Required

The documents required for the settlement of Sundry Hull claims are:

(1) A final survey Report *inter alia* incorporating the following:

(*a*) Name of the registered owner of the vessel.

(*b*) Identity of the vessel including registration details. License particulars including validity thereof wherever applicable.

(*c*) The details of loss suffered.

(*d*) The Surveyor's observation on the alleged circumstances of the loss.

(*e*) The reasonable probability of the alleged circumstances giving rise to the losses noticed and/or claimed.

(*f*) Quantification of repairs/replacement cost, salvage, sue and labour etc. where applicable.

(*g*) Cause of loss as per the Perils Clause of the Policy and the deposit to be collected by the steamer.

In lieu of cash deposit, steamer companies often accept unlimited guarantee of the Insurance Company covering the goods.

Documents for General Average Claims

1. Original Policy or certificate of insurance duly endorsed.
2. Bill of Lading (signed copy).
3. Invoice (original or signed copy).
4. A copy of Notice declaring General Average by the Shipowner/Agent.
5. General Average Deposit Receipt (GADR) on the original Lloyds form duly endorsed.

(GADR indicates the name of the steamer, details of the casualty, the Bill of Lading no., the provisional net arrived value of the goods, description of the goods, the name of the GA Adjusters, the amount of the deposit by the consignees etc.)

General Average Guarantee and Counter Guarantee

As an alternative to cash deposit shipowners are willing to accept a Guarantee from a bank or if the goods are insured from the insurers. Insurers grant this Guarantee on the behalf of the insured in terms of which they agree to pay the General Average Contribution. In such cases, a Counter Guarantee is obtained from the insured. The Counter Guarantee is required because the General Average adjustment may be based on a contributory value of the cargo which may be higher than its insured value.

Letter of Transfer

This letter is signed by the consignees whereby they:

(*i*) surrender their rights in respect of the deposit paid to shipowners by the insurers;

(*ii*) agree to transfer the deposit amount to the credit of the insurers;

(*iii*) authorize the insurers to receive from the shipowners the difference between the amount of general average as adjusted and the amount of the deposit;

(*iv*) undertake to refund to the insurers any sum deducted by the shipowners from the deposit which may not be recoverable under the insurance policy; and

(*v*) undertake to repay to the insurers, if the contributory value exceeds the insured value the proportion of general average applying to such value.

If it is reported that the General Average Act has included sacrifice of cargo, then the consignee clears the damaged cargo only after the General Average Survey is conducted by the ship's Surveyors.

Consignments by Rail/Road

In the case of sea/air/multi-modal transport/postal claims, the insured has to furnish evidence of: (1) insurance, (2) transit, (3) value and (4) loss. The following documents are required to be submitted to insurers in support of claims under rail/road transit policies:

General Documents

1. Original policy or certificate of insurance duly endorsed.
2. Invoice (original or copy)/packing list/weight specification.
3. Independent Surveyor's Report, if any.
4. Letter of Subrogation (if recovery is possible).

Other Documents Depending on the Nature of Claim

1. Original Railway Receipt (Non-delivery cases).
2. Copy of the Railway Receipt (damage claim).
3. Original Consignment Note (Non-delivery cases–Road transit claims).
4. A copy of the Consignment Note (Damage claim–Road transit claims).
5. 'Non-delivery' or 'Partial delivery' certificate from the Railways/Road Transport Operators.
6. Open Delivery/Assessment Delivery Certificate (Rail/Road).
7. Certified copy of the remarks in the Railway Delivery Book (Damage claims).
8. Certified copy of the remarks in the delivery Challan (Road Transit Claims).
9. Copy of (*a*) Notice of claim lodged on the carriers (Rail/Road), (*b*) Acknowledgement and (*c*) Subsequent correspondence with the carriers.
10. Special Power of Attorney (Rail Transit Claims).
11. Letter of Authority (Rail Transit Claims).

Marine Cargo

Documents generally required for settlement of various types of cargo claims are as under:

General

(*a*) Original insurance policy/declaration under the open policy duly endorsed by the insured. A letter of indemnity may be furnished if the original is lost.

(*b*) Original or a signed copy of sale invoice along with packing list wherever is available.

(*c*) Signed copy of Bill of Lading (in case of sea voyage)/Air Consignment Note (for air cargo/MTD/CTD for multi-modal transport)/postal receipt for sending by post.

(*d*) Triplicate or exchange control copy of Bill of entry (to facilitate verification of the date of filing to ascertain whether there has been any delay and also to check duty payment details).

(*e*) In case of General Average, GA Guarantee and Counter Guarantee of original Cash Deposit Receipt with the Letter of Transfer as the case may be. Reference be made to the separate para on GA.

(*f*) Letter of Subrogation duly stamped and executed (only where recovery from carriers/other third parties is possible).

(*g*) Special Power of Attorney (wherever recovery from Railway/other carriers is involved. In other cases as required).

16.11 Marine Cargo Losses and Frauds

Cost of Maritime frauds worldwide runs into millions of dollars.

Incidence of frauds in shipping business is not something new. The earliest incident on record goes back to 360 BC in syracuse when a shipowner tried to cheat a buyer who had advanced money to him for bringing a cargo of corn, by scutting the vessel after sailing for a few days without loading the cargo at all. In earlier times, trade between merchants of different countries was totally based on mutual trust. The transaction was invariably in cash; and as it happened sometimes unscrupulous agents or shipowners simply disappeared with the money, whilst others returned with false reports of robbery or piracy on high seas. Over the years, as trading activities increased manifold between the maritime nations, the simple process of dependence on mutual trust alone gave way to a written undertaking or pledge. It is reported that the Ventians first thought of and developed the system of trade between merchants through the mechanism not the Letter of Credit, which has, over the years undergone several changes and modifications to suit the requirements and complexities of modern trade.

Sometimes economic sanctions against some countries by other nations of the world encourage frausters to take advantage of such situations of scarcity of essential commodities and follow the path of deception to make profits from fraudulent deals.

Marine Fraud can be described as a criminal act in international trade concerning the shipping industry. The term Maritime Fraud includes a host of wrongful acts. Expert involved in the investigation of such frauds feel that such acts have increased over the years with the growth of international trade. However, only a small proportion of fraudulent acts are at all reported. In fact, a large number of cases are never reported by the affected parties for fear of delays due to protracted investigation, increase in insurance premiums, bad publicity and staffing red tape.

Criminal acts on high seas exist in a variety of ways as mentioned below:

1. *Maritime Piracy:* These are illegal acts of violence or detention of a vessel on high seas by the crew of another vessel, generally outside the jurisdiction of any state. Sometimes, acts of piracy may lead to hijacking of a vessel.
2. *Maritime Insurance Fraud:* Deliberate scuttling of overinsured vessel by the owners.
3. *Deviation Fraud:* This arises when the shipowner directs the cargo to another destination with the intention of selling the same for gain. Obviously, this involves changes of name of the importer and non-arrival of the cargo at the appointed destination.
4. *Bill of Lading Fraud:* It involves forgery of Bills of Lading in respect of non-existing goods or differences in the quantity or quality of the goods. This can be described as a fraud by the seller or buyer against shipowners or the carriers.
5. *Charters Party Fraud:* It is generally committed by the charterers against the shipowners.
6. *Agency Fraud:* It involves impersonation of agents and concealing of identities.
7. *Other Documentary Frauds:* It involves fraud in various other documents used in Maritime trade transactions.

In any international trade deal relating to export/import business, a number of parties are involved — Buyer, Seller, Shipowner, Charterer, Ship's master and crew, insurer, Banker, Broker or Agent etc. Documents form the basis of such transactions and thus, numerous possible combinations and permutations can arise for fraudulent activities. From the record of various documentary fraud cases studied and investigated during the last couple of decades, the types of fraud can be broadly categorized as under:

- Fraud committed by a trader against another trader, shipowner, banker or insurer.
- Fraud committed by a charterer against a shipowner;
- Fraud committed by a shipowner or trader against an insurer;
- Fraud committed by a charterer or shipowner against a trader.

16.12 Marine Stock Throughout Policy

STP is popularly known as 'Cradle to Grave' Coverage. This policy was introduced in mid-1970s mainly for the following reasons: to have a single policy as against multiple marine and property policies; to avoid property tariff; to expand marine premium during soft marine market; and to obtain broader coverage for static risks under marine portfolio.

Marine STP is the process of insuring both stock and transit/inventory exposures under a 'Single Policy' to ensure seamless protection to the assured on a worldwide basis.

Stock Throughput Policy is suitable for organizations that source raw materials or semi-finished goods for further value addition. These organizations then store and distribute finished goods across the world.

Inputs and Output: Raw materials, Work in Progress and Finished Goods that are in transit on world to world basis. All locations are covered such as assured's factory(ies)/Job Workers/Sub-

Contractors/Warehouses (3rd Party taken on lease or on rent) when cargoes are not in course of transit within the meaning of Marine Insurance. Movements of other items related to operations as for example:

- Import of plant and machinery on C&F/FOB or similar terms
- Import of plant and machinery on CIF terms with DIC extension
- Purchase of plant and machinery from local/domestic market
- To & Fro journey when plant or machinery sent to repairer's workshop for repairing and overhauling etc.

Stock Risk is different from Transit risks (in course of transit) is a static risk, always exposed to fire, AOG and social perils. Total exposure of inventory/stock at any point of time in a particular area/region is always greater than the single carrying limit.

Stocks are usually kept at various third party locations where different cargoes can be stored/kept (including hazardous and non-hazardous material) and warehouse keepers tend to offer less care in terms of handling and storage etc.

Severity Analysis

Line	*Claims Frequency*	*Size of the loss*
Static	Low	High
Marine	Low to Medium	Low to Medium

Risk Covered

There are two ways of underwriting a Marine Stock Throughput policy.

1. *All Risks:* All Risks of physical loss or damage from any external cause.
2. Transit Risk on All Risks basis and Static Risk other than in course of transit on named perils basis (with add-on covers).

Major Exclusions

Goods at retail outlets, insured property(ies) in the open or outbuilding, any property other than the subject-matter insured, policy deductible, consequential loss/legal liability, loss resulting from unexplained or mysterious disappearance or shortage discovered on taking inventory, misplacing or misfiling of information or clerical or accounting errors, loss or damage to goods and merchandise caused by or resulting from misappropriation, conversion, infidelity or any dishonest act on the part of the assured or other party of interest, his or their employees or agents, processing risk, theft unless following forcible and/or violent entry into or exit from the premises and act of terrorism are some of the major exclusions.

Benefits of STP from Assured's Point of View

- *Seamless Protection:* A single policy provides comprehensive protection against both, Transit (inland and Ocean Marine) and Inventory/Stock exposures.
- *Coverage:* STP offers broader coverage under static risk as against Standalone Property policy.

- *Premium Payment:* Premium can be paid in instalments in order to assist cash flow of the company.
- *Policy Administration:* This policy is very simple to administer since there is no need for declaring individual shipments. It is adjusted against final sales value/turnover achieved by the company.
- It helps in elimination of duplicity of coverage – no need for multiple policies for both transit and inventory/stock risks.
- It also eliminates dispute on concealed damage claims between Marine and Property Underwriters.

Marine STP — Challenges for Insurers

Marine Stock Throughput Policy has the following challenging features:

- Need for co-ordination between Marine Underwriter and Property Underwriter for pricing and terms for static risks.
- Continuous review of static risk in order to control accumulation for AOG/Social perils.
- Requirement of loss control effort through COPE (Construction, Occupation, Protection and Exposure) Survey where the value of stock is high in named locations.
- There is no standard policy form for Marine STP since each risk is unique and each policy needs to be tailor-made in terms of deductible, basis of valuation, price, scope of cover, exclusions, warranties etc.
- Soft market conditions force Marine Underwriters to accept undesired extensions.
- A single static risk loss can have negative impact on marine book.

The Indian insurance market needs more expertise to underwrite this specialized class of business in terms of coverage, pricing and deductible. The following are certain concerns when underwriting a STP Policy:

- *Quality Issues:* Construction/Occupancy/Protection of the Warehouse/Storage Premises.
- Nat Cat Exposures
- Social Perils
- Accumulation Control
- RI Support/Capacity

The various causes of marine losses are: (*a*) Theft Pilferage and non-delivery, (*b*) Handling and Stowage damage, (*c*) Loss from water damage and (*d*) Marine perils. Maritime frauds can be categorized as follows:

(*a*) Scuttling of ships–deliberate sinking of ships.

(*b*) Documentary Frauds–the manipulation of shipping frauds, use of forge documents.

(*c*) Chartering of vessels–fraudulent chartering companies.

(*d*) Cargo thefts–deviation of ships from standard routes, "paper shipping companies".

Apart from various measures taken by the concerned parties, following should be taken into care to reduce the frequency of frauds:

(*a*) Vessels approved by GIC (entered in IRS) should be used.

(*b*) Exercise of reasonable care and diligence wile dealing with unknown parties or parties new in the business.

(*c*) Payments should be affected by confirmed IRLC.

(*d*) The agents involved in the whole process should be reliable.

(*e*) Reputed charterer should be hired.

Exhibit 16.1
Marine Insurance Statistics

Business Generated (Gross Direct Premium — ₹ in crore)

Companies	*1993-94*	*1994-95*	*1995-96*	*1996-97*	*1997-98*	*1998-99*	*1999-2000*
GIC	141.01	154.32	175.69	176.23	181.75	189.92	193.51
NIC	136.05	128.02	154.55	140.26	151.75	155.69	148.70
OIC	122.19	125.27	152.25	141.94	142.17	149.60	146.33
NIAC	195.39	189.86	222.93	219.88	212.64	227.40	216.44
UII	155.72	150.95	182.84	163.98	173.88	169.73	176.94
Total	750.36	748.42	888.26	842.29	862.19	892.34	881.92

Profits (₹ in Crore)

Companies	*1993-94*	*1994-95*	*1995-96*	*1996-97*	*1997-98*	*1998-99*	*1999-2000*
GIC	45.42	39.50	38.71	58.38	70.82	72.97	57.20
NIC	6.04	-11.62	11.52	-3.88	4.19	-17.82	2.65
OIC	15.54	14.39	-13.06	42.77	10.67	15.74	4.11
NIAC	9.23	-1.13	51.74	7.98	72.71	77.39	34.69
UII	19.65	15.53	-13.24	40.04	8.15	32.51	30.21
Total	95.88	56.67	75.67	145.29	166.54	180.79	128.86

Profit %age

GIC	32.21%	25.60%	22.03%	33.13%	38.97%	38.42%	29.56%
NIC	4.44%	-9.08%	7.45%	-2.77%	2.76%	-11.45%	1.78%
OIC	12.72%	11.49%	-8.58%	30.13%	7.51%	10.52%	2.81%
NIAC	4.72%	-0.60%	23.21%	3.63%	34.19%	34.03%	16.03%
UII	12.62%	10.29%	-7.24%	24.42%	4.69%	19.15%	17.07%

Exhibit 16.2
Marine Insurance (Gross Direct Premium Income)

Company	*2000-01*	*2001-02*	*2002-03*	*2003-04*	*2004-05*	*2005-06*	*2006-07*	*2007-08*	*2008-09*
National	203.80	207.16	219.06	187.18	251.29	173.43	204.89	174.98	200.78
New India	313.84	339.30	344.40	259.21	252.49	299.78	321.02	437.28	446.10
Oriental	187.90	205.65	228.07	218.93	235.41	325.11	347.83	339.06	332.59
United India	279.56	255.21	339.14	300.14	243.80	203.97	263.95	300.83	338.02
ECGC*	-	-	-	-	-	-	-	-	-
GIC*	-	-	-	-	-	-	-	-	-

Royal Sundaram	-	2.78	13.02	13.38	16.80	18.29	18.44	19.55	19.97
Reliance	-	1.74	8.91	13.19	12.70	10.74	17.85	34.24	37.00
IFFCO-Tokio	0.05	31.02	18.41	24.49	30.87	46.13	128.26	66.43	113.70
TATA AIG	-	9.18	27.33	30.89	40.85	47.88	70.15	97.86	111.82
ICICI Lombard	-	-	8.91	43.59	82.53	85.71	155.24	216.72	216.47
Bajaj Allianz	-	1.36	7.41	20.72	44.96	54.33	71.25	75.18	88.17
Cholamandalam	-	-	0.16	5.82	15.90	17.00	26.56	32.66	36.56
HDFC-Chubb	-	-	-	-	0.50	1.72	2.41	3.29	8.29
Future Generali	-	-	-	-	-	-	-	0.72	6.63
Universal Sompo	-	-	-	-	-	-	-	-	0.54
Shriram	-	-	-	-	-	-	-	-	-
Bharti AXA	-	-	-	-	-	-	-	-	0.61
Total	**985.15**	**1053.40**	**1214.82**	**1117.54**	**1228.10**	**1284.09**	**1627.85**	**1798.80**	**1957.25**
Market Share									
Private Co. Share	99.995%	95.626%	93.073%	86.392%	80.042%	78.054%	69.889%	69.610%	67.313%
Public Co. Share	0.005%	4.374%	6.927%	13.608%	19.958%	21.946%	30.111%	30.390%	32.687%

Key Terms

- ❐ General Average
- ❐ Particular Average
- ❐ Sue and Labour Charges
- ❐ Maritime Frauds
- ❐ Extraneous Risk
- ❐ Ex. T.L.
- ❐ Hull Insurance
- ❐ Cargo Insurance
- ❐ Annual Policy
- ❐ Institute Clauses
- ❐ Voyage Policy
- ❐ Extra Charges
- ❐ Constructive Total Loss
- ❐ Partial Loss
- ❐ Slip Rate
- ❐ Base Premium
- ❐ GRT
- ❐ Average
- ❐ ICC Clauses
- ❐ Declaration Policy
- ❐ Package Policy
- ❐ Open Cover

Questions for Review

1. Distinguish between:
   (*a*) Open Cover and Open Policy
   (*b*) General Average and Particular Average
   (*c*) Total Loss and Constructive Total Loss.
2. Briefly explain the various types of marine losses and maritime frauds and methods to prevent them.

3. List the documents required for settlement of:
   (*a*) Cargo claims
   (*b*) Hull claims
4. Trace the history of marine insurance. Is marine insurance a profitable business in India? If so, why?
5. Briefly explain the various types of marine insurance covers available in India.
6. Briefly discuss the various insurance principles as applied to insurance business in India.
7. Briefly discuss the various factors considered for underwriting of cargo insurances.
8. List the various items of information in Hull Insurance proposal form.

Suggested Readings

1. Marine Insurance Claims, IC66, Insurance Institute of India, Mumbai, 2005.
2. IRDA Annual Reports.
3. *IRDA Annual Report 2001-02.*
4. *Marine Insurance,* IC67, Insurance Institute of India, Mumbai.
5. Barry Supple, *A History of British Insurance,* Cambridge University Press, 1970.
6. *The ET Knowledge Series,* Insurance, 2001-02.

❑❑❑

MOTOR INSURANCE

Chapter Objectives

- Overview of The Losses Due to Automobile Ownership and Usage
- Need for Automobile Insurance
- Types of Motor Insurance Policies
- Factors Considered for Premium Rating
- Motor Insurance Claims

Introduction

Motor losses to insurance company arise from the legal liability due to negligence, Bodily injury, Property damages and or theft of vehicles etc. The All India Motor Tariff governs motor insurance business in India. According to the Tariff, all classes of vehicles use two types of Policy Forms. They are Form A and Form B. Form A, or what is commonly known as Act Policy, covers Act Liability, which is a compulsory requirement of the Motor Vehicles Act. No vehicle can be used without this minimum insurance cover. Use without such insurance is a penal offence.

Form A covers unlimited liability towards Third Party bodily injury, Third Party Property Damage bodily injury of passengers of the vehicle and Liability towards employees of the owner of the vehicle while traveling in or using it, against bodily injury, to the extent required under the Workmen's Compensation Act. Form B, or what is commonly known as Comprehensive Policy, is an optional cover, which takes care of the additional losses and liabilities- own damages.

Motor Tariff, which governs the Motor Insurance business in India, classifies the motor vehicles broadly in three categories, viz., Private Cars, Motorized Two Wheelers and Commercial Vehicles. The factors considered for premium rating in motor insurance are Driver Classes, Territory, Vehicle

Classification, type of vehicle, value of vehicle, geographical area of operation and the claims experience. Depending upon the type of policy, the motor claims may be own damage claims or third party claims.

17.1 Overview of the Losses Due to Automobile Ownership and Usage

The major sources of loss exposure arising from the automobile accidents are:[1]

- Legal liability for harm caused to others as a result of negligence
- Bodily injury
- Property damages and or theft of vehicles

Risk managers realize that insurance should be considered within the context of all available risk management tools. There are several ways to lower losses from automobile accidents:[2]

(1) reduce the frequency and severity of accidents,

(2) restrict payments, and

(3) redistribute expenses and losses.

Loss Control and Prevention

The loss to the automobile insurance service providers is mainly in the form of claims arising from accidents. Accidents can be minimized by providing better infrastructure in terms of roads, limit on speed and other sophisticated traffic control measures. Also, automobile manufacturers must be encouraged to continuously pursue enhancement of the safety measures in the vehicles.

Globally speaking, there has been a demand for smaller, light-weight vehicles, which has resulted in increased severity of accidents and consequential losses.

Restriction on Claims

Putting restrictions on the insured's claims in the sense the fraudulent claims can be easily detected and effectively reduce the cost to the insurers. Another way is to incentivize the good clients by way of attractive rates and discounts.

Redistribution of Losses and Expenses

The auto liability claims, which frequently arise from driver's negligence, can be tackled through redistributions. In such a mechanism, first the guilty party is to be determined and then the guilty party pays to the suffered party the amount of loss. Such processes are generally channelled through the judicial system.

---

1. Harrington & Neihaus, *Risk Management and Insurance,* McGraw-Hill, 1999, p. 533.
2. J.S. Triechmann, S.G. Gistavson and R.E. Hoyt, *Risk Management and Insurance,* South-Western College Publishing, 2001, pp. 270-272.

Automobile Coverages[3]

The coverage for automobiles differs in countries. However, in most of the developed countries following types of coverage are available:

Automobile Liability Insurance

Automobile Liability Insurance protects the insured against the loss arising from legal liability when his or her automobile injures someone or damages another's property.

Medical Payments Coverage

Automobile Medical Payments coverage reimburses the insured and members of the insider's family for medical expenses that result from automobile accidents. The protection also applies to other occupants of the insured's automobile.

Physical Damages Insurance

Automobile Physical Damage Coverage insures against the loss of the policyholder's own automobile. The coverage is written under the two insuring agreements (also called as Comprehensive coverage) and Collusion — which indemnifies for collusion losses. Physical damage coverage applies to the insured auto regardless of the default. If the other driver is at fault, the insured that carry collusion coverage has the option of proceeding against the other driver or collecting under his or under policy coverage. In India, the GIC offers two types of policy coverage. Form A policy cover is legally compulsory under the Motor Vehicles Act, while Form B policy is optional, known as comprehensive cover. Both of these are discussed in Section 14.3 of this chapter.

17.2 Need for Automobile Insurance[4]

In Indian conditions, the vehicles are subject to many hazards like potholes, open manholes, puddles, untarred roads, traffic management system, poor pedestrian management, absence of footpaths for pedestrians, jaywalkers, increasing number of accidents etc. which accentuate the need for automobile insurance. Some of these hazards are discussed below:

Footpaths

As footpaths are encroached by hawkers, pedestrians have a tough time dodging between vehicles to reach the other end of the road. Large potholes and manholes are a common sight and during the monsoon the situation can get only worse causing untold damage to your vehicle.

Drunken Driving

Drunken driving is another very common feature. Be it a car, a two-wheeler, or even a truck, drunken driving is one of the major reasons for increase in accidents. Though drunken driving is a punishable offence, the penalty has hardly proved to be a deterrent.

---

3. Vaughan and Vaughan, *Essentials of Risk and Insurance Management and Insurance,* John Wiley and Sons Inc., 2001, pp. 435-436.
4. www. Insuremagic.com/Auto Insurancebasics — Need for Automobile Insurance.htm

Reckless Driving

Besides, rash driving by youngsters is another of the dangerous realities that you should consider. Majority of the youngsters drive recklessly caring little for the law, causing serious accidents resulting in loss of life or limb.

Theft

Cases of stolen cars are on the rise. Experts in stealing cars are well aware of the loopholes that can be exploited and accordingly have also been successful in manipulating with the chasis number of vehicles in order that they are not traced.

Fire

Other than these there is also a danger of fire or theft of vehicle. Therefore, vehicle insurance under such unsafe conditions is a must not only to cover risks towards the owner and the vehicle but also to cover the financial liability that may arise from an accident in which the other party is injured. The cost of repairs that you would have to pay to the other party in case of an accident may be exorbitant. Besides if the accident involves hospitalization too, the expenses can go through the roof. It would be a great burden if all these costs are borne by the individual. The insurance company can indemnify against such losses and the financial liability arising thereof.

Should Auto Insurance be made Compulsory?

If the auto insurance is not made compulsory, there is a strong possibility that some may not buy these voluntarily. This is because most of them think that the cost of accidents or losses will fall on others or they underestimate the risk of loss. "Economic arguments for compulsory insurance laws in these people to consider more of the costs of their actions when deciding whether to drive, what kind of car to buy, how safely to drive, and so on."[5]

The economic rationale for insurance may be that it affects people's decision to drive. Some people are likely to forgive driving if the insurance is made compulsory since it acts as a financial disincentive. Another could be that it encourages people to drive safely, which may reduce cost of risk. Those who criticise compulsory auto insurance plead that it results in lowering the disposable income or it results in a shift of income from lower group to the higher group. Also, the success of the compulsory law depends on its enforcement and way it is perceived by the insureds. In India, most of the insurance companies are facing huge losses due to false/heavy claims, the insurance being used for dubious advantages.

17.3 Types of Motor Insurance Policies

The All India Motor Tariff governs motor insurance business in India. According to the Tariff, all classes of vehicles use two types of Policy Forms. They are Form A and Form B. Form A, or what is commonly known as Act Policy, covers Act Liability, which is a compulsory requirement of the Motor Vehicles Act. No vehicle can be used without this minimum insurance cover. Use without such insurance is a penal offence. The following liabilities can be covered in this policy:

5. Harrington & Neihaus, *op. cit.*, pp. 553-554.

- Unlimited liability towards Third Party bodily injury;
- Liability towards Third Party Property Damage to the extent of ₹ 6000/- only;
- Unlimited liability towards bodily injury of passengers of the vehicle;
- Liability towards employees of the owner of the vehicle while travelling in or using it, against bodily injury, to the extent required under the Workmen's Compensation Act.

Form B, or what is commonly known as Comprehensive Policy, is an optional cover, which takes care of the following additional losses and liabilities:

- Loss or damage to the vehicle and its accessories and extra fittings, protection and removal costs, and towing disabled vehicles (only for commercial vehicles).
- Liability towards Third Party Property Damage, in excess of ₹ 6000/-.
- Liability towards employees under Common Law and Fatal Accidents Act, over and above the liability under Workmen's Compensation Act.
- Personal Accident Benefits for the owner, passengers and employees.

The above losses or liabilities can be separately covered in conjunction with the liabilities covered under the Act Policy, by taking a Comprehensive Policy paying an additional premium.

17.3.1 Form A Policy

As per the provisions of Motor Vehicles Act, all the vehicles plying in the Territorial Limits of India must possess an ACT POLICY at all times. The violation is punishable with fine etc., as per Motor Vehicle Act (as prevalent at the time of detection). As described earlier, this policy covers:

(1) Third Party Property Damage/Bodily Injury (Fatal or Non-fatal) when Insured vehicle is used in a public place,

(2) Insured's legal liability, as per Motor Vehicle Act, arising out of accident caused by or arising out of the use of the vehicle anywhere in India, and

(3) Such liability as above in respect of injury (fatal or non-fatal) to any third party and damage to any third parties' property.

The owners of the vehicle having insurable interest in it undertake this policy. The period of the cover is generally a period of 12 months from the date of inception. However, Short period covers are also available at higher rates. Subject to limit of liability laid down in the Motor Vehicle Act, the policy pays the insured's legal liability for death/disability for third party, loss or damage to third party property. Also, the liability for claimant's cost is also met (Maximum ₹ 6,000/-) unless additional premium for opting unlimited cover is paid. In addition, all costs and expenses incurred with insurer's written consent are paid.

In case of death of the Insured/Person entitled to compensation for a liability incurred under this policy, his legal heirs will be indemnified as in the case of the Insured, subject to the limitations of use of the vehicle provided that the Driver was holding a valid and effective driving license.

Third Party (A person other than Insured and the Insurer) who is injured/dies due to an accident with the Insured Vehicle, the amount of compensation adjudged by the Motor Accident

Claims Tribunal is made good by the insurers and is payable to the legal heir of the deceased or the injured. The amount of compensation is unlimited/has no preset limit.

All costs and expenses are incurred by the insured with Insurer's written consent. The compensation payable to Third Party for damage to its property (movable or fixed) is restricted to ₹ 6000/- {Rupees Six Thousand Only}, irrespective of the amount adjudged by the Motor Accident Claims Tribunal/Court. This compensation limit can be increased to Unlimited by paying of an additional Premium at the time of taking insurance. All costs and expenses incurred by Insured with Insurer's written consent.

Claims arising out of and in the course of employment of a person in the employment of the Insured are compensated to the extent of ₹ 20,000 when an Employee (other than paid driver) is in the driving seat.

When vehicle is used outside the geographical area, when used contrary to limitation as to use, driven by a person other than the driver as stated in the clauses mentioned in the policy of insurance.

17.3.2 Form B Policy[6]

Form B is an optional cover, which offers some specific advantages. Although the Act Policy Form A is identical for different classes of vehicles, the comprehensive policy cover differs for various classes of vehicles. For private cars and motorcycles, there are two Sections in the Comprehensive Policy. Additionally, Section III is provided for commercial vehicles.

SECTION I

It concerns loss or damage to the vehicle and covers the risks like:

- Fire, Explosion, Self-ignition and Lightning
- Burglary, Housebreaking and Theft
- Riot, Strike, Malicious and Terrorism Damage
- Earthquake
- Flood, Typhoon, Hurricane, Storm, Tempest, Inundation, Cyclone, Hailstorm
- Accidental External Means
- Transit by road, rail, inland waterway, lift, elevator or air.

For motorcycles and commercial vehicles, the risk of frost damage is also covered. From the above coverage, for all classes of vehicles, the risks of riot, strike, malicious and terrorism damage, earthquake and flood and storm; can be opted out of with a consequent discount in premium. In addition to these, cover is also available for 'Protection and Removal Costs' and 'Authorization of Repairs'. If a motor vehicle is disabled as a result of loss or damage due to the perils mentioned above, the insurance company bears the reasonable cost of protection and removal to the nearest repairer and the cost of redelivery to the owner/insured subject to a maximum limit, in respect of any one accident. The limits for various class of vehicles are as follows:

---

6. www. Insuremagic.com/Auto Insurancebasics — Risk covered by a Comprehensive Policy.htm

Motorcycles/Scooters:	₹	300
Private Car & Taxis	₹	1,500
Other Commercial Vehicles	₹	2,500

The owner/insured is also allowed to authorize repair expenses upto ₹ 500/- per accident.

SECTION II

It covers the liabilities towards third parties, i.e., liabilities of bodily injuries and property damage.

SECTION III

It is applicable to commercial vehicles. It covers the vehicle while it is being used for the purpose of 'Towing Disabled Vehicles.' This section covers Third Party Liabilities that the insured vehicle or the one being towed for reward/remuneration. Further, the insurance company is also not liable for damages to the towed vehicle or any property being conveyed thereby.

Benefits of Comprehensive Policy Cover – An Illustration

Mr. Tom has an Act only policy covering his private car. He employs a paid driver. While driving the vehicle, after dropping Mr. Tom at his office, the vehicle collides with a truck and the driver dies on the spot. Being an old car, Mr. Tom had nothing much to lose and that is why he had not taken a Comprehensive Policy. However, the family of the driver lost their breadwinner.

As an employer, Mr. Tom is liable to compensate for the driver, since he was driving the vehicle in course of employment. The Motor Vehicles Act, 1988 makes it compulsory to insure liabilities under Workmen's Compensation Act.

Accordingly, the legal heir of the deceased driver filed an application to the Labour Commissioner and an Award of ₹ 1,50,000 was passed against the employer. Mr. Tom, equipped with an Act Policy, approached the insurance company, who in turn satisfied the Award. The legal heir of the driver received the compensation from the Labour Court soon after and everyone was happy.

The liability for compensation as per the Workmen's Compensation Act, depends on the wages of the employee and his age, and represents mainly the loss of earnings. However, other losses representing mental pain and agony for the family, loss of consortium, future expenses on dependents and loss of prospective earnings are not accommodated in this compensation.

The legal heir of the driver, in the instant case then approached the Motor Accident Claims Tribunal, demanding a compensation of ₹ 1,00,000 towards these losses. The Tribunal passed an award of ₹ 50,000, found reasonable as per provisions of Common Law and Fatal Accidents Act. Mr. Tom had an Act Policy, which did not cover this liability, and he was saddled with the responsibility of satisfying the Court Order. You can imagine the financial burden he had to bear. Had he taken a Comprehensive Policy, covering his driver by payment of a small premium, he would not have to face this difficulty. The insurance company would have paid this additional amount of compensation too. It is, therefore, always beneficial and advisable to take a comprehensive policy covering these liabilities.

Exclusions to the Comprehensive Insurance Cover

This insurance does not cover loss or damage caused due to:

(*a*) Driver being under intoxication

(*b*) Vehicle being driven by a person not holding an effective, valid licence.

It also does not cover:

(*a*) Damage to tyres (unless the vehicle is also damaged).

(*b*) Wear and tear, mechanical breakdown.

Calculation of Premiums

In the case of Comprehensive Insurance Cover, for the purpose of premium, vehicles are categorized as follows:

Private Car

This is used for personal purposes. The premium is computed on the following basis:

- Geographical area of use and cubic capacity
- Value of the vehicle.

Accessories are to be specified separately under electrical and non-electrical items.

Two-wheeler

It is used for personal purposes only. Premium is calculated on cubic capacity and value of vehicle. Accessories are to be specified. Theft of accessories is not covered, unless the vehicle is stolen at the same time.

Commercial Vehicle

This is a vehicle used for hire and is classified as follows:

Goods-carrying commercial vehicle: In this case, premium is calculated on carrying capacity — gross vehicle weight and value of the vehicle. Accessories extra, as specified.

Passenger-carrying commercial vehicle: In this case, premium is calculated on carrying capacity of the vehicle — number of passengers and value of the vehicle. Accessories extra, as specified.

17.3.3 Auto Policy in United States

The personal auto policy, famous in the US includes four main types of coverage:[7]

(*a*) "third party" liability coverage for liability to third parties harmed by negligence of an insured person;

(*b*) "first party" medical payments coverage for the insured, or in states with no fault or related laws, personal injury protection coverage for the insured's medical expenses and loss of income;

---

7. Harrington & Neihaus, *Risk Management and Insurance,* McGraw-Hill, 1999. p. 534.

(*c*) uninsured and under insured motorists coverage for losses caused to an insured by drivers without liability insurance and drivers with comparatively low liability insurance limits; and

(*d*) coverage for physical damage to or theft of insured autos.

The auto liability coverage in the personal auto policy provides broad coverage for liability for bodily injury and property damage to other parties arising out of the use of an automobile by an insured person. As is customary with the liability insurance, the insurer also agrees to defend the insured and bear the defence costs and is responsible for negotiating and setting the claims. Personal auto liability coverage may be sold with a "single limit" that specifies the maximum amount that the insurer will pay for all damages from a single accident.

Under the first party auto medical payments coverage, the auto owner can receive payment for medical expenses arising out of an accident. Coverage is for the medical expenses for the named insured and family members hurt in any auto and other persons that are hurt while occupying a covered auto. Coverage limits under such policies are comparatively low.

In US with no fault or related laws, the personal auto policy includes personal injury protection coverage for the named insured, family members, and parties hurt while occupying a covered auto instead of medical payment coverage.

17.4 Factors Considered for Premium Rating

Automobile insurance pricing has always been a matter of controversies to the consumers, service providers and the regulators. Auto claims have increased significantly in India since last 10 years. Auto insurance rates charged to different customers reflect differences in the discounted expected costs of providing coverage. In order to classify different persons into homogeneous groups with respect to expected claim costs, insurers generally use rate classification system that include (1) driver classes that reflect the characteristics of individual insureds, and (2) territorial rating to reflect expected differences in claim costs for people that live in different geographical areas (holding individual characteristics constant). Of course, physical damage rates also depend upon the value and type of vehicle. Liability insurance rates sometimes also depend on the type of vehicle, given evidence that certain vehicles are more likely to be involved in at-fault accidents. The major factors considered in establishing driver classes and the use of territorial rating factors are:[9]

Driver Classes

The parameters are Age, Gender, and Marital Status, Use of automobile, driving education and driving record. The insureds in younger age group, the males, the married ones and new and inexperienced drivers have on average high accidental claims. The loading on the premium increases by the numbers and amount of accident claims.

Territorial Rating

Large cities have higher average claim costs followed by suburban areas, smaller cities, and small towns or rural areas. In India, the geographical areas have been classified into Group A and Group B.

Motor/Automobile Insurance business in India is governed by the All India Motor Tariff, which lays down the premium rates, terms and conditions. The main factors taken into consideration for rating in India are vehicle classifications on several parameters, the geographical area of operations and experiences.

Vehicle Classification

Vehicles are generally classified on the basis of its technical specifications, its value or use.

Technical Specifications ("The Type")

The typology of a vehicle is more or less based on its cubic capacity or gross vehicle weight and its carrying capacity. Heavier vehicles are more exposed to accidents since the resultant damages they incur are more. Similarly, vehicles with higher carrying capacity expose more passengers to risk. Therefore heavier vehicles attract higher premium rate. In private cars, taxis and motorcycles, the factor is the cubic capacity. The more the cubic capacity, the higher the premium rate. Whereas in goods-carrying commercial vehicles and passenger-carrying commercial vehicles, the criteria are gross vehicle weight and passenger carrying capacity respectively.

The Value of the Vehicle

The premium rate is applied on the value of the vehicle to arrive at the premium payable. It is the owner/insured who has to select a correct value of the vehicle and declare the same for insurance. This value is known as the Insured's Estimated Value (IEV) in motor insurance and represents the sum insured.

Normally, this value is arrived at by considering the age of the vehicle and its present purchase price. A Maruti 800 was purchased in 1998 for ₹ 1,80,000/- Considering the conventional 10% depreciation each year and the present purchase price of a similar vehicle at ₹ 2,00,000/- the IEV for year 2000 is ₹ 1,80,000 less 20% of ₹ 2,00,000 = ₹ 40,000.00

IEV = ₹ 1,40,000.00

However, this is not sufficient for deriving the correct IEV of the vehicle in terms of motor insurance. In motor insurance, the basis for payment of claims is the market value of the vehicle at the place and time of loss. This market value may be understood as, the price that the vehicle would fetch in the second-hand market. For certain vehicles, there is a good demand in the second-hand market. Maruti is one of them. The 1998 model mentioned above may fetch a price of say, ₹ 1,50,000. In such situations, the correct IEV for the Maruti of 1998 model should be ₹ 1,50,000.

Now take the case of a Premier Padmini car of 1998 model. The purchase price in 1998 was say, ₹ 1,80,000/-. The depreciated value in year 2000 works out to ₹ 1,40,000. But, the second-hand value would be at most ₹ 30,000, since it has virtually no demand in the market.

In this case, the correct IEV should be ₹ 30,000/- only. It is not worthwhile to insure your vehicle at a higher value since that will increase the premium payable but, in case of total loss, only the market value would be payable.

In motor insurance, the IEV is the limit of liability per accident and not for the entire period of insurance. In cases of partial loss or losses, which may be made good by repairs, there is no limit to the number of accidents in any period of insurance. Suppose the Premier Padmini car, as described above, claims for two accidents in the year 2000, the first for an amount of ₹ 20,000/- and the second for ₹ 15,000/- under its insurance policy with IEV of ₹ 30,000/-. Both these claims can be recovered from the insurance company, since their respective values are within the limit of IEV, irrespective of the fact that the insured in this process recovers more amount during the period of insurance than he was insured for.

However, if the vehicle is totally lost or damaged and cannot be repaired, the insured would be paid the market value or IEV, whichever is less. It is very important to select a correct IEV for insurance. There is a tendency of motor vehicle owners to declare a lower value for insurance to reduce the premium expenditure. Although, insurance companies check the IEV for its sufficiency before accepting the insurance, this is not a correct practice as the insured is exposed to a greater loss in case the vehicle is totally lost or damaged.

The Use of the Vehicle

Risk exposure varies in relation to the use the vehicle is put to. Private cars are lesser exposed than taxis, as the latter is used extensively for maximum revenue. Taxis, therefore, attract a higher premium rate. Similarly, goods carrying vehicles, which are used as private carriers and transport, only their owners' goods attract a lower premium, than those used as public carriers for transporting goods for hire.

The Geographical Area of Operation

The area of operation of a vehicle also has a direct bearing on the premium rate. This is so because, certain areas of operation are more congested with high densities of population and road traffic than others and poses higher exposure to accidents. For this purpose, the tariff differentiates two zones in India, i.e., Zone A and Zone B, for private cars and taxis. Zone A represents the Chennai region and Mumbai region (excluding Mumbai city) and Zone B represents the Kolkata region, Delhi region and Mumbai city. In Zone B, the densities of population and road traffic are more and hence attract a higher premium rate.

Such differential rating does not apply to commercial vehicles such as trucks and buses, as these vehicles normally travel throughout India for their operation. However, a discount is allowed on the premium for commercial vehicles used as contract carriage, school buses, public and private buses used for carrying passengers/workers and operate within a radius of 50 kilometres from the city limits.

Details of States under Zone A and Zone B

	Zone A	*Zone B*
Andhra Pradesh	Andaman & Nicobar Islands	Mumbai City
Goa, Daman, Diu	Arunachal Pradesh	Nagaland
Gujarat	Assam	Orissa
Karnataka	Bihar	Punjab
Kerala	Delhi	Rajasthan
Madhya Pradesh	Haryana	Sikkim
Maharashtra	Himachal Pradesh	Tripura
(Excluding Mumbai City)	Lakshadweep Islands	Uttar Pradesh
Pondicherry	Manipur	West Bengal
Tamil Nadu	Mizoram	

The Claims Experience

Unfavourable claims experience is obviously a bad risk. The tariff has adopted a system called the "No Claim discount", to give discounts for good claims experience and a loading for bad experience. The claim experience of expiring year's policy is the basis for allowing discount or charging a loading.

17.5 Motor Insurance Claims

17.5.1 Own Damage Claims

Documents

Following Documents generally required for settlement of motor claims. However depending on the merits of the case, a particular document may not be necessary or an alternate document could be used to serve the purpose of the Insurer.

(*a*) *Claim form* required to be completed.

(*b*) *Registration Certificate:* The details usually verified from the RC can instead be obtained from purchase details of the vehicle if the circumstances so warrant.

(*c*) *Driving License:* As per policy condition the driver is required to hold an effective driving license both in terms of the period validity and the class of vehicle that is being driven at the time of the accident. The MV Act provides for a grace period of 30 days after expiry of a license during which period the license may be accepted as effective, provided the holder has not been qualified from holding a license. For loss sustained by parked vehicles, driving license may not be relevant.

(*d*) *Load Challan/Trip Sheet:* To verify that the load carried was within the permissible limits and the trip sheet giving details of number of passengers carried in the vehicle.

(*e*) *Fitness Certificate:* The fitness certificate indicates the roadworthiness of a commercial vehicle.

(*f*) *Report to Police:* A copy of the FIR and Panchanama is required wherever third parties are involved in an accident.

(*g*) *Survey Report:* Surveyor ascertains the damage, assess the quantum of payable claim, verify vehicular documents and confirm that the loss/damage being claimed for is in conformity with the narration of the accident. Wherever replacement of parts is allowed surveyors physically verify serial numbers as appearing on major parts, which carry such numbers.

Procedure

- In order to proceed for claim, the insured immediately informs the insurer.
- The policy documents are verified to ensure that the policy is force and the loss is entered in the claims register and the claim form is issue to the insured to be completed and returned.

- The insurer, immediately on receipt of intimation of loss, either in writing or over telephone, a surveyor is appointed based on the estimate of repairs. The surveyors are supplied with the copy of the claim form, copy of policy and the repairer's estimate.
- In case of major accidents, the insured would be asked to arrange for photographs of the vehicle at the spot of the accident, showing all the external damages and the number plate of the vehicle. The photo expenses are to be reimbursed upto ₹ 500. Alternatively, the insured may inform the nearest office of the insurer to arrange for such photographs.
- The survey report is examined and settlement is done based on surveyor's recommendations.
- If reinspection after repair is considered necessary, it may be conducted by the same surveyor who has assessed the loss.
- Conventionally, the payment is made to the repairer directly.
- If for any reason, to be specified, the driving license cannot be produced, the claim may be considered only on non-standard basis. However for settlement of such claims the authority should be vested only with the Managers and above in the RO. Where the driving license is not endorsed for tourist taxis, since, different practices prevail in different states, it is necessary to check the local practice. The claim is to be treated as standard or non-standard on the basis of the practice prevailing in the state where the accident occurs and this will be decided by a Manager and above in the RO.
- The repairers are bound to keep aside the value of salvage and if the salvage is desired to be retained, the value is deducted from the claim bill.

Partial Loss Claims

A. Submission of bills/cash can be dispensed with for claims upto ₹ 50,000 in respect of private cars and two wheelers only, subject to:

(*a*) The survey report correctly indicating the cost of parts allowed for replacement.

(*b*) Claims being settled on the basis of a report of reinspection after repairs by the surveyor certifying that the repairs and replacements have been carried out as per assessment. For other classes of vehicles bills/cash memos have to be obtained and verified.

B. If surveyor confirms replacement of the engine and chassis if allowed for replacement and indicates the new numbers, claims may be settled whilst simultaneously advising the insured that:

(*a*) As per the provision of the Motor Vehicles Act, the new numbers have to be incorporated in the RC book.

(*b*) Insurance company be informed about the incorporation of the new numbers in the RC book for endorsing on the policy document to facilitate settlement of future claims.

(*c*) Where the vehicle is totally damaged or when the net cost of repairs is almost close to the market value of the IEV the claim could be considered to be a total loss. Such total loss claims should be encouraged on net of salvage basis, i.e., salvage being retained by the insured and an appropriate amount towards salvage value as determined by the surveyor in consultation with the company be deducted from the total loss amount.

(*d*) However, if the insured to retain the salvage, arrangements should be made for the safe custody of the damaged vehicle to prevent further loss or damage. The RTO should be informed by Registered AD post. An inventory on the major parts should be taken before taking possession of the vehicle. Immediate steps thereafter should also be taken for its disposal as per company's guidelines for disposal of salvage.

17.5.2 Theft Claims

1. *Partial Loss due to Theft:* Theft of parts/accessories from a vehicle should be reported to the police immediately by the insured. If parts are found missing or changed after recovery of stolen vehicle this be recorded in panchanama/recovery memo. Final police investigation report will also be required. However, if the competent authority is satisfied about the genuineness of the loss, final investigation report may be waived provided the insured sends a registered AD letter to the SP/ACP requesting that the insurer should be informed of any recovery.
2. *Total Loss due to Theft:* Unless claims settling authority is fully satisfied, investigation of the theft to be arranged by an investigator who may be appointed with specific terms of reference.
3. The following documents should be collected from the insured in addition to a certified copy of the FIR, for considering "on account" payment of the admissible claim after expiry of 90 days from the date of loss.
   (*a*) Surrender of the Registration Book and the Tax Book to the insurer duly transferred in the name of the insurers. The RTO is to be informed about the theft of the vehicle and this should be entered in Tax Book so that further tax will not accrue.
   (*b*) Letter of indemnity and subrogation.
   (*c*) Ignition keys of the vehicle.
   (*d*) Certificate of insurance and the original insurance policy, if not stolen with the vehicle.
   (*e*) Specially worded discharge voucher.
4. The balance payment may be released on receipt of the Final Police Investigation Report or on expiry of a suitable waiting period from the date of the "on account" payment, after obtaining the discharge voucher in full and final settlement of the claim.
5. The Police and the Registration authorities and the NCRB should be notified in writing about disposal of the claim on "total loss" basis following theft of the vehicle. They should be requested to advise the company if the vehicle is recovered subsequently. Immediately after receipt of advise from the Police regarding recovery of the vehicle, necessary steps for taking possession of the vehicle from the Police custody should be taken and, if necessary, an advocate should be appointed for filing recovery application in the court.

6. Municipal Authorities, where applicable and the RTO should be advised by registered Letter with Acknowledgement due to record 'non use' of the vehicle on account of theft and about the cancellation of the Insurance Certificate.
7. If the vehicle is recovered subsequently, the insured will have the option to repay the claim amount already paid and retain the recovered vehicle. If the vehicle is found damaged, the insured will be indemnified against loss of damage. The insured should be advised to obtain recovery memo from the Police and to get the vehicle surveyed at the Police Station before taking delivery, as mentioned under partial loss theft claims.
8. In cases of criminal breach of trust, each case should be dealt with an individual basis depending upon facts of each case and subject to legal opinion.

17.5.3 Third Party Bodily Injury Claims: Fatal and Non-fatal

1. *Intimation of Claim:* Intimation about an accident resulting into third party claim is received through various sources:
   (*a*) Insured directly or by mention in passing whilst lodging own damage claim
   (*b*) Claimant
   (*c*) MACT/Courts by notice
   (*d*) Through accident report from police in Form 54 prescribed under Central Motor Vehicles Rules, 1989.
2. *Investigation:* Investigation about the accident to collect the relevant data to quantify reasonable and just compensation as per the specified formats in respect of all third party claims is mandatory. The companies should ensure that this investigation helps the insurance company in finalizing out of court settlement at the earliest.
3. *Appointment of Advocate:* On receipt of notice from the MACT, a competent advocate from the panel may be appointed if necessary. The following relevant documents and information should be given to him/her immediately to enable him/her to draft written statement (w/s) on behalf of the Company and ensure that the proper defense is taken where necessary and no frivolous statements are made.
4. *Policy Copy:* Duly certified true copy of the complete policy with the relevant clauses and endorsements as actually attached with the original issued covering the vehicle at the material time of accident.
5. *Driving Licence:* In case it has been observed that driver was not duly licensed the necessary information should be given to the advocate. Though under Section 149(2) of the MV Act, 1988, Insurance Company has no liability if the driver is not duly licensed, the onus to prove that the driver was not holding a license rests on insurance company and this obligation is required to be discharged fully to the satisfaction of the court.
6. *Compliance Policy Conditions:* If a breach of a specific policy condition has been observed, it should be brought to the notice of the Advocate to enable proper defense if possible.
7. (*a*) Written statement on behalf of the insurance company incorporating all defenses available as enumerated under Section 149 of MV Act should be promptly filed.

(*b*) Wherever necessary when there is collusion between the insured and the claimants or when the insured fails to defend the claim, the company's advocate must be instructed to obtain the MACT's permission under Section 170 of the MV Act to Defend the claim on merits.

8. *Payment of No Fault Liability Claims:* If liability under affected policy is established after taking into consideration the foregoing defenses, company should take immediate steps to deposit No Faulty Liability amount as per Section 140 of the MV Act, 1988.
9. *Payment of Fault Liability Claims:* Companies may initiate action to settle such claims either through—
   (*a*) Jald Rahat Yojana
   (*b*) Lok Adalats
   (*c*) Direct negotiation with the claimant through DICC & RICC.
10. *Jald Rahat Yojana:* Section 152 of MV Act, 1988 authorizes insurance company to settle motor third party non-fatal bodily injury claims where claimant is an adult without claimants taking recourse to MACTs. Industry has already launched the Scheme since 1991.

Guidelines for Placing Claims in Lok Adalats

- Maximum participation and disposal of large number of claims in Lok Adalats sessions should be ensured.
- Companies should place the claims normally falling within the following parameters before Lok Adalat:
  (*a*) where occurrence of the accident is within the policy period.
  (*b*) where estimated liability is not expected to be exceeding ₹ 5,00,000 per application for compensation.
  (*c*) where no substantial point of law is involved.
  (*d*) where no defences are available under Section 149 of the MV Act, 1988, such as driver not holding effective driving license and breach of policy condition relating to limitations as to use.
  (*e*) where policy record shows that the driver was holding effective driving license.
  (*f*) where despite concerted efforts on the part of the insurance companies. They are not in a position to prove conclusively to the satisfaction of the court that a person drove the vehicle not duly licensed.
  (*g*) since there is a provision of automatic transfer of insurance in pursuance of Section 157 of MV Act, 1988 the companies cannot take defense of non-transfer of insurance of the vehicle on their books.
  (*h*) where more than one vehicle insured with different insurance companies is involved in an accident resulting into a third party claim, companies should agree for settlement on 50-50 basis to apportion the liability between them.

- Companies should not accept conditional settlement such as subject to verification of certain documents, production of documents etc.
- On having reached the agreement for compromise settlement concerned MACT issues a Consent Order specifying *inter alia* the period during which the agreed amount should be deposited. On receipt of such order, companies must deposit the amount as agreed to with the MACT within 30 days from the date of award as per schedule.
- In the event of lok adalat for pending appeals before High Courts is organized, such claims where quantum of compensation is in dispute may be considered.
- Appeals which are filed to decide a point of law should not be considered for placing before Lok Adalat.
- Applications for compensation filed by the paid employees may also be placed before Lok Adalat, whether wider legal liability is covered or not.

17.5.4 Motor Accident Claims Tribunals

Motor Vehicles Act, 1939 provides that a State Government may, by notification in the Official Gazette, constitute one or more Motor Accidents Claims Tribunals(MACT) for such area as may be specified in the notification for the purpose of adjudicating upon claims for compensation in respect of accidents involving the death of, or bodily injury to, persons arising out of the use of motor vehicles, or damages to any property of a third party so arising, or both:

Provided that where such claim includes a claim for compensation in respect of damage to property exceeding rupees two thousand, the claimant may, at his option refer the claim to a civil court for adjudication, and where a reference is so made, the Claims Tribunal shall have no jurisdiction to entertain any question relating to such claim.

A Claims Tribunal shall consist of such number of members as the State Government may think fit to appoint and where it consists of two or more members, one of them shall be appointed as the Chairman thereof.

110A. Application for compensation may be made to the tribunal (a) by the person who has sustained the injury or by the owner of the property or where death has resulted from the accident, 1 by all or any of the legal representatives of the deceased; or by any agent duly authorised by the person injured or all or any of the legal representatives of the deceased, as the case may be.

Every application under subsection (1) shall be made to the Claims Tribunal having jurisdiction over the area in which the accident occurred, and shall be in such form and shall contain such particular as may be prescribed.

17.5.5 Hit and Run Accidents and Solatium Fund

Motor Vehicles Act, 1939 contains special provisions as to compensation in cases of hit and run motor accidents. Section 109B and section 109C define “hit and run motor accident” means an accident arising out of the use of a motor vehicle or motor vehicles the identity whereof cannot be ascertained in spite of reasonable efforts for the purpose. The Central Government may, by notification in the Official Gazette, establish a Fund to be known as the Solatium Fund. The amount of compensation is ₹ 25,000/- in the event of death and ₹ 12,500/- for grievous injuries. The prescribed forms are available with the Mandal Revenue Officer of the respective Mandal. The applicant shall submit the application seeking the compensation in the prescribed form to the Claims Enquiry Officer of the Subdivision/Taluk or Mandal where the accident takes place.

Aggrieved party has to submit an application within 6 months from the date of accident.

An application made after 6 months but not after 12 months from the date of accident may be accepted by the Claims Enquiry Officer, if he is satisfied that there are reasonable grounds to condone the delay.

On receipt of the claim application, the Claims Enquiry Officer shall:

- Obtain a copy of the inquest report, FIR, post mortem or certificate of injury as the case may be from the concerned authorities and hold an enquiry in respect of claims arising out of hit and run accidents.
- Decide the rightful claimants.
- Submit the report to the Claims Settlement Commissioner.

On receipt of the report of the Claims Enquiry Officer, the Claims Settlement Commissioner will sanction the claim. Claims Settlement Commissioner means the District Magistrate, the Deputy Commissioner, the Collector, or other Officer in-charge of a Revenue District in a State appointed by the State Government.

The Claims Enquiry Officer has to submit his report to Claims Settlement Commissioner within a month's time from the date of receipt of the claim application.

The Claims Settlement Commissioner shall sanction the claim within a period of 15 days from the date of receipt of the report and communicate the sanction order along with the duly discharged receipt and the undertaking in the prescribed form to the Nominated Office of the Insurance Company.

Where the Claims Settlement Commissioner has any doubt in respect of the report submitted by the Claims Enquiry Officer, he shall return the report for further enquiry indicating the specific points on which the enquiry is to be made.

Claims arising out of death payment shall be made to the legal representatives of the deceased as decided by the Claims Enquiry Officer and in respect of grievous hurt the payment shall be made to the person injured.

Once the sanction order together with the discharge receipt and the undertaking in the prescribed form is received from Claims Settlement Commissioner, the Insurance Company will effect payment within 15 days from the date of receipt of the sanction order. The payment is made by cheque or demand draft through registered post with an acknowledgement due directly to the claimant.

Exhibit 17.1
Motor Insurance Statistics

Business Generated (Gross Direct Premium — ₹ in crore)

Companies	*1993-94*	*1994-95*	*1995-96*	*1996-97*	*1997-98*	*1998-99*	*1999-2000*
GIC	-	-	-	-	-	-	-
NIC	231.25	267.81	345.67	444.14	511.17	612.48	699.08
OIC	-	-	-	-	-	-	-
NIAC	451.29	532.38	629.68	-	806.76	936.68	1031.06
UII	278.46	340.69	408.94	487.64	543.78	661.03	712.11
Total	**961.00**	**1140.88**	**1384.29**	**931.78**	**1861.71**	**2210.19**	**2442.25**

Profits (₹ in Crore)

Companies	*1993-94*	*1994-95*	*1995-96*	*1996-97*	*1997-98*	*1998-99*	*1999-2000*
GIC	-	-	-	-	-	-	-
NIC	-60.69	-124.88	-83.71	-192.75	-213.19	-298.67	-309.01
OIC	-	-	-	-	-	-	-
NIAC	-70.42	-284.48	-210.04	-	-284.83	-221.48	-369.92
UII	-110.81	-209.87	-249.73	-298.08	-301.79	-334.54	-419.56
Total	-241.92	-619.23	-543.48	-490.83	-799.81	-854.69	-1098.49

Profit %age

GIC	-	-	-	-	-	-	-
NIC	-26.24%	-46.63%	-24.22%	-43.40%	-41.71%	-48.76%	-44.20%
OIC	-	-	-	-	-	-	-
NIAC	-15.60%	-53.44%	-33.36%	-	-35.31%	-23.65%	-35.88%
UII	-39.79%	-61.60%	-61.07%	-61.13%	-55.50%	-50.61%	-58.92%

Exhibit 17.2
Motor Insurance (Gross Direct Premium Income)

Company	*2005-06*	*2006-07*	*2007-08*	*2008-09*
National	1846.41	1986.58	2146.30	2146.29
New India	2174.50	2034.73	2034.30	2000.29
Oriental	1495.30	1739.79	1608.38	1491.30
United India	1138.16	1233.18	1434.90	1563.49
ECGC*	-	-	-	
GIC*	-	-	-	
Royal Sundaram	233.09	303.39	409.56	529.91
Reliance	26.52	455.51	1267.37	1164.82
IFFCO-Tokio	378.08	448.90	499.19	683.24
TATA AIG	239.82	273.09	253.25	224.79
ICICI Lombard	454.44	1142.55	1279.07	1321.29
Bajaj Allianz	536.61	843.87	1386.37	1503.39
Cholamandalam	52.35	97.16	1224.41	319.53
HDFC-ergo	158.03	138.32	140.38	158.78
Future Generali	-	-	-	94.88

Universal Sompo	-	-	-	3.92
Shriram	-	-	-	112.72
Bharti AXA	-	-	-	17.39
Total	8733.37	10697.07	13683.48	13336.03
Market Share				
Private Co. Share	76.195%	65.385%	52.793%	53.999%
Public Co. Share	23.805%	34.615%	47.207%	46.001%

Key Terms

- Bodily Injury
- Legal Liability
- Act Only Policy
- Comprehensive Policy
- Maturity Claim
- Premium Rating

Questions for Review

1. Is automobile insurance compulsory in India? What types of insurance covers are available for automobiles?
2. Write short notes on:
   (*a*) No claim discount.
   (*b*) Factors considered for premium rating.
   (*c*) Insured Declared Value.
3. Briefly explain the various documents required for settlement of own damage and third party documents.
4. Explain the major point of differences between the procedure for settlement of third party claims and own damage claims.

Suggested Readings

- Harrington & Niehaus, *Risk Management and Insurance,* McGraw-Hill, 1999.
- J.C. Trieschmann, S.G. Gistavson and R.E. Hoyt, *Risk Management and Insurance,* South-Western College Publishing, 2001.
- Vaughan and Vaughan, *Essentials of Risk Management and Insurance,* John Wiley and Sons Inc., 2001.
- *Insurance Law Manual,* Taxmann, 2001.
- *Motor Insurance,* IC 72, Insurance Institute of India, Mumbai, 2003.

❑❑❑

CHAPTER

LIABILITY INSURANCE

Chapter Objectives

- Tort Liabilities
- Specific Statutory Liabilities
- Lability Insurance

Introduction

Liability insurance covers provide indemnity to the insured in respect of financial consequences arising out of liability under the civil law. The civil liability arises either due to the operation of :

(a) Law of torts

(b) Specific Statutory Enactments

18.1 Tort Liabilities

A legal wrong is a violation of a person's legal rights, or a failure to perform a legal duty owed to a certain person or to the society as a whole. These wrongs may either be crimes (against the society), breach of contracts or torts. A tort is a civil wrong for which the law allows a remedy in the form of pecuniary damages. Tort may be of following types:

(a) Intentional Torts – frauds, infringment of rights, assault, trespass etc.

(b) Strict Liability — absolute liability in respect of loss or injury due to use of hazardous substances, occupational injury to employees etc.

(c) Negligence – failure to perform duties

Some of the specific tort liability covers are discussed in following sections.

18.1.1 Product Liability

This insurance is intended to provide an indemnity to the insured (upto the limit of liability) in the event of a claim being brought against him. This may be caused by anything harmful or defective in the products sold or supplied by the insured in connection with the business specified. The insurer in addition reimburses all costs and expenses incurred with its written consent defending such a claim for compensation. The insurance does not cover the cost of removing, replacing or repairing defective products or loss of use thereof.

Liability for injury or damage caused by a defective product may arise due to the operation of Sale of Goods Act or Consumer Protection Act. The product liability policy seeks to indemnify the insured against his legal liability to pay compensation (including claimants costs, fees and expenses) in respect of injury damage or pollution for third parties for claims arising out of accidents due to any defects in the products specified in the policy during the period of the insurance and first made against the insured during the policy period. For the purpose of determining the indemnity granted:

1. Injury shall mean death, bodily injury, illness or disease of or to any person.
2. Damage shall mean actual and/or physical damage to the atmosphere or of any water, land or other tangible property.
3. Pollution shall mean pollution or contamination of the atmosphere or of any water, land or other tangible property.
4. Product shall mean any tangible property after it has left the custody or control of the Insured which has been designed, specified, formulated, manufactured, constructed, installed, sold, supplied, distributed, treated, serviced, altered or repaired by on behalf of the Insured.
5. Accident shall mean a fortuitous event or circumstance which is sudden, unexpected and unintentional including resultant, continuous, intermittent or repeated exposures arising out of the same fortuitous event or circumstances,

The product policy is on 'Claims made' basis. This means that the accident giving rise to the claim shall occur during the period of insurance and further that the claim shall be first made against the insured during the policy period. The retroactive date is the date of commencement of the first 'Claims made' product liability policy. This date remains unaltered as long as the policy has been renewed without break and there has been no substantial material change in the risk. The policy does not cover:

Special Exclusions

1. The policy excludes liability for costs in the repair, reconditioning, modification or replacement of any part of any product which is or is alleged to be defective.
2. For cost arising out of the recall of any product or part thereof.
3. Arising out of any product which is intended for incorporation into the structure, machinery or control of any aircraft.
4. Arising out of deliberate, wilful or intentional non-compliance of any statutory provision.

5. Arising out of pure financial loss such as loss of goodwill, loss of market, etc.
6. Arising out of fines, penalties, punitive and exemplary damages.
7. For injury and/or damage occurring prior to the retroactive date shown in the schedule.
8. Arising out of deliberate, conscious or intentional disregard of the insured's technical or administrative management of the need to take all reasonable steps to prevent claims.
9. For injury to any person under a contract of employment or apprenticeship with insured where such injury arises out of the execution of such contract.
10. Arising out of contractual liability which would not have existed in the absence of the specific contract.
11. Arising out of any product guarantee.
12. Arising out of claims for failure of the goods or products to fulfill the purpose for which they were intended.

In addition, War and Nuclear Perils are specifically excluded. The policy does pays for **loss or damage due to:**

- War and war-like perils
- Wear and tear, depreciation, consequential loss
- Nuclear group of perils
- Gross and wilful negligence of Insured
- Violation of policy conditions
- Loss/damage/liability where Insured's family or Insured's employee are involved as principal/accessory
- Intentional act/self injury/influence of drug/intoxicant.

Additional Covers

- Vendors' Liability extension
- Technical collaborators' liability
- Products manufactured by subcontractors/licensed manufacturers on their own brand name can also be covered under the same policy.

Claims arising out of accidents during the policy period due to defects in the products covered by the policy are payable. The policy also covers injury to third party and pollution liability on account of products covered. Indemnity is extended to officials of the insured in their business capacity, officers, committees and members of insured's welfare associations and personal representatives of the estate. All costs, fees and expenses incurred in investigation, defense and settlement of claim made against the insured, cost of representation at any inquiry or other proceedings in respect of matters having direct relevance to the claim made against the insured are covered by the policy subject to the overall limits stated in the policy.

18.1.2 Directors' and Officers' Liability Insurance

In a recent spate of litigation, a number of adverse court verdicts regarding the liability of directors and officers of companies to a third party were passed where the directors and officers were held personally liable for payment of compensation to the third party. Ordinarily, the directors and officers are bound by duty towards the company itself, shareholders, employees, creditors, customers, competitors, members of the public, government and other regulatory bodies. Any breach or non-performance in the duties can result in claims against the companies and/or its directors of the company by reason of any wrongful act in their respective capacity. The Directors' and Officers' Liability Insurance policy has been designed specifically to meet any financial liabilities imposed upon them.

This policy provides cover for directors and officers of a company to reduce the impact of potential litigation owing to:

- Failure of supervision.
- Inaccuracy in statements of financial accounts.
- Lack of judgment and good faith.
- Mismanagement of funds.
- Misstatements in prospectuses.
- Allotment of shares.
- Unauthorized loans or investments.
- Failure to obtain competitive bids.
- Imprudent expansion resulting in a loss.
- Using inside information.
- Unwarranted dividend payment, salaries or compensation.
- Misleading statements filed with the stock exchange.
- Misrepresentation in acquisition agreement for the purchase of another company.
- Wrongful dismissal of an employee.

Risks covered

This policy covers all claims made in event of:

- Mergers, take-overs and divestment.
- Changes in control of shareholding.
- Shareholder claims.
- Trustee accountability and responsibility.
- Administrative liabilities.
- Disposal of old firm/entry of new owners.
- Liquidation.
- Share issues.
- Misdeeds of co-directors.
- Customs and excise allegations.
- Termination of employment.
- Miscellaneous litigation.

Compensation Offered

The extent of indemnity being severely restricted by the Companies' Act will reimburse the extent of legal costs expended only if the Director/Officer successfully defends the act taken against him. Also, coverage is available on a 'claims made' basis and applies only to claims made against the Board of Directors during the policy period, irrespective of when the wrongful act occurred.

The cover applies to:

- Liabilities arising from any claim made against Directors and/or Officers of the company by reason of any wrongful act in their respective capacity.
- Liabilities against the company where it is required to indemnify the Directors/Officers pursuant to common or statutory law provisions or Memorandum and Articles of Association.
- The company and its subsidiaries that are under the common control of the Directors/ Officers.

Exclusions

- The policy does not pay for the losses arising from any claim.
- Prior and pending litigation and claims submitted under previous policies.
- Bodily injury, sickness, disease, emotional distress, death, damage or destruction of tangible property including loss.
- Insured vs. Insured, viz., Directors suing each other.
- Illegal personal profit and remuneration.
- Deliberate, dishonest or fraudulent acts.
- Pollution and/or contamination.
- Insider trading.
- Outside directorship (can be covered with specific information).

18.1.3 Employer's Liability

Workmenn's Compensation Act, 1923 and the common law impose liability of an employer for employment injury (including death) of any of his employees who is a 'workman' as defined under the Act. Section 3 of the Act provides that the employer is liable for compensation if personal injury is caused to workmen by accident arising out of and in the course of employment. Also if the workman contacts any disease, specified in the Act as an occupational disease, the illness is deemed to be injury by accident arising out of and in the course of employment.

Coverage of the Policy under the WC Act,1923

- Indemnity to insured against his liability as an 'employer' to accidental injuries (including fatal) sustained by the 'workman' whilst at work.
- On extra premium — medical, surgical, and hospital expenses including the cost of transport to hospital for accidental employment injuries.
- Liability in respect of diseases mentioned in Part C/Schedule III of WC Act, on additional premium; which arise out of and in the course of employment.

The rates of insurance are prescribed by the tariff which is in two forms:

Table A – Indemnity against the legal liability for accident to employees under:

(a) Workmen's Compensation Act, 1923

(b) Fatal Accident Act, 1855

(c) Common Law

Table B – indemnity cover for legal liability arising under:

(a) Fatal Accident Act, 1855

(b) Common Law

Compensation

Subject to the provisions of WC Act, the amount of compensation/reimbursable is as follows:

- Where employment injury results in death, then 40%-50% of the monthly wages of the deceased multiplied by the relevant factor or ₹ 20,000/- which ever is more.
- *Permanent Total Disablement* — 50%-60% of the monthly wages of the injured disabled (PTD) workman multiplied by relevant factor or ₹ 24,000/- whichever is more.
- *Permanent Partial Disablement* — (a) For an injury specified in Part II of disablement (PPD) schedule. The percentage of loss of earning capacity caused applied to the compensation payable for permanent total disablement and (b) For an injury not specified in schedule — the percentage of permanent loss of earning capacity as assessed by qualified Medical Practitioners applied to the compensation payable for permanent total disablement.
- Where more than one injury caused by same accident, it shall be aggregate but in any case not to exceed the amount payable for permanent total disablement.
- Temporary disablement — A half monthly payment equivalent to 25% (total or partial) of monthly wages of the workman to be paid in accordance with the provisions of sub-section (2) of the WC Act.
- Actual medical expenses incurred in connection with on-duty accident ranging from ₹ 80/ — to 2400/- per case as per the option given at the inception of the policy by the insured and extra premium paid.
- Legal costs and expenses incurred with the Company's consent.

Exclusions

- Any injury which does not result in fatality or partial disablement for period exceeding 3 days.
- First 3 days of disablement where the total disablement is less than 28 days.
- For any non-fatal injury caused by any accident which is directly attributable to:
  - *(a)* Influence of drinks or drugs
  - (b) Wilful disobedience of an order for securing safety of the workman
  - *(c)* Wilful removal or disregard of safety guard device.

- War group and nuclear group of perils.
- Liability to employees of contractors of the insured (unless specifically declared).
- Employee who is not a "workman" as per WC Act.
- Liability of insured assumed under an agreement.
- For occupational diseases mentioned in part "C" of schedule III of WC Act, unless cover is extended on extra premium.
- Increase due to any change in statute provisions after policy had incepted under more than one statute/one forum for the same injury.

18.1.4 Professional Indemnity Policies

The Professional Indemnity Insurance Policy is available for all doctors, medical establishments, contractors, engineers, architects, interior decorators, chartered accountants, financial accountants, management consultants, lawyers, advocates, solicitors and counsellors.

Jurisdiction applicable under the Professional Indemnity policy will be within Indian Courts.

Under this cover, the policyholder will be covered for any professional act or omission occurring during the period of insurance provided the policy is renewed without interruption and is in force at the time of claim. Any claims arising out of act or omission of policyholder have to be made in writing during the policy period. The retroactive date of the policy is the period commencing from the date and hour mentioned in the policy and expiring at midnight on the expiry date mentioned in the policy. If the policyholder notifies any event or circumstance as a claim during the period of policy and if insurance company accepts it, then the insurer will deal with the claim. The **"Extended Claim Reporting Clause"** allows the policyholder a time limit up to 90 days from cancellation or non-renewal of policy to notify claims which had taken place during the period of insurance. And the only condition is that another policy does not exist.

18.2 Specific Statutory Liabilities

Public Liability Insurance

The Public Liability Insurance Act, 1991 imposes "no fault" liability in respect of use of hazardous substances as specified by the Act. The object of this Act is to provide through insurance immediate relief to persons affected due to "accident" while "handling" "hazardous substance" by the owners on "no fault liability basis". This has also been brought under Tariff. The definition of "Owner" is so comprehensive as to cover any person who owns or has control over any hazardous substance at the time of accident. This includes any Firm or its partners. Association or its members, Company or its Directors and all other persons associated and responsible to that Company in the conduct of their business. The various terms like "Accident", "Hazardous substances" as defined in Section 2 of the Act are given below.

"Accident" means an accident involving a fortuitous, sudden or unintentional occurrence while handling any hazardous substance resulting in continuous, intermittent or repeated exposure to death of, or injury to any person or damage to any property but does not include an accident by reason only of war or radioactivity.

"Handling" in relation to any hazardous substance, means the manufacture, processing, treatment, package, storage, transportation by vehicle, use, collection, destruction, conversion, offering for sale, transfer or the like of such hazardous substance.

"Hazardous Substance" means any substance or preparation which is defined as hazardous substance under the Environment (Protection) Act, 1986 and exceeding such quantity as may be specified by notification by the Central Government.

"Hazardous Substance" means any substance or preparation which, by reason of its chemical properties or handling is liable to cause harm to human beings, other living creatures, plants, micro-organism, property or the environment (as per the Environment (Protection) Act, 1986).

18.3 Lability Insurance

Public Liability All Risks Cover

Policy covers all amounts one is legally liable to pay third party during the policy period including legal costs and expenses subject to the limit of indemnity terms and conditions of the policy. This policy indemnifies against amounts one is legally liable to pay as damages to the third party victims of an accident. This includes compensation for accidental death — bodily injury or disease to third parties, damage to or loss of property belonging to third parties arising out of an accident including legal costs incurred with the prior consent of the insurer, legal and civil liabilities of the directors and officers of the company.

Additional Covers

Additional (optional) covers are available for additional premium:

1. *Pollution risks* — caused by a sudden, unintended and unexpected cause which takes place at a specific time and place during the policy period.
2. *Transportation risks* – Outside the premises arising out of an accident directly caused by dangerous materials or hazardous substances while being transported by rail, road or pipeline.
3. *Cover for multiple units* – Non-manufacturing premises of the insured such as offices, depots, godowns etc. located at different places incidental to insured's business activities can be covered.
4. *Technical Collaborators' Liability* – This can be included in the main policy subject to reinsurer's approval.

Maximum Liability

Any one accident: Minimum equal to paid-up capital upto a maximum of ₹ 5 crore.

Any one year: Three times of 'Any one accident' limit subject to a maximum of ₹ 15 crore.

In case of claim/s exceeding the above statutory limit/s, it is to be met by the Environmental Relief Fund to be set up under Section 7A of the Act and managed by the Authority appointed by the Central Government.

The liability beyond the total of the Insurance and the Relief Fund is to be borne by the "Owner". Every owner, in addition to premium, has to pay to the insurer and equivalent amount to be credited to the said fund. However, the central government has powers to exempt any establishment from compulsory insurance, if a fund has been established and maintained for an amount not less than ₹ 5.0 crore or equal to the paid-up caital of the establishment, in any nationalized bank for meeting liability under the act.

Schedule of Compensation

1. Reimbursement of medical expenses incurred upto a maximum of ₹ 12,500/- in each case.
2. For a fatal accident the relief will be ₹ 25,000/- per person in addition to reimbursement of medical expenses, if any incurred on the victim upto a maximum of ₹ 12,500/-.
3. For permanent total or permanent partial disability or other injury or sickness, the relief will be:
   (a) Reimbursement of medical expenses incurred, if any, upto a maximum of ₹ 12,500/- in each case and,
   (b) Cash relief on the basis of percentage of disablement as certified by an authorized physician. The relief for total permanent disability will be ₹ 25,000/-.
4. For loss of wages due to temporary partial disability which reduce the earning capacity of the victim, there will be a fixed monthly relief not exceeding ₹ 1,000/- per month upto a maximum of 3 months provided the victim has been hospitalized for a period exceeding 3 days and above 16 years of age.
5. In respect of damage to private property, upto ₹ 6,000/- per claim.
6. Apart from Public liability insurance Act policy, policies are also available to cover the legal liability of the insured against third parties for claims arising due to industrial accidents. Two different types of policies are available to cover accidents in industries like factories etc. and non-industries like hotels, schools, exhibitions and storage tanks etc.

Claim Procedure

- The Insured has to give written notice to the company as soon as possible of any claim made against him (or any specific event or circumstance that may give rise to a claim being made against the Insured) which forms the subject of indemnity under the policy and shall give all such additional information as the company may require.
- Every claim, writ, summons or process and all documents relating to the event shall be forwarded to the Company immediately after they are received by the Insured, along with the claim form duly filled up.
- No admission, offer, promise or payment shall be made or given by or on behalf of the insured without the written consent of the company.
- The insured will have the right to take over and conduct in the name of the Insured in defense of any claim in case of voluntary public liability policies.

- In the event of liability rising under the policy or payment of a claim under the policy, the limit of indemnity per anyone year under the policy shall get reduced to the extent of quantum of liability to be paid or actual payment of such claim.
- No claim is payable under the policy unless the cause of action arises in India and the liability to pay claim is established against the Insured in an Indian Court. It is also to be understood that only Indian Law shall be applicable in such action.

18.3.1 Other Laws

The other statutes which have a bearing on Public Liability Insurance are as follows:

Water (Prevention and Control of Pollution) Act, 1974

The Central and State Pollution Control Boards are established under the Act. The functions of the Board, *inter alia,* are to control sewage and industrial effluent discharge. The consent of the Board is required to establish any industry which is likely to discharge sewage or trade effluent.

Air (Prevention and Control of Pollution) Act, 1981

This Act is structured along the lines of Water Act but in relation to air pollution.

The Environment (Protection) Act, 1986

This is a comprehensive legislation for enforcement of measures for protection of the environment and for co-ordination of the activities of Pollution Control Boards constituted under the Water and Air Act.

The Factories Act, 1948

The 1987 Amendment–V Act has introduced special provisions relating to hazardous activities.

The Central Motor Vehicles, 1989 and 1993

These acts have fixed certain responsibilities on the consignor, the transporter and also the driver for the safe carriage of hazardous goods.

Key Terms

- Liability Insurance
- Public Liability
- Tort
- Product Indemnity

Questions for Review

1. Briefly explain the need for project insurance and the various covers available in India.
2. Write short notes on:
   (a) Banker's Indemnity Policy
   (b) Fidelity Guarantee Insurance
   (c) Legal Liability Insurance.

3. Briefly explain the provisions of Public Liability Insurance Act, 1991 with respect to compulsory insurance and the schedule of compensation.
4. Outline the cover available in the policy under the Workmen's Compensation Act, 1923.

Suggested Readings

1. *Engineering Insurance,* IC 77, Insurance Institute of India, Mumbai, 1999.
2. *Miscellaneous Insurance,* IC 78, Insurance Institute of India, Mumbai, 1991.
3. Barry D. Smith *et al.*, *Property and Liability Insurance Principles,* Insurance Institute of America, 1994.
4. G.E. Rejda, *Principles of Insurance and Risk Management,* Pearson Education, 2002.
5. *Liability and Engineering Insurance,* Insurance Institute of India, Mumbai, 2000.

Web Resources

- www.cpg.org
- www.insure.com
- www.insureitech.com
- www.pepeinsurance.com

❑❑❑

CHAPTER

RURAL AND SOCIAL INSURANCE

Chapter Objectives

- Need and Potential of Rural Insurance
- Legal Framework
- Various Rural Insurance Policies
- What is Social Insurance?
- Characteristics and Need for Social Insurance
- Legal Framework for Social Insurance
- Social Insurance in India
- Unemployment Insurance
- Salary Savings Scheme

Introduction

Rural insurance is an imperative in India. IRDA regulations have made compulsory rural insurance as a minimum percentage of total business mobilized. Rural insurance covers include a wide variety of agricultural insurance covers, low cost life and health insurances, equipment insurances. Social Insurance through various programs provides a safety net against the financial insecurity that can result from premature death, unemployment, poor health, job related disabilities and old age. These programs are especially vulnerable to individuals and families with limited incomes. However in India Social Insurance concept is in its premature stage, due to vast cultural, economic, social diversities. GIC is pioneer in social insurance. GIC has launched certain social insurance covers like Krishi Bima Yojana, Personal Accident social security scheme, hut insurance scheme. IRDA regulations have made compulsory social insurance as a minimum percentage of total business mobilized.

19.1 Need and Potential of Rural Insurance

The insurance sector has been mostly confined to cities. However, in the rural areas where human life and income-generating rural assets need more protection, there is tremendous scope for developing insurance business. The rural sector so far has been grossly neglected since last 50 years from the privileges of insurance cover, though a silent economic revolution can be seen now in the villages.

With the opening of the insurance sector to the private sector and foreign companies, the time has come when the government should pay serious attention to covering the rural areas. While it is true that access to insurance cover depends on the literacy/awareness levels and assured income, well-planned and organized efforts by committed private sector companies can yield rich dividends from the rural areas. This is because:

(1) A large number of rural districts have witnessed significant growth and prosperity;

(2) Access to reliable and authentic data and information has improved considerably, which can enable quick and correct decision-making;

(3) There are specific functionaries and agencies in the rural areas, which can help, explore and exploit insurance business in the untapped rural market.

Rural Banking as Catalyst

"With a decline in the public investment in agriculture, the rural banking system has been encouraging the farm development through provision of credit facilities for production of crops including horticulture, plantation, forestry; purchase of farm equipment; livestock and fish farming; irrigation facilities and installation of diesel engines etc. Bank credit is also provided for establishing village/cottage industries, stocking/supplying farm inputs and cattle-feed, and business and trade purposes. From 1969-70 to 1999-2000, up to ₹ 3.1 crore has been provided to the farm sector."[1]

"With enhanced incomes, and further supplemented by bank credit, the rural population is acquiring consumer durables, constructing houses, purchasing vehicles, computers, and so on.

All these assets need to be protected from damage/loss, natural or man-made. Thus, the rural areas offer enormous opportunities for committed private insurance companies in both life and non-life insurance schemes."

The efforts by the private insurance players, of course, backed by business, can have direct positive impact on rural development and the economic growth. Insurance in the farm sector can supplement the advances of science and technology.

Both the conventional players, LIC and GIC have been providing some insurance cover in rural areas. But, they are insufficient to meet the exact requirements of the rurals. There is an immense need of creating awareness among people. The rural customers often contend that the claim lodgement and settlement procedure is time-consuming and cumbersome. "Cattle insurance under the government-sponsored Integrated Rural Development Programme and crop insurance have not met with the expected results."

1. Mr. A.R. Patel, web article on Rural Insurance.

"Besides, the village profile available with each of the branches of nationalized/public sector banks contain exhaustive data on the population, cultivating households, categories of farmers, classification of workers, livestock, cropping pattern, farm equipment and machinery and so on.

There are more than 1,75,000 rural credit outlets in addition to the offices of the District Rural Development Agency, the District Industries Centre, and the District Development Manager of nationalized banks and Lead District Manager of the Lead Bank. All these institutions and agencies can offer considerable information to insurance companies."

Modus Operandi

Those willing to enter into rural insurance or improvise must do the following:

- Design tailored products.
- Establish efficient methods of premium collection and claims settlements.
- Create awareness for the need of insurance products.
- Educated unemployed youths of the villages can be trained and become valuable assets for the companies. While insurance companies are eager to build their business in the urban areas, there is a hitherto untapped potential for business in the rural areas, which can be exploited.
- The Centre and the State governments must encourage private and foreign insurance companies to enter the rural areas, and provide protection to rural assets from damage and loss due to natural and man-made calamities. For this purpose, reasonable and need-based concessions/relief in taxation and subsidies, required infrastructural facilities and administrative support must be extended, at least for ten years. The government may consider appointing an Expert Committee on Rural Insurance to work out the modalities for private and foreign companies interested in entering the rural areas.

(The paragraphs in quotes mentioned in this section are the views of Mr. A.R. Patel — a Mumbai-based rural credit specialist.)

19.2 Legal Framework

The Insurance Regulatory and Development Authority Act, 1999 (para 19; First schedule) has amended the Section 32B and 32C of the Insurance Act, 1938 as under:

Section 32B

Every insurer shall, after the commencement of Insurance Regulatory and Development Authority Act, 1999, undertake such percentages of life insurance business and general insurance business in the rural and social sector, as may be specified, in the *Official Gazette* by the authority, in this behalf.

Section 32C

Every insurer shall, after the commencement of Insurance Regulatory and Development Authority Act, 1999, discharge the obligations specified under Section 32B to provide life insurance or general insurance policies to those residing in the rural sector, workers in the unorganised sector or informal sector or economically vulnerable or backward classes of the society and other categories of persons as may be specified by the regulations made by the authority and such insurance policies shall include insurance for crops.

The IRDA Regulations 2000 makes it compulsory for the insurers, existing and new to promote the rural insurance.[2] The regulations prescribe for undertaking benchmark percentages for insurances in the rural insurance sector for the players.

The *rural sector* has been defined as a place which, as per the latest census, the population is not more than 5,000, the density of population is not more than 400 per sq. km. and at least 75% of the male working population is engaged in agriculture.

The regulations provide that those who are proposing to carry on the life insurance business in the year 2000 or later, are required by these regulations to write in the rural sector, at least 5% of the total policies written directly in the first financial year, 7% in the second financial year and so on. In case of non-life insurance, 2% of the total gross premium income written direct in that year, 3% in the second year and so on. Also, the authority may revise the obligation once in 5 years.

19.3 Various Rural Insurance Policies

Aqua Culture Insurance

Suitability: This policy is suitable for licensed farms or farms provided in accordance with the Government Notification for growing brackish water shrimp/fresh water prawns by adopting extensive/modified extensive/semi-intensive systems.

Salient Features: The Policy grants cover under two sections:

Section I: Basic cover, which covers only losses due to natural calamities.

Section II: Comprehensive cover granting cover for disease also. Policy is usually given for a period of 4½ months.

The basic cover provides compensation for total loss of shrimp/prawns due to:

Summer kill, pollution from external source, poisoning, riot, strike and malicious acts of third parties, terrorism, explosion/implosion, aircraft and aerial devices or articles dropped therefrom, impact damage, earthquake, storm, tempest, cyclone, flood and inundation, volcanic eruption and other convulsions of nature. Comprehensive cover in addition to basic cover encompasses death due to diseases except those caused by bad management and nutritional deficiencies.

Benefits: In the event of a fortuitous event resulting in a loss, the basis of loss settlement will be the sum insured, which is fixed as follows:

Sum Insured = Number of seeds released × expected survival rate (%) × expected average body weight in grams × input cost per kg.

---

2. Annexure 22-A.

For losses upto 4th fortnight stage, maximum liability shall be restricted to 80% of the input cost only. From 5th fortnight onwards, claims are admitted as a percentage of biomass.

Deductions towards salvage are made.

Where the percentage of loss at any stage equals or exceeds 80% of the total shrimps/ prawns insured, it will be treated as total loss.

Premium: Premium rates have been fixed as follows:

	Zones	*Section-I (Basic)*	*Section-II (Comprehensive)*
(a)	For highly cyclone prone zones	3%	7½%
(b)	Others	2%	6%

Requirements: The farm should obtain statutory licence for setting up and conducting aquaculture operations in the area as per Government legislation.

The ponds should be prepared as per prescribed, recommended and established standards. The seed should be healthy, of good quality, selected as per prescribed norms and obtained from well-known source. The seed should be of high quality and procured from reputed firms. Holiday period as recommended by MPEDA or such Government agency should be observed.

All matters concerning farming practices, norms, stipulations; guidelines recommended by competent Government agency, fisheries department research institutes, fisheries college etc. should be complied with.

Cattle Insurance

Suitability: This policy is suitable for the farmer — who owns the cattle and the banks/financial institutions which have financed the purchase of cattle under IDP /DRDA /DPAP schemes.

Salient Features: "Cattle" refers to Cows and Buffaloes, Stud Bulls, Bullocks, He Buffaloes, Calves and Heifers.

The Policy is usually given for a period of 12 months or for a long term of 3 to 5 years as per term of loan. The policy covers loss due to death, accident, illness or disease of the animal.

A qualified veterinary officer's certificate is necessary for accepting the proposal and also for fixing the value of the cattle which forms the basis for loss settlement. The policy also covers transit of cattle from the place of purchase to stable located within 80 km. For transit above the stipulated distance, additional premium @ 1% is charged.

Benefits: The policy pays for the market value of the animal prior to the accident or the sum insured whichever is less. A veterinary surgeon's certificate will be necessary to claim the amount in the case of death of the cattle.

Premium

Premium is charged on the market value of the cattle at the following rates.

S.No.	*Type of Animal*	*Rate of Premium*	
		For Death Cover	*Additional Rate for permanent total disability and from yielding milk*
1.	Animals financed under Government Scheme	2.25%	0.85%
2.	Non-scheme Animals	4.00%	1.00%
3.	Exotic Animals	6.00%	1.00%

Minimum Premium of ₹ 50/- per policy is chargeable. Discounts are allowed in the case where full advance premium is paid under long-term policies and group policies. However, premium is loaded in case of adverse claim ratio.

Requirements: Veterinary examination and tagging of the animals is necessary for granting insurance cover. Natural identification marks and colour should be clearly noted in the proposal form along with the veterinarian's report.

Indian economy is based on agriculture and about 75% of the population still depend on agriculture, dairy farming and agro-based small-scale industry. Sound agricultural base can only lead to economic stability. Hence, farmers have to be adequately protected against the various hazards. It is for this reason GIC has introduced various rural insurance schemes not only to offer financial protection to rural masses but also to fulfil the social objective of their upliftment. Chief among such schemes is the cattle insurance policy whereby the livelihood of the farmer is protected against accidental causes. Thus, this cover attains utmost importance amongst rural insurance policies.

Failed Well Insurance

Suitability: Wells financed by Co-operative societies, financial institutions, banks, Government sponsored schemes can be covered under this policy against the risk of low or no yield provided the selection of site is made on scientific principles and methods.

Salient Features: The well sites located in areas mapped by state geological departments having potential for borewells for yields upto 1000 gallons per hour are covered by this policy. Yield will be tested by pumping intermittently for 6 hours by a 2HP/3HP submersible pump.

If the yield is below 500 gallons, the well shall be deemed to be a total failure.

If the yield is between 500 to 1000 GPH, policy pays for the proportion the actual yield bears to assured yield.

Following types of wells are covered under this policy:

- Shallow tube wells
- Filter point wells
- Dry wells
- Borewells
- Dug-cum-borewells

Benefits: Drilling cost at ₹ 160 per metre upto a depth of 80-90 metres is payable subject to a limit of ₹ 15,000 per borewell. The following costs are included.

Transportation of equipment upto ₹ 350/-; Yield testing charges upto ₹ 500/-; Spot investigation charges upto ₹ 250; Labour charges for fixing casing pipe; cleaning and dewatering charges.

However, the following are excluded:

- Expenses incurred but not specifically covered.
- Natural calamities, riot and strike, quality of water, structural failure cessation of work, wilful act and negligence, defective design and material, bad workmanship, war and allied perils. Policy is subject to an excess of 17.5% of claim amount.

Premium: Rate of premium is 17.5% of sum insured.

Requirements: The proposal shall be accompanied by site selection report obtained from qualified geo-hydrologist approved by the insurers. The test is to be based on geophysical methods only, such as electrical relativity logging, vertical sounding etc., taking into account at least 250 m between two wells. The permission from local Municipal authority for digging the well and signature of bank wherever applicable shall be obtained. Open wells shall have a minimum diameter of 10 ft and depth of 30 ft. Borewells shall have a diameter of 6 inches and installed upto hard rock zone and properly sealed. Wells should be rested for 24 hours before testing.

It is not rare that despite the scientific exploration, yield in the wells may not match the guaranteed yield. It is in such a situation, this insurance comes to the rescue of the well owner. Thus, this cover is recommended.

Farmers' Package Insurance

Suitability: This policy is suitable for the farmers who wish to cover all their property and assets under a single package policy. The Policy can be issued either to individual farmers or a group.

Salient Features: Personal effects, household goods, village/cottage industrial units belonging to the farmer are covered under this insurance.

This Policy has 14 Sections offering coverage as follows:

Section 1: Covers the residential building of the farmer including contents and farm produce kept in the building from fire and allied perils.

Section 2: Covers the loss or damage to stock of farm produce from fire and allied perils. Stocks in godown and in open are covered.

Section 3: Covers all the contents in the premises against burglary, housebreaking and terrorist acts.

Section 4: Covers loss or damage to TV/VCP/VCR of the insured due to fire/burglary/theft, electrical or mechanical breakdown of accidental external means.

Section 5: The policy covers loss or damage to pedal cycle by accident, burglary, house-breaking, or fire.

Section 6: Covers the insured and his family against personal accident and death due to accidental reasons.

Section 7: Provides fire cover to artisans, tiny sector units, village and cottage industries.

Section 8: Cover death of animals due to diseases or accident including fire/lightning/famine.

Section 9: Covers agricultural pumpset upto 10 HP capacity from the risks of fire/theft/burglary and breakdown risks.

Section 10: Covers over 500 poultry birds in the farm located within the insured premises due to any accident.

Section 11: Covers fraud committed by any salaried employee of the insured in the premises.

Section 12: Covers accompanied baggage lost or damaged during travel anywhere in India.

Section 13: Covers animal drawn vehicle from risks of damage to the vehicle, personal accident, third party liability from accidental causes. The policy also covers the life of the driver.

Section 14: Covers loss or damage to agricultural tractors and its accessories due to accidental reasons. Unnamed passengers (upto 6) travelling on such tractors are covered.

Benefits: Policy offers compensation as per limits of liability/as per sum insured set against each section.

Premium: Rates of premium are fixed for individual sections. If more than 4 sections are covered, upto 15% discount is available. When more than 6 sections are covered, upto 20% discount is allowed.

This policy has been introduced keeping the needs of the rural farmer in view. As this policy provides a comprehensive cover against all the risks which can be envisaged and also eliminates the need to take various policies to cover different risks, the policy is extremely beneficial, economical and thus recommended.

Fish Insurance

Suitability: This policy is devised for fresh water fish rearers to cover stock of fry/fingerlings/fish/breeders of breeds like Rohu, Katla, Mrigal, Common Carp, Silver Carp or any other recognised breeds.

Salient Features: The policy covers total loss to the fish due to accident or disease during the period of insurance. The cover includes loss due to pollution, poisoning, malicious act by third parties, riot and strike. Partial loss of any kind is not covered.

Flood and allied risks are covered as an extension on payment of extra premium.

The policy can also be extended to cover the fish rearing pond, bunds, sluices etc. against fire and natural calamities on payment of additional premium.

Policy is issued for the rearing period subject to a maximum period of 12 months from the date of stocking.

Benefits: Since the value of fish increases due to growth and inputs, settlement of any loss will be effected as per the scheduled valuation fixed on fortnightly basis (the table of valuation will be attached to the policy). The value depends on the cost of fry/fingerlings, cost of input and other incidental expenses.

Premium: Insurance has to be effected on the sum insured of final stage of rearing period (Peak value). Premium will be charged @ 2.4% on the peak value. Flood perils are covered by charging 1% extra in non-flood prone areas and 2% in case of flood prone areas. Fish rearing ponds can be covered @ 0.5% of the value of ponds in non-flood prone area and 1% in flood prone areas.

Requirements: The proposal form should be duly completed and certified by the Government fishery official. If the pond is subsidised by Bank/FFDA, a copy of the techno-economic feasibility report is to be provided for deciding the sum insured/peak value/input cost for the items stated in the declaration sheet. Specimen copies of daily fish culture records are to be submitted. For flood cover to bunds, a certificate from Government fishery extension officer regarding construction and viability of bunds is to be provided.

Even though the fish farming is lucrative, offers high yields and profits, the experience during the recent years has been especially bad both for the farmers as well as the insurance companies. Insurance companies therefore adopt strict underwriting practices and compliance of warranties to minimise losses and also extend their technical assistance, which explains why it makes good sense in taking this insurance.

Floriculture Insurance

Suitability: Growers of commercial flowering plants such as rose, crysanthemum and jasmine having adequate agricultural expertise in the subject may take out this policy.

Salient Features: This policy covers only plants whilst growing in the farm/greenhouse/poly-house against total loss or damage due to:

- Fire including forest fire and bush fire
- Lightning
- Acts of terrorism, riot and strike
- Storm, hailstorm, cyclone, flood and inundation
- Earthquake
- Impact damage by rail/road/air vehicles and animals.

Additional Covers: Policy may be extended to cover risks of loss due to drought, pests, and diseases specific to flowering plants.

Benefits: The Policy covers the input costs incurred till the time of loss. These are the recurring expenses incurred to raise/maintain the plants such as soil preparation, fertilizer, manure, cost of plants/seeds/saplings, cost of planting/sowing and pruning, pesticides, insecticides, irrigation, labour charges and other costs specifically covered. Claims exceeding 50% of the total sum insured per hectare or ₹ 1,000/- whichever is less only shall be admitted. Each and every claim is subject to an excess of 20%.

Premium: Premium is charged on the sum insured opted as follows:

Risk Cover	*Rate*
Basic cover	1.25%-2.5%
Under glasshouse/GreenHouse in open field	
Additional Cover (Pests/diseases and drought)	
Under glasshouse/Greenhouse in open field	0.75%-1.5%

Requirements: At the time of taking out insurance, the plants should be at least one month old after plantation/transplantation, i.e., the plants should be well established in the soil. Insurance cover will be granted subject to pre-acceptance inspection by insurers and feasibility report from State Agricultural Directorate/Expert's opinion being received.

Floriculture requires constant supervision and maintenance. Despite all the precautions, the plants are exposed to risks from pests and unknown diseases or action of natural calamities. It is for this reason, coverage of the plantation under this policy is strongly recommended.

Lift Irrigation/Sprinkler Insurance

Suitability: This policy is suitable for the agriculturist using the lift irrigation or sprinkler installation for cultivation.

Salient Features: This policy covers loss or damage to intake well, delivery chambers, jackwell, pump-house, water storage tank, pipelines, cables, starters and motors of the lift irrigation system or sprinkler installation arising out of:

- Fire and allied perils
- Flood, earthquake and landslide
- Accidental damage to machinery and pipeline
- Bursting of pipelines
- Theft

Benefits: On the occurrence of a loss, claims will be paid for the cost of restoration to the extent of sum insured set against each item.

An excess of 1% the machinery value subject to a minimum of ₹ 1000/- per claim is applicable. Theft claims are paid on receipt of non-traceable certificate from the police.

Premium: A rate of 1% on the cost of the entire system is applicable for insurance under this policy. The sum insured shall be the new replacement cost including freight, customs duty and erection costs. Terrorist risk can be included in the cover at an extra premium.

Requirements: Duly filed in proposal giving the details of the machinery and their individual replacement costs should be submitted.

Loss due to breakdown, theft or accidental reasons to the machinery not only is a loss in itself, but also has consequential effect that the crop is affected. It is necessary that the system is repaired/reinstated to mitigate the losses. This policy comes to aid in such situations and is therefore recommended.

Plantation/Horticulture Insurance

Suitability: This policy is suitable for individual farmer-owner or tenant engaged in cultivation of horticultural trees or plantations or an association/organized and registered body of farmers engaged in cultivation of specified crops. Also bodies procuring inputs, processing/marketing of the produce can take this policy.

Salient Features: Horticultural trees/orchards such as citrus fruits (Orange, Lime, Sweet Lime), Grapes, Chikoo, Pomegranate, Banana and Plantations such as Rubber, Eucalyptus, Poplar,

Sugarcane, Betelvine, Cardamom, Sweet Chilli, Oil Palm, Teakwood, Strawberry, Tea, Apple and Coconut can be covered by this policy. The Policy covers loss or damage due to fire (including forest and bush fire), lightning, storm, hailstorm, cyclone and other such natural calamities/acts of terrorist to fruits in respect of horticultural crops.

Tree in Case of Plantations

Additional Covers: Unseasonal rains and frost in case of grapevines and tea, loss or damage by wild animals in case of sugarcane, banana; drought and disease in case of banana, flood and inundation in case of teak plantations; disease and pests in case of tea plantations and betelvine are the additional covers available.

Benefits: Claims are paid to the extent of 80% of the assessed loss subject to the overall limit of the sum insured. Sum insured shall be based on the cost of cultivation, i.e., input cost or cost of raising/development of trees. Only such claims exceeding 10% of sum insured per acre or minimum of ₹ 1000/- shall be admitted. Input costs on account of loss or damage to the horticultural crop/plantations are covered. Loss of yield is not covered.

Premium: Premium shall be charged for different crops as follows:

	Type of Crop	*Rate*
1.	Horticultural Crops	5.0%
	*Citrus fruits, Chikoo, Pomegranate, Banana, Grapes	
2.	Plantations	1.25%
	* Rubber, Eucalyptus, Poplar, Teakwood, Tea, Mango	
3.	Sugarcane	1.25%
4.	Betelvine	6.0%
5.	Sweet Chilli (Capsicum)	4.4%
6.	Coconut	
	3 months to 3 years	0.60
	4 years to 7 years	0.50
	8 years and upto 50 years	1.50%

Requirements: Intercropping may be done only if it does not interfere with normal growth and health of the trees. No smoking or cooking shall be allowed in the open fields and within 30 m of the property insured. Dry vegetation and leaves should be removed periodically.

Recommendations: Plantations are exposed to a variety of perils ranging from pests to forest fires. It becomes very difficult for the farmer to come out of the effects of loss in the absence of comprehensive insurance cover. It is for this reason, this insurance policy is devised which is very popular and hence recommended.

Poultry Insurance

Suitability: This policy is suitable for the poultry farmers, the beneficiaries of schemes sponsored by DRDA, DPAP, IRDP and financial institutions providing assistance to poultry units.

Salient Features: This comprehensive policy is issued to cover poultry consisting of Broiler chicks/Layer chickens/cocks and hens in the poultry farms. A minimum number of 100 broilers/500 layers or 200 birds per batch in the hatchery can be covered under the policy.

The policy provides compensation for loss to birds dead due to accident (including fire, lightning, flood, cyclone, earthquake, riot, strike, and terrorist act); diseases contacted or occurring during the period of insurance.

Benefits: Policy provides compensation when the mortality rate of the birds exceeds the following limits.

Bird	*Age*	*Mortality Rate*
Broilers	1 day to 6 weeks	More than 5% of the batch size
Layers	1 day to 8 weeks	More than 5% of the batch size
	9th week to 20th week	More than 3% of numbers at beginning of 9th week
	21st week to 72nd week	More than 1% of numbers at the beginning of 21st week.

In the event of death of birds, 80% of the bird value or as decided by the veterinary surgeon whichever is less is paid. There is an additional deductible of 20% in case of Gumbore disease.

Requirements: A Certificate from a qualified veterinarian is required. In case of layer farms having more than 5000 birds, insurance company's veterinary officer or panel doctor shall carry out inspection. All the birds in the farm should be insured. Standard practices of poultry rearing, record keeping shall have to be practised.

Outbreak of epidemics/natural calamities such as cyclone result in widespread loss to the poultry affecting the financial position of the poultry owner. The policy comes handy in such a situation and benefits the farmer.

National Agricultural Insurance Scheme (NAIS)

Premium: Premium rates depend on the age of the bird; whether or not they are financed under IRDP scheme as follows:

Bird	*Age*	*Premium for IRDP Scheme*	*Rate Non-IRDP Scheme*
Broilers	1 day to 8 weeks	0.25% per bird/batch	1.5% (6.0% p.a.)
	1 day to 6 weeks	1.00% per bird p.a.	1.2% (4.8% p.a.)
Layers	1 day to 20 weeks	—	3.2%
	21 weeks to 72 weeks		3.5%
	1 day to 72 weeks	0.8% per bird	5.5%
Parent stock (hatchery)	— —	5.0%	

(Rashtriya Krishi Bima Yojana - RKBY) – Coverage and Claims Settlement

The objectives of the NAIS are:

1. To provide insurance coverage and financial support to the farmers in the event of failure of any of the notified crop as a result of natural calamities, pests and diseases.
2. To encourage the farmers to adopt progressive farming practices, high value inputs and higher technology in Agriculture.
3. To help stabilize farm incomes, particularly in disaster years.

NAIS covers all farmers including sharecroppers, tenant farmers growing the notified crops in the notified areas are eligible for coverage. The Scheme covers following groups of farmers:

(a) ***On a compulsory basis***:All farmers growing notified crops and availing Seasonal Agricultural Operations (SAO) loans from Financial Institutions, i.e., Loanee Farmers.

(b) ***On a voluntary basis***: All other farmers growing notified crops (i.e., Non-loanee farmers) who opt for the Scheme.

The cover extend to yield losses due to non preventable risks, viz.:

(a) Natural Fire and Lightning

(b) Storm, Hailstorm, Cyclone, Typhoon, Tempest, Hurricane, Tornado etc.

(c) Flood, Inundation and Landslide

(d) Drought, Dry spells

(e) Pests/Diseases etc.

Losses arising out of war and nuclear risks, malicious damage and other preventable risks are excluded. There are three levels of Indemnity, viz., 90%, 80% and 60% corresponding to Low Risk, Medium Risk and High Risk areas available for all crops (cereals, millets, pulses and oilseeds and annual commercial/annual horticultural crops) based on Coefficient of Variation (CV) in yield of past 10 years' data. However, the insured farmers of unit area may opt for higher level of indemnity on payment of additional premium based on actuarial rates. The Threshold yield (TY) or Guaranteed yield for a crop in an Insurance Unit is the moving average based on past three years Average Yield in case of Rice and Wheat and five years Average Yield in case of other crops, multiplied by the level of indemnity.

Calculation of Coverage and Indemnity

If the 'Actual Yield' (AY) per hectare of the insured crop for the defined area [on the basis of requisite number of Crop Cutting Experiments (CCEs)] in the insured season, falls short of the specified 'Threshold Yield' (TY), all the insured farmers growing that crop in the defined area are deemed to have suffered shortfall in their yield. The Scheme seeks to provide coverage against such contingency. 'Indemnity' is calculated as per the following formula:

$$\frac{\text{Shortfall in Yield}}{\text{Threshold yield}} \times \text{Sum Insured for the farmer}$$

{Shortfall in Yield = 'Threshold Yield – Actual Yield' for the Defined Area}.

GIC is the implementing agency (IA) of the scheme. Loss assessment and modified indemnity procedures in case of occurrence of localized perils, such as hailstorm, landslide, cyclone and flood where settlement of claims is on individual basis, shall be formulated by IA in coordination with State/UT Govt. The loss assessment of localized risks on individual basis will be experimented in limited areas initially and shall be extended in the light of operational experience gained. The District Revenue administration will assist IA in assessing the extent of loss. The A&O expenses are shared equally by the Central Government and respective State Government on sunset basis [100% in 1st year, 80% in 2nd year, 60% in 3rd year, 40% in 4th year, 20% in 5th year and 'zero' thereafter].

Procedure for Approval and Settlement of Claims

The claims are dependent upon the yield data supplied by the states. Once the Yield Data is received from the State/UT Govt. as per the prescribed cut-off dates, claims are estimated and settled by the insurers. The claim cheques along with claim particulars are released to the individual Nodal Banks. The Banks at the grass-root level, in turn, credit the accounts of the individual farmers and display the particulars of beneficiaries on their notice board. In the context of localised phenomenon, viz., hailstorm, landslide, cyclone and flood, the IA prescribes the procedure to estimate such losses at individual farmer level in consultation with DAC/State/UT. Settlement of such claims is on individual basis between IA and insured.

To meet catastrophic losses, a Corpus Fund has been created with contributions from the Government of India and State/UT on 50:50 basis. A portion of Calamity Relief Fund (CRF) shall be used for contribution to the Corpus Fund. The Corpus Fund is managed by Implementing Agency (IA).

Selection of the Banks for claims payment has been made on the basis of Service Area Approach (SAA) of RBI or at the option of the Banks (where Co-operative Banks have good network). The Department of Agriculture, Agricultural Statistics, Directorate of Economics and Statistics, Department of Co-operation, Revenue Department of the State Government will be actively involved in smooth implementation of the Scheme.

Cattle Insurance

Cattle insurance covers indigenous cross-bred and exotic cattle owned by private owners and financial institutions, i.e., Bank financed, Military dairy farms, Co-op Dairies, Corporate dairies. The cover extends to death of cattle due to accident inclusive of flood, cyclone, famine or any other fortuitous circumstances, diseases, surgical operations, riot and strike, terrorism, earthquake. In case of transit beyond specified distance by Road or by Rail, additional premium has to be paid by the insured. The cover excludes losses due to malicious act, accident/diseases contracted prior to commencement of risk, transit by air or sea, intentional slaughter, theft or clandestine sales, missing of insured animals, war and allied perils, nuclear exclusion clause.

This policy covers the animals like cows, buffaloes, bullocks, camels, sheep, goats, horses, ponies, mules etc. Identification of animals and valuation is as per the veterinary certificate and or declaration of the purchase committee. Claims for cattle insurance are generally settled for the sum insured or market value prior to illness, whichever is less. In case of PTD of animals, the claim will be restricted to 75% of the sum insured. In order to claim, notice must be given to the insurance company with prescribed time.

Documents to be submitted at the time of the claim:

(1) Identity proof of the cattle exposed to adverse events

(2) Veterinary Doctor Certificate

(3) Claim form duly filled

Ordinarily the claims must be settled within 15 days from the lodgment and completion of formalities. Recently, the companies are using RFID tags to prevent fraudulent claims.

Livestock Insurance Scheme

The Livestock Insurance Scheme has been formulated with the twin objectives of providing protection mechanism to the farmers and cattle rearers against any eventual loss of their animals due to death and to demonstrate the benefit of the insurance of livestock to the people and popularize it with the ultimate goal of attaining qualitative improvement in livestock and their products.

Guidelines for Implementation of Livestock Insurance Scheme

1. Livestock Sector is an important sector of national, especially rural economy. The supplemental income derived from rearing of livestock is a great source of support to the farmers facing uncertainties of crop production, apart from providing sustenance to poor and landless farmers.
2. For promotion of the livestock sector, it has been felt that along with providing more effective for disease control and improvement of genetic quality of animals, a mechanism of assured protection to the farmers and cattle rearers needs to be devised against eventual losses of such animals. In this direction, the Government has approved a new centrally sponsored scheme on Livestock Insurance on pilot basis to be implemented during the 10th Plan. The continuance of the scheme beyond that will be based on a critical assessment of its performance during this period. The broad guidelines, subject to the plausible discretion of the Chief Executive Officers, to be followed by the States for implementing the scheme are detailed below:

Implementing Agency

3. Department of Animal Husbandry, Dairying & Fisheries is implementing the Centrally Sponsored Scheme of 'National Project for Cattle and Buffalo Breeding (NPCBB), with the objective of bringing about genetic upgradation of cattle and buffaloes by artificial insemination as well as acquisition of proven indigenous animals. NPCBB is implemented through State Implementing Agencies (SIAs) like State Livestock Development Boards. In order to bring about synergy between NPCBB and Livestock Insurance, the latter scheme will also be implemented through the SIAs. Almost all the states have opted for NPCBB. In states which are not implementing NPCBB or where there are no SIAs, the livestock insurance scheme will be implemented through the State Animal Husbandry Departments.

Executive Authority

4. The Chief Executive Officer of the State Livestock Development Board will also be the executive authority for this scheme. In those states where no such Boards are in place, the Director, Department of Animal Husbandry will be the Executive Authority of the scheme. The CEO will have to get the scheme implemented in various districts through the senior most officer of the Animal Husbandry Department in the district; the necessary instructions for this purpose will have to be issued by the State Government. The Central funds for premium subsidy, payment of honorarium to the Veterinary Practitioners, awareness creation through Panchayats etc. will be placed with the SIA. As Executive Authority of the scheme, the Chief Executive Officers will be responsible for execution, and monitoring of the scheme. The main functions of the CEO will be:

(*i*) Managing the Central funds carefully and in accordance with instructions issued by the Department of Animal Husbandry, Dairying and Fisheries, Government of India.

(*ii*) Calling quotations from the insurance companies for implementing the scheme, carrying out negotiations with them and selecting suitable company (companies).

(*iii*) Signing the contract with the selected insurance company/companies.

(*iv*) Payment of subsidy premium to the Insurance Company (including advance, if any and its subsequent adjustment).

(*v*) Preparing districtwise list of veterinary practitioners (Government/Private) and providing the same to the insurance company and also to concerned Panchayati Raj bodies.

(*vi*) Creating awareness among the general public as well as the officials whose services may be required for implementation of the scheme;

(*vii*) Carrying out field inspections and also facilitating field inspections by Central teams;

(*viii*) Release of funds to the District Officers in charge of the Department of Animal Husbandry for payment of honorarium to the Veterinary Practitioners.

(*ix*) Regular monitoring and preparation of reports for submission to the Central/State Governments.

(*x*) Such other functions necessarily required for efficient implementation of the scheme.

The Principal Secretary/Secretary in-charge Animal Husbandry of the State Governments/Director of State Animal Husbandry Department will ensure availability of sufficient infrastructure in terms of manpower and other logistic support to the CEO/District level officer, needed for effective implementation of the scheme. (The exact name, designation, address of CEO/District Officer in-charge for Insurance work will be made available to Central Government and same will be prominently displayed on important places within the district and especially in the rural areas of the district. Any change in the name and designation of CEO will also be properly communicated to all concerned.) For effective implementation and monitoring of the scheme, if states feel necessity, a district committee could be formed suitably involving the officers/organizations having interest in the field of Animal Husbandry. The Dairy Co-operative Societies, if interested, could also be involved and given responsibility of implementing the scheme wherever possible.

Districts in which the scheme will be implemented

5. The scheme is to be implemented during 2005-06 and 2006-07 on pilot basis in 100 selected districts. During its pilot stage, the scheme will be restricted to cross-breed and high yielding cattle and buffaloes only. The list of districts selected for this purpose based on the population of female cross-breed and high yielding cattle and of buffaloes as per 17th livestock census as the main criterion is given in Annexure-I. The scheme is to be implemented in these districts only.

Selection of Insurance Companies

6. In order to get the maximum benefit in terms of competitive premium rates, easier procedures of issue of policy and settlement of claims, Chief Executive Officer will be empowered to decide upon the Insurance company(s) and the terms and conditions. While selecting Insurance Company, besides premium rates offered, their capacity to provide services, terms and conditions and service efficiency should also be taken in to account. The CEO will invite quotations in writing from those public and private general insurance companies having a fairly wide network in the state or a considerable part of the state. The CEO should select the Insurance Company/Companies after negotiating with the insurance companies for successful and efficient implementation of the scheme and popularizing the scheme amongst the livestock owners. If any Insurance Company is offering cover for any type of disability in addition to death of the insured animal, such offer could be considered, however, no subsidy in the premium for such additional risk coverage will be provided. The entire cost of premium on account of the risk coverage other than death of the animal has to be borne by the beneficiaries. However, if any additional risk covers is offered as a package along with death cover and the premium rate is not exceeding the maximum limit of 4.5% for annual policies and 12% for three year policies, such offer could be accepted and subsidy could be provided. As mentioned above, the CEO has to ensure that the premium rate agreed to is competitive. Under no circumstances, the rate of premium should exceed 4.5% for annual policies and 12% for three year policies. Normally, a single insurance company should be entrusted for insurance with the work in a district. However, for the purposes of encouraging competition and popularizing the scheme more than one insurance company may be allowed to operate in a district, if other terms and conditions are remaining same. Default in settlement of claim or any types of deficiency in services on part of Insurance Companies could be brought to the notice of the Insurance Regulatory and Development Authority which is a nodal authority in the country in this regard.

Involvement of Veterinary Practitioners

7. The active involvement of the veterinary practitioners at the village level is required for the successful implementation of the scheme. They are to be associated with the work of identification and examination of the animals to be covered under the scheme, determination of their market price, tagging of the insured animals and finally issuing veterinary certificates as and when a claim is made. Besides, being in touch with the farmers and cattle-rearers, they may also help in promoting and popularizing the scheme. As far as possible, only the veterinary practitioners working with the state government may be involved. Private veterinary practitioners may be involved only if Government veterinary practitioners are not available. A list of such veterinary practitioners will be prepared for every district by the district officer of the Department of Animal Husbandry. The list of veterinary practitioners will be made available with the insurance company selected for the district as well as to the concerned Panchayati Raj bodies.

Commencement of Insurance Policy Cover and Adjustment of Premium Subsidy

8. In order to generate confidence among the cattle owners about the efficacy of the scheme, it is important that the policy cover should take effect once the basic formalities

like identification of animal, its examination by the veterinary practitioner, assessment of its value and its tagging along with payment of 50% of the premium to the insurance company or its agent by the cattle owner. The selected insurance company will have to agree to this. However, it is possible that the insurance company may point out a provision in the Insurance Act that insurance cover can take effect only after the whole premium is paid in advance. In order to take care of this problem, there could be an arrangement by which certain amount is paid in advance to the insurance company directly by the CEO. This amount should not exceed 50% of the premium of the number of animals expected to be insured in a period of 3 months. The insurance company, on its part, should issue instructions to their branches that as and when 50% of the premium is paid by the cattle owner, they should issue the policy by suitably adjusting the balance 50% from this advance. The insurance company should prepare monthly statements of the policies issued indicating the assessed value of each animal and the Government share for each district duly countersigned by the district officer of the Animal Husbandry Department and submit to the CEO so that, that much amount can be recouped to the insurance company by the CEO. Target of getting the number of animals insured in a three months' period for payment of advance to the Insurance Company should be on realistic basis and recouping of the advance fund should be on the basis of subsequent progress made by the concerned insurance Company. As the scheme in its present form will not continue beyond 31st March, 2007, the CEO should, as far as possible, ensure that no advance is outstanding with the insurance company beyond that period. In any case, if any such amount remains outstanding, the insurance company should be asked to pay the same forthwith in the first week of April, 2007. This should be suitably incorporated in the agreement to be executed with the insurance company.

Animals to be Covered under the Scheme and Selection of Beneficiaries

9. All those female cattle/buffalo yielding at least 1500 litre of milk per lactation are to be considered high yielding and hence can be insured under the scheme for maximum of their current market value. Animals covered under any other insurance scheme/plan scheme will not be covered under this scheme. Benefit of subsidy is to be restricted to two animals per beneficiary and is to be given for one time insurance of an animal up to a maximum period of three years. The farmers will have to be encouraged to go for a three-year policy which is likely to be more economical and useful for getting the real benefit of insurance on occurrence of natural calamities like flood and drought etc. However, if a livestock owner prefers to have an insurance policy for less than three years period for valid reasons, benefit of the subsidy under the scheme would be available to them also, with the restriction that no subsidy would be available for further extension of the policy. Field performance recording of the NPCBB could also be involved for identification of beneficiaries. The Gram Panchayats will assist the Insurance Companies in identifying the beneficiaries.

Determination of Market Price of the Animal

10. An animal will be insured for the maximum of its current market price. The market price of the animal to be insured will be assessed jointly by the beneficiary, authorized veterinary practitioner and the insurance agent.

Identification of Insured Animal

11. The animal insured will have to be properly and uniquely identified at the time of insurance claim. The ear tagging should, therefore, be foolproof as far as possible. The traditional method of ear tagging or the recent technology of fixing microchips could be used at the time of taking the policy. The cost of fixing the identification mark will be borne by the Insurance companies and responsibility of its maintenance will lie on the concerned beneficiaries. The nature and quality of tagging materials will be mutually agreed by the beneficiaries and the Insurance Company. The Veterinary Practitioners may guide the beneficiaries about the need and importance of the tags fixed for settlement of their claim so that they take proper care for maintenance of the tags.

Change of Owner During the Validity Period of Insurance

12. In case of sale of the animal or otherwise transfer of animal from one owner to other, before expiry of the Insurance Policy, the authority of beneficiary for the remaining period of policy will have to be transferred to the new owner. The modalities for transfer of livestock policy and fees and sale deed etc. required for transfer, should be decided while entering into contract with the insurance company.

Settlement of Claims

13. The method of settlement of claim should be very simple and expeditious to avoid unnecessary hardship to the insured. While entering into contract with the insurance company, the procedure to be adopted/documents needed for settlement of claim should be clearly spelt out. In case of claim becoming due, the payment of insured amount should be made within 15 days positively after submission of requisite documents. While insuring the animal, CEOs must ensure that clear cut procedures are put in place for settlement of claims and the required documents are listed and the same is made available to concerned beneficiaries along with the policy documents.

Effective Monitoring of the Scheme

14. The present scheme is a pilot scheme only. The continuance of the scheme during XI plan will be considered after critical review of the scheme during pilot stage. In view of this, there is need of strict monitoring at different stages. The monitoring should be in terms of financial releases, number of animals insured and type of insurance. Monitoring at the Central and State levels is extremely important. CEO will be required to make special efforts for effective monitoring. Secretary in-charge Animal Husbandry in State Government/Director of state animal Husbandry will take periodic review of the implementation of the scheme.

Payment of Honorarium to the Veterinary Practitioners

15. The involvement of veterinary officer in the scheme is from beginning to end. His active interest and support is essential for success of the scheme. In view of this it is essential to provide some incentive to the veterinary practitioners to motivate them to carry out these activities wholeheartedly. It has been decided to pay an honorarium of ₹ 50/- per animal at the stage of insuring the animal and ₹ 100/- per animal at the stage of issuing

veterinary certificate (including conducting post-mortem, if any) in case of any insurance claim. Central Government will provide the amount needed for payment of honorarium to the SIAs. The CEOs should ensure that Boards will pay to Veterinary Practitioners at end of each quarter depending on number of animals insured and veterinary certificates issued by them in that quarter.

Publicity

16. The scheme is new and people inclusive of the concerned officials are not much aware of the scheme. Therefore, public as well as the machinery involved in this have to be made aware of the scheme and benefits thereof. Pamphlets, posters, wall paintings, radio talks, TV clippings etc. will help in creating awareness among the farmers about the benefits of insuring their high yielding animals under the scheme. Publicity campaigns on special occasions like animal fairs etc. will also be taken up for wide publicity. The Panchayati Raj institutions will be involved in publicity in a big way. The task of disseminating information on the scheme and inviting farmers to offer their animals for identification for insurance will be entrusted to the Intermediate Panchayats. For this purpose, the CEOs are empowered to provide assistance not exceeding ₹ 5000/- for each intermediate Panchayat (in both cash and in the form of publicity material).

Commission to Insurance Agents

The active and dedicated involvement of insurance agent is most essential for efficient implementation of the scheme. The insurance company should be persuaded to pay at least 15% of the premium amount to the agent out of their premium income. While entering into contract with the Insurance Company, this has to be ensured by the implementing agency.

19.4 What is Social Insurance?

The government on a compulsory basis generally provides social insurance. It is not easy to precisely define because the government can use the power and resources to apply the insurance method or modification of it in a variety of ways. In the developed countries like US, there has been a tendency to look first to the private insurance industry for the coverage of risk that society deem important. When such risks have not been handled adequately by private insurance, social insurance programme comes into picture.

19.5 Characteristics and Need for Social Insurance

The main characteristics of social insurance are:

- Social insurance is based on the law, rather than on contract. Cost and benefit are established by and can be changed by government.
- Hence, coverage is compulsory for all persons to whom the law applies. They cannot choose to decline to participate, nor can they select the coverage or the amount of the benefits.
- The objective is to provide some minimum level of economic security for the large portion of the population. The basic ideology is to provide an economic system that stresses free

enterprise and individual initiative, people should not rely entirely upon government programs.

- The focus of social insurance is to provide maximum benefits to the lower income groups. Unless lower income groups are subsidized to high income groups, the payments of the former will not be large enough to furnish the minimum level of protection that are desired.
- Social insurance usually covers only those who are or who have been employed. Most social insurance plans are concerned for interruption of income (by death, unemployment or retirement) earned through employment.

19.6 Legal Framework for Social Insurance

The Insurance Regulatory and Development Authority Act, 1999 (para 19; First schedule) has amended the Sections 32B and 32C of the Insurance Act, 1938 as under:

Section 32B

Every insurer shall, after the commencement of Insurance Regulatory and Development Authority Act, 1999, undertake such percentages of life insurance business and general insurance business in the rural and social sector, as may be specified, in the Official Gazette by the authority, in this behalf.

Section 32C

Every insurer shall, after the commencement of Insurance Regulatory and Development Authority Act, 1999, discharge the obligations specified under Section 32B to provide life insurance or general insurance policies to those residing in the rural sector, workers in the unorganised sector or informal sector or economically vulnerable or backward classes of the society and other categories of persons as may be specified by the regulations made by the authority and such insurance policies shall include insurance for crops.

The IRDA Regulations 2000 makes it compulsory for the insurers, existing and new to promote the social insurance.[1] Similar to the requirement for the rural sector, the regulations also prescribe for undertaking benchmark percentages for insurances in the social insurance sector for the players.

The *social sector* is defined as including the unorganized sector, the informal sector, the economically vulnerable or backward classes and other categories of persons, both in rural and urban areas.

In case of social sector the requirement is compulsory underwriting of 5000 lives in the first financial year, 7,500 in the second year and so on. Also, the authority may revise the obligation once in 5 years.

19.7 Social Insurance in India

Social insurance is the baby of the social security systems prevailing in that country. Social security is the security cover which society furnishes through appropriate organization against risks to which its members are exposed. The basic idea is to use social means to prevent deprivation and vulnerability to deprivation.

In the literature on development issues, it has often been assumed explicitly or implicitly that developing countries are too poor to be able to *afford* social security systems. Public participation in social security systems can take wide variety of forms and it is very much possible even for poor countries to achieve considerable success on this front. This is not to say that economic growth and social security are not linked. However at the same time, simple economic growth alone cannot ensure improvements in living standards of people. Social intervention is necessary for improving quality of life at the micro level.

Studies carried out by UNICEF and World Bank also provide considerable evidence that it has been the direct public support rather than the average income of the population that has been the driving force behind the success of social security schemes worldwide. In fact, the countries with good primary social security systems are those which have adopted the path of support-led security (as against growth-led security) and have *not waited* to grow rich before resorting to large-scale public support to guarantee certain basic capabilities. Notable examples include China, Chile, Cuba, Jamaica and Kuwait.

Need for a Social Security System in India

A large chunk of Indian population lives under abject poverty. They barely manage to earn enough to eat. It is our social obligation to provide our underprivileged brethren with an adequate safety cover.

Only a very small percentage of the working population is employed by the organised sector, which provides benefits like the state pension. A vast majority is either self-employed or employed in the rural and unorganized sector. As a result, they are deprived of social benefits such as retirement benefits and disability or death compensation. Similarly, health care although subsidised is thinly and haphazardly spread. State support for the unemployed and disabled is negligible.

Social changes taking place in the country are also resulting into increased need for a social security system. The Joint Family System, which prevailed in India for long is losing its flavour. This system provided a natural safety cover to the members of a family. However, its break-up into nuclear families means that the death or disability of the bread-earner leaves his dependants completely exposed.

A comprehensive social security system includes social insurance, health insurance, disability compensation, unemployment compensation, old-age pension schemes, etc. In India, social security systems are an emerging concept and there is no strong base to start with. Given the constraints on funds and infrastructure availability, social insurance is the only scheme that can be launched at present. Further, opening up of the insurance sector has created increased awareness about insurance and also provides a sustainable revenue model to carry out the task of social insurance.

India — A Special Case

India is a special case compared to many other countries for the implementation of social insurance schemes. A support-led social security system is one that requires active state intervention. The main source of funds provided by the state comes from the taxes it collects. Unfortunately, India has a tiny tax-paying base. Further, social insurance is not a constitutional right of the citizens in India. The cause can again be traced to the fragile economic situation of the country that does not permit any kind of comprehensive social insurance schemes.

Social Insurance Schemes of GIC

GIC has launched certain social insurance covers like Krishi Bima Yojana, Personal Accident social security scheme, hut insurance scheme. However, the experience has been that most of these are failure in the sense these schemes failed to achieve the objectives for which these were floated. Similar is the case of LIC.

Social Insurance Schemes of LIC

Life Insurance Corporation of India (LIC) has taken the initiative and launched several social insurance schemes. Some of the schemes launched by LIC in the past are: Landless Agricultural Labourers Scheme, Group Insurance Scheme for beneficiaries of the Integrated Rural Development Program, Rural Group Life Insurance Schemes and the Krishi Shramik Samajik Suraksha Yojana (2001). Most of the social insurance schemes launched could not achieve their desired objective as a large chunk of the population covered under these schemes were not even aware of them. In August 2000, LIC launched the Janashree Bima Yojana as a single scheme to replace the older social insurance schemes. The objective of this scheme is to provide life insurance protection to the rural and urban poor living below the poverty line and marginally above the poverty line. This is a group insurance scheme and the minimum size of the group is 25. The annual premium is ₹ 200 per member per annum. The member/nodal agency/state government pays half the premium and the remaining half is borne out of the Social Security Fund. There are 40 occupational groups, which can be covered under Janashree Bima Yojana. They range from beedi workers and handloom tailors to construction workers and safai karmacharis.

Creation of a Separate Body for Social Insurance

The Central Government of India created the Social Security Fund in 1988. LIC was given the responsibility for managing the Fund. However, performance data for the past five years on the social insurance front is not encouraging.

Exhibit 19.1

Description	*1996-97*	*1997-98*	*1998-99*	*1999-00*	*2000-01*
Existing lives renewed	44,86,884	47,57,476	47,72,082	46,23,797	46,62,281
New Lives	4,48,143	2,62,456	1,28,158	3,26,190	74,610
Total	49,35,027	50,19,941	49,00,240	49,49,987	47,36,891

The number of new lives covered in the last one year is less than the number of people born in India in one day. Providing social insurance to all is a mammoth task and requires a set-up fully dedicated to this task. On the front of social insurance, various recommendations have been made by researchers extracts of which are follows:

- Cost minimization is a basic requirement on which any social security system is built. Instead of all the insurance companies complying with the social requirement (as imposed by IRDA) individually, it has been proposed that a common pool of funds be generated and channelled towards the same objective. This will prevent duplication of work and thereby reduce administrative and implementation costs.

- At the same time, with the entry of private insurance players in the country, it is all the more difficult for LIC to do justice to both — its commercial insurance business and meeting social obligations. The need for a separate body dedicated to social insurance is therefore obvious.
- The biggest concerns in implementation of social schemes are being able to reach the target population and cost-effectiveness. Therefore only group insurance can be introduced in such schemes. It is a time-tested fact that Government bodies have not been able to make inroads among the masses in a cost-effective manner. Further, given that India has a very narrow tax base and low tax revenue, work-based and community-based social insurance systems should be encouraged.
- Decentralization, i.e., participation of local people in administration and implementation of such schemes is essential. Therefore, it is necessary to have a nodal agency that can interact with people on behalf of the insurer and with the insurer on behalf of the group. The *introduction of a nodal agency* would also reduce the administrative overheads of the insurer thereby reducing overall cost. There arc several advantages of the use of a nodal agency for implementation of social life insurance schemes.
    - *(a)* Local level participation and ownership ensures that implementation would suit local requirements and hence there are higher chances of success.
    - *(b)* This structure combines advantages of centralized policy making with localized implementation.
    - *(c)* It effectively bypasses poor functioning of the public sector hierarchy.

However, these recommendations pertain only to the delegated authority and not devolved authority. The insurer will collect the premium directly from the nodal agency and the nodal agency will do the collection in parts or at one time from the group members.

Registered bodies like co-operatives, unions (such as taxi unions etc.), associations (such as fishermen associations), self-help groups and registered NGOs etc. are ideally suited to act as nodal agencies.

Co-operatives

As per statistics of the National Co-operative Union of India, there are 1.4 lakh primary agricultural co-operatives and 3.6 lakh primary non-credit co-operatives. The agricultural co-operatives cover 13.7 crore people whereas the non-credit co-operatives cover 6.4 crore people. In the present scenario, co-operatives fit very well to act as the nodal agency and offer immense potential for reaching out to the masses of India.

Associations

Associations are widely spread across the country in different occupational groups and hence provide a platform to tap the people associated with such associations.

Self-help Groups

Self-help Group is a concept utilized by NABARD to develop the habit of thrift saving among very poor people who are devoid of any sort of financial system. At present, their main function is to collect money in small instalments from members at regular intervals and form a common pool. It also provides credit to its members, when required. These groups are linked to the local bank either directly or through NGOs. Through NGOs, government bodies and banks, vast number of self-help groups have been established in the recent years. Fuelled by enthusiasm at all stakeholder levels, it has expanded rapidly throughout India, including marginal and tribal areas. In light of the above facts, Self-help Groups can also be used as nodal agencies.

Critical Success Factors in Selection of Nodal Agencies

- *High level of mutual trust*

  People should have faith in the nodal agency, especially when targeted people are less educated and are from the low-income group.

- *Monetary transactions*

  The existence of a monetary transaction is the single most critical operational factor for success. In the case where existing interactions between the individuals and the nodal agency involves monetary transactions, it becomes much easier to collect money efficiently and on time.

- *Frequency of interaction of nodal agency with the group*

  High frequency of interaction adds to mutual understanding between the individuals and the nodal agency.

- *Organizational structure of the nodal agency*

  The organizational structure of the nodal agency should be conducive to the implementation of social insurance schemes. The structure should ensure simplicity of the process for the individuals covered. The nodal agency's structure should also ensure the transparency of its operations. This would help in inspiring trust among the people.

- *Interests of the nodal agency*

  From the nodal agency's perspective, the implementation of any such scheme should be in line with its objectives. It has been observed that in case of most co-operatives, the primary intention was to help its members. However, some NGOs were looking for monetary incentives to cover their costs.

19.8 Unemployment Insurance

Unemployment Insurance is designed to provide short-term protection for regularly employed persons who lose their jobs and who are willing and able to work. Unemployment insurance has several basic objectives:

- Provide cash income during involuntary unemployment
- Help unemployed workers find jobs
- Encourage employers to stabilize employment
- Help stabilize economy.

Unemployment insurance is a popular concept in developed countries like US where they have well-defined laws and regulations. However, in India it will take a long time to come.

19.9 Salary Savings Scheme

Under this scheme, the premium is deducted from the salary of the employee at source and net is paid to him. The Employer to the insurer remits to the amount so collected. The Salary Savings Scheme can be introduced in an institution or establishment subject to specified terms and conditions.

The scheme is of great benefit to the insurer because the payments of the premium is assured, as long as the employee is in service and the procedures of accounting become simple because there is only one transaction for all the employees under one employer. The minimum number of members is 15 and there is no maximum limit. Since the payment of premium is consistent and guarrateed, the loading on monthly premiums is not charged in SSS policics. The SSS policies can be issued only after the employer has agreed to make deductions regularly from the salaries of the employees and remit the premiums to the insurer. The employee has to authorize the employer to deduct the premium from his salary and such authorisation letters are collected along with the proposal for insurance and are sent to the employer by the insurer.

Logically, there may be a gap between the time the policy is completed and the notice for pemium sent to the employer. Therefore, first two premiums are collected in advance.

Shiksha Sahayog Yojana

It is a scholarship scheme launched by LIC on 31.12.2001 for the benefit of children of members of Janashree Bima Yojana. It is for the students studying in IX to XII standards, whose parents are covered under Janashree Bima Yojana. If a student fails and is detained in the same standard, he will not be eligible for scholarship for the next year in the same standard.

Under this scheme, the scholarship of ₹ 300/- per quarter per child will be paid for maximum period of 4 years. The benefit is restricted to two children per member (family) only. No premium is charged for the scholarship. A Nodal Agency specified for the purpose, identifies the students. The member of Janashree Bima Yojana whose child is eligible for scholarship has to fill up an application form (available with Nodal Agency) and submit to the Nodal Agency. The applications duly filled up and certified will be sent along with the list of the beneficiary students by the Nodal Agency to the concerned LIC, P&GS Unit for disbursement of scholarship/s. The scholarship/s is disbursed to the beneficiary students through the concerned Nodal Agency. As only a limited number of beneficiaries will be provided scholarship under the scheme, the selection for eligible students will be made on the basis of poorest of the poor.

The scheme is administered through Pension and Group Schemes Department of LIC of India.

Janashree Bima Yojana

It was launched by LIC to provide life insurance protection to the rural and urban poor persons below poverty line and marginally above the poverty line in the age group of 18 to 58 years belonging to a member of any of the approved vocation/occupation groups, e.g., a government department which is concerned with the welfare of any such vocation/occupation group, a Welfare Fund/ Society, Village Panchayat, NGO, Self-help Group, etc. The minimum number of members is 25.

Key Terms

- ❒ Rural Banking
- ❒ Rural Insurance Covers
- ❒ Acqua Culture Insurance
- ❒ Cattle Insurance
- ❒ Failed Well Insurance
- ❒ Farmer's Package Insurance
- ❒ Floriculture Insurance
- ❒ Lift Insurance
- ❒ Horticulture Insurance
- ❒ Poultry Insurance
- ❒ Social Insurance Schemes
- ❒ Self-help Groups
- ❒ Unemployment Insurance
- ❒ Nodal Agency

Questions for Review

1. Briefly explain the various rural insurance covers available in India.
2. List the IRDA provisions on obligations of insurers to rural sectors.
3. Define social insurance and state its main features. List the various provisions of IRDA Regulation on social insurance.
4. Critically evaluate the state of social insurance scheme in India what steps can be taken to make them more effective?

Suggested Readings

1. N.K. Rustagi, *Crop Insurance in India — An Analysis,* B.R. Publishing Corporation, 1988.
2. K.N. Rao, *Crop Insurance: Past, Present and Future, An Article Published in Vision,* Journal published by MDI, Gurgaon, July-Dec. 2002.
3. Syed M. Ahsan, *Agricultural Insurance: A New Policy for Developing Countries,* Gower Publishing Co. Ltd., 1985.
4. Strategies for Rural Markets, Anabil Bhattacharya, *Insurance Time,* Kolkata, October 2002.
5. Irving Pfeffer and David R. Klock, *Perspectives on Insurance,* Prentice-Hall, Englewood Cliffs, 1974.
6. IRDA Annual Reports.
7. Mark D. Dorfman, *Fundamentals of Insurance,* Prentice-Hall, 2002.

Web Resources

- www.bimaguru.com
- www.bimaonline.com
- www.irdaindia.org

Annexure 19-A

INSURANCE REGULATORY AND DEVELOPMENT AUTHORITY

New Delhi, the 14th July, 2000

(Obligations of Insurers to Rural and Social Sectors) Regulations, 2000

In exercise of the powers conferred by Section 32C read with Section 32B of the Insurance Act, 1938, (4 of 1938), the Authority, in consultation with the Insurance Advisory Committee, hereby makes the following regulations, namely:-

1. Short Title and Commencement

(1) These regulations may be called the Insurance Regulatory and Development Authority (Obligations of Insurers to Rural or Social Sectors) Regulations, 2000.

(2) They shall come into force from the date of their publication in the *Official Gazette*.

2. Definitions

1. In these regulations, unless the context otherwise requires —

(a) *"Act"* means the Insurance Act, 1938 (4 of 1938);

(b) "*Authority*" means the Insurance Regulatory and Development Authority established under the provisions of Section 3 of the Insurance Regulatory and Development Authority Act, 1999 (41 of 1999);

(c) *"Rural sector"* shall mean any place as per the latest census which has — (*i*) a population of not more than five thousand; (*ii*) a density of population of not more than four hundred per square kilometre; and (*iii*) at least seventy-five per cent of the male working population is engaged in agriculture;

(d) *"Social sector"* includes unorganized sector, informal sector, economically vulnerable or backward classes and other categories of persons, both in rural and urban areas;

(e) *"Unorganised sector"* includes self-employed workers such as agricultural labourers, bidi workers, brick kiln workers, carpenters, cobblers, construction workers, fishermen, hamals, handicraft artisans, handloom and khadi workers, lady tailors, leather and tannery workers, papad makers, powerloom workers, physically handicapped self-employed persons, primary milk producers, rickshaw pullers, safai karmacharis, salt growers, seri-culture workers, sugarcane cutters, tendu leaf collectors, toddy tappers, vegetable vendors, washerwomen, working women in hills, or such other categories of persons;

(f) *"Economically vulnerable or backward classes"* means persons who live below the poverty line;

(g) *"Other categories of persons"* includes persons with disability as defined in the Persons with Disabilities (Equal Opportunities, Protection of Rights, and Full Participation) Act, 1995 and who may not be gainfully employed; and also includes guardians who need insurance to protect spastic persons or persons with disability;

(*h*) All words and expressions used herein and not defined herein but defined in the Insurance Act, 1938 (4 of 1938), or in the Insurance Regulatory and Development Authority Act, 1999 (41 of 1999), shall have the meanings respectively assigned to them in those Acts.

3. Obligations

Every insurer, who begins to carry on insurance business after the commencement of the Insurance Regulatory and Development Authority Act, 1999 (41 of 1999), shall, for the purposes of Sections 32B and 32C of the Act, ensure that he undertakes the following obligations, during the first five financial years, pertaining to the persons in —

(a) **Rural sector,** (*i*) in respect of *a life insurer* — (I) five per cent in the first financial year; (II) seven per cent in the second financial year; (III) ten per cent in the third financial year; (IV) twelve per cent in the fourth financial year; (V) fifteen per cent in the fifth year; of total policies written direct in that year; (*ii*) in respect of *a general insurer*, — (I) two per cent in the first financial year; (II) three per cent in the second financial year; (III) five per cent thereafter, of total gross premium income written direct in that year.

(b) **Social sector**, in respect of all insurers, — (I) five thousand lives in the first financial year; (II) seven thousand five hundred lives in the second financial year; (III) ten thousand lives in the third financial year; (IV) fifteen thousand lives in the fourth financial year; (V) twenty thousand lives in the fifth year;

Provided that in the first financial year, where the period of operation is less than twelve months, proportionate percentage or number of lives, as the case may be, shall be undertaken. Provided further that, in case of a general insurer, the obligations specified shall include insurance for crops. Provided further that the Authority may normally, once in every five years, prescribe or revise the obligations as specified in Regulation 3.

4. Obligations of Existing Insurers

(1) The obligations of existing insurers as on the date of commencement of IRDA Act shall be decided by the Authority after consultation with them and the quantum of insurance business to be done shall not be less than what has been recorded by them for the accounting year ended 31st March, 2000.

(2) The Authority shall review such quantum of insurance business periodically and give directions to the insurers for achieving the specified targets.

CHAPTER

PROJECT AND ENGINEERING INSURANCE

Chapter Objectives

- Risks Associated with New Projects
- The History of Engineering Insurance
- Engineering Insurance
- Engineering All Risks Insurance
- Contractor's Plant and Machinery Insurance Policy
- Deterioration of Stock Insurance

Introduction

Every project leader within the corporate sector knows that nothing but an unqualified success of a project can ensure the repayment of costs involved or loans availed. In case of any delays or failure of a project, liquid funds will have to be made available to replace the costs incurred as well as repay the loans taken. Ever since India has been ushered into the era of liberalization, privatization and globalization, Project insurance has emerged as the need of the hour. The demand for Project insurance is increasing with major emphasis placed on infrastructure projects, besides other large projects.

At times, tried and tested risk management tactics have proved themselves effective in stemming the risks. But now, every Risk Manager would rather look for a new technique that could reflect the changing times. Everyone is looking for a modern and up-to-the-mark risk management strategy. Since the industrial scenario is changing so quickly, Risk Managers in India have been forced to steel themselves for a challenging albeit an interesting assignment that should ensue within this new millennium by

- Adapting to the 'Global Scenario' and 'Modern Technology'
- Providing the latest Risk Management tactics as well as sustained risk
- Management support for the development of industry within the Indian sub-continent.

Although new technology results in optimization of productivity and production, it also creates new and unheard of risks. Introducing new technology is similar to developing a new subculture in engineering, erection, construction, commissioning and innovation in handling and transport of materials. Since automation also intensifies the chances of risks occurring due to human error, the repercussions are bound to be costly. Since Risk Management means efficiently managing the risks, it should be oriented towards the prevention rather than the cure, itself.

20.1 Risks Associated with New Projects

Risks, which might have a significant impact on the construction or operation of a project, can be grouped as—

1. *Commercial Risks:* Related to potential problems during construction resulting in delays and escalation of costs.
2. *Operational Risks:* Poor performance that translates in failure in generating adequate cash to pay the lending financial institutions.
3. *Risks of Disparity:* Difference between supply and markets resulting in the inability to produce assured capacity.
4. *General Risks:* Vendor's inability to utilize power generated.
5. *Political Risks:* Most likely to affect non-Indian investors as they are mere spectators to the ongoing bureaucratic scenario.

Basically, Risk Management is aimed at analyzing risks, controlling and financing them. Ideally, the Risk Manager must review the efficiency of the risk management decisions taken and also make appropriate changes that ensure proper handling of risks.

20.2 The History of Engineering Insurance

The development of engineering insurance began in England around the middle of the 19th century in the wake of the Industrial Revolution.

The Industrial Revolution had been triggered by the inventions of steam boilers by Papin in 1690 and by Newcomen in 1725, and the double-acting industrial steam engine by James Watt in 1781. The increasing use of steam boilers and steam engines permitted the switch from manual labour in workshops to machine-based production in factories, thus changing the face of technology and society.

The factory worker joined the craftsman and gradually replaced him. The explosion of steam boilers and the rupture of the large flywheels of steam engines were new and unfamiliar types of property damage that also led to personal injuries in the factories and their surroundings.

As a result, the British boiler operators founded the Manchester Steam Users' Association in 1854 with the aim of regularly inspecting its members' steam boilers for deficiencies and instructing the operating personnel on how to use them properly.

This established the institution of technical inspection and, at the same time, the profession of an inspection and later of an insurance engineer. The number of boiler explosions declined considerably, and design methods and materials were improved. Manufacturers' production operations were supervised by independent experts, as were erection and commissioning.

In 1859, a number of engineers had the idea not only of preventing damage by way of inspections but also of offering insurance protection for property damage and personal injuries, and founded – likewise in Manchester– the Steam Boiler Assurance Company.

Just seven years later, in 1866, the Hartford Steam Boiler Inspection & Insurance Company came into being in the USA, originally with the intention of offering inspections and insurance protection for the locomotives of the private railway companies. This company has since become the largest insurance and inspection company for engineering risks in the USA.

A host of inventions in the 19th century accelerated the process of industrialization and the demand for adequate insurance protection. Electric motors, generators, transformers, water and steam turbines, gas engines, petrol and diesel engines resulted in the flourishing of power engineering and the energy industry.

The supply of electricity in Germany began with the decentralized generation of electricity in industrial companies to drive the machines and in the municipalities for lighting the streets. The year 1900 witnessed the first steam turbine installation with an output of 1 MW at the power station in Elberfeld. From these origins, the electricity supply system based on the pioneering ideas and successful trials of Oskar v. Miller in the second half of the 19th century developed into a central and now trans-European grid with ratings of up to 1,300 to 1,500 MW in nuclear power stations in Germany and France.

As a result of the progress made in compressor and pump construction, together with hygienic sewage disposal in conurbation areas, the gas and water industries led to the establishment of modern gas, water and sewage systems for the rapidly growing cities. The new machinery being used needed adequate insurance protection. In the UK and the USA, the steam boiler insurers started providing this cover under the name of "engine insurance".

20.2.1 Machinery Insurance

In Germany, this boom in economic development began, somewhat later, in the second half of the 19th century. Rapid growth and confidence in the ability to realize new business ideas led to a wave of new businesses being set up in what came to be known as the "founder era" ("Gründerzeit").

One of these successful founders was the 36-year-old Karl Thieme, who, in co-operation with respected industrialists and bankers from Munich, founded the Münchener Rückversicherungs-Gesellschaft in Munich in 1880 and Allianz Versicherungs-AG in Berlin in 1890. In 1898, one of his employees, Chief Engineer Fritz Böhrer, who had gathered extensive experience with losses in his time as technical director of a printing company, suggested something that had not been available in Germany up to that time – an innovative "insurance for machines and mechanical devices for all industrial companies, electricity, gas and water works, etc.".

In 1898/99, Böhrer carried out a written survey among various commercial and industrial companies in Bavaria. Following an analysis of this survey, which confirmed the need for machinery insurance, the new product was introduced in conjunction with other participating insurance companies and marketed as "accident insurance" for machinery supplementary to an existing public liability insurance policy.

All risks cover with named exclusions

Thieme, who was always open to new ideas and greatly interested in innovative insurance schemes for his young company and its clients, backed Böhrer's idea entirely. From the very outset, this machinery insurance was designed as all risks cover with named exclusions – quite the opposite of the policies for steam boilers, which only offered insurance protection for property damage caused by named perils, e.g., explosion.

On 1st January 1900, what was then the Munich Branch of Allianz Versicherungs-AG was granted a licence to sell this machinery insurance – initially for the Kingdom of Bavaria. The Imperial Supervisory Office in Berlin later extended this licence to several primary insurers all over Germany in 1903 and 1904.

With this product, the then still young Munich Re wanted to offer its cedants an insurance cover designed to meet the needs of the flourishing commercial and industrial business. With the help of specially selected agents, business with the new product was rapidly expanded and offered for machinery in virtually every sector. More and more insurers became active in the new class.

20.2.2 Global Ventures

Munich Re also marketed machinery insurance outside Germany – in Austria, Hungary, Italy, Switzerland, Norway, Denmark, the Netherlands and, ultimately, also overseas. Thieme continued to support Böhrer's idea of machinery insurance through various difficulties of the pioneering years. In this way, the fortuitous meeting of Thieme, the courageous entrepreneur, and Böhrer, the visionary engineer, helped machinery insurance become a success. To put the new class of insurance on a broader footing, insurance for financial losses resulting from insured machinery losses – known at that time as operating loss insurance – was introduced on 15th August, 1910 as an early forerunner of machinery loss of profits insurance.

20.2.3 Project Insurance

All Risk Project Insurance Policy: Project Insurance is an all-inclusive insurance cover for any damage to project material whilst in transit, risks of damage on site and while being erected or commissioned under an "All Risks Project Insurance Policy." This policy has been designed after bearing in mind the various risks associated with erection of a factory right from the shipment of the first consignment, the subsequent storage, civil construction, erection of plant and machinery, commissioning and trials until the end of the trial period when commercial production commences. Any damages or injury to the third party is covered under this policy. This policy is more commonly known as *Marine-cum-Erection* policy.

Marine-cum-Erection Insurance: Although people tend to think that there are major differences between Project insurance and Marine-cum-Erection insurance, they are essentially the one and the same since the scope of cover is strikingly similar in both. This is also an "All Risks Insurance" which provides cover against the *loss* or damage to the consignments during transit or damage during storage, handling, erection, testing and commissioning stages. This policy also covers Third Party Liability due to indemnifiable accidents at project site. The cover commences right from the moment goods leave the manufacturer's/supplier's premises (warehouse) in a foreign country and remains in force during voyage to any Indian port and thereafter during inland transit to the site of erection; during storage at site; during shifting of goods for the purpose of erection and continues to be in force until completion of erection, testing and commissioning.

While availing this cover, the proposer (insured) must ensure the following:

• While availing the policy, insured should take care of the insurance obligations under the contract. The provision and contents in the relevant portion of the Tender have to be taken.	• Document are to be examined and appropriate policy will have to be taken.
• The sum insured will have to be properly arrived at, since the Prime Cost of the Plant and Equipment will not be a subject-matter for adjustment. • In respect of imported equipment's invoice value in Foreign Currency and Exchange Rates are to be furnished, based on which the value of the equipment's in Indian Rupees will be arrived at.	• Any extension of Policy Period or Testing Period will be costlier as compared to such period being included in the anticipated period, while selecting the policy period at inception. • Even if the extension of the policy is required to be taken at a later date, it would be more economical to opt for a longer extension period than several extensions of small periods.
• The Project period selected for insurance purpose will have to take into account possible delays during execution and accordingly it is advisable to have buffer period to take care of shippage.	• The possibility of having higher excess under the policy has to be considered, which will have the facility of discount in the premium rate.
• The testing period selected will also have to take into	

Escalation

In order to take care of increase in value due to escalation in the basic project cost, duties appreciation in Foreign Currency and fluctuation in the Exchange Rate, the escalation provision may be availed at the inception of the policy. The maximum permissible limit is 50 per cent escalation and premium is charged on half the escalation amount.

Basic Insurance Cover

This insurance cover under Project Insurance Policy comprises of two parts:

1. The first is coverage for transit to take care of the interest during the transit from the various suppliers' warehouses to the site of erection.
2. The second is the storage-cum-erection coverage to take care of the interest during storage, erection, testing and commissioning.

The transit risks covered are "All Risks" plus war, strike, riot and civil commotion for imports and strike, riot and civil commotion for inland transit.

For the erection portion, the risks covered are any accident, fire, riot and strike, lightning, malicious damage, storm, tempest, flood and inundation, earthquake, act of God perils, tearing apart due to centrifugal forces, shortcircuiting, faults in erection, lack of skill and carelessness, and theft and burglary of property stored at the site of erection. It also covers damages to equipment during the commissioning and testing, till handed over to the principals.

Additional Covers

The risks of one project differ from another. In order to meet the particular requirements of the project concerned, care should be taken to check on which additional coverage/s out of those listed below is/are required and action taken thereon.

- Dismantling Cover
- Third Party Liability Cover
- Deletion of 60 days Clause in Ocean Policy
- Maintenance Period
- Additional Transits
- Additional Customs Duty.
- Express Delivery
- Testing of Second-hand Machinery
- Cross Liability Cover
- Terrorism Cover
- Clearance and Removal of Debris

Storage Risks at Fabricators' Premises/Workshop

In short, the cover is against all risks of physical loss or damage arising out of operation of any one or more of the following perils:

- *Location Risks:* Fire, Lightning, Theft and Burglary.
- *Handling Risks:* Impact from falling objects, Collision, failure of Cranes or Tackles.
- *Operational Risks:* Failure of safety devices, Leakage of Electricity, Insulation failures, Short-circuit, Tearing apart on Account of centrifugal forces. Explosion.
- *Human Risks:* Carelessness, Negligence, Faults in erections, Malicious Element, Damage, Strikes and Riots, Terrorism
- *Acts of God:* Earthquake, Storm, Tempest, Hurricane, Flood.
- Subsidience: Landslide, Rockslide.

Insurance policies that are required after completion of project are:

- Fire Insurance
- Machinery Breakdown Insurance
- Advance Loss of Profit
- Public Liability Insurance

20.3 Engineering Insurance

Shortly after World War I – and mainly because of the instability of the currency resulting from the hyperinflation in the fateful crisis year of 1923 – the capital goods industry began to look for the most comprehensive insurance protection possible against risks to the calculated earnings of the contracting companies and their suppliers during the construction of technical facilities.

This demand was met by erection all risks insurance (EAR), which was launched on the market by Atlantic-Versicherung and Allianz in 1924 with the support of Munich Re. Erection all risks insurance offered the contractor the benefit of having simple, complete cover based on the all risks model, encompassing inter alia the risks of fire, explosion and natural hazards.

The advantages of the new product were so convincing that erection all risks insurance rapidly asserted itself in continental Europe, but also in the UK and the USA, either under the name construction insurance or as builders' risk insurance. In recent years' this property insurance has been supplemented by the corresponding financial loss insurance, named advance loss of profits insurance (ALoP) or delay in start-up (DSU) insurance.

The worldwide spread of risks by way of reinsurance helped this difficult class of business become a success, even though erection all risks insurance is exposed to major losses to a far greater extent than machinery insurance. As erection all risks insurance was designed to protect contractors during the erection and test testing of facilities, there was still a need for insurance to cover the risks to be borne by the contractor under his guarantee obligation after handing over the machinery to the operator.

The machinery guarantee insurance required for this purpose was introduced in 1927. This insurance covers the costs of repairing consequential damage to insured property caused by faulty design, materials, erection, etc. Machinery guarantee insurance offers a further supplement to the comprehensive range of engineering insurance products, but antiselection makes it very difficult for the insurance industry to operate profitably in this class.

Apart from various covers available for projects before and after implementation, specific covers are also available for various items of plant and machinery and equipments. Some of these are discussed as below.

(a) Boiler Insurance

(b) Erection Insurance

(c) Storage-cum-Erection

(d) Marine-cum-Erection

(e) Loss of Profits (Machinery) Insurance

(f) Contractors all risk policy

(g) Machinery Breakdown insurance.

Civil Engineering Completed Risks Insurance Policy

This cover is provided to owners and operators of civil engineering structures can have comprehensive insurance protection against loss or damage after the construction work has been completed and the facilities are taken over. This policy is suitable for completed works such as runways, railway lines, bridges, flyovers, jetties, tunnels, dams, canals, harbours, dry docks, water pipe lines, irrigation systems, reservoirs, etc. The policy offers cover against loss or damage due to:

1. Fire
2. Lightning
3. Explosion/implosion
4. Riot, strike & malicious damage
5. Impact by any rail, road or water borne vehicle or animal
6. Storm, cyclone, typhoon, tempest, hurricane, tornado, flood and inundation, wave action
7. Subsidence, landslide and rockslide
8. Earthquake, fire and shock, tsunami
9. Frost, avalanche, ice

Extra Covers

Further hazards depending on the location and type of risk can be included like bush fire, volcanic action, blasting operations, cover for removal of debris following a loss at additional premium.

In case of damages which can be repaired, the policy provides for payment of costs necessary to restore the items to their condition immediately before the occurrence of the damage. In case of total loss, the actual value of the items immediately before the occurrence of the loss is payable to the extent the costs are included in the sums insured. Since the policy is on indemnity basis, only incurred costs are payable. Loss assessment is subject to adjustments for under insurance, salvage and policy excess. Premium is charged for the type of civil works covered, the earthquake zone in which the property is located, the additional covers required and the past claims experience. The insured has to file a proposal form giving full description of the civil works proposed to be insured, the geographical conditions, exposure to the risks, maintenance details and the values for which insurance is required need to be submitted. The documents generally required for processing engineering claims are as under:

(a) Copy of the policy complete with terms, conditions and warranties.

(b) Claim form duly completed by the insured.

(c) Survey report should include —

  (i) Clear indication of the cause of loss

  (ii) Extent of damage and loss

  (iii) Establishment of liability

  (iv) Assessment of loss occurrence of riot is in the public knowledge, production

  (v) Confirmation of compliance of policy terms, conditions and warranties

  (vi) Admissibility of the claim.

(d) Photographs (if necessary)

(e) Police report, and (if necessary)

(f) Fire Brigade report (if necessary)

The steps involved in the loss adjustment are as under:

Gross loss assessed

(a) Less: depreciation, if any,

(b) Less: Salvage

(c) Less: Under Insurance

(d) Less: Excess

(e) Net Claim Payable

Note: Items (e) and (f) may be waived if the survey report is clear and does not cause any doubt on the occurrence as well as the extent of loss. Where occurrence of riot is in the public knowledge, production of Final Police Investigation Report and Fire Brigade report may be waived.

In case of the theft losses it is necessary to collect a copy of the first information report or proof of complaint lodged by the insured with the police, such as Registered A/D letter. Final Investigation Report may be waived depending upon the merits of the case.

20.4 Engineering All Risks Insurance

The first record of insurance specifically for building structures, contractors' all risks insurance (CAR), dates back to 1929 and the construction of Lambeth Bridge over the Thames in London. In Germany, this type of insurance was introduced in 1934 under the name of "Bauleistungsversicherung", when severe restrictions were imposed on the possibilities for creating reserves for outstanding losses to the detriment of the building contractors.

The insurance terms and conditions were derived from erection all risks insurance, with which the companies had already acquired ten years of experience. Nowadays, contractors' all risks insurance cover is increasingly extended by a corresponding loss of profits cover, which provides compensation for the financial losses suffered by principals as a result of delays in completion caused by property damage.

EAR policy is designed to protect the interest of civil contractors and Firms involved in construction activity against the damage or destruction of various civil engineering projects undertaken by them. The policy is suitable for all types of civil engineering construction works ranging from small buildings to massive dams as they are susceptible to damage by a variety of external and internal causes during the course of construction. This is a comprehensive policy designed to cover all risks associated with civil works right from the time of commencement of works at site till the contract works are taken over or put into use. The policy covers:

1. Fire/lightning.
2. Accidental damage during construction like dropping or falling, defective workmanship and material, lack of skill, negligence, malicious act and human error.
3. Act of God perils such as flood and inundation, earthquake.
4. Collapse, collusion, impact.
5. Theft and burglary, malicious and terrorist damage.

Policy may be extended to cover air freight, additional customs duty, express freight, over time wages, expenses for clearance an removal of debris, damage to surrounding property, third party liability, escalation in costs, contractor's plant and machinery at the construction site, defects in construction which surface during maintenance period for which the contractor is liable under the terms of agreement with the principal. Claims are payable at the prevailing market rates for restoration of affected property to the condition immediately before the occurrence of damage. Cost of any improvement and modifications will not be admitted. The amount of loss payable is subject to under insurance if any, and the policy excess. Premium chargeable depends on the nature of the project, the project cost, the project period, geographic location and the period of testing. Discount in premium is allowed for large projects with sum insured more than ₹ 100 crores, the higher deductibles opted and for the fire protection available at the site. Premium may be paid in installments where the project period exceeds 1 year. In case of early completion of the project also, refund of premium may be claimed for the balance period of insurance.

20.5 Contractor's Plant and Machinery Insurance Policy

This policy is suitable for contractors involved in construction business for covering all kinds of construction equipment like compressors, heavy duty cranes, boring machines, bulldozers, pipe jacking, and hauling equipment, pavers, excavators, loaders, road rollers, tunnel boring machines etc. can be covered under this policy. The policy offers cover against loss or damage due to sudden unforeseen eventualities such as:

1. Fire, lightning, explosion/implosion/aircraft damage, riot, strike, malicious and terrorist damage, earthquake, subsidence, landslide, rockslide, storm, tempest, hurricane, typhoon, tornado, flood and inundation as are covered by the fire policy.
2. Burglary and theft.
3. Damages while at work due to faulty handling, dropping or falling, collision and impact.

The policy can be extended to cover the additional risks of third party property damage and injuries; loss or damage to surrounding property, expenses incurred on overtime, express freight, air freight, additional customs duty, clearance of debris following a loss for additional premium. In the event of a loss, costs necessarily incurred for restoration or repairs of the damaged equipment including transportation costs to and fro repair shop, customs duties, taxes etc to the extent included in the sum insured are paid. Policy also covers transit risk of the equipment within the project site. However, damages to exchangeable parts, electrical or mechanical breakdown, and accidents resulting from over load or similar tests are excluded. The policy is subject to excess as stated in the policy. Rate of premium depends on the type of equipment and the location at which it operates. Premium is charged on the reinstatement cost of the equipment. The potential insured has to submit a proposal form giving details of contractor's plant and machinery item wise, the individual values proposed for insurance and the geographical location of the project site where the equipment shall be used. In case additional covers are required, they should be specifically mentioned.

At the time of claim settlement the validity of the policy at the time of occurrence and identification of damaged equipment/item is verified. The surveyor generally confirms the accidental damage to the equipment. For items fabricated by the contractor and replacement values not available, the surveyor assesses the loss on the basis of actual costs incurred by the insured.

20.6 Deterioration of Stock Insurance

Breakdown and cold storage machinery may cause rise in temperature of cold storage chambers leading to Deterioration of stock. This policy covers such losses to the stocks in cold storage. The policy is suitable for the owner of the cold storage (individual or a cooperative society) or those who take the cold storage on lease or hire for storage of perishable commodities.This policy covers loss or damage to the stocks in cold storage following breakdown of the cold storage plant. The deterioration of the stocks can be due to:

1. Rise in temperature
2. Sudden and unforeseen escape of refrigerants into the cold storage rooms.

However, the following causes are not covered:

1. Shrinkage, inherent defects or diseases, natural putrefaction, etc.
2. Improper storage, damage to packing material, insufficient air circulation
3. Any willful act or gross negligence of insured or his representatives
4. Loss due to overloading of plant
5. Fire perils including riot, strike, malicious and terrorism damages, war perils
6. Loss arising out of failure of any part requiring periodical renewal; wear and tear parts
7. Operation of fuses and similar devices

Policy can be extended to cover damage to stocks resulting from failure of public electric supply. In the event of a loss, the market value of the commodities lost and reasonable expenses incurred to avoid or minimize such loss or damage, say for transferring the goods from one cold storage to the other are paid. In case of a total loss, claim is paid subject to the overall limit of sum insured under the policy. The sum insured should represent the maximum value of stocks in the cold storage at any given time. Certificates issued by Government authorities that the stocks are unfit for consumption should be provided in support of the claim made. Premium depends on the nature and value of goods stored, the age and condition of the refrigeration plant, stand by/repair and/or replacement facilities, nature of refrigerant, alternative storage facilities available, past claims experience and similar other factors. Proposal form should be submitted duly filled giving the nature of commodities stored, details of the refrigeration plant, stand by /maintenance and repair facilities available. The refrigeration plant should be covered under machinery breakdown insurance policy. Following loss minimization measures are insisted by the surveyors while settlement claims:

(i) No fresh stock should be loaded in the cold storage chambers.

(ii) Cold storage doors should be sealed to maintain temperature and avoid temperature rise.

(iii) If possible, the insured should be requested of shift stocks to some other running cold storage premises preferably in cool evening/night period or by refrigerated vans.

(iv) The insured should be requested to carry out repairs to the refrigerator plant most expeditiously.

(v) If there is no possibility of completing the repairs immediately, the insured should be advised to unload stocks from cold chamber for disposal in the local market as quickly as possible, and at the best available price in association with the surveyor/local authorities.

20.6.1 Erection All Risks Insurance

This policy is suitable for the principal or contractors of a project being erected as the project is exposed to various external risks during the construction period and damage to plant and machinery and the supporting structures due to accidents cause financial loss apart from delay in implementation of the project. Interest of all the subcontractors may be covered by one policy for operational flexibility. This is a comprehensive insurance policy designed to cover any sort of contingency right from the moment the materials are unloaded at the project site and continues during the entire project period until the project is tested, commissioned and handed over. The policy covers the following perils:

1. Location risks: Fire, lightning, theft and burglary.
2. Handling risks: Impact from falling objects, collision, failure of chains or tackles.
3. Operational risks: Failure of safety devices, leakage of electricity, failure of insulation, short circuit, explosion, etc.
4. Risks of human element: Negligence, carelessness, faults in erection, malicious damage, riots and strikes.
5. Act of God: Storm, tempest, hurricane, flood, inundation, landslide, rockslide, and earthquake.
6. Extra covers: Cover for contractors plant and equipment, third party liability, surrounding property, removal of debris, escalation, express freight, overtime charges, additional customs duty are provided at suitable additional premium.

Claims are payable at the prevailing market rates for restoration of affected property to the condition immediately before the occurrence of damage. Cost of any improvement and modifications will not be admitted. The amount of loss payable is subject to under insurance if any, and the policy excess. Premium chargeable depends on the nature of the project, the project cost, the project period, geographic location, the period of testing. Discount in premium is allowed for large projects with SI more than ₹ 100 crore, the higher deductibles opted and for the fire protection available at the site. Premium may be paid in installments where the project period exceeds 1 year.

20.6.2 Industrial All Risks Insurance

This coverage is provided to all major industrial units (other than petrochemical risks) having over all sum insured of ₹ 100 crore and above in one or more locations in India are eligible to take Industrial All Risks Insurance Policy. The policy offers cover against damage due to all perils covered by:

A. Fire and special perils policy.
B. Burglary insurance policy.
C. Machinery Breakdown/Boiler explosion/Electronic equipment Insurance.
D. Business Interruption due to fire and special perils policy.

Losses due to the following are excluded:

1. Faulty material/workmanship/defective design and material.
2. Inherent vice, defects, deteriorations, and normal wear and tear.

3. Collapse or cracking of buildings.
4. Pollution, contamination, shrinkage, rust, corrosion, scratching, and temperature changes
5. Larceny, fraud, dishonesty, inventory losses, shortage on delivery
6. Wilful act, negligence; wars and nuclear risks.

Machinery loss of profit cover is optional. Debris removal, escalation and other covers available as extensions to fire policy can be covered for additional premium. The policy offers widest range of cover compared to that provided by individual operational policies. Under insurance to the extent of 15% is ignored. Sine the insurance is on reinstatement value basis; all expenses for restoration of the damaged property will be covered to the full extent. The policy is however, subject to an excess of 5% of claim amount with a lower limit of ₹ 5 lakh and upper limit of ₹ 50 lakh. Premium rates for the policy are based on:

1. The cover opted
2. Claims experience
3. Deductibles opted
4. Risk assessment report of the engineer (for MLOP)

20.6.3 Machinery Insurance Policy

This policy is suitable for every industry which operates on machines and for whom breakdown of plant and machinery is of serious consequence. Monetary costs involved for restoration of machine to its original state are covered by the machinery (breakdown) insurance policy. The policy offers cover against loss or damage to the plant and machinery due to sudden and unforeseen reasons whilst the machinery is at work or at rest caused by:

1. Faulty material, design, construction or erection.
2. Vibration, mal-adjustment, mal-alignment
3. Defective lubrication, loosening of parts, stress, molecular fatigue, heating, centrifugal force, explosion/implosion.
4. Electrical faults and failures.
5. Failure of connected machinery or protective devices.
6. Lack of skill/carelessness of the operators
7. Falling, impact, collision and the like
8. Obstruction or entry of foreign bodies into the machine

Additional expenses required to repair and restore the damaged machinery like overtime, express freight, surrounding property, third party liability, additional customs duty, air freight can be covered on payment of necessary additional premium.

In case of partial loss, all expenses necessary for restoration of the affected machinery will be paid to the extent insured in the policy. Claims will be paid in full provided the machine is adequately insured. Depreciation is not applied except for parts with limited life or which are subject to wear and tear. Excess at 1% of sum insured shall be deducted from all claims. Where the repair cost exceeds the cost of the machine, loss will be dealt on 'total loss basis', i.e., claim will be settled for the depreciated cost of the machine as on the date of loss. Premium is charged on the reinstatement value of individual machinery. The machine as a whole should be insured. Premium rates depend on the type of machine; the industry in which it is used and its value. Discounts are offered based on factors such as stand-by facilities, spares available and claims experience provided the value of all machinery at a particular location exceeds ₹ 10 crore. While sett,ling claims, the test reports of the damaged parts if deemed necessary by the surveyor and/or suggested by the insurers is to be submitted to the insurer/surveyor. The claim payable may include costs of dismantling transportation to the repairer's shop, repairs and retransportation and re-erection and other incidental expenses. If damaged equipment being sent out is covered under a Marine Transit Policy, the cost of such insurance may also be reimbursed. If repeated losses are reported on the same equipment, the underwriting office can take the help of an outside expert to ascertain the precise cause of repeated losses and suggest measures for avoidance/minimization of reoccurrence of breakdown/loss. The exclusion of damage to Belts, Ropes, Chains, Rubber Tyres, Dyes, Moulds, etc. is to be considered. As to the oil and other operation media in the transformer and equipment, these may be reimbursed when specifically covered under the policy.

The losses under the other extensions like additional custom duty, air freight, express freight, etc., are to be assessed separately and the underwriting office should confirm the availability of additional sum insured specifically for such items of expenditure while recommending the claim for settlement. If the assessment involves additional expenses for repair/replacement, the surveyor should confirm that the expenses are reasonable.

20.6.4 Loss of Profits Policy

This policy is suitable for industries where interruptions or delays as a result of machinery breakdown or boiler explosion result in huge consequential losses. Where the time lag between the breakdown or loss and the restoration is large, this policy compensates for the loss of profits during the intervening period.

The policy offers cover against consequential losses following loss or damage to the property insured under machinery breakdown and/or boiler and pressure plant insurance. This policy covers actual financial losses suffered by the insured due to business interruption arising from:

1. Reduction in turnover and
2. Increase in cost of working

The standard policy thus insures the loss of gross profits in the business following accident to the machinery, boiler and pressure plant, as a result of material damage loss covered under the corresponding machinery breakdown and boiler explosion policies. The losses as a result of reduced turnover because of the machinery damaged and the additional expenditure necessarily incurred for avoiding or reducing the fall in turnover for the interruption period are compensated under this policy. However, the policy is subject to a time excess of 7 days (14 days in case of petrochemical risks) which means that interruptions for periods less than or equal to these periods are not covered. Premium rates depend on the critical nature of the machinery covered by the breakdown or explosion policies; their relative importance and contribution to final output; the repairs, maintenance and stand by facilities available and the indemnity period opted.

Key Terms

- ❒ Engineering Insurance
- ❒ Stock Insurance
- ❒ EAR Insurance

Questions for Review

1. Briefly explain the need for engineering insurance and the various covers available in India.
2. Write short notes on:
   (a) Engineering All Risk Policy
   (b) Loss of Profits Policy

Suggested Readings

1. *Engineering Insurance,* IC 77, Insurance Institute of India, Mumbai, 1999.
2. *Miscelleneous Insurance,* IC 78, Insurance Institute of India, Mumbai, 1991.

Web Resources

- www.cpg.org
- www.insure.com
- www.insureitech.com
- www.pepeinsurance.com

❑❑❑

CHAPTER

MISCELLANEOUS INSURANCE

Chapter Objectives

- Aviation Insurance
- Other Insurances

Introduction

This chapter illustrates some special classes of insurance.

21.1 Aviation Insurance

Aircraft Comprehensive Insurance Policy

The Policy covers: *(a)* Loss or damage to the aircraft, *(b)* legal liability to the third party and passengers, *(c)* Legal liability for freight, mail etc. carried, *(d)* Personal accident risk to the pilots, crew and ground staff and *(e)* Loss of professional licence of pilots and other crew members.

Airline Insurance (Hull and Liability)

The hull policy covers loss and accidental damage (including emergency landings) to air and ground risks; the liability policy covers the airline against legal action from third parties or customers in respect of death, injury or physical damage to property. Most airlines have 'manuscript' wordings devised by the brokers, insurers and purchasers to reflect individual needs, circumstances and preferences. Hull claims are quickly determined and settled. Liability losses are usually complex, as accidents often result from a combination of factors. Often liability will be split with other parties, such as airports and particularly, manufacturers.

Airline Insurance (Hull War)

These policies provide cover to airlines for loss of or damage to their property (aircraft and spares). The risks covered are excluded from hull all risks policies and arise from war or war-related activities including:

— War invasion, hostilities, civil war, rebellion, attempted coups etc.

— Strikes, riots, civil commotion or labour disturbances.

— Sabotage.

— Hijacking (attempted or actual) or seizure of control (including pilot suicide).

— Acts for political or terrorist purposes.

— Confiscation, naturalisation, detention etc. for the use of any government or public authority.

Product Liability

Product liability covers an insured's legal liability to third parties for injury and loss or damage arising out of the defective design or manufacture of an aircraft product. It encompasses all types of aircraft products, for example, airframes, engines, seats and minor components.

General Aviation

General aviation is the insurance of "all aircraft other than commercial and military aircraft, and commercial aircraft capable of carrying less than 40 passengers." Different insurers use different definitions. Often planes that can carry between 40 and 60 passengers may be included in either this book or the airline book, depending on the insurer's reinsurance programme.

Miscellaneous Covers

There are a number of other types of aviation cover available. Long-term policies (of up to 3 years) are common for each of these types of covers.

Aviation Insurance can be purchased in two ways: (1) from a "direct writing" company where the insured contacts the company direct; or (2) through an independent insurance agent who represents several companies. The Indian aviation insurance business is worth around $20 million. In India, the major chunk of this business is owned by GIC. However, hardly 2 per cent of the same is retained by it since the premium is large, various complexities are involved and as the risk is huge and it will have to be reinsured. On a global basis, the loss ratio in general aviation insurance has exceeded 1.1 to as much as 1.25 or more for the last several years. The key reasons that the insurance companies have been losing money in aviation business are:

1. The cost of repairs is increasing fast.
2. The number of insured accidents is up.
3. The value of the aircraft is soaring.

To keep insurance costs under control in the current difficult environment, aircraft and aviation business owners have to think on the following aspects:

- Self-insurance
- Matching equipment to needs
- Optimize maintenance costs
- Promote revenues
- Promote personal aviation
- Focus on safety.

Additional Covers

The risks of one project differ from another. In order to meet the particular requirements of the project concerned, care should be taken to check on which additional coverage/s out of those listed below is/are required and action taken thereon.

- Dismantling Cover
- Express Delivery
- Third Party Liability Cover
- Testing of Second-hand Machinery
- Deletion of 60 days Clause in Ocean Policy
- Cross Liability Cover
- Maintenance Period
- Terrorism Cover
- Additional Transits
- Clearance and Removal of Debris
- Additional Customs Duty.

Storage Risks at Fabricators' Premises/Workshop

In short, the cover is against all risks of physical loss or damage arising out of operation of any one or more of the following perils:

- *Location Risks:* Fire, Lightning, Theft and Burglary.
- *Handling Risks:* Impact from falling objects, Collision, failure of Cranes or Tackles.
- *Operational Risks:* Failure of safety devices, Leakage of Electricity, Insulation failures, Short-circuit, Tearing apart on Account of centrifugal forces, Explosion.
- *Human Risks:* Carelessness, Negligence, Faults in erections, Malicious Element, Damage, Strikes and Riots, Terrorism
- *Acts of God:* Earthquake, Storm, Tempest, Hurricane, Flood. Subsidience: Landslide, Rockslide.

Other Insurance Policies that are required are:

- Empoyer's Liability/Workmen's Compensation
- Employee's Sickness and Accident/Travel Insurance

- Office/Documents/Cash/Computers, etc.
- Motor damage and Third Party
- Public and Product liability.

21.2 Other Insurances

The various other classes of insurance are:

A. Burglary Insurance

The various covers available in this category are:

- Burglary (Business Premises) Policy
- Burglary (Private Residences) Policy
- Burglary All Risks Policy
- Money-in-transit Insurance
- Baggage Insurance Policy

B. Jewellers' Block

The policy is specially designed to take care of all risks of a jeweller whose business involve sale of articles of high value in small bulk like jewelry gold and silver articles, diamonds and precious stones, wrist watches etc. This is a package policy covering risks like fire, lightning, explosion, strike, riot, malicious damage, burglary, housebreaking, theft, robbery and hold ups. For risks up to a sum insured of ₹ 25 lakh the stocks are to be kept in Standard Safes after business hours and in the case where sum insured is up to ₹ 10 crore, stocks should be kept in Burglar Proof safe after business hours and in case of values insured being above ₹ 10 crore, the stocks should be kept in a number of Burglar Proof Safes, after business hours.

C. Banker's Indemnity

This policy is suitable for Banks, NBFC's and other institutions who deal with operations involving money. The policy provides contingency against the following contingencies:

1. Loss in premises due to fire, riot and strike, burglary or house breaking or hold up resulting in loss to money/securities at the premises.
2. Lost, stolen, mislaid, misappropriated or made away either due to negligence or fraud of employees of the insured whilst in transit.
3. Direct financial loss by bogus, fictitious or forged or raised cheque/drafts/FDRs or forged endorsements.
4. Loss to money and/or operations by dishonesty.
5. Loss due to fraud and/or dishonesty or criminal act of the insured's employees.
6. Loss by robbery, theft or by other courses to the parcels insured with the post office.
7. Infidelity or criminal acts by appraisers on the approved list.
8. Infidelity or criminal acts by Janata Agents/Chhoti Bachat Yojana Agents/Pygmy Collectors.

The indemnity provided under this policy in respect of direct losses shall not exceed the sums insured set against each cover. Excess is applicable except for fire and burglary claims. By charging appropriate premium, the sum insured under the policy is maintained constant so as to have full cover even after a claim. The insured is required to lodge a complaint with the police and take all practical steps to recover the property lost/apprehend the guilty person/take departmental action in the event of a loss.

D. Fidelity Guarantee Insurance

Fidelity guarantee covers are provided to indemnify the pecuniary loss suffered by the acts of dishonesty, fraud, forgery, larany, default etc. by employees occupying the positions of trust. These policies can be taken by individuals for self (Individual policy guaranteeing one name) or by employees, for the specific employees' as group, (collective policy) or for employees unnamed, for group as a whole (floater policy). The policy can be taken for specific positions rather than names e.g., accountant, cashier etc. (Positions policy). Blanket covers are also available for entire staff or group of employees. Guarantee policy-missing documents indemnity are also available in respect of people who may be in possession of voluminous documents like shares and bond certificates; bank deposits, real estate and there is a high degree of risk in possession of those documents.

E. Business Insurances

Business Guard Sanjeevani: Suitable for Business establishments with needs for sum insured in excess of ₹ 10 lakh and up to ₹ 1 crore. It is a comprehensive and specially designed policy, offering different limits of coverage permitting insured to select a cover as per his specific requirement. It covers fire, public liability, burglary, money in safe and personal accidents.

Business Guard Jyothi: It is a comprehensive package which covers losses arising out of a variety of perils including fire, public liability, burglary and money-in-safe. Additionally, it offers the business owner a personal accident insurance.

Trade Protector: This Policy is suitable for shops, retail agencies, dealers, restaurants, hair dressers, boutiques, beauty parlours, laundries, video game parlours, hotels, guest houses or any other business establishments who want to take comprehensive insurance protection under one package policy.

F. Personal Accident Insurance

These covers are non-tariff. These policies provide for accidental injury to body which results in death or disablement. The scope of these covers can be extended to medical expenses. The popular ones are:

(a) Bhagyashree Child Welfare — to cover the cost of education of one girl child if one or both the parents die, during an accident.

(b) Janata personal accident policy — a low cost policy covering death or loss of limbs due to accident for sum assured upto ₹ 25,000.

(c) Personal accident — covers death or bodily injury due to an accident.

Other than these covers, specific covers are available for road or rail accidents (Traffic Accident Policy), NRIs and their family (NRI accident insurance policy), womens (Rajrajeshwari Mahila Kalyan), accident cover and cash compensation for leave (Executive Guard etc.)

G. Other Policies

- Horse Insurance
- Cycle Riskshaw Insurance
- Pedal Cycles Insurance
- Plate Glass Insurance
- Household Appliances Insurance
- Shopkeepers' Policy (Composite)
- Carriers' Legal Liability
- LPG Dealers
- Office Umbrella
- Special Contingency
- Electronic Equipment Policy
- Gun Insurance
- Baggage Insurance

Other Miscellaneous Insurance Statistics

Business Generated (Gross Direct Premium — ₹ in crore)

Companies	*1993-94*	*1994-95*	*1995-96*	*1996-97*	*1997-98*	*1998-99*	*1999-2000*
GIC	353.05	424.50	517.55	622.11	691.69	816.79	911.38
NIC	172.18	188.42	254.06	299.65	321.43	393.46	425.13
OIC	472.21	532.34	645.78	755.63	856.39	1045.95	1174.43
NIAC	303.37	335.09	384.59	1231.12	516.42	619.63	681.18
UII	243.32	236.85	291.59	352.80	397.87	481.69	496.23
Total	**1544.13**	**1717.20**	**2093.57**	**3261.31**	**2783.80**	**3357.52**	**3688.35**

Profits (₹ *in crore)*

Companies	*1993-94*	*1994-95*	*1995-96*	*1996-97*	*1997-98*	*1998-99*	*1999-2000*
GIC	-72.44	-198.95	-147.01	-197.37	-220.78	-264.08	-378.35
NIC	20.37	-30.68	21.18	2.01	17.62	30.30	-23.88
OIC	-47.95	-190.43	-252.40	-242.17	-224.99	-361.36	-354.74
NIAC	41.00	55.45	42.88	-185.01	75.66	-26.84	1.68
UII	38.99	4.29	3.31	2.41	8.03	39.40	-59.63
Total	**-20.03**	**-360.32**	**-332.04**	**-620.13**	**-344.46**	**-582.58**	**-814.92**

Profit %age

GIC	-20.52%	-46.87%	-28.40%	-31.73%	-31.92%	-32.33%	-41.51%
NIC	11.83%	-16.28%	8.34%	0.67%	5.48%	7.70%	-5.62%
OIC	-10.15%	-35.77%	-39.08%	-32.05%	-26.27%	-34.55%	-30.21%

NIAC	13.51%	16.55%	11.15%	-15.03%	14.65%	-4.33%	0.25%
UII	16.02%	1.81%	1.14%	0.68%	2.02%	8.18%	-12.02%

Miscellaneous Insurance (Gross Direct Premium Income)

Company	*2000-01*	*2001-02*	*2002-03*	*2003-04*	*2004-05*
National	1505.99	1666.47	2136.67	2688.15	3010.98
New India	2073.09	2313.14	2709.38	3011.27	3169.44
Oriental	1540.49	1719.16	2042.7	2089.18	2288.42
United India	1635.42	1763.86	2024.74	2136.73	2109.75
ECGC*	-	338.52	374.78		
GIC*	280.08				
Royal Sundaram	0.24	50.44	132.26	193.85	250.89
Reliance	0.13	29.87	121.34	101.49	95.41
IFFCO-Tokio	2.09	3.34	91.39	154.86	292.99
TATA AIG	-	49.91	156.69	234.17	323.68
ICICI Lombard	-	16.13	70.82	203.68	513.89
Bajaj Allianz	-	112.71	228.43	335.5	587.24
Cholamandalam	-	9.31	65.77	105.57	
HDFC-Chubb	-	9.49	112.57	173.32	
Total	**7037.53**	**8063.55**	**10108.00**	**11327.22**	**12921.58**

Market Share

Private Co. Share	99.965%	92.548%	88.183%	87.624%	81.868%
Public Co. Share	0.035%	7.452%	11.817%	12.376%	18.132%

Miscellaneous Insurance - Underwriting Experience

Company	*2000-01*	*2001-02*	*2002-03*	*2003-04*	*2004-05*
National	393.71	-319.32		76.29	-164.35
New India	496.33	-632.59		-295.92	-53.05
Oriental	-312.66	-476.32		61.85	76.29
United India	-488.69	-248.1		-114.14	-181.75
ECGC*	**	**			
GIC*	-487.36	-501.37		-323.52	56.7
Royal Sundaram	**	**		-9.96	-7.1
Reliance	**	**		-6.05	-6.37
IFFCO-Tokio	**	**		-5.6	-6.49
TATA AIG	**	**		-16.15	3.07
ICICI Lombard	**	**		-4.3	-10.42
Bajaj Allianz	**	**		3.13	24.96
Cholamandalam	**	**		-16.8	-10.42
HDFC-Chubb	**	**		-29.58	-11.6
				-680.75	-290.53

** Details Not Provided/Available

Key Terms

- Project Insurance
- Fidelity Insurance
- Aviation Insurance
- Business Insurance

Questions for Review

1. Write short notes on:
   (a) Aviation Insurance
   (b) Banker's Indemnity Policy
   (c) Fidelity Guarantee Insurance

Suggested Readings

1. *Miscellaneous Insurance*, IC 78, Insurance Institute of India, Mumbai, 1991.
2. Barry D. Smith *et al.*, *Property and Liability Insurance Principles*, Insurance Institute of America, 1994.

Web Resources

- www.cpg.org
- www.insureitech.com
- www.insure.com
- www.pepeinsurance.com

❑❑❑